Microsoft Office 95 Shortcut Keys

The Microsoft Office 95 shortcut keys can be used in Word, Excel, PowerPoint, and Access.

Working with Files	Shortcut
Open a new file	Ctrl+N
Open an existing file	Ctrl+O
Save a file	Ctrl+S or Shift+F12
Open Save As dialog box	F12
Print the active document	Ctrl+P
Exit the application	Alt+F4

Editing	Shortcut
Undo last action	Ctrl+Z
Redo/Repeat last action	Ctr'
Clear the selection or character to right	
Clear the selection or character to left	
Cut the selection to the Clipboard	
Copy the selection to the Clipboard	
Paste from the Clipboard	
Select all	..trl+A
Find	Ctrl+F
Repeat last find or Go to	Shift+F4
Find and replace	Ctrl+H

Moving	Shortcut

Note: Hold Shift down while you use any of the following movement keys to select that area.

One character/field left	Left arrow
One character/field right	Right arrow
One line/row up	Up arrow
One line/row down	Down arrow
One word right while editing	Ctrl+Right arrow
One word left while editing	Ctrl+Left arrow
To beginning of line or row	Home
To end of line or edit entry	End
One screen up	Page Up
One screen down	Page Down
Beginning of document/worksheet/field	Ctrl+Home
End of document/worksheet/field	Ctrl+End
Next cell/column/field	Tab
Previous cell/column/field	Shift+Tab
Go to a location	F5 or Ctrl+G

Formatting	Shortcut
Bold on/off	Ctrl+B
Italic on/off	Ctrl+I
Underline on/off	Ctrl+U

Formatting

	Shortcut
Activate font button in toolbar	Ctrl+Shift+F
Activate point-size button in toolbar	Ctrl+Shift+P

Working with Windows

	Shortcut
Switch to next application	Alt+Tab
Switch to previous application	Alt+Shift+Tab
Open Start menu	Ctrl+Esc
Close current document window	Ctrl+F4 or Ctrl+W
Restore document window to previous size	Ctrl+F5
Switch to next open document in application	Ctrl+F6
Switch to previous open document in application	Ctrl+Shift+F6
Move document window	Ctrl+F7
Resize document window	Ctrl+F8
Maximize document window	Ctrl+F10
Maximize application window	Alt+F10
Go to next window pane	F6
Go to previous window pane	Shift+F6

Working with Menus

	Shortcut
Choose menu	Alt+underlined letter
Choose item on open menu	Underlined letter
Activate menu bar/cancel a menu	F10 or Alt
Activate document control menu	Alt+- (minus)
Activate application control menu	Alt+Spacebar
Display shortcut menu	Shift+F10

Working in Dialog Boxes

	Shortcut
Choose next tab in tabbed dialog box	Ctrl+Tab
Choose previous tab in tabbed dialog box	Ctrl+Shift+Tab
Move to next option in dialog box	Tab
Move to previous option in dialog box	Shift+Tab
Choose active command button or check box	Spacebar
Select item with underlined letter	Alt+letter
Choose default command button	Enter
Cancel choices and close dialog box	Esc
Choose toolbar button in Open/Save dialog box	Alt+number (order of buttons)

Other Shortcuts

	Shortcut
Get online help	F1
Get context-sensitive help pointer	Shift+F1
Start spell-check	F7
Start Thesaurus	Shift+F7

Using Microsoft Office 95, Second Edition

201 W. 103rd Street, Indianapolis, Indiana 46290 (317) 581-3500

Copyright© 1998 by Que® Corporation

Using Microsoft® Office 95

Second Edition

Patty and Rick Winter

que®

A Division of Macmillan Computer Publishing, USA
201 W. 103rd Street
Indianapolis, Indiana 46290

Contents at a Glance

Using Microsoft® Office 95, Second Edition

Library of Congress Catalog No.:97-81317

ISBN: 0-7897-1622-4

99 98   6 5 4 3 2 1

Interpretation of the printing code: The rightmost double-digit number is the year of the book's printing; the rightmost single-digit number, the number of the book's printing. For example, a printing code of 98-1 shows that the first printing of the book occurred in 1998.

All terms mentioned in this book that are known to be trademarks or service marks have been appropriately capitalized. Que cannot attest to the accuracy of this information. Use of a term in this book should not be regarded as affecting the validity of any trademark or service mark.

Screen reproductions in this book were created using Collage Plus from Inner Media, Inc., Hollis, NH.

Executive Editor
Jim Minatel

Acquisitions Editor
Jill Byus

Development Editors
Rick Kughen
Melanie Palaisa

Technical Editor
Doug Klippert

Managing Editor
Thomas F. Hayes

Project Editor
Lori A. Lyons

Copy Editors
Amy Lepore
San Dee Phillips
Tom Stevens
Marilyn Stone

Indexer
Ginny Bess

Production
Jeanne Clark
John Etchison
Christy M. Lemasters
Heather Stephenson

Cover Designers
Dan Armstrong
Ruth Harvey

Book Designers
Nathan Clement
Ruth Harvey

Contents

Contents

Using Outline View **374**
Using Slide Sorter View **374**
Using Notes Pages View **377**
Using Slide Show View **378**

Saving a Presentation **378**

Opening an Existing Presentation **379**

Closing a Presentation **379**

17 Entering Slide Content 381

Reviewing AutoLayout **382**

Entering and Editing Text **383**
Typing the Content for Your Slides **383**
Creating New Text Objects **385**
Changing Text and Correcting Errors **386**
Checking Your Spelling in PowerPoint **387**

Inserting Clip-Art Pictures **388**

Letting PowerPoint Choose Art for You **390**

Inserting a Word Table or an Excel Worksheet **391**

Inserting an Organization Chart **393**

Inserting Other Objects **395**

18 Enhancing a Presentation 399

Working with Templates **400**
Choosing a Template **400**
Altering a Template **403**
Applying a Different Template **404**

Enhancing Text **405**
Choosing a Font, Style, and Color for Text **406**
Changing Line and Paragraph Spacing **407**

Aligning Text **408**
Adding Bulleted Text **409**

Working with Colors and Line Styles **411**
Choosing Fill and Line Colors and Line Styles **411**
Using Shading and Patterns **414**
Adding Shadows to Objects **416**
Copying Attributes from One Object to Another **417**

Working with Color Schemes **417**
Changing Individual Colors in a Color Scheme **418**
Choosing a Different Color Scheme **418**

19 Creating Output and Doing the Show 421

Checking Slides Before the Presentation **422**

Choosing a Setup for Presentation Components **425**

Printing Presentation Components **427**
Making Settings in the Print Dialog Box **427**
Printing Different Kinds of Output **429**

Setting Up and Running a Slide Show Onscreen **432**
Running a Slide Show **433**
Setting Transitions and Slide Timings **435**
Automating a Slide Show **436**
Annotating a Slide Show **438**
Building Slide Text **439**
Animating Objects on a Slide **439**
Interacting with Objects During a Presentation **442**

IV Using Access

20 Creating a Database 445

What Is a Database? **446**
What Are Primary and Foreign Keys? **447**

About the Authors

Patty Winter is a Senior Partner at PRW Computer Training and Services. She shares her home with Molly, her daughter, many local teens who need a safe haven, two dogs, a cat, and the wildlife that comes visiting. She has worked with computers since 1982, training adults, testing programs, developing course material, and creating solutions for user productivity. She has trained thousands of adults on the use of personal computers. Her emphasis has been on peopleware. She is the author of *Microsoft Word 97 Quick Reference, Excel 5 for Windows Essentials;* lead author of *Special Edition Using Microsoft Office 97* and *Special Edition Using Microsoft Office Professional for Windows 95;* contributing author of *Special Edition Using Microsoft Office,* and co-author of *Excel for Windows SureSteps, Look Your Best with Excel,* and *Q&A QueCards.*

Rick Winter is a Senior Partner at PRW Computer Training and Services. He shares his home with Karen, his wife, Danny and Jimmy, Honey Bear (a dog), and the wildlife that doesn't want to go to Patty's house. He is a Microsoft Certified Trainer and Certified Professional for Access and has trained thousands of adults on personal computers. He is the author of *Microsoft Access 97 Quick Reference;* lead author of *Special Edition Using Microsoft Office 97 Small Business Edition, Special Edition Using Microsoft Office 97,* and *Special Edition Using Microsoft Office Professional for Windows 95;* co-author of *Excel for Windows SureSteps, Look Your Best with Excel, Q&A QueCards* and many other books for Que. Rick has a B.A. from Colorado College and an M.A. from University of Colorado at Denver. In conjunction with Ideas Unlimited Inc., Rick also travels throughout the U.S. doing computer-aided group facilitation and strategic planning.

PRW Computer Training and Services, nested in Idaho Springs, in the mountains of Colorado, is a recognized leader in training, training materials, and consulting. PRW provides classes in the Denver area on Microsoft Office and onsite training, programming, and consulting across the country. PRW won the prestigious Rocky Mountain Chapter Society for Technical Communication's Distinguished Award for its work on Que's *Excel for Windows SureSteps* in 1994.

For information on course content, onsite corporate classes, or consulting, contact PRW at the following address:

PRW Computer Training and Services
491 Highway 103
Idaho Springs, Colorado 80452
(303) 567-4943 or (303) 567-2987 Voice (8-5 MST)
prwtrain@compuserve.com

Dedication

To my friend Peggy Jagoda. Thank you for all you do for me! Without your support during this book, I probably would have gone nuts, or worse yet, gotten stuck at the computer forever.

Patty Winter

To all the teachers of Clear Creek County. Your dedication, enthusiasm for learning, and time creates a positive future for all our children. I would like to give a very special thank you to my oldest son's first teacher, Judy Lenardson, for helping Danny and his parents learn what a teacher can and should be.

Rick Winter

Acknowledgments

We would like to thank Rick Kughen and Melanie Palaisa, Development Editors, for being available to discuss ideas, make suggestions, and help us complete this project.

Thanks also to Jill Byus, Acquisitions Editor, and Chris Van Buren, our agent, for conversing between themselves to handle all the administrative work that goes into this type of project.

We also appreciate all the hard work of the editing team headed by Lori Lyons, Production Editor. Thanks also to Copy Editor Tom Stevens for his attention to details, and to our Technical Editor, Doug Klippert, for his valuable knowledge. Thanks also to the production team who had to put this all together in book form.

We appreciate everyone's willingness to give up time with family, miss weekends, and work long nights to help get this project to bed.

We'd Like to Hear from You!

Que Corporation has a long-standing reputation for high-quality books and products. To ensure your continued satisfaction, we also understand the importance of customer service and support.

Tech Support

If you need assistance with the information in this book or you have feedback for us about the book, please contact Macmillan Technical Support by phone at **317-581-3833** or via e-mail at support@mcp.com.

Orders, Catalogs, and Customer Service

To order other Que or Macmillan Computer Publishing books, catalogs, or products, please contact our Customer Service Department:

Phone: 1-800-858-7674

Fax: 1-800-835-3202

International Fax: 1-317-228-4400

Or visit our online bookstore: http://www.mcp.com/.

S O MUCH TO LEARN, SO LITTLE TIME. Corporations continue doing more with less (meaning *you* have to do more in less time). Computer software packages continue to add more and more features and come out faster with new releases. The job you have today looks nothing like the one you had five years ago. The information age accelerates and you are expected to keep up.

Using Microsoft Office 95, Second Edition, packs as much information in as little space as possible. In the space that it takes to describe one application, this book packs in information about many applications. *Using Microsoft Office 95, Second Edition,* discusses Microsoft Word, Excel, PowerPoint, Access, and the various applets such as WordArt, ClipArt Gallery, and Organization Chart.

The authors are Patty and Rick Winter, a sister-brother team who have owned their own business for over ten years. Patty and Rick have corporate, nonprofit, small business, and consulting experience. Each has trained over 3,000 adults on how to use software. This varied experience provides a well-rounded foundation to help answer your questions about Microsoft Office. We also hope to provide you with the best information about how to get the most out of your applications.

Who Should Use This Book?

The *Using* series is for today's typical computer user, who may or may not know how to use this specific technology. They are not afraid of computers (as they have to use them on a day-to-day basis) or of new technology if it relates to getting work done. They want answers as quickly as possible so they can get on with their lives, and have no great desire to understand the inner workings of a technology. They learn best by asking, then doing.

Using Microsoft Office 95, Second Edition, is the right choice for executives, management staff, home users, small business owners, marketing personnel, human resources staff, professional secretaries, assistants, and coordinators—anyone using any of the Office 95 suite applications and wanting to get up to speed quickly on the Office applications.

This book assumes that you are familiar with Microsoft Windows 95 or Windows NT but not familiar with all the applications in the Office suite.

Using Microsoft Office 95, Second Edition, is the ideal companion volume to *Using Microsoft Word 95*, *Using Microsoft Excel 95*, *Using Microsoft PowerPoint 95*, *Using Microsoft Access 95*, and *Using Windows 95*—all from Que. For more details on any individual applications, you can also look at the Que *Special Edition* title for each of these applications (*Special Edition Using Microsoft Word 95*, for example).

How This Book Is Organized

The authors designed *Using Microsoft Office 95, Second Edition*, to complement the documentation that comes with Microsoft Office. They aim for giving you, the reader/user, more information about actually *using* the applications, not just documenting their features. After you become proficient with one or more of the applications within Office, you can use this book as a desktop reference.

Using Microsoft Office 95, Second Edition, is organized as follows:

Chapter 1, "Overview of Office," introduces you to Microsoft Office and creates the foundation you need for working with all the Office applications. You learn about the features shared by the Office applications that enable you to move from program to program without starting all over every time you begin learning a new application. In addition, this chapter includes working with toolbars and menus, managing your files, and printing.

Chapters 2–7 in Part I, "Using Word," cover the essentials of Word 95. This includes the basics of Word from typing, editing, and formatting a letter to more advanced topics such as tables, mass mailings, and large report documents.

Chapters 8–14 in Part II, "Using Excel," cover the essentials of Excel 95. You create, edit, and format worksheets but also discover the power of working with functions, formulas, and what-if analysis features.

Chapters 15–19 in Part III, "Using PowerPoint," cover the essentials of PowerPoint 95. You create a presentation that you can display on your computer, overhead transparencies, or 35mm slides. These chapters cover creating and formatting slides, inserting artwork and other visual object features, and creating interesting transition effects.

Chapters 20–25 in Part IV, "Using Access," cover the essentials of Access 95. You learn basic database definitions and what is required for planning a database. You also learn how to create tables for storing your data, queries to sort and find data, forms to input data, and reports for printing data.

Conventions Used in This Book

Commands, directions, and explanations in this book are presented in the clearest format possible. The following items are some of the features that will make this book easier for you to use:

- *Menu and dialog box commands and options.* You can easily find the onscreen menu and dialog box commands by looking for bold text such as you see in this direction: Open the **File** menu and click **Save**.

- *Hotkeys for commands.* The underlined keys onscreen that activate commands and options are also underlined in the book, as shown in the previous example.

- *Combination and shortcut keystrokes.* Text that directs you to hold down several keys simultaneously is connected with a plus sign (+), such as Ctrl+P.

- *Graphical icons with the commands they execute.* Look for icons like this ▣ in text and steps. These indicate buttons onscreen that you can click to accomplish the procedure.

- *Cross references.* If there's a related topic that is prerequisite to the section or steps you are reading, or a topic that builds further on what you are reading, you'll find the cross reference to it after the steps or at the end of the section, such as this:

SEE ALSO

➤ *To learn about window elements common across applications, see page 14*

- *Glossary terms.* For all the terms that appear in the glossary, you'll find the first appearance of that term in the text in *italic* along with its definition.

- *Sidebars.* Information related to the task at hand, or "inside" information from the author, is offset in sidebars so as not to interfere with the task at hand and to make it easy to find this valuable information. Each of these sidebars has a short title to help you quickly identify the information you'll find there. You'll find the same kind of information in these that you might find in notes, tips, or warnings in other books, but here the titles should be more informative.

Your screen may appear slightly different from the examples in this book because of your installation and hardware setup. The screen items and functionality may change due to what applications and portions of applications are installed as well as your hardware and network options. You may see slight changes for menus, dialog box options, and toolbars.

Overview of Office

What's included in Office 95

Learn common features in Microsoft Office Applications

How to determine which application to use

Find a file by name, contents, or properties

Preview and print documents

What's Included in Office 95

The professional edition of Microsoft Office 95 includes the following applications and new features:

- Microsoft Word for Windows 95, Version 7.0
- Microsoft Excel for Windows 95, Version 7.0
- Microsoft PowerPoint for Windows 95, Version 7.0
- Microsoft Access for Windows 95, Version 7.0
- Microsoft Schedule+, Version 7.0
- Microsoft Office Binder
- Getting Results Book
- Microsoft Office Shortcut Bar
- Microsoft Bookshelf '95

No Access or Bookshelf in standard edition

The standard edition of Office 95 does not include Microsoft Access or Microsoft Bookshelf '95.

Using Common Features in Microsoft Office Applications

The goal of Microsoft Office is to provide users with the following features:

- A common user interface (standardized operation of menus, toolbars, and dialog boxes)
- Quick access from one Office suite application to another
- Data shared across applications
- Resources shared across applications
- Information shared across workgroups
- In the future, a common task automation language

Many of the core applications underwent (and continue to undergo) revisions to meet these goals. In the long run, a common user interface across applications increases efficient and effective use of all applications.

Another book about Microsoft Office 95?

This book was written for those users who are using Microsoft Office 95 and not a newer release of the product. We are not attempting to cover everything in Office 95. For instance, if you need more information about common Windows tasks or features, you might consider Que's book *Using Windows 95*. We wrote this book using the Microsoft Office 7.0a version. For those of you who have not upgraded to 7.0a, a free update is available. Contact Microsoft or your local vendor for more information.

Providing a Common User Interface

A clear benefit of a common user interface across applications is that by learning one application in the suite, you know the operational basics of the other applications. Figure 1.1 illustrates the similarity between Excel and Word menu bars and toolbars. Notice that Word has a **Table** menu option, but Excel has a **Data** menu option. Although the goal is to provide one common user interface, some degree of uniqueness remains in each application. Key common features, however, such as the **File**, **Open** and **Edit**, **Find** commands can be found in exactly the same place in each application.

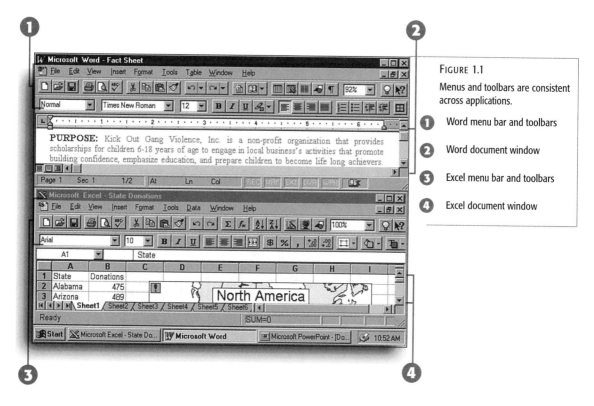

FIGURE 1.1

Menus and toolbars are consistent across applications.

1. Word menu bar and toolbars

2. Word document window

3. Excel menu bar and toolbars

4. Excel document window

Microsoft Office applications provide consistency in more than just similar toolbars and menus. Dialog boxes, customizable features, and operational features are similar. Additionally, online help is available in several forms in Office 95 applications:

- Help application
- Answer wizards
- The use of wizards
- Tip wizards and Tip of the Day
- Getting Results Book

Quick Access to Other Applications

Microsoft Office provides the Microsoft Office Shortcut Bar. By default, this toolbar appears in the upper-right corner of the Windows 95 desktop (see Figure 1.2).

FIGURE 1.2

The Microsoft Office Shortcut Bar provides easy access to opening and creating documents and Office Manager features.

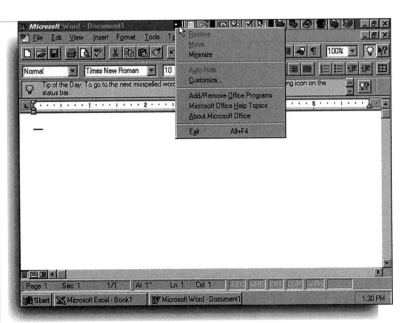

You can use the Shortcut Bar to do the following:

- Start new files based on templates and wizards.
- Open existing files and automatically launch the related application.
- Add tasks, make appointments, and add contacts.
- Use Office features such as Setup and Answer Wizards.

- Add other applications to the Office Shortcut Bar.
- Switch between Microsoft Office applications.
- Launch Microsoft Office applications.

The Shortcut Bar is just one way that Microsoft Office provides quick access to applications. In each Microsoft Office application, you find OfficeLinks, which are toolbar buttons or menu choices that provide direct access to pertinent features of other applications. For example, in Word you can insert an Excel Worksheet into a document by simply clicking a toolbar button. Doing so launches Excel and provides the full features of Excel for that embedded worksheet (see Figure 1.3). Note that, without having to leave Word, the menus and toolbars change to Excel's when you edit the worksheet.

Use Auto Hide on the Shortcut Bar

If you get frustrated with the Microsoft Office Shortcut Bar, you can activate the Auto Hide feature so that it is visible only when you want to see it. Point to an open spot on the Shortcut bar and right-click, and select **Auto Hide** from the shortcut menu. When you click inside an application window, the Shortcut Bar disappears. To see it, move the mouse pointer to the edge of the screen where the Shortcut Bar is located.

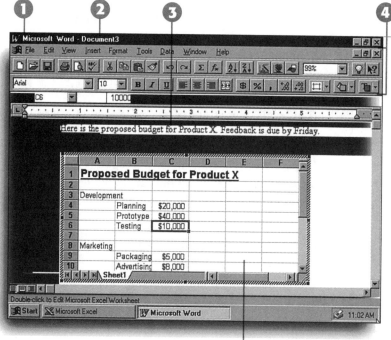

FIGURE 1.3

Connectivity between applications enables you to insert an Excel worksheet into a Word document and edit the worksheet using Excel menus and toolbars without leaving Word.

1. Word title bar
2. Word document name
3. Word document window
4. Excel menu bar, toolbars, and formula bar
5. Excel document window

Sharing Data Across Applications

Microsoft Office products provide several methods of sharing data between applications:

Method	Description
Copying	Copies the data from the source application to the target application using the Clipboard
Linking	Links a copy of the data from the source document to the target document (and saves data with the source document)
Embedding	Embeds data from the source document into the target document (saves data with the target document)

The Microsoft Office applications share data effortlessly. When you copy a table from Excel or Access to Word, for example, you get a Word table that retains all the fonts and formats from Excel or Access. You do not need to reformat your table, as you might with some other products.

Linking and embedding features take advantage of Microsoft Windows *object linking and embedding (OLE)* specifications. Linked documents automatically update when a source document changes. Embedded documents provide access to the source application while storing the data in the target application. Each feature has its pros and cons and serves a specific purpose.

Microsoft Office extends the data sharing beyond application integration by providing workgroup integration with Microsoft Exchange. Users can mail documents, spreadsheets, and data files from within the source application. Routing slips can be attached to files that Exchange then broadcasts to the group— or routes to each person, in sequence, one at a time.

Microsoft Exchange and OLE are not covered here

The focus of this book does not include Microsoft Exchange. For more information about Exchange, refer to Que's *Special Edition Using Microsoft Exchange Server 5.5*. We also have not covered OLE in great detail. If you need more information on OLE, consider Que's *Special Edition Using Microsoft Office for Windows 95*.

Sharing Resources Across Applications

A key element in Microsoft Office is the recognition that certain resources are needed by more than one application. Clip art is needed to perform word processing tasks, spreadsheet tasks, and presentation graphic tasks, for example. Rather than duplicating program overhead, Microsoft Office provides an auxiliary application, Microsoft ClipArt Gallery, for use with all applications. The same is true of the need for a query engine (to ask questions of your data), a graphing tool (see Figure 1.4), and an organization chart drawing tool.

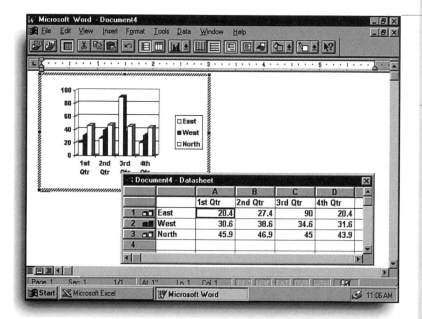

FIGURE 1.4

Microsoft Graph, one of the auxiliary applications that ships with Microsoft Office, is used by all applications to draw graphs.

Providing a Common Language

Providing a common language across applications is the most challenging goal of Microsoft Office. In the past, each product had a different programming or macro language. Excel Version 5.0 is the first Microsoft Office suite product to provide what is now the common language of the Office products: Visual Basic for Applications (VBA). Access for Windows 95 now also includes Visual Basic for Applications. (VBA uses OLE and can send keystrokes to other applications making it possible for VBA to run a cross-application process) Until VBA is added to the other suite products, however, users have to learn WordBasic and VBA to automate common office tasks.

Determining Which Application to Use

Table 1.1 lists some common office tasks and suggested application tools to accomplish each task.

TABLE 1.1   Common Office tasks

Task	Application	Comments
Create letters, memos, reports, term papers	Word	Use Word for projects that are word-intensive.
Create budgets, invoices, income tracking, statistics	Excel	Use Excel for projects that have a lot of numbers and calculations.
	Access	Alternatively, use Access for large lists when you're searching for a lot of information and making many reports off the same set of data.
Create slides, overheads, presentations	PowerPoint	Use PowerPoint for presentations when you want to produce 35mm slides, transparencies, audience handouts, or computer-run presentations.
Maintain mailing lists	Word, Access, Excel, or Schedule+	Maintain data in Word, Access, Excel, or Schedule+.
Create mailouts or personalized cover letters	Word	Merge mailing-list data into Word to print documents, letters, brochures, and labels.
Create a table of financial data to be used in a Presentation	Excel	Create a table in Excel.
	PowerPoint	Embed a table into into a PowerPoint slide.
Send a document to a group of people for feedback, and receive a response	Word, Excel Access, PowerPoint	Create the document, spreadsheet, report, or presentation in the desired application(s).
	Exchange	Send the file(s) using the Exchange routing feature.

Task	Application	Comments
Track client contacts, log phone support, and follow up with forms	Access	Create a contact database in Access with related tables for clients, phone calls, projects, letters and correspondence. Create forms for data entry. Optionally print letters (reports) directly from Access.
	Word	Optionally, merge client contact data into Word and print follow-up form letters from Word.
Provide audit trail between supporting spreadsheet data and annual report document	Excel	Create the supporting schedules needed in Excel.
	Word	Create the annual report document in Word. Use OLE to link the data from Excel to the Word document. Whenever the spreadsheet data changes, the annual report document is updated automatically.
Create, print, and distribute a department newsletter	Word	Create a newsletter in Word.
	Exchange	Distribute a newsletter electronically using Exchange's Send feature.

With four or five new software applications so tightly integrated, deciding on which product to use for which task could be difficult. Experience with each application is the best guide to combining the powers of each application to meet your needs.

Viewing Parts of the Window

One of the best features of Windows and Microsoft Office is the similarity between different applications. After you learn one program, the next and subsequent programs are easier to learn. This point is especially true because parts of the window are similar.

SEE ALSO

➤ *For more information about Word, see page 50*

➤ *For more information related to Excel, see page 190*

➤ *For more information about PowerPoint, see page 348*

Understanding Common Window Elements

Each application usually displays the application window itself and at least one document window. Figure 1.5 shows a review of the elements on a screen. Table 1.2 describes the common elements on the application window and the document window.

TABLE 1.2   Window features common to Office applications

Feature	Description/Use
Control-menu icon	The Microsoft program icon in the upper-left corner of the window. If the document window is maximized, the document icon is located directly below the program Control-menu icon. If the document window is not maximized, the document Control-menu icon is in the upper-left corner of the document window.
	Double-click to close the application or the document. Single-click to open the Control menu and choose the **Restore**, **Minimize**, **Maximize**, or **Close** commands.
Title bar	At the top of the window. The title bar is dark if the window is active, grayed if another window is active. (The color may be different if you have changed colors in the Display Properties of the Control Panel.)
	Shows the name of the program or document. If the document window is maximized, the program title bar shows the name of the application and of the document. Double-click to toggle between maximize and restore. If a window is restored (not full screen), drag the title bar to move the window.
Minimize button	The first button in group of three buttons in the upper-right corner of the document or program window.
	Click to shrink the window to an icon. The Program Minimize button shrinks the program to an icon on the taskbar. The Document Minimize button shrinks the document to an icon in the work area above the status bar (and probably behind another document).

Minimize all open windows

You can minimize all open programs by clicking the right mouse button in an empty spot on the taskbar and choosing **Minimize All Windows**.

Feature	Description/Use
Maximize button	The second button in the group of three buttons in the upper-right corner of the document or program window. It looks like a full-screen window (a rectangle with thick black line on top).
	When window is restored (not full screen), click the button to change the window to the largest possible size. This action causes the button to change to the Restore button.
Restore button	The second button in the group of three buttons in the upper-right corner of the document or program window. It looks like two windows cascaded.
	When the window is maximized, click this button to change the window to the last smaller-sized window. This action causes the button to change to the Maximize button.
Close button	The third button in the group of three buttons in the upper-right corner of the document or program window. An X appears on this button.
	Click this button to close the window. If you have not saved your work, you are prompted to save and continue or close without saving.
Menu bar	The line below the title bar starting with File.
	Click one of the words to select a menu or press Alt and then type the underlined letter on the menu.
Window border	Thin gray line surrounding a window that is not maximized.
	Move the mouse pointer until a double arrow appears and then drag it to change the size of window.
Window corner	A textured box in the bottom-right corner of the window.
	Move the mouse pointer until a double arrow appears and drag it to change both the width and height of the window.

Some items generally occur just on application windows (and not document windows) but are common to most applications. Table 1.3 discusses these items.

FIGURE 1.5

The screen provides many choices that you can make with the mouse.

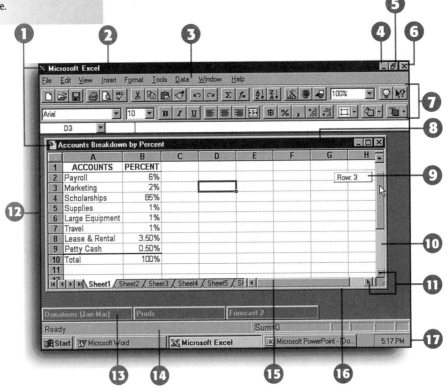

①	Control-menu icons	⑩	Scrollbars
②	Application title bar	⑪	Scroll arrows
③	Menu bar	⑫	Document window
④	Minimize button	⑬	Document icon
⑤	Restore button	⑭	Status bar
⑥	Close button	⑮	Scroll box
⑦	Toolbars	⑯	Window border
⑧	Document title bar	⑰	Taskbar
⑨	ScrollTip		

TABLE 1.3   Window features common to application windows

Feature	Description/Use
Toolbar(s)	Picture buttons below the menu bar or other places onscreen.
	When you move the mouse pointer to a button, a ToolTip description appears on the button and the status bar describes the button in more detail. Click the button for the most frequently used commands. Sometimes the button gives you only one feature for a command. Use the menu for more options on a feature.
Status bar	The bottom line of the application window.
	The status bar may provide information about the insertion point location on the document and the status of some toggle keys on the keyboard, such as the Insert/Overwrite or Num Lock key. In some programs, the status bar describes a menu or toolbar choice in more detail. In some programs, you can double-click the status bar to accomplish tasks.
Document window	The area between the toolbars and the status bar.
	Shows an open document, scrollbars, and possible title of the document in the title bar.
Document icon	The icon at the bottom of the screen above the status bar, visible if the document window is not maximized.
	If the document is minimized, double-click it to open a document window.

Most document windows also have features common to each other. Table 1.4 shows some of the features common to document windows across applications.

TABLE 1.4   Window features common to document windows

Feature	Description/Use
Scrollbar	The gray area between the scroll arrows on the right and bottom of the document window. Click above or below the scroll box on the vertical scrollbar or to the left or right of the scroll box on the horizontal scrollbar to move the view of the document a full screen up, down, left, or right.

continues...

TABLE 1.4   Continued

Feature	Description/Use
Scroll box	The gray square or rectangle box inside the scrollbars. Drag the scroll box to position the view of the document.
Scroll arrows	Arrows on either side of the scrollbar. Click an arrow to move the view one line in the direction of the arrow. Hold down the mouse pointer on an arrow to scroll quickly.
ScrollTip	Description that appears when you drag a vertical scroll box. In Excel, this shows the row number, in Word, the page number, in PowerPoint, the slide number, and in an Access table, the record number when you drag the vertical scroll box.
Document window	The area inside the window. The location where the document resides and where editing takes place.

Using Toolbars in Microsoft Office Applications

One of the improvements Microsoft made with the Office 95 upgrades of Word, Excel, and PowerPoint was to reorganize and improve the toolbars so that the tools are more consistent across the Microsoft Office applications. Although some buttons are unique to each application, many buttons are common to all or some of the applications. You now can choose from more than one toolbar in all the applications. You also can customize the toolbars by adding or removing buttons.

Activate or deactivate a toolbar

1. Click the right mouse button on an active toolbar.

   A pop-up menu shows a list of the potential toolbars. Microsoft displays those toolbars with a checkmark to the left of the name. (Figure 1.6 shows a list of the toolbars for each application described later in this chapter.)

2. Click the toolbar that you want to activate or deactivate. If the toolbar is floating, you can also click the toolbar's Control-menu icon to close the toolbar.

No toolbars are visible

If the program does not show any toolbars, choose the **View** menu, select **Toolbars,** and select the toolbar(s) that you want to display.

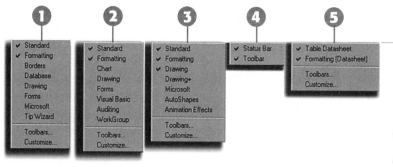

FIGURE 1.6

When you click the right mouse button on a toolbar, a menu appears, showing the active and available toolbars.

1 Word toolbars

2 Excel toolbars

3 PowerPoint toolbars

4 Schedule+ toolbars

5 Access toolbars

Some buttons have drop-down choices. For example, the Font button displays a list of available fonts. The drop-down buttons are indicated by a down arrow next to the button. Some of the drop-down buttons have two choices: You can click the button for the current choice or click the down arrow next to the button to change the current choice. (In Figure 1.8, shown later, the Highlight button in Word and Back Color button in Access work this way.)

Some buttons change on toolbars when you change the view. For example, Word adds an Outline toolbar when you change to Outline view. Excel adds a Charting toolbar when you use the Chart Wizard.

Access Toolbars

Microsoft Access menus and toolbars change depending on which portion of the program you are in. For example, if you just enter Access and show the database window, the Database toolbar displays. If you are designing a form, the Form Design toolbar displays; if you view the form, the Form View toolbar displays. You can find the name of the toolbar(s) displayed by clicking the right mouse button in the toolbar and seeing the name(s) shown with checkmarks. (In Figure 1.6, the Access toolbars visible are Table Datasheet and Formatting-Datasheet). If a button is dimmed, the button is not currently available. (For example, the Access Database toolbar in Figure 1.7 shows a dimmed Format Painter button, which means that you cannot use this button in the current view.)

To show some of the similarities between toolbars, Figures 1.7, 1.8, and 1.9 show some of the available toolbars in each of the applications.

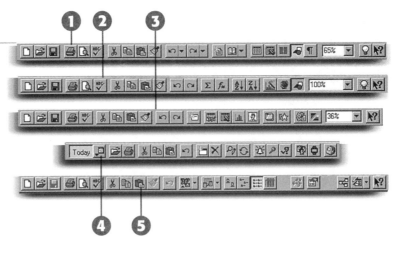

FIGURE 1.7

The Standard toolbars for Word, Excel, PowerPoint, Schedule+, and the Access database toolbar show many similarities.

1 Word Standard toolbar

2 Excel Standard toolbar

3 PowerPoint Standard toolbar

4 Schedule+ toolbar

5 Access Database toolbar

Standard Toolbars

Figure 1.7 shows the Standard toolbar for each Microsoft Office application. Notice how many of the buttons are the same. Table 1.5 shows the common buttons and their purposes.

TABLE 1.5   **Common buttons on the Standard toolbars**

Button	Word	Excel	PowerPoint	Access	Schedule+	Use
New	X	X	X	X		Create a new, blank document.
Open	X	X	X	X	X	Open an existing document.
Save	X	X	X	X		Save the active document on-screen.
Print	X	X	X	X	X	Print the document.
Print Preview	X	X		X		Preview the document as it will look when printed.
Spelling	X	X	X	X		Check the spelling of the document.

Button	Word	Excel	PowerPoint	Access	Schedule+	Use
Cut	X	X	X	X	X	Remove the selection from the document and place a copy in the Clipboard.
Copy	X	X	X	X	X	Copy the selection from the document and place a copy in the Clipboard.
Paste	X	X	X	X	X	Copy the contents of the Clipboard into the document at the location of the insertion point.
Format Painter	X	X	X	X		Copy the format-ting from the selected items to the next selection.
Undo	X	X	X	X	X	Reverse your last action.
Redo	X		X			Redo the last action or actions that were undone.
Repeat		X				Repeat the last action or redo the last undone action.
Insert Microsoft Excel worksheet	X		X			Insert a Microsoft Excel worksheet into the document.
Zoom Control	X	X	X			Change the size of your display (does not affect printing).
TipWizard	X	X				Show or hide the TipWizard tool-bar, which lists tips of the day and help for your procedures.

continues…

TABLE 1.5 **Continued**

Button	Word	Excel	PowerPoint	Access	Schedule+	Use
Help	X	X	X	X		Click the toolbar button or menu option for help on that choice. Double-click to search for help on a topic that you type.

Formatting Toolbars

Just as Standard toolbars have common buttons, Formatting toolbars also have many similar buttons. Figure 1.8 shows the formatting toolbars for Word, Excel, PowerPoint, and the Access Form/Report Design Formatting toolbar. Table 1.6 lists the common buttons and their purposes.

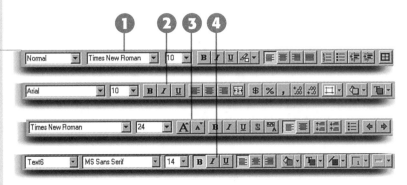

FIGURE 1.8

The Formatting toolbars for Word, Excel, PowerPoint, and Access show many similarities.

1 Word Formatting toolbar

2 Excel Formatting toolbar

3 PowerPoint Formatting toolbar

4 Access Form/Report Design Formatting toolbar

TABLE 1.6 **Common buttons on the formatting toolbars**

Button	Word	Excel	PowerPoint	Access	Use
Font	X	X	X	X	Click the arrow to the right of the font name to display a list of typefaces. Click the desired font.
Font Size	X	X	X	X	Click the arrow to display and choose the desired size for text.

Button	Word	Excel	PowerPoint	Access	Use
Bold	X	X	X	X	Bold the selected text.
Italic	X	X	X	X	Italicize the selected text.
Underline	X	X	X	X	Underline the selected text.
Align Left	X	X	X	X	Align the items so that the left side of each is lined up.
Center	X	X	X	X	Align the items so that each is centered.
Align Right	X	X		X	Align the items so that the right side of each is lined up.
Bullet	X		X		Place a bullet before each line of the selected text.

Drawing Toolbars

The drawing toolbars for Word, Excel, and PowerPoint also have common buttons. (These are shown in Figure 1.9. Table 1.7 lists the common buttons and their purpose.) The similar buttons on Access are called the Toolbox, which is available when you are designing a report or a form. (Figure 1.9 and Table 1.7 also show these Access buttons.)

TABLE 1.7 Common buttons on the Drawing toolbars

Button	Word	Excel	PowerPoint	Access	Use
Line	X	X	X	X	Click and drag to start and draw the line. Release the mouse button to end the line. Use the Shift key to draw lines at 0, 30, 45, 60, and 90 degree angles (depending on the program).

continues…

TABLE 1.7   **Continued**

Button	Word	Excel	PowerPoint	Access	Use
Rectangle	X	X	X	X	Click and drag from one corner to the opposite corner. Release the mouse button to complete the rectangle. Use the Shift key to draw a square.
Ellipse	X	X	X		Click and drag from one corner to the opposite corner. Release the mouse button to complete the ellipse. Use the Shift key to draw a circle.
Arc	X	X	X		Click and drag to start and draw the arc. Release the mouse button to end the arc.
Freeform	X	X	X		Drag the mouse to draw. Double-click to end the drawing.
Selection Tool	X	X	X	X	To select multiple objects, drag the mouse from upper left corner to bottom right and release mouse. Black boxes (selection handles) indicate that the object is selected.
Bring to Front/Bring Forward	X	X	X		With two objects stacked on each other, bring the selected object to the top (or front).
Send to Back/ Send Backward	X	X	X		With two objects stacked on each other, send the selected object to the bottom (or back).
Group Objects	X	X	X		Combine more than one drawn object into a single object for editing and moving.
Ungroup Objects	X	X	X		Uncombine grouped objects back into their original drawings.

Button	Word	Excel	PowerPoint	Access	Use
Flip Horizontal	X		X		Flip an object from top to bottom.
Flip Vertical	X		X		Flip an object from right to left.
Reshape	X	X			Drag black selection handles to reshape a freeform object.
Drop Shadow		X	X		Apply a shadow to the bottom and right of an object.

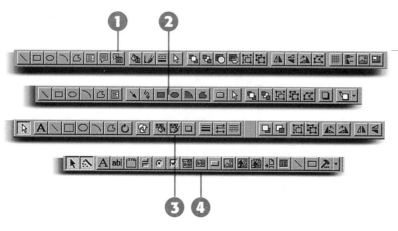

FIGURE 1.9

The Drawing toolbars for Word, Excel, and PowerPoint, and Access's Toolbox show many similarities.

1 Word Drawing toolbar

2 Excel Drawing toolbar

3 PowerPoint Drawing and Drawing+ toolbars

4 Access Toolbox

Shortcut Menus

Microsoft has shortcut menus for Word, Excel, PowerPoint, Access, and Schedule+. To access a shortcut menu, select the item that you want to change and click the right mouse button in the selected area. The menu that appears gives you options for only the selection. You don't have to wade through the menu bar to figure out which menu items go with what you are doing.

In addition to shortcut menus for toolbars, Microsoft has shortcut menus for selected text, drawing and graphics objects, rows, columns, and others, depending on your application. Figure 1.10 shows an example of the shortcut menus for selected text in each of the applications. Notice that each of the shortcut menus has Cut, Copy, and Paste, but each menu also has items specific to the application.

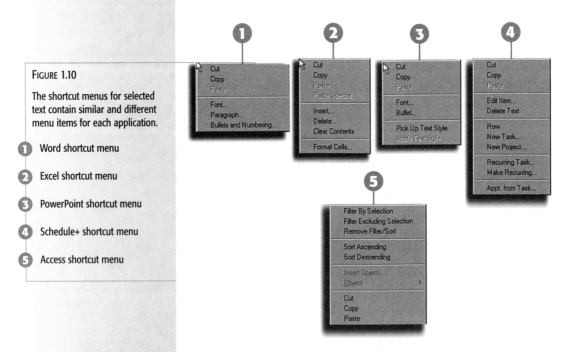

FIGURE 1.10

The shortcut menus for selected
text contain similar and different
menu items for each application.

1 Word shortcut menu

2 Excel shortcut menu

3 PowerPoint shortcut menu

4 Schedule+ shortcut menu

5 Access shortcut menu

Finding Files

You can use the Open a Document button on the Microsoft Office Shortcut Bar to open a document and launch the program that created the document at the same time. After you click the Open a Document button, the Open dialog box appears. This dialog box is the same one that appears when you are in a program and use the **File** menu and select **Open**.

When you get to the Open dialog box, you have many options to narrow or expand your search. You can change the display and order of the files, use wildcards in file names, choose a file type, or identify a file by its contents, date, or other properties. These options in the Open dialog box replace the Find File feature from the previous version of Microsoft Office.

Displaying File Lists

After you have selected a computer, drive, and folder through the **Look in** drop-down list, you see a list of files (and possibly other folders) in the contents list box. You have four options for viewing this file list (see Table 1.8). Figures 1.11 through 1.14 show the different views of the files.

TABLE 1.8   File list views

Button	Name	Purpose
	List	Shows filenames with a file type icon only.
	Details	Shows filenames, file type icon, size of file, file type, and modified date and time.
	Properties	Shows user-added summary information, such as title, author, keywords, and others.
	Preview	Shows what the first part of the file looks like.

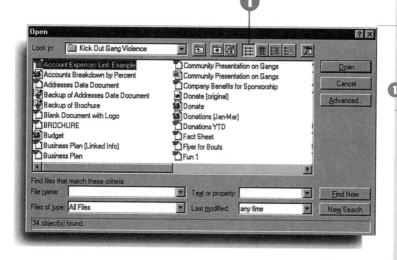

FIGURE 1.11
Click the List button to display filenames.

① List button

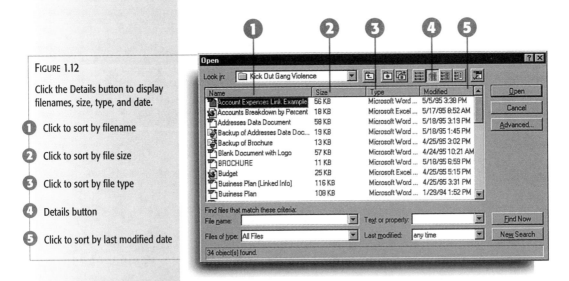

FIGURE 1.12

Click the Details button to display filenames, size, type, and date.

1 Click to sort by filename

2 Click to sort by file size

3 Click to sort by file type

4 Details button

5 Click to sort by last modified date

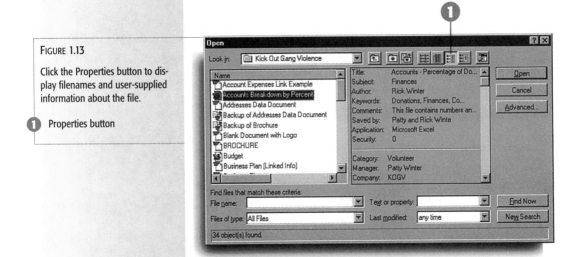

FIGURE 1.13

Click the Properties button to display filenames and user-supplied information about the file.

1 Properties button

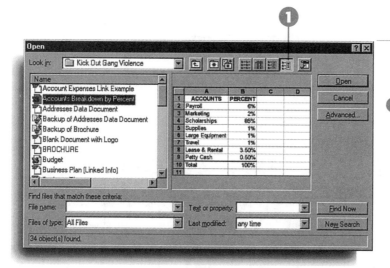

FIGURE 1.14

Click the Preview button to see a picture of the file.

1 Preview button

Technically, the Access database window (see Figure 1.15) is not a file dialog box. You can, however, picture the database window as a permanently open file dialog box with the list of all the objects (parts) of the database. To see a list of one type of object, click the (Tables, Queries, Forms, and so on) tab at the top of the database window. To open up the object, double-click the object name in the list. You can also display the object names in different views with the four buttons on the toolbars (see Table 1.9). These buttons are similar to the file dialog buttons.

TABLE 1.9   These buttons change the view of icons

Button	Name	Purpose
	Large Icons	Displays the object names with large icons and names underneath the icons.
	Small Icons	Shows object names with small icons and names to the right of the icons and alphabetizes the list from left to right and then top to bottom.
	List	Shows object names with small icons and alphabetizes the list from top to bottom and then left to right.

continues…

TABLE 1.9 **Continued**

Button	Name	Purpose
	Details	Shows a small icon, description of the object (from clicking the right mouse button and filling in properties), and the dates the object was modified and created. Like the Details button of the file dialog box, you can also sort the list by clicking the column headers.

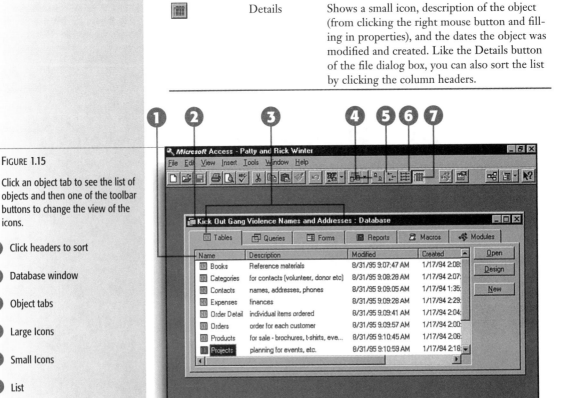

FIGURE 1.15

Click an object tab to see the list of objects and then one of the toolbar buttons to change the view of the icons.

1 Click headers to sort

2 Database window

3 Object tabs

4 Large Icons

5 Small Icons

6 List

7 Details

Sorting the File List

When you choose the Details button ▦, the list of files displays with the filename, size, type, and modified date and time. The top of the contents list box shows column headers—Name, Size, Type, and Modified (shown previously in Figure 1.12).

Sort the list of files

1. From the File Open dialog box, click any of the column headers to sort the list ascending by that category. For example, to sort the files by date, click the **Modified** header.

2. Click the column header again to sort the list descending by that category. Click again to sort the files with the latest date at the top of the list.

Using Wildcards to Shorten the File List

If your file list is particularly long, you may want to limit the list by the file name. Two wildcards can help you limit the list by characters in the name of the file: * (asterisk) and ? (question mark). The asterisk means replace any number of characters. The question mark means replace one character.

Limit the file list using wildcards

1. In the **File name** text box of the Open dialog box, type the text with wildcards.

2. Choose the **Find Now** command button. The following list shows some examples:

Type	To Display
B*	All files that begin with B
Rev??	Rev95, Rev96, Rev97
Don	Reasons to Donate, Donations YTD, Orientation to Donors, Don Campbell's Resume

3. To remove the wildcard and all restrictions on the file list, choose the **New Search** command button.

Finding a File by Date

When your list is long and you do not remember the exact filename but you do remember the approximate time that you last worked on the file, you can limit the file list to just those files modified at a certain time.

Find files by date modified

1. On the Open dialog box, use the **Last Modified** drop-down list and select **yesterday, today, last week, this week, last month,** or **this month** (see Figure 1.16).

2. Click the **Find Now** command button to limit the file list by time.

More use for wildcard asterisks

Unlike the DOS wildcard, you can use multiple asterisks within filenames.

FIGURE 1.16

To display only those files meeting
data criteria, choose the Last
Modified drop-down list.

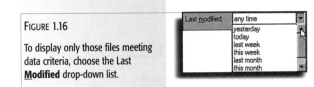

3. To return the file list to show all dates, select any time at the
bottom of the list.

Finding a File by Contents

You may remember where you put a file but don't have a clue as
to what you called it. You can look for a file by the contents
inside the file or by the summary information that you added to
the file.

Find a file using the contents of the file

1. On the Open dialog box, in the **Text or Property** text box,
type some text that you put in the file—such as who you
addressed the file to, the subject, or maybe an expense category. (Figure 1.17 shows all the files containing Rick, which
means that Rick can be typed in the file, an author of the
file, or part of any other file property.)

FIGURE 1.17

All files that have Rick as part of
the document or a property are
shown here.

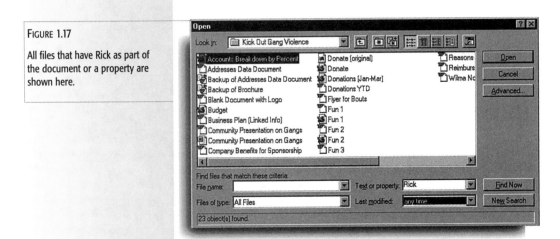

2. Choose the **Find Now** button.

3. To reset the Open dialog box, choose the **New Search** command button.

Expanding the Search to Include Subfolders

If the search text isn't found in the current folder, you can expand your search to other folders on the hard drive.

Broaden the search

1. On the Open dialog box, choose the highest level that you want to search (for example, the C drive) in the **Look in** drop-down list.

2. Select the Commands and Settings button 🖳 to display the drop-down menu.

3. Select **Search Subfolders** (shown in Figure 1.18).

4. Now when you do any of the search procedures such as using the **File name**, **Text or property**, **Last modified**, **Files of type**, or **Advanced** searches, subfolders display as well as the files.

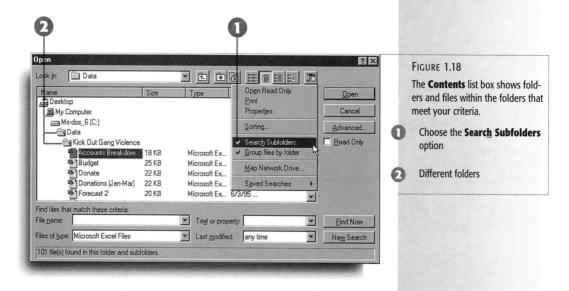

FIGURE 1.18

The **Contents** list box shows folders and files within the folders that meet your criteria.

❶ Choose the **Search Subfolders** option

❷ Different folders

5. To group files by their subfolders, check the **Group files by folder** option on the Commands and Settings button.

6. To again display only the contents of the **Look in** choice, uncheck the **Search Subfolders** option.

Displaying Types of Files

If you enter the Open dialog box through the Open a Document button on the Microsoft Office Shortcut Bar, the dialog box shows files of all types. If you enter the Open or Save As dialog boxes through a specific program such as Word, Excel, PowerPoint, or Access, the default is to show only those files created by that program.

Display all or different file types

1. On the Open or Save As dialog boxes, choose the **File of type** drop-down list.

2. Select **All Files**. You also can display files from different word processors such as WordPerfect, spreadsheets such as Lotus 1-2-3, or database programs such as dBASE IV.

This capability is helpful if you want to open a file created by a different program or if you want to save a file in a different format for use in a different program. Figure 1.19 shows some of the **Files of type** choices for the Excel Open dialog box. These types include text files, different spreadsheet formats, older versions of Excel, and database file formats.

You usually change the file type when you want to convert a file from one kind of worksheet (Lotus 1-2-3 to Excel), word processing document (WordPerfect to Word), or database (dBASE to Access) to another. In some cases, however, you may want to open a different kind of file. For example, you can open an Excel worksheet file in a Word document. (Table 1.10 shows some possibilities for opening different kinds of files.)

TABLE 1.10   File types that you can open in a different application

Application Opening File	File Type	Result
Word	Excel worksheet	Word table (can be a merge data document)
PowerPoint	Word (outline)	Heading 1 = slide title, Heading 2, 3 = points and subpoints
PowerPoint	Excel worksheet	Each row becomes the title of the slide

When you try to open a file of a different type, if your application can't convert the file type, an error message appears stating that the file format is not valid.

In Access, you don't use File Open to open a different type of file. You can, however, use the **File** menu, select **Get External Data**, and choose **Import** to import an Excel worksheet into Access. You have options indicating the range and whether the first row contains field names or not. You can also export a table, query, form, or report to Word or Excel using the OfficeLinks button ⊞ ▾ on the toolbar.

Using Advanced File Find Capabilities

Although the **Text or property** option searches for the contents of the file or any property, you may want to limit your search to one property or use many properties at one time.

Use the advanced search capabilities

1. Click the Open button ⊞ on your program's standard toolbar.

2. If you want, fill out the **File name**, **Text or property**, **Files of type**, and **Last modified** options as described earlier.

3. Choose the **Advanced** button. The Advanced Find dialog box appears with any choices you made in the Open dialog box.

4. Choose the **Property** drop-down list and select the property that you want (shown in Figure 1.20).

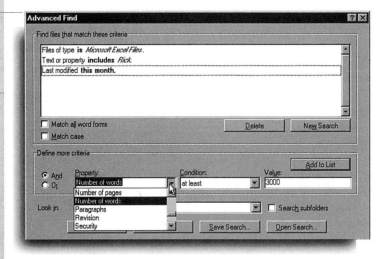

5. In the **Val̲ue** text box, type the text for which you are looking.

6. Choose the **A̲dd to List** button.

7. If you want to add another condition, choose the **An̲d** option button (both conditions must be true) or the **O̲r** option button (either condition must be true) and complete steps 2-6.

8. When you finish filling in the Advanced Find dialog box, choose the **F̲ind Now** button on the bottom left of the Advanced Find dialog box.

You return to the Open dialog box with the list of files that meet your criteria in the contents list box. (Some of the other options in the Advanced Find dialog box are listed in Table 1.11.)

TABLE 1.11   Other options in Advanced Find dialog boxes

Option	Description
Match a̲ll word forms checkbox	For contents, comments, and other item searches, you can find files that match different forms of the word. For example, if the Value is *to be*, the search looks for *to be*, *are*, *is*, *am*.
M̲atch case checkbox	For contents, comments, and other items in the **Property** choice, you find only those items that match capitalization (uppercase and lowercase) the way you typed the options in the **Val̲ue** text box.

Option	Description
Delete button	Click one of the items in the **Find files that match these criteria**, and then choose the **D**elete button to remove that criteria.
Ne**w** Search button	Clear all search criteria and start over.
Condition drop-down list	This list changes depending on the **P**roperty selected and enables you to find matches that contain the entire **Val**ue choice, a portion of it, one of the items in the **Val**ue choice, items greater or less than a date, and others.
Look in drop-down list	The same as **Look in** on the Open dialog box; it enables you to change the location of your search.
Searc**h** subfolders checkbox	Same as the menu choice on the Commands and Settings menu in the Open dialog box; it enables you to include files from the current folder and any sub-folders that you want.
Save Search button	Save any search criteria with a name for later retrieval.
Open Search button	Choose one of the named searches you created with the **Save Search** command.
Cancel button	Don't do any of the Advanced Find options and return to the Open dialog box the way you left it.

Saving and Using Saved Search Criteria

If you continually search for the same kinds of files, you may want to save your search settings. After you identify the file-name, location, property information, text, or date search criteria, you can save these settings.

Save search criteria

1. If you are in an Open dialog box, choose **Advanced** to open the Advanced Find dialog box.
2. Choose the **S**ave Search button.
3. Type the name of the search and choose the **OK** button.

Use saved search criteria

1. If you are in an Open dialog box, choose **Advanced** to open the Advanced Find dialog box.

2. Click the **Open Search** button to display the Open Search dialog box.

3. Select the named search from the list and choose the **Open** button.

4. To delete the search, choose the **Delete** button. To give the search a different name, choose the **Rename** button. (Figure 1.21 shows a list of saved searches.)

FIGURE 1.21

Select saved searches in the Saved Searches list box.

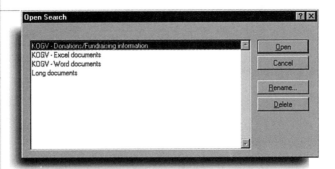

Saving Your Favorite Files and Folders

If you use the same files or folders over and over, you may want to save them in a special folder called Favorites.

Add a file or folder to favorites

1. In an Open dialog box, select your favorite file or folder and click the Add to Favorites button.

2. From the drop-down menu, select **Add [*Folder Name*] to Favorites** or **Add Selected Item to Favorites**.

3. When you want to see the Favorites files and folders, click the Look in Favorites button in any file dialog box.

Copying and Moving Files, Printing, and Other Hidden Features

When you are in an Open or Save dialog box, you have other options that are hidden and do not display as a choice in the dialog box. Access these options by selecting a file or files and then clicking your right mouse button (see Figure 1.22).

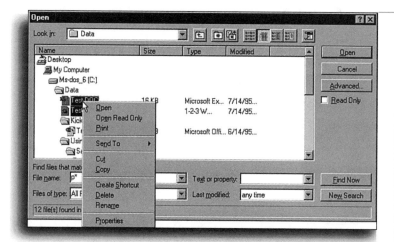

FIGURE 1.22

Select saved searches in the **Saved Searches** list box.

You can select files in one of several ways:

- Click one filename.
- Hold down the Ctrl key and click any files to select more than one file.
- Click the first file, hold down the Shift key, and click the last file to select a group of adjacent files.

After you have selected your file(s), click the right mouse button in part of the selection and choose one of the following:

- Choose **Open** to open all the selected files.
- Choose **Open Read Only** to open the files, but you need to give a new name if you want to save the files.
- Choose **Print** to print the files. (This is not available in Access).

Copy files to My Briefcase

My Briefcase is a Windows 95 feature that enables you to keep your documents up-to-date between your desktop computer and a laptop computer.

- Choose **Send To**, and choose a floppy drive to copy the file, Fax Recipient to fax the file, Mail Recipient to send a mail version of the file, or My Briefcase.
- Choose **Cut** to move the files to the Clipboard (and remove the original files).
- Choose **Copy** to copy the files to the Clipboard (and keep the original files in place).
- Choose **Create Shortcut** to create another icon in the directory that is a shortcut to the file. (Click the right mouse button on the shortcut name and choose **Properties** to give the shortcut a keyboard shortcut. The shortcut name starts with "Shortcut to.")
- Choose **Delete** to remove the files to the Recycle Bin.
- Choose **Rename** to give the file a new name.
- Choose **Properties** to give a keyboard shortcut to a shortcut file or see file information such as DOS filename, date created, file attributes, summary information, and statistics.

Restore files that you think are gone

If you accidentally delete files, you can get them back if you haven't emptied the Recycle Bin. With all programs minimized or closed, choose Recycle Bin on the Windows Desktop. Select the filename, choose the **File** menu, and select **Restore**.

If you choose **Cut** or **Copy**, choose the location where you want the file to go, click the right mouse button, and choose **Paste** from the shortcut menu.

Printing Documents

Access is different

In Access, you select the object in the database window or double-click the item to open it, choose the **File** menu, and select **Print**.

To print or preview the current document, you can use menu commands, toolbar buttons, or shortcut keys. As mentioned in an earlier section, you can print one or more files by clicking the right mouse button on a file name in an Open dialog box and then choosing the **Print** command.

Printing All or Part of the Document

Print the current document

1. Choose the **File** menu, and then select **Print**. The Print dialog box (similar to Figure 1.23) appears, displaying more choices.

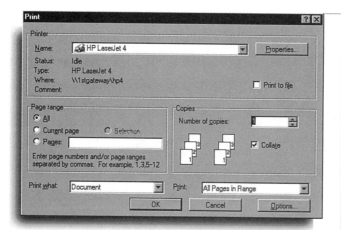

2. Make selections on the dialog box, and choose **OK**. Options in the Print dialog box enable you to print the entire document or workbook, the current page, specific pages, selected sheets, or selected text. You also can specify the number of copies to print. In the **Pages** text box in Word or **Slides** text box in PowerPoint, you can skip pages (you can type 1-2, 4-7, or just 13- to print page 13 to the end of the document).

Changing Printing Options

If you want to make additional printing choices, use the Page Setup dialog box (shown in Figure 1.24). The options in this dialog box enable you to set margins, print headers and footers, specify the print orientation, and change the printer settings.

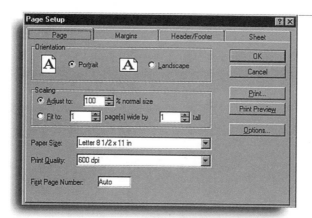

To change margins, paper size, and other features, use the following commands:

Application	Menu Command
Word	**File, Page Setup**
Excel	**File, Page Setup**
PowerPoint	**File, Page Setup**
Access	**File, Page Setup**

To change the printer, choose the printer from the drop-down list in the **Printer** section of the Print dialog box.

Using Print Preview

Although your screen shows what you will see on the printed page, Word, Excel, and Access have a Print Preview option that enables you to see the entire page (or more than one page), including headers and footers, page numbers, and margins. You enter the preview by choosing the **File** menu, and the **Print Preview** command. (Table 1.12 shows the features available while you are in Preview mode.)

TABLE 1.12   Print Preview options

Option	Word	Excel	Access
Change margins		X	
View Ruler (to change margins, indents, and tabs)	X		
Magnify/Zoom	X	X	X
Zoom to different sizes	X		X
Multiple pages	X		X
Shrink to fit	X	X	
Print	X	X	X
Edit	X		
Next (go to next page)	X	X	X

Option	Word	Excel	Access
Previous (go to previous page)	X	X	X
Setup (go to setup dialog box)	X		
Go to specific page/ first or last page			X
OfficeLinks (Output to Word or Excel)			X

Figure 1.25 shows Print Preview for Word; Figure 1.26 shows Print Preview for Excel; and Figure 1.27 shows Print Preview for Access.

Change margins in Excel or Word

1. Click the **Margins** button (Excel) or View Ruler (Word) button 📑.
2. Move the mouse pointer to the top or side until the pointer changes to a double-headed black arrow, and then drag the margin.

Magnify the document

1. Click the Magnifier 🔍 (Word) or **Zoom** (Excel) button.
2. Click the document where you want magnification.
3. To deactivate magnification, click the document again.

Edit the document in Word

1. Click the Magnifier button 🔍 to deactivate magnification and activate editing.
2. Make changes as if you were in Normal or Page Layout view.

Use shrink to fit in Excel

1. Choose the **Setup** button.
2. Click the Page tab, choose **Fit To,** and fill in the Page(s) Wide by Tall text boxes.

FIGURE 1.25

The Word Print Preview can show more than one page at a time.

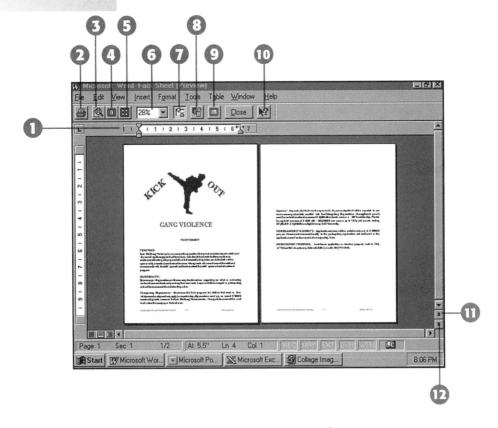

1	Use ruler to change margins	**7**	View Ruler
2	Print	**8**	Shrink to Fit
3	Magnifier	**9**	Full Screen
4	One Page	**10**	Help
5	Multiple Pages	**11**	Previous Page
6	Zoom Control	**12**	Next Page

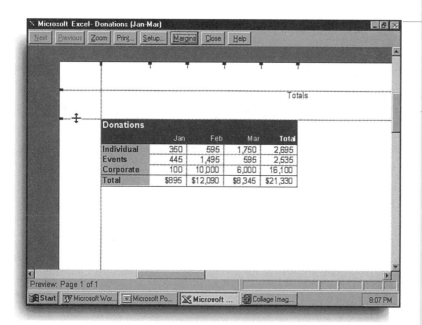

FIGURE 1.26

You can change margins and view a document in Excel's Print Preview. Just drag double-headed arrow to change margins

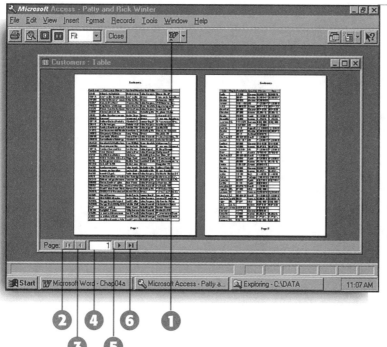

FIGURE 1.27

In Access, Print Preview can show one or two pages at a time.

1. OfficeLinks (send to Word or Excel)
2. First page
3. Previous page
4. Specific page
5. Next page
6. Last page

Creating and Editing Documents

Identify the parts of the Word screen and the toolbar buttons

Enter and edit text using a variety of Word tools from the menu, toolbars, and shortcut keys

Use AutoText entries to quickly insert repetitive text in your document

Use your mouse, keyboard, or a combination of both to select text

Learn the difference between the Save As and Save commands for saving your document

Understanding Word Basics

Of all the applications included with Microsoft Office, Word may be the one you use most. You need a word processor to produce at least letters and envelopes in your everyday work. Using Word, you also can create memos, fax cover sheets, reports, newsletters, mailing labels, brochures, tables, and many other business and personal documents. Not only does Word offer many commands and features that help you complete your work quickly and easily, but you almost don't need to know how to type anymore. Word provides easy graphics handling, outlining, calculations of data in tables, the capability to create a mailing list, list sorting, and efficient file management. In addition, you can perform many desktop publishing tasks, such as formatting fonts, creating display type, aligning text, adding shading, and adding graphic borders.

If you are familiar with Windows 3.1 or Windows 95 applications, you probably already know quite a bit about operating Word. You know, for example, how to use such features as the Control menu icon, the Window menu, and Help. Additionally, you understand the use of the mouse, including the right-click to display the shortcut menu, scrollbars, dialog boxes, and other features of a Windows application.

Using the Word Screen

When you start the program, Word displays specific screen elements as defaults, including the title bar, menu bar, two toolbars, a ruler, scrollbars, and the status bar. Word is so flexible that you can, of course, hide these elements or show different components, at any time, by choosing a command from the **View** menu or the **Tools** menu. By default, Word is trying to give you the most common tools that you need to begin your word processing adventure. (Figure 2.1 shows the default Word screen and indicates the components of the screen.)

SEE ALSO
➤ To get more information about window elements, see page 13

➤ If you need more information about working with menus, see page 25

Don't forget about the powerful help feature

As you are working with an application like Word, you may find that you don't know how to do something. Remember the powerful online help built into Word. Choose **Help** from the menu bar, and then select one of the commands from the menu provided.

FIGURE 2.1

Using Word's screen elements can help you complete tasks quickly and efficiently.

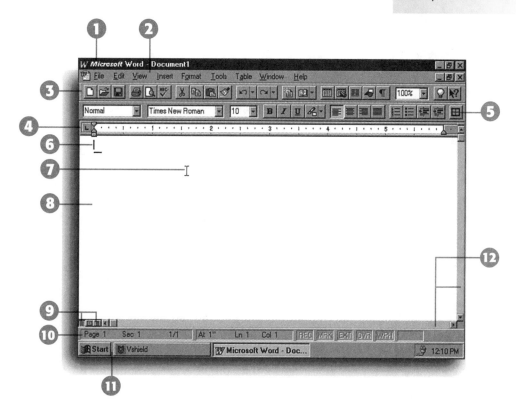

1	Title bar	7	Insertion point
2	Menu bar	8	Workspace
3	Standard toolbar	9	View Buttons
4	Ruler	10	Status bar
5	Formatting toolbar	11	Taskbar
6	End-of-file marker	12	Scrollbars

The following list describes Word's screen elements:

- *Title bar.* The title bar contains the name of the program, the name of the document, the Control menu icon, and the Minimize, Maximize/Restore, and Close buttons. Additionally, the title bar can contain the Microsoft Office Shortcut Bar.

- *Menu bar.* The menu bar contains specialized menus containing related commands. Choose commands from the **Format** menu, for example, to change fonts, set tabs, add a border, and so on.

- *Standard toolbar.* This toolbar contains buttons that you click to perform common tasks, such as starting a new document, saving a document, checking spelling, and undoing an action. The buttons in the Standard toolbar provide shortcuts for common menu commands. When you leave the mouse pointer on a button, a ToolTip appears with the mouse pointer, giving the name of the button.

- *Formatting toolbar.* The buttons in the Formatting toolbar provide shortcuts for choosing character or paragraph formatting such as changing fonts, font sizes, styles, alignments, and so on. Use this toolbar to format text quickly as you work.

- *Ruler.* The ruler provides a quick and easy method of setting tabs and indents in your text.

- *Workspace.* The workspace consists of a blank page in which you enter or edit text, place pictures and graphics, and work with your document.

- *Insertion point.* The insertion point shows you where the text, pictures, and graphics will be placed. In other programs it is known as a *cursor*.

- *Scrollbars.* Use the scrollbars to move quickly to another area of the document.

- *Status bar.* The status bar lists information and displays messages as you work in Word. When you double-click the page, section, or line reference area, the Go To tab on the Find and Replace dialog box is displayed.

You can use the status bar to turn options on and off

When you double-click the REC, EXT, OVR, and WPH boxes on the status bar, you can quickly turn the associated feature on or off. REC is Macro Record, EXT is Extend Selection Mode, OVR is Overtype mode, and WPH is WordPerfect Help.

- *Taskbar*. The taskbar is part of Windows 95 and enables you to start applications through the Start button and to switch between applications that have been launched by clicking the button for the application.

- *End-of-file marker*. The short horizontal line indicates the end of the document. You cannot move past this marker. You see this only in Normal and Outline Views of the document.

- *Mouse pointer*. As you move your mouse, the mouse pointer moves onscreen. The mouse pointer may change shape depending on the screen location (I-beam, left-pointing white arrow, right-pointing white arrow, and so on), indicating that you can accomplish different tasks.

- *View buttons*. To the bottom left of the horizontal scroll bar are three View buttons (Normal View, Page Layout View, Outline View). These buttons enable you to change your view to include margins, headers and footers, or show additional organizing tools.

While you are working on or reviewing a document you may want to see more of the document window and less of the Word program window. You can hide the ruler, toolbars, scrollbars and even the ToolTips that are displayed when you point to a button on a toolbar.

SEE ALSO

➤ *To learn more about toolbars, see page 18*

➤ *To learn more about formatting paragraphs, see page 84*

➤ *For more information about the ruler, see page 88*

➤ *For more detailed information on window elements, see page 13*

➤ *For more information about views, see page 74*

Hiding rulers

1. Choose the **View** menu.

2. Select **Ruler** to turn the ruler off.

Hiding scrollbars

1. Choose the **T**ools menu and then select **Options.** The Options dialog box is displayed.

2. Select the View tab in the Window section of the dialog box and click the **Hori**z**ontal** or **V**ertical scrollbar option to turn off either scrollbar.

3. Choose **OK** to apply the changes and to return to your document.

Hiding toolbars and tooltips

1. Choose the **V**iew menu and then select **Toolbars** to display the Toolbars dialog box.

2. Click the check box of the toolbar that you want to hide to remove the check mark from the box.

3. Click the **Show ToolTips** option to turn it off.

4. Choose **OK** to apply your changes and to return to the document.

When you are ready to use these same screen elements again, turn the options back on by performing the same procedure as explained to turn them off.

Entering Text in a Word Document

When you start the Word program, Word supplies you with a new, blank document (named Document1 in the title bar). You can begin to type at the blinking insertion point. When you enter text, that text appears in the workspace at the insertion point. (This section describes the basic techniques of entering text, moving around in a document, and selecting text for editing.)

Typing Text

When entering text, you type as you would in any word processor. Word automatically wraps the text at the end of a line—you do not have to press Enter to begin a new line. Press Enter only when you want to start a new paragraph or to create a blank line. Word defines a paragraph as any number of letters, words, or sentences ending with a paragraph mark. As you type, Microsoft Word indicates words that it does not recognize by underlining them with a red wavy line (see Figure 2.2).

A paragraph mark is a nonprinting character inserted whenever you press Enter. You can view paragraph marks by clicking the Show/Hide ¶ button ¶ in the Standard toolbar. To hide paragraph marks, click the Show/Hide ¶ button again. Figure 2.2 shows paragraph marks and the Show/Hide ¶ button on the Standard toolbar. In addition, the right indent marker in the figure is set at 4 1/2 inches so that you can see the automatic word wrap.

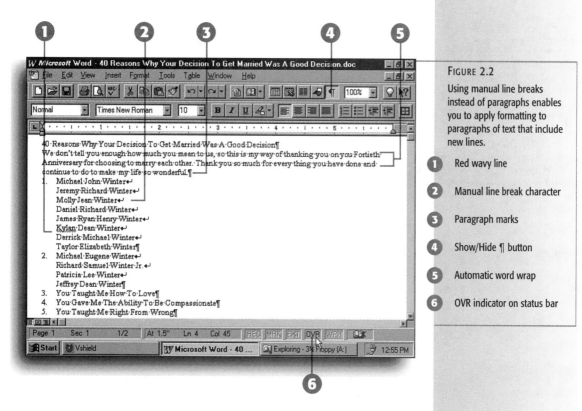

FIGURE 2.2

Using manual line breaks instead of paragraphs enables you to apply formatting to paragraphs of text that include new lines.

1. Red wavy line
2. Manual line break character
3. Paragraph marks
4. Show/Hide ¶ button
5. Automatic word wrap
6. OVR indicator on status bar

The following list contains some useful shortcuts and features that you can use when entering text in Word:

- If you make a mistake while typing, press the Backspace key to erase a character to the left of the insertion point.

- Press the Delete key to remove a character to the right of the insertion point.

- To repeat the text that you just typed, choose **Edit** and then select **Repeat Typing**, or press Ctrl+Y.

- To erase the text that you just typed, choose **Edit** and select **Undo Typing**, or press Ctrl+Z. You also can click the Undo button ↶▾ in the Standard toolbar.

- To start a new line without inserting a paragraph mark, press Shift+Enter. Word inserts a line break character. This is helpful when you want the new line to retain the formatting of the paragraph.

- Double-click the OVR indicator in the status bar to use Overtype mode, which enables you replace existing text with the text that you enter. Double-click the indicator again to turn off Overtype mode.

SEE ALSO

➤ *For more information about paragraph spacing, see page 84*

➤ *To add bullets and numbering see page 93*

Taking Advantage of the AutoText Feature

The *AutoText* feature enables you to automate entering information that you use frequently. You can create an AutoText entry that includes text only, formatted text, or graphics. Rick and I have found that we use AutoText entries for text that we would have created a macro for in other applications.

Don't confuse the AutoText feature with AutoCorrect. AutoText entries use abbreviations and the F3 key to insert text where you want it. You control when to insert the item. On the other hand, *AutoCorrect* entries also use abbreviations to insert text, but this automatically happens when you type the abbreviation and then press the Spacebar. AutoCorrect is intended for misspelled words but can easily be used for common text needs. For example, prw could be used to insert the company name "PRW Computer Training & Services" every time you type prw and press the Spacebar. You could also have an AutoText entry named prw that would insert both the company name and the address when you type prw and press F3. The AutoCorrect item helps minimize typing text in paragraphs, while the AutoText

Nonprinting characters are similar to WordPerfect's reveal codes

To see the codes for paragraphs, spaces, and tabs in your document, you can turn on the Show/Hide option to display these nonprinting characters. This is similar to WordPerfect's reveal codes. To learn more about the differences and similarities between Word and WordPerfect, choose the **Help** menu and then the **WordPerfect Help** command.

entry enables you to use a standard format for company letter-head.

SEE ALSO

➤ *To learn more about AutoCorrect, see page 102*

Creating and using AutoText entries

1. Create the text or graphics that you use repeatedly.

2. Select the text you just created.

3. Choose the **Edit** menu and select **AutoText.** The AutoText dialog box is displayed (shown in Figure 2.3).

4. Type a name for the AutoText entry in the **Name** box.

5. Click the **Add** button to create the entry.

6. To use the AutoText entry that you just created, move the insertion point to the place where you want the text inserted.

7. Type the name for the entry and press F3. The text is inserted at the insertion point.

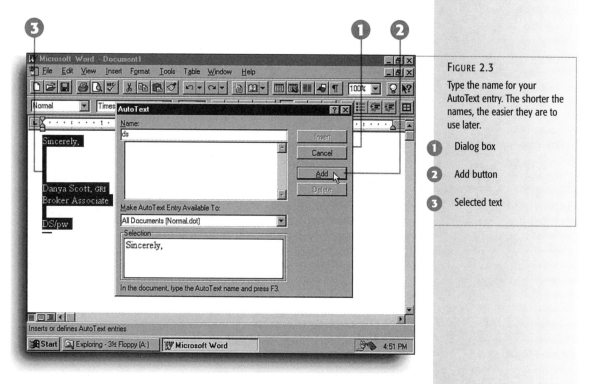

FIGURE 2.3

Type the name for your AutoText entry. The shorter the names, the easier they are to use later.

① Dialog box

② Add button

③ Selected text

Positioning the Insertion Point

To move the *insertion point*, move the I-beam mouse pointer to the new location and click the left mouse button. You can position the insertion point anywhere in the text area except below the end marker (the short horizontal line displayed in the text area). You can move the end marker by inserting paragraph marks (pressing Enter) before the end marker.

If you want to move the insertion point to a location that doesn't appear in the current window, you can use the horizontal or vertical scroll bar to move to the new location. When the new location appears in the window, place the I-beam pointer where you want to position the insertion point and click the left mouse button.

Additionally, you can press certain keys on the keyboard to move the insertion point quickly to a new location. Rick and I feel that using the keyboard to move around in a document is sometimes faster and easier than using the mouse. Table 2.1 lists keys that you can use to move around in your documents.

What happened when I clicked the mouse?

The insertion point always stays within the text area. If you click outside the margin boundary on the right, Word places the insertion point in the nearest text. If you click outside the boundary on the left, you select text in the document.

TABLE 2.1   **Keyboard shortcuts to move the insertion point**

Key	Moves Insertion Point
Arrow keys	One character or line up, down, left, or right
Page Up/Page Down	One screen up or down
Ctrl+ ←/→	One word to the left or right
Home/End	Beginning or end of a line
Ctrl+Home/End	Beginning or end of the document
Ctrl+Page Up/Page Down	Top left or bottom right of screen
Alt+Ctrl+Page Up/Page Down	Top of the previous or next page

Selecting Text

After entering text, you may want to delete or move a word, sentence, or paragraph. In addition, you may want to format the text by changing the font or font size, indenting text, and so on. Before you can perform one of these actions on the text in your document, you must select the text. Selecting the text shows

Word where to perform the action. After you select text, the selected text temporarily changes to white text on a black background. If you have changed the text or the background to a different color, the selected text may appear different, for instance, white text with a blue background, or yellow text with a black background.

You can select text by using the mouse, the keyboard, or a combination of methods, depending on how much text you want to select. Table 2.2 describes some of the methods of text selection.

TABLE 2.2 Selecting Text

To Select	Do the Following
One word	Position the I-beam pointer anywhere in a word and double-click. The word and the space following the word are selected. When you are changing the font characteristics for one word, you need only place the insertion point in the word, not select the entire word.
Multiple Words	Position the insertion point at the beginning or end of a word. Hold down the Ctrl and Shift keys and press the right- or left-arrow key repeatedly to select multiple words.
One sentence	Hold down the Ctrl key while clicking anywhere in the sentence. Word selects all words in the sentence to the ending punctuation mark, plus the blank space(s) following the punctuation mark.
One paragraph	Triple-click the paragraph, or place the mouse pointer in the selection bar, and double-click. The selection bar is a vertical white space to the left of the workspace. When you point the mouse in the selection bar, the I-beam pointer changes to a right pointing arrow (see Figure 2.4).
Specific text	Click and drag the I-beam pointer over one character, one word, or the entire screen.
One line of text	Place the mouse pointer in the selection bar to the left of the line and click once.
Whole document	Hold down the Ctrl key while clicking the selection bar. Alternatively, press Ctrl+A to select the entire document.

continues…

TABLE 2.2 **Continued**	
To Select	**Do the Following**
A vertical block of text	Hold down the Alt key while you click and drag the mouse pointer across the text. (Figure 2.5 shows a vertical block of selected text.)
Text using the arrow keys	Position the insertion point where you want to start selecting, press and hold down the Shift key, and then press the appropriate arrow key to move up, down, left, or right.
To the end of a line	Position the insertion point where you want to start selecting and then press Shift+End. Alternatively, select to the beginning of the line of text by pressing Shift+Home.
A block of text	Position the insertion point where you want to start selecting, move the mouse pointer to the end of the text you want to select, hold down the Shift key, and click the left mouse button.
Deselect text	Click anywhere in the workspace of a document or press an arrow key.

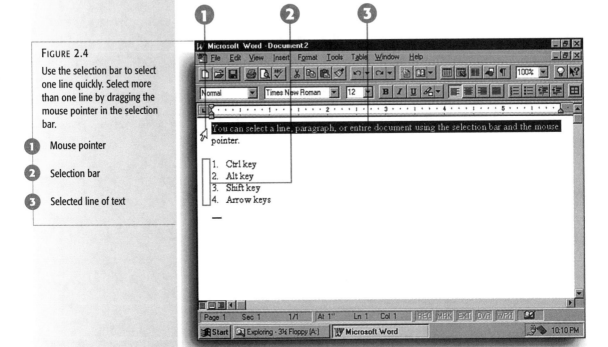

FIGURE 2.4

Use the selection bar to select one line quickly. Select more than one line by dragging the mouse pointer in the selection bar.

1 Mouse pointer

2 Selection bar

3 Selected line of text

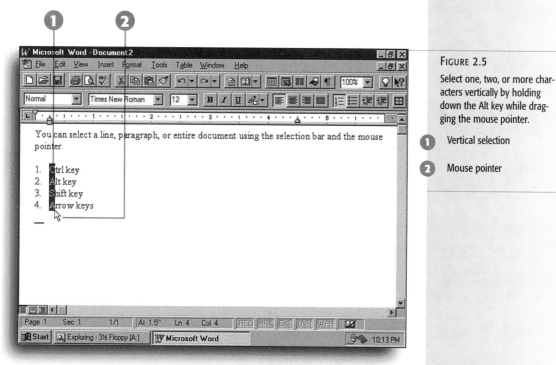

FIGURE 2.5

Select one, two, or more characters vertically by holding
down the Alt key while dragging the mouse pointer.

1 Vertical selection

2 Mouse pointer

Editing Text in a Word Document

With Word, changes and corrections are easy to make. You can
select any text in your document and delete it, copy it, or move
it. You also can make other changes easily. How many times have
you typed text only to discover that the Caps Lock feature was
on? Don't type the text again; use Word's Change Case command. This section shows you how to edit your document quickly and easily. You can use the Backspace and Delete keys to edit
one character at a time, or you can select text first and then edit
it. Table 2.3 summarizes the keyboard shortcuts, toolbar buttons,
and shortcut menu commands that are most productive for me.

**Caution: Accidentally deleting
selected text**

If you have text selected and
press the Spacebar or any character key, the selected text is
deleted and is replaced by the
characters that you typed. Use
the **Edit**, **Undo** command or
click the Undo button on the
Standard toolbar to reverse the
last action.

TABLE 2.3   **Procedures for editing selected text**

	Delete	**Copy**	**Move**	**Undo**	**Redo**
Keyboard	Delete or Backspace	Ctrl+C then Ctrl+V	Ctrl+X then Ctrl+V	Ctrl+Z or	Ctrl+Y or F4

continues…

TABLE 2.3   **Continued**

	Delete	Copy	Move	Undo	Redo
Toolbar buttons	✂	📋 then 📋	✂ then 📋	↺ ▾	↻ ▾
Right mouse button	Cut	Copy then Paste	Cut then Paste		

SEE ALSO

➤ *For more information on typing text, see page 61*

For more information on typing text, see page 61

Undoing a Mistake

Remember simple steps

If you make a mistake while typing text, pressing Backspace or Delete to delete the mistake may be easier than using Undo.

You can reverse many mistakes by using the Undo command. Suppose that you type a sentence and decide that you don't like the way it reads. You can delete the sentence by choosing **Edit** from the menu bar and choosing the **Undo** command. If you make a correction and change your mind, you can use the Undo command to reverse the action.

Word also provides a ↻ **Redo** command (also on the **Edit** menu) you can use to reverse the last Undo. Both the Undo and Redo commands describe the action that you just performed, like Undo Typing, Redo Clear, and so on.

The **Edit**, **Undo** ↺▾, or **Edit**, **Redo** ↻ menu commands work only on the last task that you performed. If, for example, you delete a sentence and decide that you want it back, you must choose the Undo command before carrying out another task. However, Word supplies Undo and Redo buttons in the Standard toolbar that enable you to undo or redo other recent actions. (Figure 2.6 shows the Undo drop-down list displaying six of the most recent actions.)

Copying, Moving, and Deleting Text

This is an instance where Word offers many ways to accomplish the same command. Which method you prefer is a matter of personal preference.

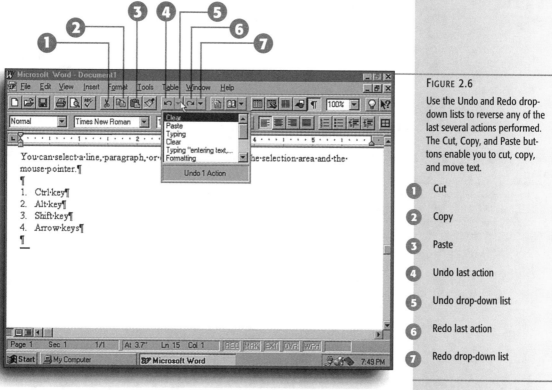

FIGURE 2.6

Use the Undo and Redo drop-down lists to reverse any of the last several actions performed. The Cut, Copy, and Paste buttons enable you to cut, copy, and move text.

① Cut

② Copy

③ Paste

④ Undo last action

⑤ Undo drop-down list

⑥ Redo last action

⑦ Redo drop-down list

Delete text

1. Select the text.

2. To delete the text, press the Delete key.

Copy or move text

1. To copy or move the text, click the Copy 📋 or Cut ✂️ button on the Standard toolbar. Word places a copy of the selected text on the Clipboard.

2. Position the insertion point where you want the text copied or moved.

3. Click the Paste 📋 button on the Standard toolbar. A copy of what is on the Clipboard is placed at the insertion point.

You also have the shortcut menu commands available. After you select the text, you can right-click the selection, and select the **Cut**, **Copy**, or **Paste** commands from the shortcut menu.

Delete is really delete, not cut

When you press Delete, the text is erased; the only way to recall the text is to choose the Undo command.

Tools or keyboard shortcuts for moving text

Use the Cut button on the Standard toolbar, or the Shift+Delete keyboard shortcut to remove text instead of the Delete key. You can bring back the last deletion without undoing any other work by positioning the insertion point and clicking the Paste button.

Copying text or other elements in your documents, such as pictures and charts, is one way to share data between applications. The Windows Clipboard is used by all the Microsoft Office applications. You can, for example, create text in Word, copy it, and paste it in PowerPoint. You also can copy a worksheet from Excel and paste it as a table in Word.

Drag-and-Drop Editing

Another method that you can use to move or copy text is called *drag-and-drop* editing. Word supplies this shortcut for moving or copying selected text. You also can use drag-and-drop editing to copy or move graphics or other objects.

Using drag-and-drop editing

1. Select the text or graphics that you want to move.

2. Point to the selected text or graphic and hold down the left mouse button. The drag-and-drop pointer appears (see Figure 2.7).

Create a copy while you drag and drop

To copy the text or graphic instead of moving it, hold down the Ctrl key as you point to the selected text or graphic, and drag the dotted insertion point to a new location.

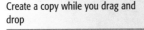

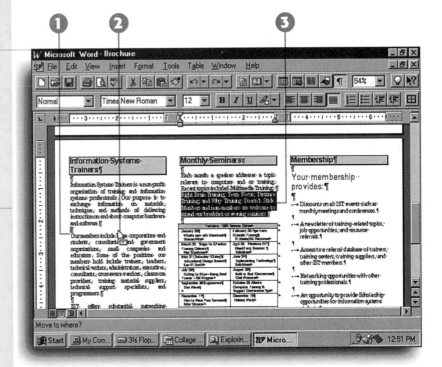

FIGURE 2.7

By using the drag-and-drop pointer, drag the selected text or graphic to a new location.

1 Dimmed Insertion Point

2 Drag-and-Drop Pointer

3 Selected Text

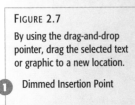

3. Drag the pointer and the dimmed insertion point that appears to the new location, and release the mouse button.

Converting Case

Word includes a handy command you can use to convert the case of text you entered earlier. If you decide that you do not want a heading to appear in all caps, you can select the text that you want to change, choose the **Format** menu, and select **Change Case**. The Change Case dialog box appears. Select one of the following options:

- *Sentence Case*. Capitalizes only the first letter in selected sentences.

- *Lowercase*. Changes all selected text to lowercase.

- *Uppercase*. Converts all selected text to all capital letters.

- *Title Case*. Capitalizes the first letter of each word of selected text.

- *Toggle Case*. Changes uppercase to lowercase and lowercase to uppercase in all selected text.

If a sentence or multiple sentences are selected, initial caps changes the first word of the sentence. If a phrase is selected, initial caps capitalizes the first letter of every word, as in book titles.

Saving, Closing, and Opening Word Documents

This section shows you how to save and close a document, open an existing document, and start a new one. (The following discussion is specific to Word; for information about basic file management, refer to Chapter 1, "Overview of Office.")

As in other Microsoft Office programs, you save a Word document by assigning it a name and a location in your drive and folder list. After naming the file, you can save changes made in that document, without renaming the file, by pressing a shortcut key or clicking a button in the Standard toolbar.

Change the default editing options in Word

The drag-and-drop editing option is activated by default. If you do not want to use drag-and-drop editing, you can turn the feature off by choosing the **Tools** menu and selecting **Options**. In the Edit tab, select **Drag-and-Drop Text Editing** to turn off the option.

You also can use the shortcut key to change case

Select the text and press Shift+F3. Each time you press the shortcut key, Word cycles through lowercase, uppercase, and initial caps.

Caution: Save your work often

Save your documents early in their creation, and save often as you work on them. If a power failure occurs while you are working on your document and you have not saved it as a file, you lose the document.

Saving a Word Document

When you save a document, Word places the file in the My Documents folder on your hard drive, unless you specified a different folder for Word when you installed Microsoft Office or changed the file location with the Tools, Options command. In addition, Word's default file type is Word Document. Word also suggests a filename for the document. You can accept the suggested name or rename the document to suit yourself by typing a new name in the **File Name** text box.

The name Word suggests depends on the text in your document. If you have short lines at the top of the document, Word uses the first phrase of text up to a punctuation mark, new line character, or paragraph mark and suggests Word Document for the file type.

Word filenames

A Word filename can have as many as 255 characters and can include spaces and some punctuation marks. Stay away from using forward slash (/), backslash (\), greater-than sign (>), less-than sign (<), asterisk (*), question mark (?), quotation mark ("), pipe symbol (|), colon (:), or semicolon (;).

Save a document

1. Click the Save button 💾 on the Standard toolbar. The Save As dialog box is displayed (shown in Figure 2.8).

FIGURE 2.8

Use the Save As dialog box to identify the document name in the **File Name** text box or accept Word's default name.

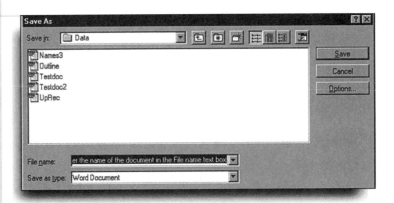

2. Type the name of the file in the **File Name** text box or accept Word's suggested filename.

3. Click the pull-down arrow for the **Save in** list and select the drive or folder that you want to save the file in, or click the Up One Level 📤 button. You can choose to save a file to a hard drive, floppy drive, network drive, and so on; available drives are in the **Save in** list. (See Table 2.4 for a description of the buttons on the dialog box.)

4. If you didn't choose a folder in step 3, select a folder by double-clicking the folder name in the list.

5. If you want to change the type of file that this document is saved as, select a format other than Word in the **Save as Type box**. This is extremely useful if you want to use the file in another application, such as DOS Text, WordPerfect 5.1, Word 2.x for Windows, or Word for Macintosh.

6. Choose **OK** to save the document.

TABLE 2.4	**Dialog box buttons**	
Button	**Name**	**Function**
	Up One Level	Changes the folder in the **Save in** prompt to the folder above.
	Look in Favorites	Changes the folder in the **Save in** prompt to the Favorites folder.
	Create New Folder	Enables you to create a new folder in which to save documents. The new folder is located under the folder you are currently in.
	List	Changes the display of file and folder names to a list.
	Details	Changes the display of file and folder names to a detailed list with column headings and file information.
	Properties	Changes the display of file and folder names to a list with a properties section on the right of the list. Select a document name to see more detailed information about the document.
	Commands and Settings	Displays a pull-down menu with the **Properties**, **Sorting**, and **Map Network Drive** commands.

> **Use the Details button to sort a document list**
>
> Click the Details button to display file details and then click the Modified column heading to sort your file list in descending and then ascending date order.

Saving Changes to a Named Document

After you save your document the first time by assigning it a name and location on the disk, you can continue to work on it. The changes that you make are not saved, however, unless you save them. When you are ready to save again, you simply click the Save button ▣. Word quickly saves the changes, and you are ready to proceed.

Saving All Open Documents

To save all open documents, choose the **File** menu and select **Save All**.This command saves all open documents and any open templates, macros, and AutoText entries. When you use the **Save All** command, Word displays a message box, asking you to confirm that you want to save each open document. If you have not named a document, Word displays the Save As dialog box so that you can name the document.

Closing All Open Documents

When you save your documents, they remain open until you choose to close them. You can close one document at a time by choosing the **File** menu and selecting **Close**. If you want to close all the open documents at one time, you can hold down the Shift key, select the **File** menu, and choose the **Close All** command. The Shift key changes the command to Close All.

Changing AutoSave Settings

As mentioned earlier, Word has an AutoSave feature that is automatically turned on. The default is to save your document every 10 minutes. If you leave this option on, you will most likely not lose as much as you would without it. If you would like to AutoSave more often than every 10 minutes, you can change the option by choosing the **Tools** menu and selecting **Options**. In the Save tab, select the **Automatic Save Every *x* Minutes** text box and decrease the number of minutes by using the increment buttons or typing a different number in the text box.

Opening a Word Document

To open a saved document in Word, click the Open button 📑 on the Standard toolbar. Word displays the Open dialog box (see Figure 2.9).

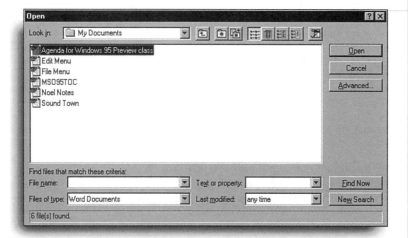

FIGURE 2.9

Select the file from the list of files and choose **Open** to open the document.

In the Open dialog box, select the filename from the list of files, if you saved it in Word's default folder. Otherwise, you can change the drive and folder, or even the file type, to access the file you want. (You can also use your shortcut menu in the Open dialog box to perform many commands.)

Open, print, copy, or delete a document

1. Locate the document in the Open dialog box.

2. Right-click the document name to display the shortcut menu.

3. Select a command from the shortcut menu.

4. If you choose **Cut** or **Copy** from the shortcut menu, you then need to change to the folder to which you want to copy or move the document.

5. Right-click the dialog box and select **Paste** from the shortcut menu.

SEE ALSO

➤ For more information about finding files, see page 26

Starting a New Word Document

You can start a new document at any time by clicking the New button 🗋 on the toolbar. When you use the New button or

Ctrl+N, a blank document appears using default fonts and other settings from Word's Normal template.

Create a new document from the New dialog box

1. Choose the **File** menu and select **New**. The New dialog box appears (see Figure 2.10).

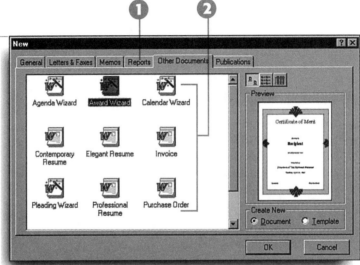

2. Select one of the tabs on the New dialog box. See Table 2.5 for a description of the templates that come with Word.

3. Double-click the template that you want to use to create a new document.

TABLE 2.5   Templates on the New dialog box

Tab	Template
General	Blank Document
Letters & Faxes	Contemporary Fax
	Contemporary Letter
	Elegant Fax
	Elegant Letter

Tab	Template
	Fax Wizard
	Letter Wizard
	Professional Fax
	Professional Letter
Memos	Contemporary Memo
	Elegant Memo
	Memo Wizard
	Professional Memo
Reports	Contemporary Report
	Elegant Report
	Professional Report
Other Documents	Agenda Wizard
	Award Wizard
	Calendar Wizard
	Contemporary Resume
	Elegant Resume
	Invoice
	Pleading Wizard
	Professional Resume
	Purchase Order

The templates listed in your New dialog box may vary from the list provided based on installation choices.

The Normal template is Word's default. The Normal template has the following characteristics:

- Uses an 8 1/2-by-11-inch portrait-oriented page
- Includes 1-inch top and bottom margins and 1 1/4-inch left and right margins

The quickest way to start a new document

Using the shortcut Ctrl+N or the New button in the Standard toolbar skips the New dialog box and bases the new document on the Normal template.

- Uses Times New Roman 10-point body text
- Supplies three heading styles: Arial 14-point bold, Arial 12-point bold italic, and Arial 12-point. All three heading styles are left-aligned and use single line spacing. They all add a 12-point space above and a 3-point space below the heading.

Formatting Documents

Learn different document views and understand their elements

Format text by changing fonts, font size, font styles, and copy formats

Adjust line and paragraph spacing, set tabs, use indents, adjust alignment, and use bullets and numbered lists

Change page size and orientation, set margins, and create columns

Understanding Views

Word enables you to view your document in a variety of ways. Each view—Normal, Outline, Page Layout, Master Document, and Print Preview—offers advantages for text editing, formatting, organizing, and similar tasks. You may prefer one view, but you also may want to use other views while formatting documents. The following list briefly describes each view:

- Normal view is mainly for entering and editing text.
- Page Layout view is perfect for formatting the text and page.
- Outline view enables you to collapse documents to heading levels so that you can move or copy text easily to reorganize long documents. (Outline view is covered in detail in Chapter 6, "Working with Large Documents.")
- Master Document view is a method of viewing and organizing several documents at one time. (This view is not discussed in this book. For more information, see Que's *Special Edition Using Microsoft Word 97*.)
- Print Preview shows how the document is formatted and enables you to make changes without having to go back to an Edit mode. (Print preview is discussed in detail in Chapter 4, "Proofreading and Printing Documents.")

This section covers the two most commonly used views: Normal and Page Layout.

In addition to views, Word provides magnification options for viewing a document. You can magnify the view to 200 percent, for example, or reduce it to fit the entire page (or even the entire document) onscreen. Finally, you can remove or display the various screen elements to produce a better view.

Changing views does not affect the insertion point

No matter what view or magnification you use, the insertion point remains where it was in the preceding view.

SEE ALSO
➤ *For more information on Print Preview, see page 109*
➤ *For more information on Outline view, see page 146*

Viewing the Document in Normal View

Normal view—the default view in Word—shows the basic document and text. Although you can view various fonts and font sizes, tabs, indents, alignments, and so on, you cannot view formatted columns, page margins, or headers or footers (see Figure 3.1). Use Normal view for entering and editing text or for formatting text. (Figure 3.1 shows the Normal View button.) You can use the view buttons in the horizontal scroll bar to switch between views quickly. (You learn about the other view buttons in the following sections.)

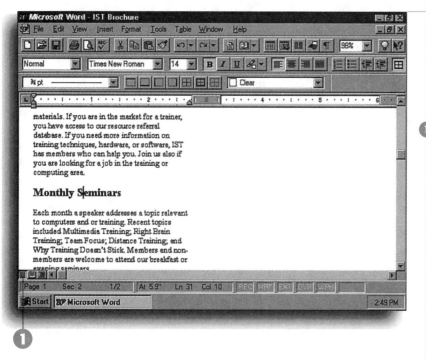

FIGURE **3.1**

The text in columns appears as one column per page in Normal view, meaning that you won't be able to see the actual layout of formatted columns.

1 Normal View button

Using Page Layout View

Page Layout view shows how the text, columns, margins, graphics, and other elements look on the page. Page Layout view provides the *WYSIWYG* (what-you-see-is-what-you-get) view of your document. Editing and formatting may be slower in Page Layout view, but you can get a better idea of how your document looks as you format and when you finish formatting. (Figure 3.2 shows the same document as Figure 3.1, but in Page Layout view.) In Page Layout view, the vertical scroll bar adds two extra buttons to move up or down a page at a time.

FIGURE 3.2

You can view columns and page margins in Page Layout view, meaning that your documents appear onscreen just as they do when printed.

1 Page Layout View button

2 Previous page button

3 Next page button

4 Page margins

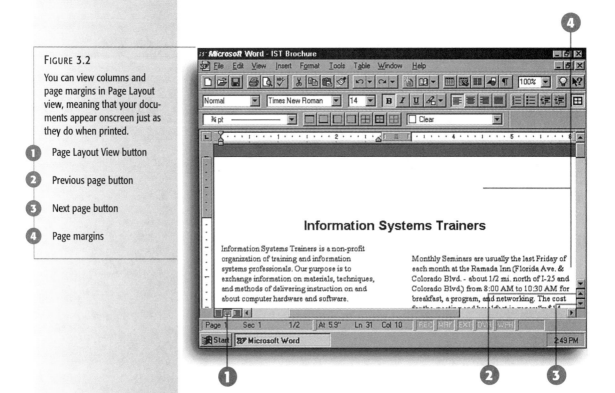

To change views by using the View menu, use one of these options:

- Choose **View**, **Normal** for text editing and entering.

- Choose **View**, **Page Layout** to format the text and page.

Hiding Screen Elements

In addition to changing views, you can display or hide the screen elements so that you can see the document design better. Use the **View** menu to remove the rulers and toolbars. You also can choose **View** and select **Full Screen** to view a document with nothing else onscreen but the Full Screen button (shown in Figure 3.3). You can enter and edit text in this view as well as move pictures and objects. To return to Normal or Page Layout view (depending on which view you were using when you switched to Full Screen view), press the Esc key or click the Full Screen button.

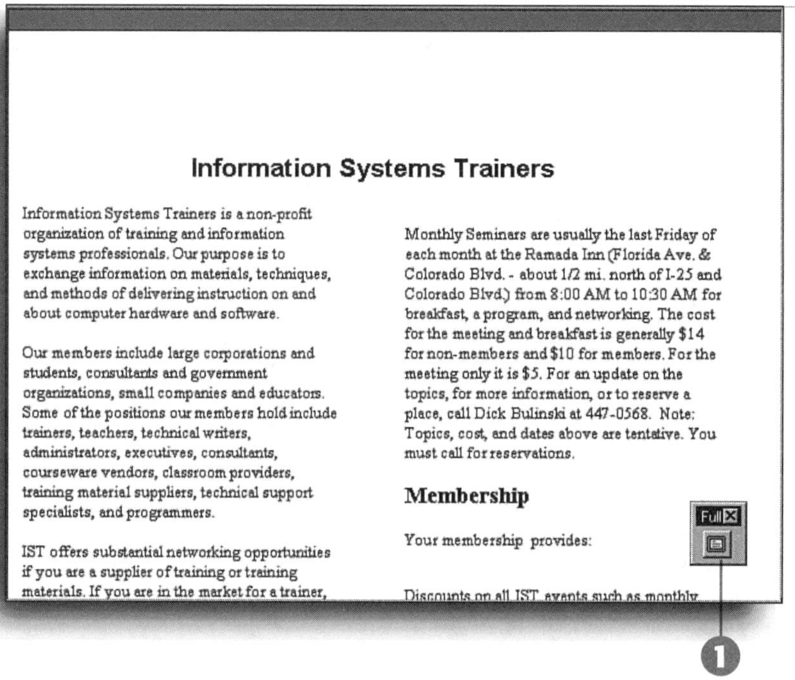

Information Systems Trainers

Information Systems Trainers is a non-profit organization of training and information systems professionals. Our purpose is to exchange information on materials, techniques, and methods of delivering instruction on and about computer hardware and software.

Our members include large corporations and students, consultants and government organizations, small companies and educators. Some of the positions our members hold include trainers, teachers, technical writers, administrators, executives, consultants, courseware vendors, classroom providers, training material suppliers, technical support specialists, and programmers.

IST offers substantial networking opportunities if you are a supplier of training or training materials. If you are in the market for a trainer,

Monthly Seminars are usually the last Friday of each month at the Ramada Inn (Florida Ave. & Colorado Blvd. - about 1/2 mi. north of I-25 and Colorado Blvd.) from 8:00 AM to 10:30 AM for breakfast, a program, and networking. The cost for the meeting and breakfast is generally $14 for non-members and $10 for members. For the meeting only it is $5. For an update on the topics, for more information, or to reserve a place, call Dick Bulinski at 447-0568. Note: Topics, cost, and dates above are tentative. You must call for reservations.

Membership

Your membership provides:

Discounts on all IST events such as monthly

FIGURE 3.3

Full screen view enables you to see and work with your document with no screen elements or obstructions.

1 Full Screen button

Magnifying the View

You can change the magnification of the view to better control how much of your document you see onscreen at any time. Word provides two methods of changing views: choosing **View** and selecting **Zoom** or clicking the Zoom Control button `100%` on the Standard toolbar. (Figure 3.4 shows a document at 115% magnification in Page Layout view).

Change magnifications by using the Zoom dialog box

1. Choose the **View** menu and select **Zoom**. The Zoom dialog box appears (shown in Figure 3.5).

Use Zoom Control to set the magnification best for you

To set your own magnification, click the down arrow next to the Zoom Control button, and then select a percentage or enter any number between 10 and 200.

More control with the Zoom dialog box

The Zoom dialog box enables you to view more than two pages at a time in Page Layout view.

FIGURE 3.4

You can format the text and document at any view magnification.

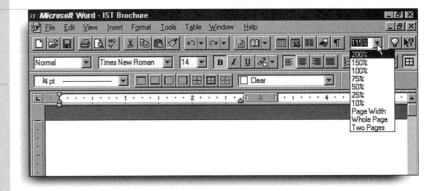

FIGURE 3.5

Choose Page Width to see an entire line of text in the Zoom dialog box.

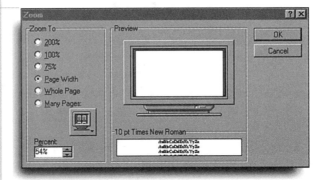

Zoom options depend on the view you are in

The Zoom dialog box and Zoom Control button may appear differently depending on which view (Normal or Page Layout) you are in when you choose the **Zoom** command.

2. In the Zoom To area, select the magnification that you want or enter a percentage in the **Percent** box; click the monitor button under the **Many Pages** option, and choose the number of pages that you want to view.

3. Choose **OK** to close the dialog box.

Formatting Text

Word, like the other programs in Microsoft Office, provides many options for formatting text. You can select a variety of fonts, sizes, and styles to enhance your documents. In addition, Word provides a Formatting toolbar that makes text formatting easy. Alternatively, you can use the Font dialog box, described later in this section. If the Formatting toolbar is not on, right-click a visible toolbar and click **Formatting** on the shortcut menu.

You can format text by first selecting the text and then making the formatting changes. Alternatively, you can position the insertion point, make the formatting changes, and then enter the text. All text entered from that point on is formatted according to your specifications until you change the formatting again or move the insertion point to another part of the document.

SEE ALSO

➤ *For more information about using toolbars, see page 18*

Changing Fonts in Word

Font is the typeface of the text. A typeface can, for example, be Times New Roman or Helvetica. The font that you choose helps create an impression or set the mood for the document. Suppose that you want to create an informal flyer for a sale. You can use a fun font, such as Comic Sans MS, Curlz MT, or Ransom. Formal, sophisticated fonts are those such as Arial, Matura MT Script Capitals, or Britannic Bold.

The following are three basic types of fonts:

- *Serif.* This font has strokes (sometimes called "feet") at the ends of letters—Times New Roman, Palatino, Bookman
- *Sans serif.* This font has no strokes—Helvetica, Arial, Avant Garde
- *Specialty.* Symbols and script fonts—Wingdings (symbol) Curlz MT (script).

Select the font that you want to use from the Formatting toolbar's Font drop-down list (shown in Figure 3.6).

When you are looking at the list of available fonts, Microsoft tries to show you where the fonts are coming from. The TT symbol stands for TrueType; this means the font is a scalable font and prints just as it appears. The printer icon next to the font name means that the font is generated by the printer definition that you have installed. Some fonts don't have anything next to them; those are screen fonts and may or may not print.

Changing Font Size

Font size is measured in points. Points and picas are typesetting measurements used for measuring spacing, line thickness, and so on. Twelve points equal a pica, and six picas equal an inch; therefore, 72 points equal an inch.

Use the right mouse button to display toolbars

To display additional toolbars, right-click an open space on any visible toolbar and select **Formatting**, **Borders**, **Drawing**, or any of the toolbars that do not display a checkmark.

FIGURE 3.6

Word lists the most recently used fonts at the top of the list so that you can find them quickly. The rest of the available fonts are listed in alphabetical order.

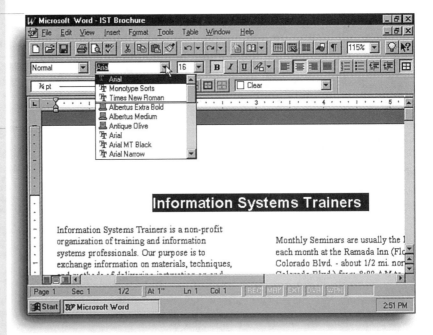

All text that you enter in a new, Normal template document is 10-point Times New Roman by default. You can, of course, change the type size. Use the Font Size drop-down list [10 ▼] on the Formatting toolbar to select the size that you want. The font sizes available in the Font Size drop-down list depend on your printer. If you know that your printer can print a size that is not listed in the box—15 point, for example—type the number in the Font Size text box and press Enter.

Choosing Font Styles

Font style keyboard shortcuts

The keyboard shortcuts for bold, italic, and underline are Ctrl+B, Ctrl+I, and Ctrl+U. After you select the text or before you type the text, simply press the keyboard shortcut to apply or remove the font enhancement.

Character formats, also called font *styles*, change the appearance of text. The Formatting toolbar supplies buttons for three font styles: bold **B**, italic *I*, and underline U. To apply any of these attributes, simply click the appropriate button. You can apply one, two, or all three attributes.

Besides these three font styles, Word supplies several effects—including strikethrough, superscript, subscript, small caps, and all caps—in the Font dialog box.

Using the Font Dialog Box

Choose the **Format** menu and select **Font** to display the Font dialog box. Use this dialog box to format the text all at once; for example, you can use the dialog box options to change the font, size, and font style of the selected text. (Figure 3.7 shows the **Font** tab of the Font dialog box.)

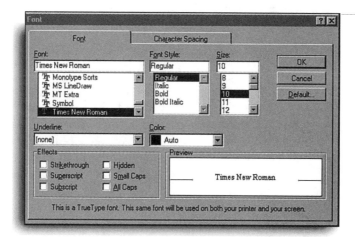

Figure 3.7

Use the Font dialog box to perform many changes at one time on selected text.

Using the **Font** tab of the Font dialog box, you can select a font and font style. A sample of the formatting style appears in the **Preview** box. The **Font** tab also enables you to choose from more attributes than are available in the Formatting toolbar, including single, words only, double, and dotted underlines and colors. After you select the options that you want, choose **OK** to close the dialog box.

Changing the Default Font

You may decide that you don't like the default font determined by Microsoft (Times New Roman, 10 point). If that is the case, you can change the default font by using the **Format**, **Font** command.

Change the default font

1. Choose the **Format** menu and select **Font** to display the Font dialog box.

Using styles for formatting

You can also format text by using Word's styles and your own to format text the same way over and over. Then when you want to change formatting in multiple places, you can change the style, and Word changes it everywhere the style appears. (For more information on using Word styles, see Chapter 6.)

2. Make any of the necessary changes in the dialog box.

3. Click the **Default** button on the dialog box.

4. Word prompts you to make sure that you want to change the default font. Click **Yes** to make your changes, or **No** to cancel the changes.

Copying Formats

Word makes formatting text easy with the Format Painter ![icon], which enables you to format an entire document quickly and easily.

When you format text—such as a heading, complicated tabs, or indents—and you need to format other text in the document the same way, you can save time by copying the formatting of the original text. Suppose that you formatted a heading as 18-point Universal, bold and italic, center-aligned, and with five-points spacing below the heading. Rather than select and format each heading in your document separately, you can use the Format Painter to copy the format to another heading.

Using the Format Painter to copy formats to other text

1. Select the formatted text—the text with the format that you want to copy.

2. Click the Format Painter button ![icon] in the Standard toolbar. The pointer changes to a paintbrush and I-beam (as shown in Figure 3.8).

3. Select the text to be formatted, and that text automatically changes to the original text format.

   (Alternatively, if you have more than one section of text that you want to copy the format to, you can double-click the Format Painter button and select each section to change.)

4. When you finish copying the format, click the Format Painter button again or press the Esc button to deactivate it.

Adding Highlighting to a Document

Another feature for making text stand out in a document is high-lighting (similar to using a highlighter pen to mark text in a

---

Use Format Painter for multiple locations

You can copy formatting to multiple locations using the Format Painter. Select the formatted text that you like, and double-click the Format Painter button to copy the format. For each location that you want to apply the format, select the text. Click the Format Painter button again or press Esc when you're finished.

Disabling the Highlight Feature

To disable Word's highlighting features, choose the **Tools** menu, select **Options**, and on the **View** tab, deselect the **Highlight** checkbox.

printed document). You highlight in the same way that you make text bold, italic, or underlined. First, select the text that you want to change and then click the Highlight button [icon] on the Formatting toolbar. The background behind the text changes to a different color.

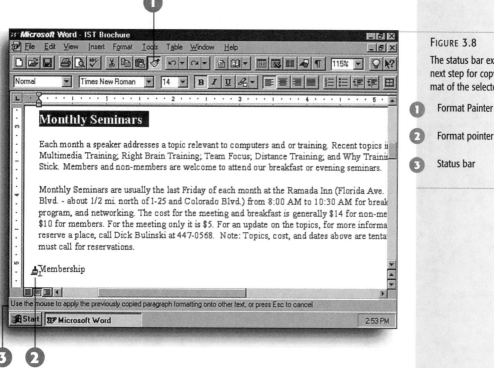

If you want to change the highlight color, click the drop-down arrow to the right of the Highlight button [icon] and choose a different color. The other option is to choose the highlight color first. Your mouse pointer changes to a highlighter tool. Click and drag to select the text that you want to highlight. When you release the mouse, the selected text is highlighted. To stop highlighting, simply click the Highlight button. To remove highlighting from a specific section of text, select the highlighted text and click the Highlight button.

Remove all highlighting in your document

Suppose that you want to remove all highlighting in the document. You can first select the entire document by pressing Ctrl+A, click the pull-down arrow on the Highlight button on the Formatting toolbar, and select the None option.

What is a paragraph?

Word's definition of a paragraph is any amount of text—one character or several sentences—ending with a paragraph mark. The paragraph mark is a nonprinting character that you can display by clicking the Show/Hide button ¶ on the Standard toolbar. Every time you press Enter, a paragraph mark is inserted at the position of the insertion point.

Leading adjusts the amount of text that fits on a page

Adjusting the leading is a sneaky way to add more or less text to a page. If you need to produce a one page document and your document runs into two pages with a little bit of text on the second page, for example, you can adjust the leading to force all the text on to one page. On the other hand, if you are a student writing a term paper that has to be *x* number of pages, you could adjust the leading to have more space between the lines.

Caution: Be careful changing leading (line spacing)

In most cases, don't use different line leading sizes in one document (see Figure 3.9). Different leading sizes confuses the reader and makes the text hard to read.

Formatting Paragraphs

A large part of formatting a page of text is formatting the paragraphs of body text, headings, lists, and so on. When producing an attractive, professional-looking document, you want to present a unified arrangement of the text elements. You can accomplish this by specifying line, word, and paragraph spacing; aligning the text; setting tabs and indents; and specifying how the text flows on the page.

Word enables you to select a paragraph of text and change its format by choosing commands or clicking buttons in the Formatting toolbar and the Tables and Borders toolbar. This section shows you how to format paragraphs of text.

Adjusting Line Spacing

You can use spacing to change the design and readability of your text. For the most part, Word's default spacing works quite well for most documents, but you may sometimes want to apply specific spacing. This section shows you how to change line and paragraph spacing and gives you a few tips on when to adjust spacing.

Line spacing, also called *leading* (pronounced LED-ing), is the space that separates a line of text from the text above and below it. Without line spacing, uppercase letters, ascenders (the top strokes of t, b, d, and so on), and descenders (the bottom strokes of g, j, y, and so on) in one line would touch those in the next line.

Word's default line spacing is single. Word measures spacing in points or in lines. Text typed in 10-point uses approximately 12-point spacing, or one line (single). Text typed in 12-point uses 14-point spacing, which still is one line. The line spacing depends on the size of the type. The larger the type size, the greater the line spacing: 24-point text, for example, uses about 27-point line spacing. Typesetting guidelines generally call for leading to be about 120 percent of the point size of the text.

Word enables you to change the line spacing in your text. You can set spacing to single, double, or one-and-a-half lines; or you can set a specific measurement in points. (Figure 3.9 shows four paragraphs of text with different leading—line spacing).

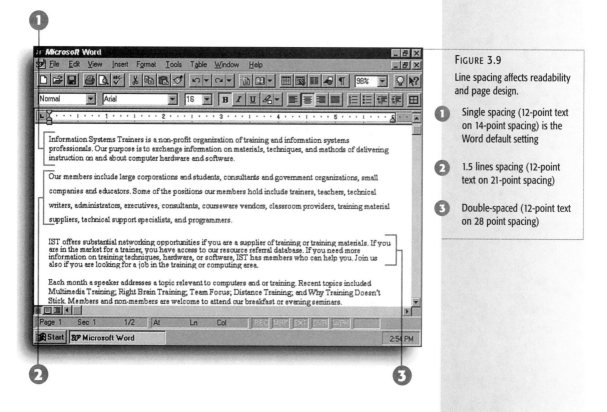

FIGURE 3.9

Line spacing affects readability and page design.

1. Single spacing (12-point text on 14-point spacing) is the Word default setting

2. 1.5 lines spacing (12-point text on 21-point spacing)

3. Double-spaced (12-point text on 28 point spacing)

Changing line spacing

1. Place the insertion point in the paragraph that you want to format, or select multiple paragraphs. Leading changes to any character in a paragraph cause the leading of the entire paragraph to be changed.

2. Choose the **Format** menu and select **Paragraph**. The Paragraph dialog box appears (see Figure 3.10).

3. Select the **Indents and Spacing** tab.

4. In the **Line Spacing** drop-down list, select the option that you want. Enter a value in the **At** box, if necessary. (These options are described in Table 3.1.)

5. Choose **OK** to close the dialog box.

Keyboard shortcuts for line spacing

If you want to use one of Word's standard leading (spacing) values, three keyboard shortcuts save time: Simply place your cursor anywhere in the paragraph (or select multiple paragraphs) and press Ctrl+2 for double spacing, Ctrl+1 for single spacing, and Ctrl+5 for 1.5 spacing.

FIGURE 3.10

The Paragraph dialog box
enables you to control line
spacing, either by using one of
Word's standard line spacing
values or by inserting your
one-line spacing.

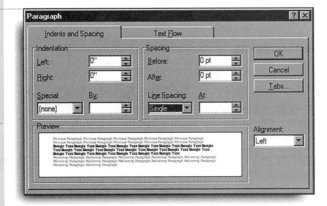

TABLE 3.1   **Line-spacing options**

Option	Result
Single	Default line spacing (two to five points larger than text size).
1.5 Lines	Spacing that is one-and-a-half times the size of the normal spacing. For 12-point spacing, the spacing is 18 points.
Double	Spacing that is twice the size of the normal spacing. For 12-point spacing, the spacing is 24 points.
At Least	Accommodates larger font sizes within a line of text. In the **At** box, enter a specific line-spacing amount that Word can use as minimum spacing. To allow for a larger font, for example, 12-point text that includes some 18-point characters, the spacing is 20; if you enter **20** in the **At** box, spacing is adjusted to 20 points.
Exactly	Limits Word to a certain amount of spacing, which you enter in the **At** box. If you use this option and then change the Font size to a size too large to display, characters are cut off.
Multiple	Decreases or increases line spacing by the percentage that you enter in the **At** box. To increase spacing by 20 percent, for example, enter **1.2**; to decrease spacing by 20 percent, enter **.8**.

Modifying Paragraph Spacing

You can add extra space between paragraphs to improve read-ability in your documents and to add valuable whitespace. Whitespace, or areas of a page that contain no text or graphics, provides rest for the reader's eyes and prevents the page from looking too crowded. Readability often is improved when you add space between paragraphs.

Use extra paragraph spacing instead of a first-line indent when you use left-aligned body text (shown in Figure 3.11). The reader's eyes can find the beginning of a paragraph easily without the indent. You also can add more spacing after headings or subheadings, between items in a list, within tables, and in outlines.

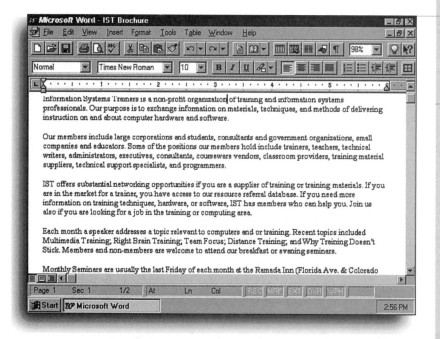

FIGURE 3.11
Extra spacing makes the beginning of each paragraph easy to find and provides valuable whitespace.

Add extra paragraph spacing

1. Place the insertion point in the paragraph that you want to format, or select multiple paragraphs.

2. Choose the **Format** menu and select **Paragraph**. The Paragraph dialog box appears (refer to Figure 3.10).

3. Select the **Indents and Spacing** tab.

4. In the Spacing area, you can add space before or after the paragraph to create more whitespace. Enter a value in the **Before** box, the **After** box, or in both boxes. To add half a line before or after the paragraph, type **6 pt** in either box. A full line would be 12 pt.

5. Choose **OK** to close the dialog box.

Setting Tabs

You can set *tabs* in a document by using either the Tabs dialog box or the ruler. Using the ruler to set tabs is quick and easy. The ruler also is handy for other kinds of paragraph formatting, such as indenting text and changing margins.

Looking at the ruler, you see gray vertical hash marks every 1/2 inch across the ruler. These are the default tab stops in Word set at 1/2 inch. Not only can you change tabs for the document on which you are working, you can change the default tab stops too. If you add your own tab stop positions, the default tabs up to that point disappear.

Change the default tabs

1. Choose the **Format** menu and select **Tabs**.

2. In the **Default tab** stops text box, change the setting to the interval that you prefer. For instance, .75 places the default tabs every 3/4" across the ruler.

3. Choose **OK** to return to the document.

If you want to change the default tab stop positions on all new documents, you need to modify the Normal.dot template file. This is the template on which all your new documents are based if you don't choose another template.

Modify the Normal.dot template file

1. Click the Open button 📂 on the Standard toolbar.

2. In the **Files of type** list box, select **Document Templates (*.dot)**.

3. In the **Look in** prompt, navigate to the MSOFFICE\ TEMPLATES folder. (The folder name for MSOffice may be different.)

4. Double-click the NORMAL.DOT file to open the template file.

5. Make the changes to default tabs as explained above.

6. Save and Close the document template.

The next time you create a new document based on the Normal template, the default tab stop positions reflect your changes.

To use the ruler to set tab stops in your text, first position the insertion point in the paragraph that you want to format or select multiple paragraphs and click the tab alignment button on the horizontal ruler (as shown in Figure 3.12) until the type of tab that you want appears. Then click the place on the ruler where you want to set the tab stop.

Setting and using tabs in your documents makes typing lists and editing and formatting changes much easier. If you set and use tabs instead of pressing the tab key or the Spacebar repeatedly to move the insertion point where you want it, making changes is much easier. Word offers four common types of tabs to make typing with tabs easier. Some of the uses for the different tab styles are as follows:

- Left-aligned tabs are useful for Names, Addresses, Lists, and Tasks.

- Centered tabs are useful for Headings, Titles, Cover Pages, Sections, and Invitations.

- Right-aligned tabs are useful for Numbers (without decimals), Page numbers, and Header and Footer information.

- Decimal tabs are useful for Numbers with decimals, Percentages, Product Codes, and Currency.

One of the biggest formatting problems that I have run into is fixing documents in which the user typed information without tabs defined—for example, a list of employees names, with department and extension number. The list was typed using the Spacebar to line up the information in columns. When the typist wanted to distribute the list and print it, the columns were not lined up. Had the list been typed using tabs, all the columns would have lined up just fine. To fix the list, I had to delete all the extra spaces, define tab stop positions, and type tabs to move the text.

You can reposition any tab stop in the ruler by clicking and dragging the tab marker to a new location. To remove a tab stop, drag the tab marker off the ruler and straight down into your document.

Setting tabs with leaders

A tab *leader* is made up of characters that fill in the space between the end of the text and leads up to the left side of the tab position. If you want to use leaders with tabs, first choose **Format**, select **Tabs,** and then select tab stop position, alignment, and leader options (none, dots, dashes, or underline) in the Tabs dialog box. If you are setting more than one tab, click the **Set** button after each tab definition.

FIGURE 3.12

Click the ruler to set a tab
stop; drag a tab marker in the
ruler to reposition the tab
stop.

1️⃣ Tab alignment button

2️⃣ Left tab

3️⃣ Center tab

4️⃣ Right tab

5️⃣ Decimal tab

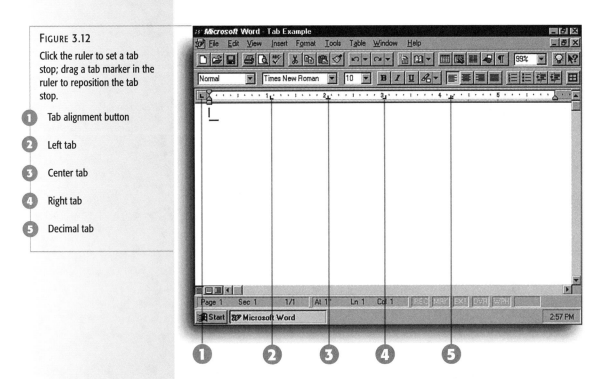

**Noticing formatting information in
the ruler**

When you position the insertion
point in any paragraph of text, tab
and indent settings for that paragraph appear in the ruler.

Indenting Text

You can use the ruler or the Paragraph dialog box to set indents
for text. Using the ruler, you can indent the left side, the right
side, or only the first line of a paragraph. (Figure 3.13 shows
indents for selected text.)

Word also supplies Increase Indent 🔲 and Decrease Indent 🔲
buttons (shown in the Formatting toolbar in Figure 3.13). Each
time that you click one of these buttons, you indent the selected
text to the next tab stop or to the preceding tab stop.

A hanging indent (see Figure 3.14) is commonly used for bulleted or numbered lists. I use hanging indents to draw attention to
information in correspondence. The first line of the text hangs
to the left of the body of the paragraph. To create a hanging
indent, position the insertion point anywhere in the paragraph
and drag the left indent marker (the rectangle and up-pointing
triangle on the bottom of the ruler) to the position where you

want to indent the paragraph beginning with the second line. Then drag the first-line indent marker (the down-pointing triangle on the top of the ruler) to the point at which you want the overhanging line to start.

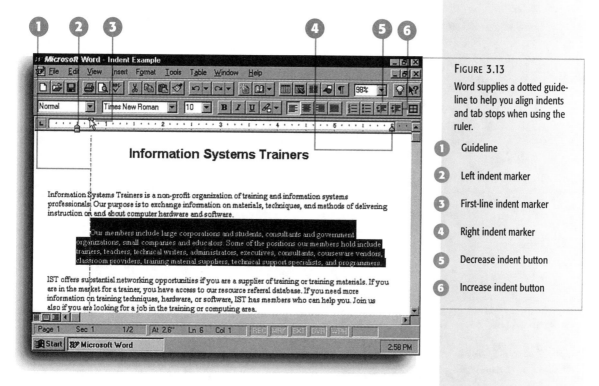

FIGURE 3.13

Word supplies a dotted guideline to help you align indents and tab stops when using the ruler.

1. Guideline

2. Left indent marker

3. First-line indent marker

4. Right indent marker

5. Decrease indent button

6. Increase indent button

Adjusting Text Alignment

Setting the *alignment* is a way of organizing your text. The way you align the text in a document makes the text easy to read, decorative, eye-catching, formal and sophisticated, or casual and flexible. Word enables you to left-align, right-align, center, or justify the text in your documents. (Figure 3.15 shows the four alignments and the corresponding toolbar buttons.)

Quickly aligning text

The keyboard shortcuts for aligning text are: Ctrl+L for Left aligned, Ctrl+E for Centered, Ctrl+R for Right aligned, Ctrl+J for Justified, and Ctrl+Q to change back to normal (left aligned, single space, no indents). Remember, just as when applying line spacing, text alignment applies to whole paragraphs.

FIGURE 3.14

Create a hanging indent by first dragging the left indent marker and then dragging the first-line marker into position.

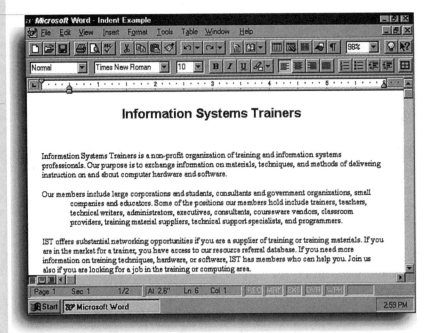

FIGURE 3.15

Align your text so that the reader can easily follow the message and so that the page is attractive.

① Align Left

② Center

③ Align Right

④ Justify

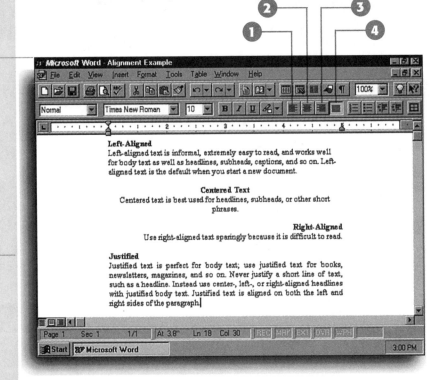

Adding Bullets and Numbering

Using Bullets and Numbering enables you to pull out information in your documents by making lists easier to read. You can bring emphasis to text by applying either bullets or numbering to lists (see Figure 3.16).

To create a bulleted list, you simply type the list, select the list after it is typed, and click the Bullet button ⊞ on the formatting toolbar. Alternatively, you can type the first line with an asterisk (*) and a space at the beginning of the line and press enter at the end of the line. (The asterisk and space convert to a bullet with an indent.) You can also choose to activate the bullets before you type the list. In this case, click the Bullet button on the formatting toolbar and type the list, clicking the bullet button again when you finish to deactivate bulleting.

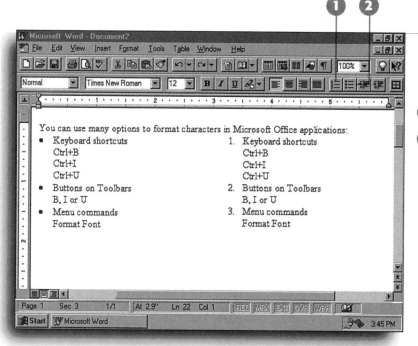

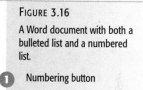

FIGURE 3.16

A Word document with both a bulleted list and a numbered list.

1 Numbering button

2 Bullets button

To create a numbered list, simply type the list, select the list after it is typed, and click the Numbering button ⊞ on the formatting toolbar. Or, you can type the first line with a number and a space at the beginning of the line and press Enter at the end of the line. (The number and space convert to a numbered list with an indent.) You can also activate numbering before you type the list. In this case, you click the Numbering button on the Formatting toolbar, type the list, and click the Numbering button again, when you are finished, to deactivate numbering (refer to Figure 3.16).

If you want to insert a blank line or lines without bullets in your list, use Shift+Enter to create manual line breaks. The line following the manual line break does not have a bullet. To add more lines with bullets, press Enter to create a new paragraph (see Figure 3.17). When you are ready to stop a numbered or bulleted list, press Enter twice to stop the numbering.

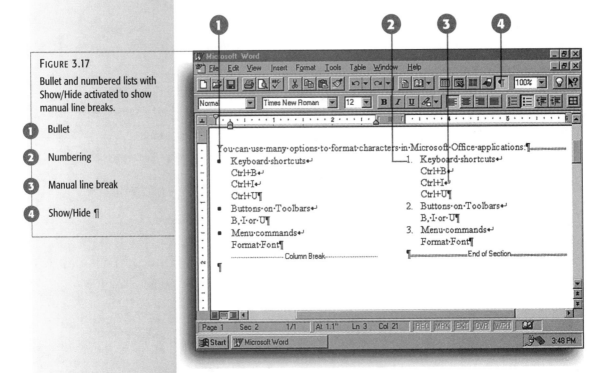

FIGURE 3.17

Bullet and numbered lists with Show/Hide activated to show manual line breaks.

1. Bullet

2. Numbering

3. Manual line break

4. Show/Hide ¶

Formatting the Page

Formatting the page includes changing paper size and orientation, setting margins, creating columns, and formatting tables.

The way you format the page depends on the amount of text, the size and orientation of graphics, the type of document, and so on. Keep in mind that you want to create an attractive, eye-catching page of easy-to-read text.

Suppose that you have several drawings of cars to be inserted into an advertisement with very little text. You can create the ad in *landscape* (wide) orientation with one-inch margins. On the other hand, if your text contains two long lists of items and no graphics, you can use *portrait* (tall) orientation with two columns and half-inch margins.

Word's page-formatting commands are flexible and easy to use. You can change the page to fit your text so that you present the most professional-looking document possible.

Changing Paper Size and Orientation for Word Documents

The size and orientation of the paper that you use depend mostly on your printer. Some printers take 8 1/2-by-11-inch sheets only; others can print sheets ranging from small envelopes to legal-size paper. Most laser and inkjet printers can print in either orientation. Check your printer manual before changing paper size and orientation.

Changing paper size and orientation

1. Choose the **File** menu and select **Page Setup**. The Page Setup dialog box appears (see Figure 3.18).
2. Select the **Paper Size** tab.
3. Select a size from the **Paper Size** drop-down list.
4. In the Orientation area, select **Portrait** or **Landscape**.
5. Choose **OK** to close the dialog box.

Setting Margins

You can change the margins of your document from the default settings to any margin that you want. Word's Normal template uses 1-inch top and bottom margins and 1.25-inch left and right margins. You can set the margins by using the Page Setup dialog box (see Figure 3.19). Keep in mind that your printer may limit the page margins you can select.

FIGURE 3.18

Choose paper size and orientation, and then view the change in the Preview box.

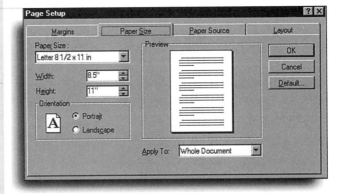

FIGURE 3.19

You can change the margins to shorten the line length and add valuable whitespace.

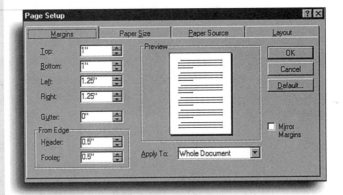

Multiple margin changes in one document

When you set margins, you can control the area of the document to change by using the **Apply to** option on the **Margins** tab of the Page Setup dialog box. This option enables you to apply margin settings to the entire document, specific sections, or only apply margin settings to the document from the insertion point forward.

SEE ALSO

➤ *For more information about section breaks, see page 164*

Changing the margins of your document

1. Choose the **File** menu and select **Page Setup**. The Page Setup dialog box appears.

2. Select the **Margins** tab.

3. Use the spinner buttons to increase or reduce the margins in one-tenth-inch increments, or enter specific values in the **Top**, **Bottom**, **Left**, **Right**, and **Gutter** fields. Setting a gutter margin is described in the next section.

4. Select the area of text to change in the **Apply to** drop-down list.

5. Choose **OK** to close the dialog box.

SEE ALSO

➤ *For more information about section breaks, see page 164*

Creating Columns

You can divide the page into one, two, three, or more columns to make the text well organized and easy to read. Documents such as books, magazines, catalogs, newsletters, brochures, and even advertisements often are divided into columns. Word makes dividing your documents into columns easy. To see your text formatted in columns, you must be in Page Layout view or Print Preview.

Format the columns in your document

1. If you have different numbers of columns throughout your document or if only a portion of your document is to have columns, select the text for which you want to change columns.

2. Choose the **Format** menu and select **Columns**. The Columns dialog box appears (see Figure 3.20).

3. In the Presets area, select the number or type of columns that you want. **One**, **Two,** or **Three** creates that number of equal columns. **Left** or **Right** creates two unequal columns with either the left or right column smaller than the other. You can add additional columns through the **Number Of Columns** increment box.

4. Use the other options in the dialog box to customize columns. You can adjust the width of the columns in the Width and Spacing section.

5. Choose **OK** to accept the changes and close the dialog box.

You divide a document into columns by using the Columns dialog box (see Figure 3.20). You can select a preset number of columns and designs or enter a number of columns and each column width, if you prefer. When you enter your own column width, you must specify spacing, called **gutter space**, between the columns.

Limit the number of columns to keep reading easy

Normally, you divide an 8 1/2-by-11-inch portrait-oriented page into no more than three columns; divide the same-size landscape-oriented page into no more than five columns. When you use too many columns on a page, the lines of text become too short and are hard to read.

FIGURE 3.20

You can make one column wider than the other for an interesting effect. View the result in the Preview box before choosing OK.

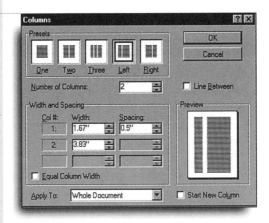

FIGURE 3.20

You can make one column wider than the other for an interesting effect. View the result in the Preview box before choosing OK.

If you like, you can add a line, or rule, between the columns by selecting the **Line Between** option. Word even enables you to start a new column at the insertion point by selecting the **Start New Column** option. Preview your column choices in the Preview box before accepting or rejecting the changes in the dialog box.

SEE ALSO

➤ *For more information about lines, borders, and shading, see page 179*

Proofreading and Printing Documents

Learn about Automatic Spell Checking, the Spelling command, and AutoCorrect

Use the Grammar command to clean up your document

Use the Thesaurus to enrich your word power

Learn how to use Find and Replace productively

Use Print Preview tools to change your document

Understand the print options on the Print dialog box

Learn how to print envelopes

Introducing Proofing Tools

Word supplies several tools that make proofreading easy. You can use Word's Spelling, Grammar, and Thesaurus commands to proofread your documents and supply suggestions for improvement. You can also use the Find and Replace commands to help you review or change text. No matter how long or short a document is, using the Spelling and Grammar commands is well worth the time it takes. Word quickly reviews the text and alerts you if it finds a misspelled word or any grammatical errors. Additionally, you can use Word's Thesaurus to find alternative words so that your text is not monotonous and repetitive.

After your document is complete, you can print it. Word has a special print preview mode in which you can view the document and make last-minute changes in the design before printing. Finally, you can print your document by using Windows defaults or by setting options in Word.

Using Automatic Spell Checking

Automatic Spell Checking, if activated, checks your spelling as you type. When Word encounters a misspelled word, the word is underlined with a wavy line. To check the word, simply point to it and click the right mouse button. The shortcut menu is displayed with suggested replacement words in bold type at the top of the menu. You may also choose from **Ignore All**, **Add**, and **Spelling** commands. You can choose any of the commands by clicking the left mouse button. If you choose any of Word's suggested replacements, Word automatically substitutes the replacement word for the misspelled word.

Using the Spelling Command in Word

To check spelling in a document, click the Spelling button ![ABC check icon] on the Standard toolbar (see Figure 4.1). The Spelling dialog box appears. Word highlights a questionable word, displays the word in the **Not in Dictionary** text box, and suggests a change in the **Change To** text box (see Figure 4.2). If you want, you can choose another word from the **Suggestions** list box or edit the word in the **Change To** box. After you select the proper word, you can click the **Change** button to change this one

Use the status bar to move through misspelled words

On the right side of the status bar is a book icon–the Spelling and Grammar Status tool. A check mark on the book is displayed if there are no errors in the document. An **X** is displayed if there are errors. To jump from one spelling or grammar error to another without scrolling, double-click the icon to move to the next error. A shortcut menu automatically appears offering the options mentioned earlier in the chapter.

Other ways to begin checking spelling

You can check the spelling in a document by choosing the **Tools** menu and selecting **Spelling** or by pressing F7. If you're not sure of the spelling of a particular word, highlight it and press F7. If the word is misspelled, the Spelling dialog box appears. If the word is spelled correctly, a dialog box appears indicating that Word is finished checking the selection. You have the option to continue spell checking or returning to your document.

occurrence or click **Change All** to change all occurrences of the misspelling throughout your document. When a repeated word is detected, you can choose to **Delete** the second occurrence of the word or **Ignore** the repetition. If the word is correct and not in the dictionary (such as a person or company's name), you can choose to **Ignore** this one occurrence, **Ignore All** occurrences in the document, or **Add** the word to the dictionary so that the Spelling command does not stop at the word again. If you want the program to correct the spelling automatically when you type it wrong, choose the **AutoCorrect** button.

The Spelling command is not a replacement for proofreading

The spelling command finds only unrecognized words. If you are like me, you may type the word incorrectly with a real word. For instance, I type `form` when I mean to type `from` and vice versa. The spelling tool does not find that mistake.

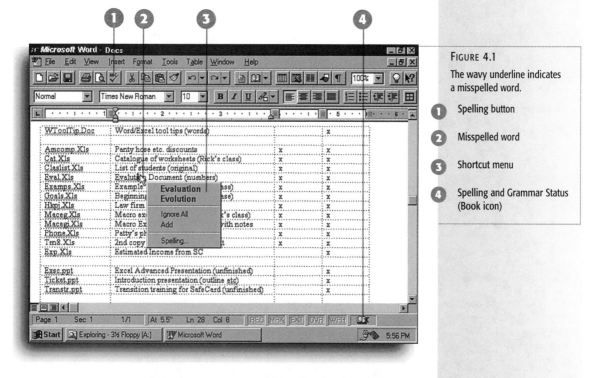

FIGURE 4.1

The wavy underline indicates a misspelled word.

1. Spelling button

2. Misspelled word

3. Shortcut menu

4. Spelling and Grammar Status (Book icon)

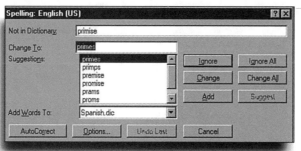

FIGURE 4.2

Select a word in the **Suggestions** box or enter the correct word in the **Change To** text box to correct the mistake in the text.

Add jargon to the dictionary

If you happen to type words that are not recognized but are specific to your occupation, you may want to add them to the dictionary so that the spell checker does not stop at each occurrence of the word. Those of you in the legal, medical, or publishing professions may find this particularly helpful.

SEE ALSO

➤ *For more information about replacing information quickly, see page 107*

Using AutoCorrect

The *AutoCorrect* feature automatically corrects spelling mistakes and formatting errors or replaces characters that you enter with specific words or phrases. This feature saves you time. Suppose that you consistently type anohter instead of another or WHen instead of When. You can enter these common mistakes into AutoCorrect, and the next time that you make the mistake, Word corrects it automatically.

To set options and make entries for AutoCorrect, choose the **Tools** menu and select the **AutoCorrect** command. Figure 4.3 shows the AutoCorrect dialog box with a new entry. The AutoCorrect dialog box lists options that you can activate or deactivate. If you need to type words that include two initial capital letters, deactivate the **Correct TWo INitial CApitals** option. The **Replace** and **With** text boxes enable you to enter your own items, and the list at the bottom of the AutoCorrect dialog box displays Word's default list plus any items that you add. You can add or delete items at any time.

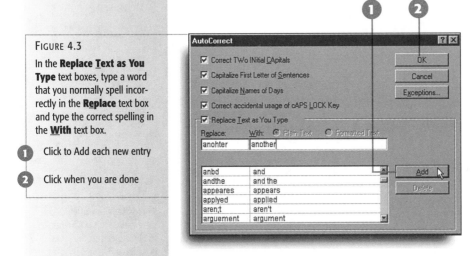

FIGURE 4.3

In the **Replace Text as You Type** text boxes, type a word that you normally spell incorrectly in the **Replace** text box and type the correct spelling in the **With** text box.

❶ Click to Add each new entry

❷ Click when you are done

You can also use AutoCorrect to save time and expand an abbreviation every time you type one. For example, you can have adr expand to include your address. You type adr and press the Spacebar, and adr is replaced with your home or business address—for example, 720 Skyline Drive, Idaho Springs, CO 80452.

Add the incorrect and correct spelling to AutoCorrect using the AutoCorrect dialog box

1. If the misspelled word is on the document that you have open, select the word.

2. Choose the **Tools** menu and select **AutoCorrect** to display the AutoCorrect dialog box.

3. If the word does not appear in the **Replace** text box, type the word incorrectly in the **Replace** text box.

4. Press tab to move to the **With** text box and type the word correctly.

5. Choose the **Add** button to add to the AutoCorrect list.

6. Repeat steps 3 through 5 for other words that you want to add.

7. When you are finished adding words to AutoCorrect, choose **OK** to close the dialog box.

Checking Grammar

If you have problems with your writing, Word may be able to help you. Word's Grammar Checker reviews text in your document and reports possible problems, such as passive verbs, pronoun errors, punctuation errors, jargon, and double negatives. You can review the error and suggestion, and then decide whether to change the text. You can even ask for a further explanation of the grammar rule.

To check the grammar in a document, choose **Tools** from the menu bar and select the **Grammar** command. The Grammar dialog box appears (see Figure 4.4). Grammar dialog box options are explained in Table 4.1.

Caution: Using abbreviations

Don't include words or abbreviations that you ever use intentionally in the **Replace** text box; if you do, every time you type the word, it changes! In this case, you probably want to use the AutoText feature (see "Taking Advantage of the AutoText Feature," in Chapter 2).

Don't blindly trust the Grammar Checker

You must read the suggestions carefully. You may find that the suggestion is not valid and that the problem, as the Grammar Checker sees it, is not really a problem.

FIGURE **4.4**

You can choose to ignore or change the problem, ignore the rule for this document, or ask for an explanation of the problem.

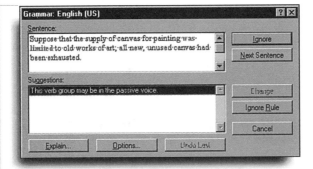

TABLE 4.1 **Grammar dialog box options**

Option	Explanation
Sentence	The sentence in question appears in this text box, where you can edit the sentence.
S**u**ggestions	Word defines the problem and may suggest alternative solutions.
Ignore	Choose this command button if you want to ignore the problem and move to the next grammar problem, which can be in the current sentence.
Next Sentence	Choose this button to look for potential problems in the next sentence, ignoring any other problems that may be in the current sentence.
Change	Choose this button to change the sentence if an alternative suggestion was made in the **Suggestions** text box or if you made changes in the sentence box.
Ignore **R**ule	Choose this button if you want to ignore a specific rule for the rest of the document.
Cancel/Close	Cancel closes the dialog box without making a change. After you make a change, the Cancel button changes to Close. Choose **Close** to return to your document.
Explain	This button displays a message box that further explains the rule and often offers examples (see Figure 4.5).
Options	This button enables you to customize rules and styles for the Grammar Checker.
Undo **L**ast	Choose this button if you change your mind about the last grammar change that you made.
Start	Appears in place of the Ignore command button when you click the document. The Grammar dialog box remains onscreen while you edit your document. Choose **Start** to continue the grammar check.

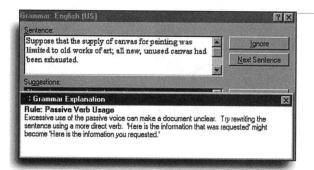

FIGURE 4.5

Choose **Explain** to learn more about the grammar rule in question. Click the **X** close button on the grammar explanation dialog box to close the message box.

Using the Thesaurus

Much like a printed thesaurus, Word's Thesaurus feature supplies a variety of synonyms and antonyms you can use to replace the word that you are looking up.

Use the Thesaurus

1. Position the insertion point in the word that you want to look up.

2. Choose the **Tools** menu and select the **Thesaurus** command (or press Shift+F7). Word automatically highlights the word, and the Thesaurus dialog box appears (see Figure 4.6).

3. In the **Meanings** list, select the meaning that you want to use. Double-click a synonym or meaning to display more synonyms.

4. In the **Replace with Synonym** list, select the word that you want to use as a replacement.

5. Choose **Replace** to close the dialog box, and substitute the new word (the one in the **Replace with Synonym** text box) for the old one, or choose **Cancel** to close the dialog box without replacing the word.

Options available in the Thesaurus dialog box are explained in Table 4.2.

Utilizing the Meanings list box

Suppose that you want to find a synonym for the word second. Using the words in the **Meanings** list box, you can look up either next or moment (see Figure 4.6).

Looking up another word

If you want to look up a word that is different from the original word, position the insertion point in the **Replace with Synonym** text box, type a new word, and choose **Look Up**.

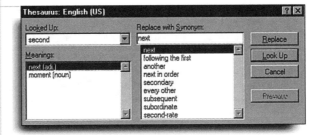

TABLE 4.2   **Thesaurus dialog box options**

Option	Description
Loo**k**ed Up/**N**ot Found	A drop-down list of all the words you have looked up since you opened the Thesaurus dialog box. The list disappears when you close the dialog box. The text-box name changes to **Not Found** if the word is not in the Thesaurus.
Meanings/**A**lphabetical List	Definition and part of speech of the selected word. Selecting a different meaning results in a new list of synonyms. **Alphabetical List** appears if the selected word is not in the Thesaurus.
Replace with **S**ynonym	The word in the text box is the selected word that you can **Look Up or Replace** when you choose either of those command buttons. The list of words below the text box is a list of synonyms from which you can select.
Replace with **A**ntonym	If Antonyms is available in the **Meanings** list box, you can highlight it and then select an antonym (opposite in meaning) from this list box.
Replace	Choose this button to substitute the selected word (in the Replace with Synonym text box) for the original word in the text.
Look Up	Displays meanings and synonyms for the selected word (in **the Replace with Synonym** text box).
Cancel	Closes the dialog box.
Previous	Displays the last word that you looked up. Works only in the current Thesaurus dialog box.

Using Find and Replace

You may find that reviewing a document is easier if you can quickly locate specific text or formatting in different sections of the document. The **Find** command enables you to search for specifics in your document. If you use the **Replace** command instead, you not only find what you are looking for, but you can then replace what you found with something else.

Use the **F**ind command

1. Choose the **Edit** menu and select the **Find** command (or press Ctrl+F). The Find dialog box appears.

2. In the **Fi**nd **What** text box, type the text that you need to find. You can choose one or more options in the Find dialog box to enhance your search (see Figure 4.7). You can also add the Replace option to the dialog box by clicking the **Replace** button. (These options are described later in Table 8.3.)

3. Choose the **Find Next** button to find the text.

4. When you get to the first occurrence of the item in the **Fi**nd **What** text box, you can choose **Find Next** again, **Cancel**, or the **Replace** button.

5. If you choose the **Replace** button, type the text that you want to use in the **Replace With** text box (see Figure 4.8). You can choose one or more options in the Find and Replace dialog box to enhance your search.

6. Click the **Replace** button again to replace and look for the next occurrence of the found text.

Fix mistakes quickly throughout the whole document

Using the Replace command helps you to quickly fix the same mistake made many times. For instance, if you misspelled a person's name the same way throughout the entire document, you could find each occurrence and replace it with the correct spelling. You choose the **Replace All** button when you get to the first misspelled word.

FIGURE 4.7

To make a number of identical changes throughout a document, click the **Replace** button to add the **Replace With** option to this dialog box.

FIGURE 4.8

The Find dialog box changes to the Replace dialog box when you click the **Replace** button.

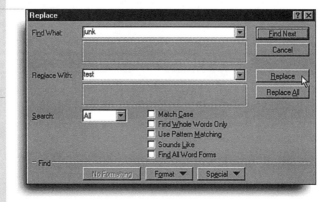

Use the Replace command first

You can choose to use the Replace command, by choosing the **Edit** menu and selecting **Replace** to begin your search instead of using the **Find** command first. If you close the Find dialog box and then later realize that you want to perform the same find, simply press Shift+F4 to perform your last find again.

Replace words that you typed incorrectly or that you don't need

You may consistently type words incorrectly that are real words. For instance, form for the word from or vice versa. You can find every occurrence of each of these words and see whether you typed it correctly. If you use the **Replace** command, you can pick and choose when to replace the word. Make sure that you use the **Find Whole Words Only** option.

When you are finding or replacing text, you have a number of options for your search. Table 8.3 describes these options on the Find and Replace dialog boxes.

TABLE 8.3   **Find and Replace options**

Option	Description
Search	Searches forward (Down), backward (Up), or through the entire document (All).
Match Case	Matches capitalization (uppercase or lowercase) when searching for text.
Find Whole Words Only	Finds a match that is an entire word only (if you are looking for the, Word doesn't find other or their).
Use Pattern Matching	Use with special characters (? is a wildcard for any one character, and * is a wild card for any number of characters). S?t finds Sat, Sit, Set. S*t finds all the preceding items as well as Soot, Sachet, Saddest, and others.
Sounds Like	Searches for different spellings of words that sound the same. If you're looking for there, Word finds their, there, and they're.
Find All Word Forms	Searches for all the different grammatical forms of a word. If you type is in the **Find What** text box, Word finds is, are, be, and am.
No Formatting	Removes formatting from the search criteria if any formatting is added with the **Format** button.
Format	Searches for format item in the **Find What** text box that includes fonts, styles, and other formatting.

Option	Description
Sp**e**cial	Searches for special characters such as paragraph marks, tabs, line breaks, and others.

Previewing a Document

Sometimes when you format a page of text in Normal view, problems are revealed when you print the document. The margins may be too wide, a headline may break in an odd place, a paragraph may be indented by mistake, and so on. You can save time, effort, and paper if you view your document in Print Preview before you print it. You can either click the Print Preview button 🔍 on the Standard toolbar, or choose the **File** menu and select **Print Pre**v**iew**.

Figure 4.9, which shows a document in print preview, reveals a document with too much information jammed onto one page. You can quickly fix the problems in this view before you print. First, you may want to fix the bullets in the first column of the table. Move the mouse pointer to the top of the table above the first column until you see the black down arrow pointer and click to select the entire column. Now you can choose **View** and select **T**oolbars to turn on the Formatting toolbar, and then click the bullets tool to turn off the bullets. You can make any other changes necessary and see what the document will look like before you print to paper.

SEE ALSO
➤ *For more information about printing documents, see page 40*

Using the Rulers

By default, Word does not display the rulers in print preview. You can, however, choose the **View** menu and select **Ruler** to display both the horizontal and vertical rulers. Use the rulers as you would in any other view to set tabs, adjust indents, and change the margins.

To adjust the margins, indents, or tabs by using the ruler, click the Magnifier button 🔍 on the toolbar (to deactivate the

---

You can replace formatting too

A very powerful option of the **Replace** command is the capability to replace formatting. Suppose that you have used the style Heading 3 repeatedly in your document and that Heading 4 is better. Using the **Format** button on the Replace dialog box, you can select **Styles to Find** and **Styles to Replace**.

Edit and format in Print Preview

You can edit and format your document in Print Preview just as you can in Page Layout or Normal view. Use the menus and commands or display any of the toolbars to use as shortcuts. You first need to deactivate the magnifier in print preview by clicking the Magnifier button 🔍 in the Print Preview toolbar.

magnifier), and position the insertion point at the place in the text you want to change. Any changes affect the current section.

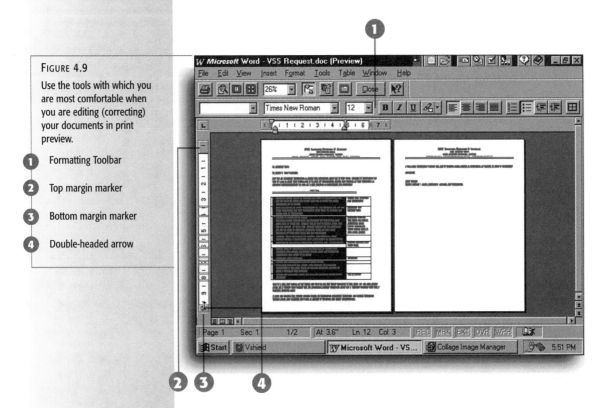

FIGURE 4.9

Use the tools with which you are most comfortable when you are editing (correcting) your documents in print preview.

1 Formatting Toolbar

2 Top margin marker

3 Bottom margin marker

4 Double-headed arrow

Change the margin

1. Move the mouse pointer over the margin marker (the point where the white ruler meets the light gray area) until the mouse pointer changes to a black double-headed arrow (refer to Figure 4.9). If you wait a little longer, you see a ScreenTip indicating the name of the object to which you are pointing.

2. Click and drag the arrow left or right (in the horizontal ruler) or up or down (in the vertical ruler) to change the margin.

Change the indent or tab

1. Point to the indent or tab marker on the ruler until the mouse pointer changes to a white arrow.

2. Click and drag the arrow left or right on the horizontal ruler to change indent or tab positions. A dotted guideline appears across the page as you drag any of the markers (see Figure 4.10). Use the guideline to align elements on the page.

SEE ALSO

➤ *For more information about setting tabs, see page 88*

➤ *For more information about indenting text, see page 90*

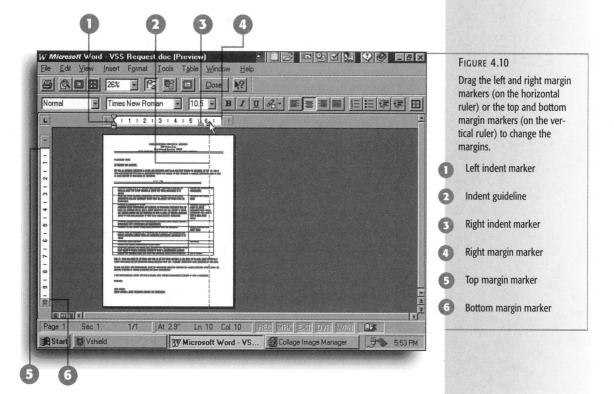

FIGURE 4.10

Drag the left and right margin markers (on the horizontal ruler) or the top and bottom margin markers (on the vertical ruler) to change the margins.

1 Left indent marker

2 Indent guideline

3 Right indent marker

4 Right margin marker

5 Top margin marker

6 Bottom margin marker

Using the Preview Toolbar

Undoing mistakes while in Print Preview

Choose the **Edit** menu and select **Undo** (or press Ctrl+Z) to reverse the Shrink to Fit operation (the Preview toolbar doesn't include an Undo button).

Print Preview includes a special toolbar that you can use to edit your document. The Preview toolbar works in much the same way the other toolbars work. You can place the mouse pointer on a toolbar button to view the ScreenTip and the description of the button in the status bar. You can use a toolbar button to print your document, view one page or multiple pages, display or hide the ruler, view the full screen (without screen elements such as the title bar, scrollbars, and so on), close print preview, and get help on a specific topic. Two toolbar buttons are particularly useful: Shrink to Fit and Magnifier (see Figure 4.11).

The Shrink to Fit button 📋 adjusts elements in a document, such as line and paragraph spacing and margins, so that you can fit a little more on the page. Suppose that your document fills one page, and one or two sentences overflow to a second page as shown in Figure 4.9. The status bar, on the left shows you the page you are on and the total number of pages in the document. Try clicking the Shrink to Fit button to squeeze all the text onto the first page (see Figure 4.10).

The Magnifier 🔍 enables you to toggle between the normal mouse pointer and the magnifier pointer. When the magnifier pointer contains a plus sign (+) as shown in Figure 4.11, you can magnify a portion of the document to 100 percent. When the magnifier pointer contains a minus sign (–), clicking the page reduces the view to Whole Page view. To change the magnifier pointer back to the normal pointer, click the Magnifier button again.

Clicking the Print button 🖨 on the Preview toolbar prints the document using the default options in the Print dialog box. (If you want to make changes to any printing options, see the following section, "Printing Word Documents.")

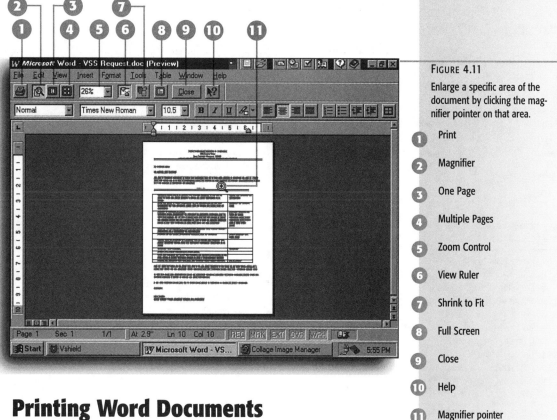

FIGURE 4.11

Enlarge a specific area of the document by clicking the magnifier pointer on that area.

1. Print
2. Magnifier
3. One Page
4. Multiple Pages
5. Zoom Control
6. View Ruler
7. Shrink to Fit
8. Full Screen
9. Close
10. Help
11. Magnifier pointer

Printing Word Documents

When you print from Word, you generally use the defaults set up in Windows. The default options print one copy of all the pages in the document. You can, however, change these defaults in the Print dialog box, which is opened by choosing the **File** menu and selecting **Print** (see Figure 4.12).

Options in the Print dialog box are described in Table 4.4.

TABLE 4.4 **Print dialog box options**

Option	Description
Printer Section	
Name	Choose this drop-down button to select another printer on which to print this document.

continues...

TABLE 4.4   Continued

Option	Description
Printer Section	
Properties	Choose this button to change the properties of the selected printer (including paper size, paper orientation, and graphics resolution). The properties are in effect for all documents printed with the printer (not just this document).
Print to fil**e**	Choosing this option prints the document to a file on disk so that you can transport the file to another computer or service bureau.
Page range Section	
All	Prints all pages in the document.
Curre**nt page**	Prints only the page in which the insertion point is located.
Pag**es**	Prints the specified pages. Enter a page range in the text box. Separate individual pages with commas (1,4,5); indicate a page range with a hyphen (1-5); and indicate pages in a section with P and S (p1s2).
Selection	Select text in the document before choosing to print and click **S**election to print only the selected text.
Copies Section	
Number of c**opies**	Prints specified number of copies. Enter the number of copies to be printed.
Collat**e**	Select this option to print copies in order. If you want two copies of a five-page document, the first copy of pages 1 to 5 prints and then the second copy prints.
Other Options	
Print w**hat**	Specify what to print: the document, document properties information, comments, a list of styles, AutoText entries, or key assignments.
Pr**int**	Specify which pages to print: all pages, even pages, or odd pages in the page range.
Options	Click this button to customize printing options.
OK	Click this button to send the selected pages to the printer.
Cancel	Click this button to cancel all changes and close the dialog box without printing the document.

Print your file on a color printer even if you don't have one

You can use the **Print to fi**l**e** option to print your color document to a disk file and then take the disk to a computer that has a color printer attached to it. You need to select the color printer that you will print to in the **Name** list box, choose the **Print to fi**l**e** option, and then take the disk to the other computer. This is particularly useful if you need to take your document to a print shop.

SEE ALSO
➤ *To learn how to print a document, see page 40*

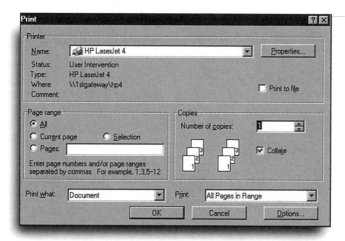

FIGURE 4.12
To print using the default options in the Print dialog box, choose OK.

Printing Envelopes

In many word processing programs, printing envelopes can be a cumbersome chore. Word offers an easy and quick way to print envelopes. Using Word you can print individual envelopes (not attached to a document), envelopes attached to a document, and envelopes as part of a mail merge.

SEE ALSO
➤ *For more information about printing envelopes as part of a mail merge, see page 142*

Print an envelope in Word

1. Insert an envelope into the printer.

2. Choose **Tools** from the menu bar, and then **select Envelopes and Labels**. The Envelopes and Labels dialog box appears.

3. Choose the **Envelopes** tab.

4. Enter a **Delivery Address** and **Return Address** (see Figure 4.13). If you have an address on the document, Word may find the address and place it in the **Delivery Address** area. You can also click the Insert Address button for either address and choose an address from your Personal Address Book.

Printing a mailing list

You can merge many addresses at one time with the mail merge feature (see Chapter 5, "Creating Mass Mailings").

5. Select envelope and feed options, if necessary.

6. Choose **Print**.

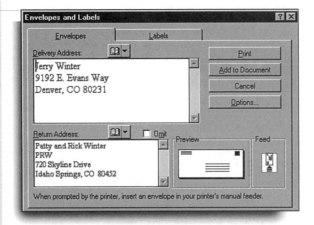

Options found in the Envelopes and Labels dialog box are described in Table 4.5.

TABLE 4.5   **Envelopes and Labels dialog box**

Option	Description
Delivery Address	Enter the name and address to which the envelope will be mailed.
Return Address	Enter your name and address. If a name and address are displayed, this is from the information you entered when you installed the program. You can change the default information by choosing the **T**ools menu, selecting the **Options** command, and clicking on the **User Info** tab.
O**m**it	Choose this option to exclude the return address.
Preview	Click the envelope in the Preview box to display the Envelope Options dialog box and the **Envelope Options** tab. Select the size, bar code, placement, and font for the addresses in this dialog box.
Feed	Click the Feed box to display the Envelope Options dialog box and the **Printing Options** tab. Select the method of feeding envelopes that best fits your printer.
Print	Choose this button to send the envelope to the printer.

Option	Description
Add to Document	Adds the envelope style and contents to the document so that you can save it for later use.
Cancel	Click this button to cancel your choices and close the dialog box without printing the envelope.
Options	Displays the Envelope Options dialog box.

Make your own changes to the envelope

If the Envelope Options tab does not give you enough flexibility to change what you need to on an envelope, return to the Envelopes and Labels dialog box and choose **Add to Document**. Word places a new page at the beginning of your document, formatted for the envelope. Change this page as you would any other document.

CHAPTER
5

Creating Mass Mailings

Create a mail merge main document

Develop your mail merge data source

Use merge fields in your main document

Merge the main document and the data source into a customized form letter

Use data from an Excel spreadsheet as your data source

Use data from an Access database as your data source

Select data from the data source based on specific criteria

Understanding Mail Merge

Mail merge is the process of creating a document once, then sending it to many different people so it looks as if you typed each document separately. If you need to send more than one person the same document, you can create the document, build a data source (a list of names and addresses), and then merge the two files. That way, the next time you need to send a document to many people, you can create the new document and use your existing data source.

The document you create is called a *main document*. In this document, you type any information meant for all recipients. You also can add *merge fields* specific to each person or company. Next you create a *data source*, which stores the information specific to each individual or company (similar to a database). Finally, you merge, or combine, the two documents to create the mail merge.

Word's Mail Merge capabilities enable you to automate and personalize correspondence—such as announcements, change of address notifications, advertisements, personal letters, and so on—by composing the document and including merge fields for information that varies. Each document probably needs different company names, individuals' names and addresses, and even notes specific to an individual or company. You can place a merge field anywhere in the document—address lines, the salutation, and even the body of the document. Figure 5.1 shows an example of a completed mail merge document.

Word has simplified performing a mail merge into three simple steps.

Create a mass mailing

1. Create the main document (such as a form letter, envelopes, or mailing labels).

2. Attach the data source (name and address file).

3. Merge the main document with the data source.

You can use Word to create the data source, or you can use an existing file from another program such as Access, Excel, a personal address book, or your Schedule+ contact list.

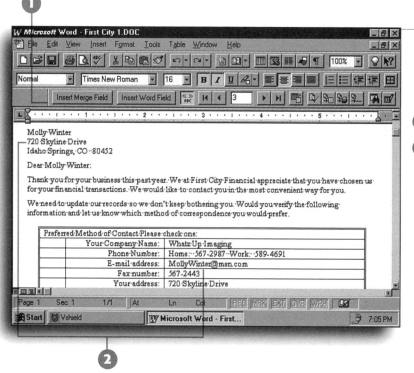

FIGURE 5.1

This main document contains merge fields for the name and address, the salutation, and the right column of the table.

1 Mail merge toolbar

2 Merged fields

Creating a Main Document

The first step in creating a mass mailing is to write the letter you want to send. In other words, create a main document.

A main document includes the standard text and graphics to be included as part of each letter. Word has simplified this process with the Mail Merge Helper, which takes you step by step through creating a main document and a data source. You don't need to memorize and repeat the steps for creating custom documents; just follow Word's lead.

Create a main document using Mail Merge Helper

1. Choose the **Tools** menu and select **Mail Merge**. The Mail Merge Helper dialog box opens (see Figure 5.2).

2. Under step 1, Main Document, click the **Create** button.

3. From the drop-down list, choose **Form Letters**. The dialog box in Figure 5.3 opens.

FIGURE 5.2

The only option currently available is the Create option in step 1, Main Document.

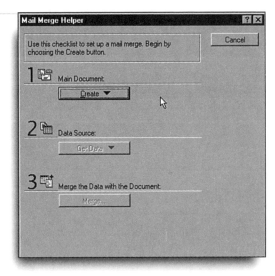

FIGURE 5.3

Use this dialog box to tell Word whether you want to use the **Active Window** or begin a **New Main Document**.

4. If the letter you want to use is in the active window, click **Active Window**. If you want to create a document to use as your main document, click **New Main Document**.

5. After you chose either **Active Window** or **New Main Document**, you return to the Mail Merge Helper. You now have the option to select the **Data Source**.

The type of document you selected (form letters, in this example) and the name of your main document are now listed under step 1, as shown in Figure 5.4.

Editing the Main Document

You now have two choices in the Mail Merge Helper dialog box (see Figure 5.4). You can choose to **Edit** the main document in step 1, or you can choose to **Get Data** in step 2. The latter option enables you to attach the data source to the main document. If you have created and named a main document but have not created your data source, you first should edit the main document to add your body text.

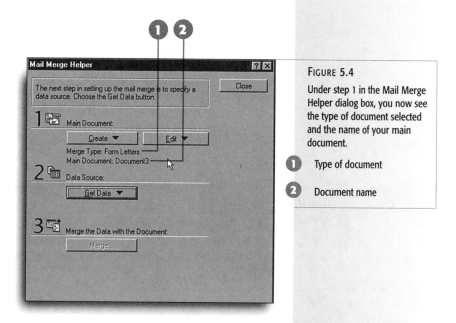

FIGURE 5.4

Under step 1 in the Mail Merge Helper dialog box, you now see the type of document selected and the name of your main document.

1 Type of document

2 Document name

To enter or edit text in the main document, click the **Edit** button in step 1. The filename appears in the pull-down list. Click the name of your main document to open it.

If you are creating a letter from scratch, enter the information that will be standard in all letters. Be sure to leave room for items such as name, address, city, state, zip code, and so on. You can even use these items as placeholders. That way, when you are ready to add the merge fields, you know where they belong. You'll insert these items as merge fields later in this chapter.

When you have finished creating the standard body of your letter, select the **Tools** menu and choose **Mail Merge** to return to the Mail Merge Helper.

> **Working with an existing letter**
>
> Remember that a main document includes the standard text and graphics to be part of each letter. If you are reusing an existing letter, you need to delete the name and address of the previous recipient and use place holders for this information.

Creating a Data Source

A *data source* can be a Word table, an Excel worksheet, an Access database, an address book, or another file that holds the variable

Adding the current date to your main document

If you want to include the current date each time you use a main document, position your cursor on the line where you want the date to appear. Then choose **Insert** from the menu bar and select **Date & Time**. Locate the date format you want to use and select **Update Automatically** at the bottom of the Date and Time dialog box. Each time you open the main document, the current date will now appear.

Too much is better; plan ahead

As you begin creating your data source, it is better to have too many fields than to have too few. Adding one forgotten field of information to thousands of records is time-consuming and increases the chance of data entry errors. Deleting an unnecessary field takes a few simple keystrokes.

information used to customize your letter. The data source, for example, can hold the names, addresses, phone numbers, and account information of your customers.

Planning Your Data File

Planning is the most important step of creating a data source. The most important feature of the data source (database) is flexibility. Take the time to identify all the information that you could possibly ever need about recipients when sending a mass mailing. Group that information into fields.

A *field* is a category of information. A phone book, for example, has fields for last name, first name, suffix (M.D., Sr., III), city (sometimes), and phone number. Your document might include fields such as first name, last name, salutation, address, city, state, zip code, account number, and the previous year's sales. All fields related to one person or company are called a *record*.

When designing your data source, consider how you plan to arrange, or sort, your data. Do not include more than one piece of information in each field. If you want letters to print alphabetically by last name, for example, you need at least two fields in your data source: first name and last name. One field called Name does not provide the flexibility to sort by last name.

SEE ALSO

➤ *For more information about creating a database in Access, see page 527*

Create the fields in your Word data source

1. Open your main document.

2. Choose the **Tools** menu, then select **Mail Merge** to open the Mail Merge Helper dialog box.

3. Under step 2, click the **Get Data** button.

4. To create a new data source, click **Create Data Source**. A list of common field names appears on the right side of the Create Data Source dialog box (see Figure 5.5).

5. Remove unwanted field names by selecting the name and clicking the **Remove Field Name** button. Repeat this until only the field names you want to use are listed on the right.

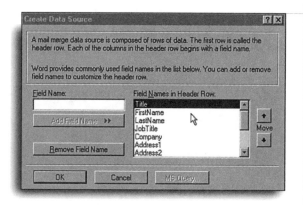

6. To add a field name that is not listed, type the name in the **Field Name** box and click the **Add Field Name** button.

7. To rearrange fields, select a field name and click the up- or down-pointing Move arrow to the right of the field names list.

8. When all your field names are listed and are in the correct order, choose **OK**.

9. When prompted to save your data source, type a filename. The data source is separate from the main document, however, so be sure to give it a different name.

10. If you are ready to add data to your data source, click **Edit Data Source** in the dialog box. If you want to return to the main document, click **Edit Main Document**.

> **Do not use spaces in field names**
>
> When adding new fields, do not use spaces between words. Instead, use the underscore character (as in **Zip_Code**) or uppercase letters (as in **ZipCode**) to make field names easier to read.

Adding Information to Your Data Source

Now that you have created the data source file to store variable information, you are ready to add specific information to this file. The data source file is where you place data related to each individual or company. After you enter all your data, you can create the merged document.

Add information to your data source

1. Open your main document.

2. Click the Edit Data Source button 📝 on the Mail Merge toolbar. The Data Form dialog box opens, as shown in Figure 5.6.

FIGURE 5.6

Enter variable information for your mailing in the Data Form dialog box.

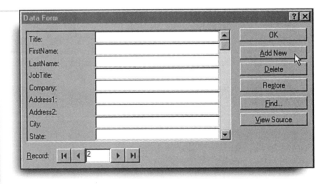

3. Type any applicable information in the first field. Press Enter or Tab to move to the next field. Repeat this process until you have completed all applicable fields. You do not need to enter information in every field. If a field does not apply, leave it blank.

4. To add another record, click the **Add New** button. Repeat data entry until all records are entered.

5. After you have entered all applicable records, choose **OK**.

Use Enter to start a new record

When you get to the last field in the record, you can press Enter to start a new record form so you don't have to click the **Add New** button.

Editing a Data Source

After you have entered all your data into the data source document, you'll probably need to delete records or change data periodically. Editing a data source document is just like editing any Word document. One advantage, however, is that the Mail Merge Helper has a Find feature that eliminates the hassle of scrolling and searching for a specific record.

Locate the record you want to edit

1. You can view any record in the data form by clicking the Edit Data Source button 🖹 on the Mail Merge toolbar.

2. Click the **Find** button on the right of the Data Form dialog box.

3. Identify a unique piece of information about the record you want, such as the last name or zip code. Type that information in the Find box.

4. In the **In Field** drop-down list, select the field in which this information is located.

5. Click **Find First** to locate the first record that meets the criteria you specified.

6. Click **Find Next** until you get to the record you want. Click the **Close** button in the Find dialog box.

With the record displayed, make the necessary changes. Then choose **OK** to return to your document.

After locating a record, you might decide to delete it. To delete a record, click the **Delete** button on the right side of the Data Form dialog box.

Inserting Merge Fields

After the standard elements of your letter are complete and your data source has been created, you are ready to identify where in the main document to place the variable pieces of information. This process involves inserting merge fields.

In Figure 5.7, First City Financial is using mail merge to send letters to clients requesting updated information.

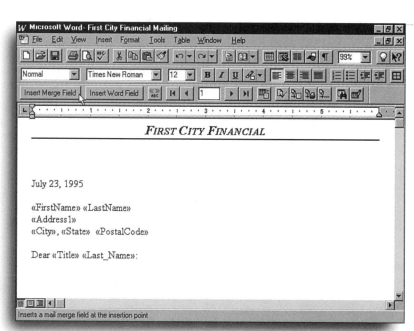

Minimize what you type

You can type just part of the information to find more records. Type **win** in the last name field, for example, to find all records in which "win" is part of the last name. Try to be specific enough to get only the results you want.

FIGURE 5.7
Merge fields enable you to make a form letter look like a personal letter.

Merge fields are the categories of information included in your data source, such as first name, city, state, and so on. Merge fields tell Word specifically where to place each variable piece of information in the letter.

Insert merge fields into your main document

1. Open your main document.

2. Place the insertion point where the first variable piece of information should appear, or you can select a placeholder such as name, address, city, and so on.

3. Click the Insert Merge Field button on the Mail Merge toolbar.

4. Select the name of the field you want. The name of the field appears in angle brackets (<< >>) in your document.

5. Type any words, spaces, or punctuation required between fields.

6. Insert the next merge field. Repeat until all fields are entered.

Be sure to include punctuation between fields

When creating a letter, include punctuation in places such as the salutation. A standard letter contains the following line when all merge fields are included:
```
Dear <<Title>>
<<LastName>>:
```

Sorting Records in Your Data Source

Using Word to perform a mail merge enables you to sort your records before you print letters. If the mailing is for your business, making the job easier for postal workers is to your advantage. When you print hundreds of letters and take them to the post office, if they are sorted in order of zip code (even if you don't have a bulk mail permit), they probably will get to the recipients faster.

Another reason to sort before you print is that if the printer jams, you are able to begin printing from where the problem occurred.

Although planning your sort is not required to perform a merge, it can save you time in the end. If you do not identify sort fields ahead of time, you might find yourself sorting and re-sorting until you get the results you want.

You can select up to three fields for sorting. Choose only one field, however, if that's all you need.

The first field is the primary sort or biggest grouping. The second field specifies how records should be sorted within the first group. The third field specifies how records should be sorted within the second group.

Suppose that your data source has fields for First Name, Last Name, and Sales Region. If you want records sorted alphabetically by Sales Region, your first field (primary sort) would be Sales Region, your second field would be Last Name, and your third field would be First Name.

Sort data according to fields you specify

1. Open your main document.

2. Click the Mail Merge Helper button ![icon] on the Mail Merge toolbar to open the Mail Merge Helper dialog box.

3. Under step 3 of the Mail Merge Helper dialog box, click the **Query Options** button to open the Query Options dialog box (see Figure 5.8).

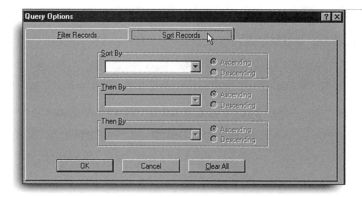

FIGURE 5.8
Use the **Sort Records** tab to organize your data source before you merge your document.

4. In the Query Options dialog box, click the **S**ort **Records** tab.

5. Select the first field you want as your primary sort in the **S**ort **By** category, and then press the **Tab** key.

6. Select the second field in **Then By** category, and then press the **Tab** key.

7. Select the third field in the second **Then By** field and choose **OK**.

8. Click the **Close** button after you finish with the Mail Merge Helper.

Whenever you view your data or perform a merge, the sort criteria you defined are applied.

Viewing the Order of the Data

You should view your data source to verify that your sort criteria produced the results you want.

View your data source

1. Click the Edit Data Source button 📝 on the Mail Merge toolbar.

2. Click the **Next Record** button ▶ at the bottom of the Data Form dialog box to scroll through the records.

3. Choose **OK** to return to your main document.

Merging the Main Document and the Data Source

Viewing merge results onscreen is helpful

If you are merging a new main document for the first time, merging to a new document 📄 enables you to see the results before you use paper. Your custom documents do not always turn out as you anticipate after all the variable information is entered. Merging data to a new document you can view onscreen can save many reams of paper and trips to the printer.

After you have created the main document and data source, the next step is to combine the two components into form letters.

You have the following three options when merging the files:

- You can merge the files directly to the printer.

- You can merge them to a third file of form letters that appears on your screen.

- You can merge them directly to a fax or email list.

Checking for Errors

No matter which merging option you choose, you first should check to make sure that the merge works properly. You run the risk of wasting both time and material if you print hundreds or thousands of letters without checking them first. You can encounter many different errors, but Word helps you locate and identify the problem. In other words, follow Word's lead.

Check a mail merge for errors

1. Open the main document.

2. From the Mail Merge toolbar, click the Check for Errors button ![icon].

3. In the Checking and Reporting Errors dialog box, click the **Simulate the Merge and Report Errors in a New Document** option. Word indicates that no errors were found if that is the case. If errors do exist, Word gives you the option to correct them now or later. Either way, Word takes you directly to the field or record with the problem.

Merging to a New Document to View Onscreen Before Printing

If you don't want your letters to print just yet, you can merge the two documents to a third document and view it before printing.

Merge to a third document

1. Open the main document.

2. On the Mail Merge toolbar, click the Merge to New Document button ![icon].

3. View the new document, called Form Letters by default. Scroll through the first several pages to ensure that merge fields went to the right place and that page breaks worked.

4. If everything is in place, choose the **File** menu and then select **Print** to print to your default printer.

5. Make any necessary changes in the Print dialog box and choose **OK**.

Merging Directly to the Printer

If your job shows no errors, you can merge a main document and the data source directly to the printer. When choosing this option, understand that your entire merged file is sent to the printer. This means you risk wasting lots of paper if you are not certain the mail merge is correct.

Merging to a new document saves time and paper

If you are working with a main document for the first time, you might want to merge to a third document instead of directly to the printer. It's not uncommon for merged form letters to look different than expected after all the custom information is included.

Printing specific letters

In the Print dialog box, you can use the **Pages** option in the Page Range section to identify which letters to print. You can type **p1s5, p1s7**, for example, to print the fifth and seventh letters of the merged document. This is extremely helpful if the printer jams or crunches one of your letters. A merged document is one page with many sections.

Edit your main document and data source, not the merged form letter

If you merge two documents and do not get the results you expected, don't try to edit each page of the document individually. You can save time if you close the form letter document without saving it, edit the main document or data source, then perform the merge again. Use the View Merged Data button 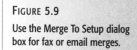 on the Mail Merge toolbar.

Merge directly to the printer

1. Open the main document.

2. On the Mail Merge toolbar, click the Merge to Printer button 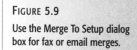.

3. Choose **OK** to send the merge directly to your printer.

Merging to a Fax or Email Address

If you want to fax or email a mail merge document, use the **Merge** button in the Mail Merge Helper dialog box to select which electronic means you want to use.

Email or fax a mail merge document

1. Open the main document.

2. Click the Mail Merge Helper button 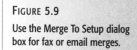 on the Mail Merge toolbar to open the Mail Merge Helper dialog box.

3. Under step 3 of the Mail Merge Helper dialog box, click the **Merge** button to open the Merge dialog box.

4. Select **Fax** or **Electronic Mail** from the **Merge To** drop-down list.

5. Click the **Setup** button to define which data field to use for the address. The Merge To Setup dialog box opens (see Figure 5.9).

FIGURE 5.9

Use the Merge To Setup dialog box for fax or email merges.

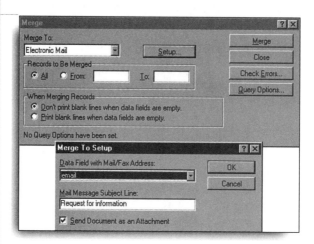

6. From the **Data field with Mail/Fax Address** drop-down list, select the field that stores the mail or fax address.

7. In the **Mail Message Subject Line** text box, type a subject for the email or fax message.

8. If you want to send the document as an attachment, click the **Send document as an Attachment** check box.

9. Choose **OK** to close the Merge To Setup dialog box, then click the **Merge** button to perform the merge.

Merging Data from an Excel Worksheet

Suppose that you already have data in an Excel worksheet. Fortunately, you don't have to retype the data. If you have many names to enter, you can use Excel to create a data source from scratch. For large numbers of records, Excel has a greater capability to manage, sort, and edit than a Word table does. (An Excel database holds up to 16,384 records.)

Create a database in an Excel worksheet

1. Open or switch to Excel.

2. Choose the **File** menu and select **New**, or click the New button on the Standard toolbar.

3. Your field names are the column headings of your worksheet. Type the name of your first field in cell A1. Press the Tab key or the right arrow on your keyboard, or click in cell B1.

4. Type the second field name in cell B1. Press the Tab key or the right arrow on your keyboard. Repeat until all field names are listed as column headings.

5. Click in cell A2. Begin typing your data and save often.

SEE ALSO

➤ *For more information about creating worksheets, see page 189*

➤ *For more information about editing information in Excel worksheets, see page 210*

Type the information, don't worry about order

Don't worry about the order of the data. Your first goal should be accuracy. You can sort the database later.

Use your Excel worksheet as a mail merge data source

1. Return to Word.

2. Open your main document.

3. From the Mail Merge toolbar, click the Mail Merge Helper button 🔲.

4. Under step 2, click **Get Data**.

5. Choose **Open Data Source**.

6. In the **Files of type** drop-down list, select **MS Excel Worksheets** (see Figure 5.10).

The Mail Merge toolbar

If you don't see the Mail Merge toolbar, make sure a merge document is open. The Mail Merge toolbar is available only when you are in a mail merge document.

FIGURE 5.10

The Open Data Source dialog box looks and works just like the Open File dialog box.

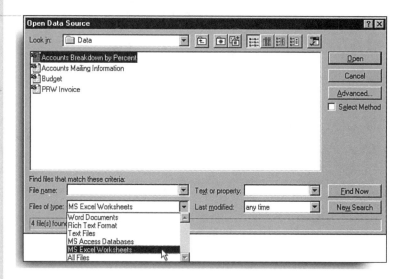

7. Select the Excel file in which your data is saved.

8. Click the **Open** button.

After you attach your Excel file as the data source, you can insert merge fields. Perform the merge as you would with any other data source. For more information, refer to the sections "Inserting Merge Fields" and "Merging the Main Document and the Data Source" earlier in this chapter.

Using Access Data as a Mail Merge Data Source

Another tool for managing data is Microsoft Access. If you have many fields and records, Access might be more appropriate for your data than a Word table or an Excel worksheet. This is especially true if you need to answer many questions about the data and make many different reports. You can use Access to create a query that sorts and searches your mailing list instead of specifying your data selection rules through Word.

Use Access as your mail merge data source

1. Open your main document in Word.
2. From the Mail Merge toolbar, click the Mail Merge Helper button ▦.
3. Under step 2, click **Get Data**.
4. Choose **Open Data Source**.
5. In the **Files of type** drop-down list, select **MS Access Databases**.
6. Click the Access file in which your mailing information is saved.
7. Click the **Open** button.
8. The Microsoft Access dialog box eventually opens, as shown in Figure 5.11. Select either the **Tables** or **Queries** tab, then select the name of the Access object and choose **OK**.

Use an existing Access query

Use a Microsoft Access query that already has your information selected and sorted for your mail merge.

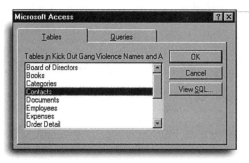

FIGURE 5.11

The Microsoft Access dialog box enables you to choose existing Access tables or queries for your data source.

After you attach your Access table or query, you can insert merge fields. Perform the merge as you would with any other data source.

SEE ALSO

➤ *For more information about inserting merge fields and merging the main document and the data source, refer to the sections "Inserting Merge Fields" and "Merging the Main Document and the Data Source" earlier in this chapter.*

Using the Address Book for Merging

You can use the Contact List from Schedule+ or the Personal Address Book from Microsoft Exchange as your data source. Microsoft Exchange enables you to create a Personal Address Book that can be used to send electronic mail (email) or paper mail. One of the features of Schedule+ is the Contact List. You can create and maintain a list of names and addresses and can use this list to contact business associates, friends, and family. If you have a list of names and addresses in the Contact List of Schedule+ or in the Personal Address Book of Microsoft Exchange, you can attach this list to your merge document.

Use an address book for your data source

1. Open your main document.

2. From the Mail Merge toolbar, click the Mail Merge Helper button 📇.

3. Under step 2, click **Get Data**.

4. Select **Use Address Book**. The Use Address Book dialog box opens, as shown in Figure 5.12.

FIGURE 5.12

Select which address book you want to use.

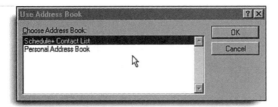

5. In the **Choose Address Book** list, select the list you want to use and choose **OK**.

6. In the Mail Merge Helper dialog box, click **Close**.

After you make your address book the data source, you can insert merge fields. Perform the merge as you would with any other data source. For more information, see the sections "Inserting Merge Fields" and "Merging the Main Document and the Data Source" earlier in this chapter.

Specifying Data Selection Rules

If your data source is in Word, Excel, Access, Schedule+, or the Personal Address Book, you can specify criteria that each record must meet to be included in the mail merge. This selection process enables you to maintain information in one location instead of having multiple databases, or worse yet, having the same name in multiple databases.

Deciding Which Fields Have Rules

Creating selection rules can be tricky. When using more than one rule, you need to connect the rules with an And or an Or. If you use the wrong word or the wrong Compare To condition, you might not have any records merged. Before exploring Word's query options, write down which records you want and which field holds the information you will be searching. You can specify one rule (such as all zip codes beginning with 8) or multiple rules (such as all last names beginning with B that have zip codes beginning with 5). You can specify up to six rules.

If you want to use multiple rules and merge only records that meet all the rules, use And. If you want to merge records that meet either rule, use Or. The preceding example would use And to meet both conditions.

The other problem you might encounter is narrowing your search too much. In the preceding example, you get all the records in which the last name begins with B and the zip code begins with 5.

Identifying Data Criteria

To use a large database for multiple merge operations, you might want to determine specific rules for the records you will select.

Specify rules within your data source

1. Open your main document.

2. On the Mail Merge toolbar, click the Mail Merge Helper button 🖳.

3. Under step 3 of the Mail Merge dialog box, click **Query Options**. The Query Options dialog box opens (see Figure 5.13). It contains two tabs, **Filter Records** and **Sort Records**.

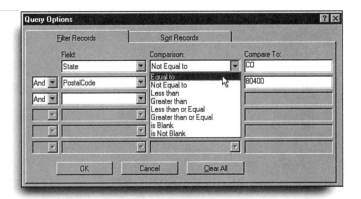

4. Click the **Filter Records** tab.

5. In the **Field** column, click the down arrow to display the names of your fields. Select the field name for which you want to create a rule.

6. In the **Comparison** column, click the comparison you want Word to make (such as **Not Equal to** or **Equal to**).

7. In the **Compare To** column, type the value you want Word to check records against. If you want Word to locate all records with a zip code of 80400, for example, enter **80400** (see Figure 5.14).

8. Choose **OK**.

9. Click the **Close** button in the Mail Merge Helper dialog box.

10. Click the View Merged Data button 🔳 on the Mail Merge toolbar.

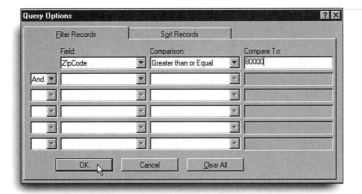

FIGURE 5.14
Enter criteria to determine which records to merge into form letters.

You can use the View Merged Data button to toggle between merged data in your letter and the letter with the merge fields displayed onscreen.

Creating Labels Using Mail Merge

After you create your letters, you might want to create labels to mail them. You might even want to send a preprinted postcard as a follow-up to everyone who received a specific mailing.

Creating labels isn't difficult. You just need to know which type of label you are using. You then create a label document and make it your main document. You can reuse the data source you created for your letters.

Creating the Main Document for Mailing Labels

After your letters are printed, you might want to create labels for the outside of the envelopes.

Create mailing labels using Mail Merge

1. Choose the **Tools** menu and select **Mail Merge**. The Mail Merge Helper dialog box opens.

2. Under step 1, click **Create**.

3. From the drop-down list, choose **Mailing Labels**. A message dialog box from Word displays.

4. Click **New Main Document** to create the document that will serve as your label template.

Setting Up the Labels Merge

You need to tell Word where your data is stored, what style of label you are using, and where to place specific merge fields.

Start the labels merge

1. From the Mail Merge toolbar, click the Mail Merge Helper button ⊞.

2. Under step 2, click the **Get Data** button and choose **Open Data Source**.

3. Select the name of the file that contains your data.

4. After you select a file, Word prompts you to set up the main document for labels. Click **Set Up Main Document** to specify the label size and type. The Label Options dialog box appears (see Figure 5.15).

FIGURE 5.15

Use the Label Options dialog box to set up your label document.

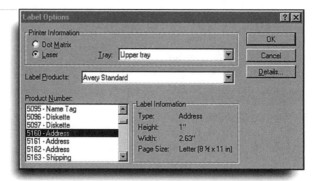

5. In the **Printer Information** section, select the type of printer you have (**Dot Matrix** or **Laser**).

6. In the **Label Products** drop-down list box, select the brand of labels you have.

7. Under **Product Number**, select the style of labels you have. (The style number is on the outside of the box.) Choose **OK**. The Create Labels dialog box opens (see Figure 5.16).

8. To add merge fields to your label, click **Insert Merge Field**. Locate and select the name of the first field from your data source. Repeat this until all the fields you want on the label are listed. When you add merge fields to a label, make sure

---

Moving quickly in a list box

To quickly find a specific product number, make sure the highlight bar is in the **Product Number** list box and type the first digit of the product number you want to find. The list moves to the beginning of the section where those labels should be listed. To find Avery 5160 address labels, for example, type **5** and then scroll down to that number.

to include all spaces and punctuation you want to appear on each label.

FIGURE 5.16
Use the Create Labels dialog box to insert merge fields for your labels.

9. Choose **OK**.
10. Click **Close** in the Mail Merge Helper dialog box.

Editing the Format of a Label

After you create the initial format for your label, you might want to make formatting changes. You can go back and edit the format of a label at any time.

Return to the label setup process

1. Open your main document.
2. From the Mail Merge toolbar, click the Mail Merge Helper button .
3. Under step 1, click the **Edit** button and select the Mailing Label document from the pull-down list.
4. Make formatting changes as you would with any other Word document.

Printing Labels

To print labels, follow the steps outlined in the earlier section, "Merging the Main Document and the Data Source." You also can use the Merge to New Document ⬚ or Merge to Printer ⬚ buttons on the Mail Merge toobar to print your labels.

Creating Envelopes Using Mail Merge

You can create envelopes rather than labels to address your form letters. Creating envelopes is not difficult, but you need to consider whether your printer tray automatically feeds envelopes. If it doesn't, you might find it easier to use labels than to manually feed hundreds of envelopes.

Creating the Envelopes File

If you want to print envelopes, you first need to create a main document that identifies both the size of the envelope and the location of the merge field.

Create envelopes using Mail Merge

1. Choose the **Tools** menu and select **Mail Merge**. The Mail Merge Helper dialog box opens.

2. Under step 1, click **Create**.

3. From the drop-down list, choose **Envelopes**. A message dialog box from Word displays.

4. Click **New Main Document** to create the document that will serve as your envelope template.

Setting Up the Envelopes Merge

You need to tell Word where your data is stored, what style of envelope you are using, and where to place specific merge fields.

Start the envelopes merge

1. From the Mail Merge toolbar, click the Mail Merge Helper button ⬚.

2. Under step 2, click the **Get Data** button and choose **Open Data Source**.

3. Select the name of the file that contains your data.

4. After you select a file, Word prompts you to format the main document for envelopes. Click **Set Up Main Document** to specify the envelope size and type. The Envelope Options dialog box appears.

5. Click the **Envelope Options** tab (see Figure 5.17).

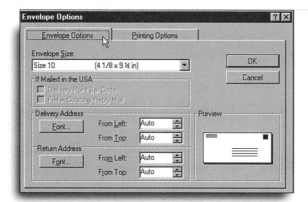

FIGURE 5.17
Use this dialog box to set up your envelope options.

6. In the **Envelope Size** drop-down list box, select the size of envelope you are using.

7. Under **Delivery Address**, type specific top and left margins if your requirements are different from a standard envelope.

8. Under **Return Address**, type specific top and left margins if your requirements are different from a standard envelope.

9. Click the **Printing Options** tab (see Figure 5.18).

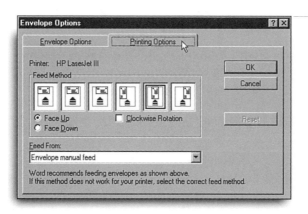

FIGURE 5.18
Use the Printing Options tab in the Envelope Options dialog box to set up your envelope print options.

10. Under **Feed Method**, select the way your envelopes feed into your printer.

11. In the **Feed From** drop-down list box, select whether your printer feeds envelopes from a print tray or requires a manual feed. Choose **OK**.

12. To add merge fields to your envelope, click the Insert Merge Field button [Insert Merge Field] on the Mail Merge toolbar. Locate and select the name of the first field from your data source. Repeat this until all the fields you want on your label are listed. Choose **OK** after you insert all the fields for your envelope.

13. Click the **Close** button in the Mail Merge Helper dialog box.

Editing the Format of an Envelope

Don't forget punctuation

When formatting your main envelope document, make sure to include all standard spacing and punctuation in your sample envelope.

You can edit the format of an envelope just as you do any Word document. You can change the location of merge fields, for example, or the size of the envelope you want to use.

Return to the envelope setup process

1. Open your main document.

2. From the Mail Merge toolbar, click the Mail Merge Helper button .

3. Under step 1, click the **Edit** button and select the Envelope document from the pull-down list.

Printing Envelopes

To print envelopes, follow the steps outlined in the section "Merging the Main Document and the Data Source" earlier in this chapter. You also can use the Merge to New Document or Merge to Printer buttons on the Mail Merge toolbar to print your envelopes.

Working with Large Documents

Learn how to create and edit an outline

Use existing styles to format text in a document

Use AutoFormat and Style Gallery

Create and edit your own styles

Add headers and footers to each page of your document

Create endnotes, footnotes, and annotations for document notations

Add bookmarks and cross-references to your document

Outlining a Document

When creating a large document, use an outline and Outline view to get an overview of how the document is put together. You can also easily rearrange headings and text to better suit the flow of information. Finally, use outlining in long documents to quickly move to a specific location and view the text.

To outline a document, you assign headings to the text to signify different levels of topic development. You can create up to nine different levels of text, including body text. Word formats and indents each level so that you can organize the text quickly. The headings remain formatted in other views as well, although the indents shown in outline view disappear in Normal and Page Layout views. You can also assign any of the predefined heading levels in Normal or Page Layout view.

Figure 6.1 shows an initial outline for a document. As you enter more headings and body text, you can format the text, arrange the headings, and move text around to better organize the document.

Word provides an outline view in which you can organize your documents. Outline view provides an Outline toolbar (see Figure 6.1) that enables you to assign headings to your text, hide body text or headings, and rearrange your outline. You can outline an existing document or create a new document in Outline view. (Table 6.1 gives a brief description of each tool in the Outline toolbar.)

Using a Word outline in PowerPoint

Create an outline first in Word and then use the outline as the basis for a PowerPoint presentation (see Chapter 17).

TABLE 6.1   **Outline toolbar button descriptions**

Button	Button Name	Description
⬅	Promote	Elevates a heading to a higher level.
➡	Demote	Reduces a heading to a lower level.
⏩	Demote to Body Text	Reduces the heading to body text.
⬆	Move Up	Repositions the selected heading(s) up one heading in the outline.
⬇	Move Down	Repositions the selected heading(s) down one heading in the outline.

Button	Button Name	Description
+	Expand	Shows subheadings and body text under selected heading.
–	Collapse	Hides subheadings and body text under selected heading.
8	Show Headings	Expands or collapses the outline to a specific level.
All	All	Expands or collapses the entire outline or hides all body text.
≡	Show First Line Only	Shows all body text or only the first line of the body text.
	Show Formatting	Shows or hides character formatting.
	Master Document view	Changes to Master Document view or back to simple outline view. If Master Document view is selected, the Master Document toolbar appears to the right of the Outline toolbar.

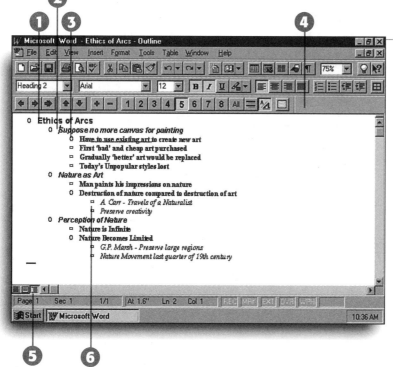

FIGURE 6.1

You can plan a document from scratch in Outline view, assigning levels of importance to headings as you write.

1   Heading Level 1

2   Heading Level 2

3   Heading Level 3

4   Outlining Toolbar

5   Outline view button

6   Heading Level 4

Creating an Outline

You create an outline by entering, formatting, and assigning headings in Word's Outline view. The view provides helpful features you can use to organize your document. After creating your outline, you easily can change heading levels, add text, and otherwise edit your document by using the Outline toolbar and other features of Outline view.

Use the View buttons on the horizontal scrollbar

To change to Outline view, simply click the third view button in the horizontal scrollbar (refer to Figure 6.1).

To start creating an outline, choose the **View** menu and select **Outline**. In Outline view, use the Outline toolbar to specify various levels of headings and body text. Word indents each heading and its text and formats the text for you.

SEE ALSO

➤ *For more information on viewing the document, see page 74*

Entering Text

You can enter text as you normally do by typing paragraphs, heading text, and so on in Normal, Page Layout, or Outline view. You can assign heading styles to existing text by using the Formatting toolbar.

Using Styles to change heading level formats

You can reformat any text formats easily by using styles. (For more information, see "Formatting with Styles," later in this chapter.)

The Formatting toolbar includes a drop-down list of styles (see Figure 6.2). In the Normal template—the default template for documents—Heading 1 style is used for the broadest topics, Heading 2 is used for the subdivisions of Heading 1 topics, and so on. To view or change the style, click the I-beam mouse pointer anywhere in the paragraph and use the Formatting toolbar.

Alternatively, you can designate outline levels as you enter text. Simply select a heading style from the drop-down list in the Formatting toolbar and type the heading. Then change the style, if necessary, and type the next heading or body text.

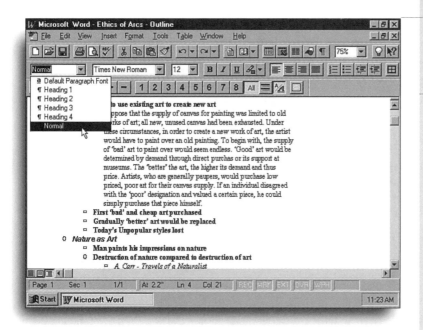

FIGURE 6.2
You can assign heading styles by using the Formatting toolbar.

SEE ALSO

➤ *For more information on entering text, see page 54*

➤ *For more information on formatting text, see page 78*

➤ *Normal style is the same as body text style except that it uses 6-point leading after the paragraph. For more information, see page, 152*

Selecting Text

Outline view provides a slightly different method of selecting text than do the other views. Each paragraph of text, whether that text is a heading or body text, is preceded by a hollow plus sign (+) or a hollow minus sign (-). If you position the mouse pointer on one of these symbols, the pointer changes to a four-headed arrow. When the pointer changes shape, click the plus sign or minus sign to select the associated paragraph and any lower-level headings and body text below it.

Suppose that you click the hollow plus sign preceding the text designated as Heading Level 1 (refer to Figure 6.1). By doing so, you select all text from that point to the next Level 1 heading.

More information visibly available

The plus and minus signs also indicate whether more text has been entered under that level of the outline. A hollow plus sign before a Heading 1 entry, for example, means that other headings or body text have been entered under that heading. A hollow minus sign appears if there are no headings or body text associated with this level. A small, hollow box precedes body text.

(In this case, all the text is selected.) Similarly, if you click the plus sign preceding the Level 2 head, you select all text from that point to the next Level 2 heading. You also can select text by clicking the selection bar (to the left of the text area) or by dragging the I-beam pointer across specific text. After you select the text, you can then choose the level of the heading that you want to assign.

Promoting and Demoting Headings

After assigning various heading levels to your text, you may decide to change those levels. You can do so by using the Promote ⬅ and Demote ➡ buttons in the Outline toolbar. Simply select the text and then click the Promote or Demote button.

The Promote button—the first button from the left in the Outline toolbar—looks like an arrow pointing left. Each time you click the button, the selected text moves up one level (until it reaches Level 1) and displays with less indentation. Similarly, the Demote button—an arrow pointing right—bumps the selected text down one heading level at a time (until it reaches Level 9) and displays with further indentation toward the right. Remember that when you select a heading, you select all text and subheadings within that heading. When you promote or demote the heading, all subheadings follow suit.

To change a selected heading to body text in a single step, click the Demote to Body Text ➡ button—a double arrow pointing right.

Collapsing and Expanding Outlines

Double-click is a great shortcut

Double-click the plus sign that precedes a heading to display all the text below that heading. Double-click again to hide all the text.

You can edit an outline by adding, deleting, or rearranging body text and headings. In Outline view, you can add or delete text as you do in any view. But Outline view also provides two features that make it easier for you to rearrange your text: viewing and moving outline levels. You can use the Outline toolbar to view specific levels of the outline. In addition, you can rearrange topics easily without cutting and pasting text.

You can view various levels of an outline by using the Show Heading buttons—the buttons numbered 1 through 8 in the Outline toolbar. If you click the Show Heading 1 button, for example, only Heading 1 text appears onscreen. If you click the Show Heading 2 button, you see only Heading 1 and Heading 2 text.

If you show only headings with no body text, you are collapsing the outline. Expanding the outline means just the opposite. If only Heading 2 text is showing, for example, click the Show Heading 3, Show Heading 4, or All button to expand the outline.

Figure 6.3 shows a collapsed outline. The hollow plus sign next to each heading indicates that more text levels exist within that heading. If a hollow minus sign appears next to a heading, the heading contains no further text levels.

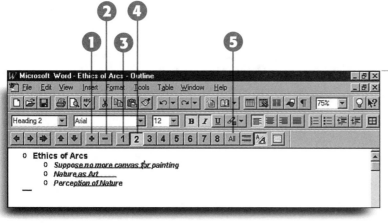

FIGURE 6.3

Use the Expand and Collapse buttons to reveal text below the selected head.

1 Expand

2 Collapse

3 Show Heading 1

4 Show Heading 2

5 All

Rearranging Headings and Text

You can rearrange topics in your document by selecting and moving headings in Outline view. The easiest method is to collapse the outline to the level to be moved, select the heading you want to move, and drag the heading to its new position. Subheads and body text move with the selected heading.

Figure 6.4 shows how the screen looks when you move a heading (and its subheadings and body text) to a new position. The mouse pointer changes to a double-headed arrow, and a guideline moves with the mouse to help you position the heading.

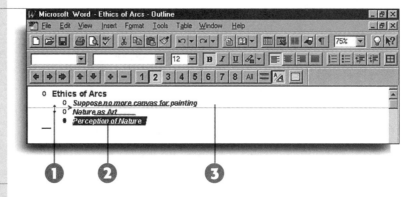

FIGURE 6.4

For the most efficient and easiest rearranging of topics, collapse the outline to the heading level to be moved.

❶ Double-headed mouse pointer

❷ Dragging heading up

❸ Guideline

SEE ALSO

➤ To learn about using drag-and drop to move text, see page 64

Formatting with Styles

A *style* is a collection of formats that you can assign to selected text in a document. Each style includes attributes such as font, type size and style, spacing, leading, alignment, indents, and tabs. Styles enable you to format your documents quickly and consistently. Word provides a large number of ready-to-use styles. You also can create your own styles as you work.

Word has two types of styles:

- *Paragraph styles*. If you position the insertion point or select any portion of a paragraph and apply a paragraph style, the entire text of the paragraph changes to reflect the new style.

- *Character styles*. If you position the insertion point or select any point or select any portion of a paragraph, only the text selected is changed.

In the Style pull-down box on the Formatting toolbar (refer to Figure 6.2), the paragraph symbols before the style name

---

Caution: Select all text to be moved

If you do not collapse the outline before moving the text, you may leave some body text behind. Be sure to select all text to be moved.

Print any level of the outline

To print the outline at any level, choose the **File** menu and select **Print**, or click the Print button.

indicate paragraph styles. Style names marked with an under-scored letter a̱ indicate a character style. One of Word's para-graph styles, for example, is the Heading 1 style used to outline a document. Using the Normal template, heading 1 text initially appears in 14-point Arial, bold, and left-aligned. You can assign this style, or any other style, as often as necessary in your documents.

Word's styles are associated with its *templates*, which are a preset collection of page, paragraph, and character formatting styles that you can use to develop a particular type of document. Each time you start a new document, the New dialog box lists many different templates. The Normal template (Word's default) offers three heading formats and a body-text format. Other templates, such as the Invoice, Letter, and Memo templates, provide differ-ent styles for your use.

Styles are particularly useful when you are working on a large document. Rather than moving from page to page and separately formatting each heading, list, tab setting, and so on, you can for-mat a style one time and then assign the style to each portion of text that you want to format. After you assign styles, you may decide you want to change all occurrences of text formatted with a particular style. Rather than reformatting each occurrence sep-arately, you only need to edit the style.

SEE ALSO

➤ *For more information about formatting text, see page 78*

➤ *For more information about formatting paragraphs, see page 84*

➤ *For more information about changing fonts, sizes, and styles, see page 79*

➤ *For more information about creating a new document, see page 69*

Using Word's Styles

To apply a style, first select the text that you want to format. Then open the Style drop-down list in the Formatting toolbar and select the style that you want to apply (see Figure 6.5).

Use the Style Gallery to get a sneak peek at Word's built-in templates

You can examine some of Word's templates by working with the Style Gallery (see "Using Style Gallery" later in this chapter). From the menu bar, choose the **Format** menu and then choose **Style Gallery**. Choose the template that you want to review in the **Template** list box. In the Preview section, choose **Style Samples**. The styles for the template display with the style name and associ-ated formatting.

Viewing Style Names in the docu-ment is extremely helpful

To see the style names in the left margin, from Normal or Outline view, choose the **Tools** menu, select **Options,** and change the **Style Area Width** on the **View** tab to **.7**.

FIGURE 6.5

The Normal Template's Heading 2 style is 12-point Arial, bold italic, left-aligned, with spacing set at 12 points before and 3 points after the paragraph.

1 Level 2 heading

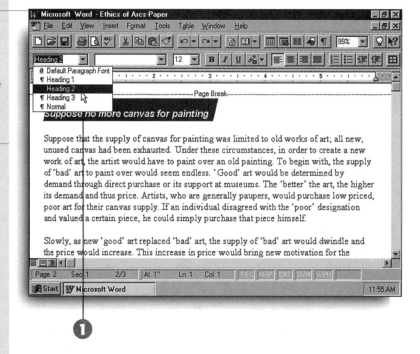

You can change the format of text after applying a style. You could, for example, change the Level 2 heading in Figure 6.5 to 14-point or center-aligned. Changing the format of a particular heading, however, does not change the style itself or other headings to which you apply that style.

SEE ALSO

➤ *For more information about changing the attributes of styles, see page 155*

Creating a Style

Creating your own styles in Word is easy. Suppose that you want to create a heading style for use throughout your document; you want the style to be 18-point Times New Roman, bold, and center-aligned. You can create this style, add it to the Style drop-down list, and use it as you do any other Word style.

Creating your own style

1. Select the text on which you want to base your style, and apply the desired formatting.

2. With the text still selected, click the Style box in the Formatting toolbar to select the current style name. Which style name you choose does not matter.

3. Type your own name for the style (see Figure 6.6).

4. Press Enter to add the name to the Styles list.

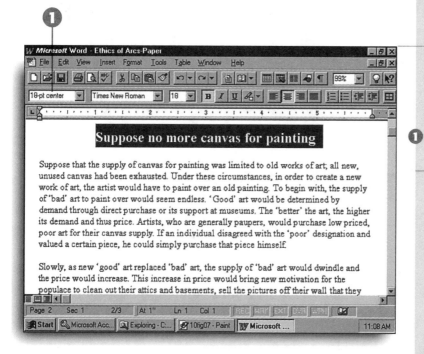

FIGURE 6.6

When you enter a new name in the Style box, you do not actually delete the original style; you are just adding a new style to the list.

1. Type the style name in the Style box

Editing a Style

You can edit any style by changing font, size, alignment, tab stops, and so on, whether it is a preset style provided with Word or a style you created.

Editing a style

1. Choose the **Format** menu and select **Style**. The Style dialog box appears (see Figure 6.7).

2. In the **Styles** list box, select the style that you want to modify. Samples of the text as it is now formatted appear in the Paragraph Preview and Character Preview boxes.

3. Choose the **Modify** button to edit the style. The Modify Style dialog box appears (see Figure 6.8).

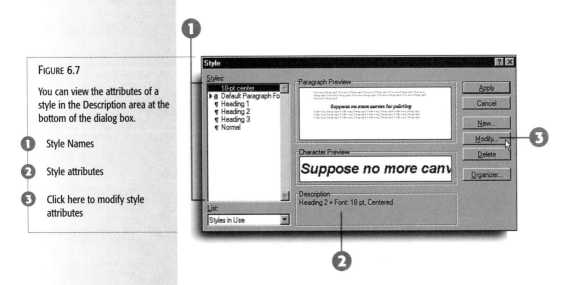

FIGURE 6.7

You can view the attributes of a style in the Description area at the bottom of the dialog box.

1 Style Names

2 Style attributes

3 Click here to modify style attributes

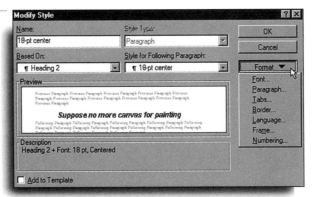

FIGURE 6.8

Modify a style by selecting an option in the **Format** drop-down list.

4. Click **Format** to display a drop-down list of the style attributes that you can edit.

5. Select an attribute—**Font**, **Paragraph**, **Tabs**, and so on—from the list. Make the desired changes in the dialog box that appears. (The dialog box that appears is exactly like the one that appears when you choose the corresponding command from the **Format** menu.) Choose **OK** to return to the Modify Style dialog box.

6. Repeat step 5 as often as necessary to modify additional style attributes.

7. After making all desired changes, choose **OK** in the Modify Style dialog box. You return to the Style dialog box.

8. Choose **Close** to exit the Style dialog box. All text that has been formatted with your style is changed throughout your document.

Using AutoFormat

AutoFormat is a feature of Word that analyzes your document and automatically applies styles (such as headings, subheadings, bulleted lists, and tabs) to your document when you use the AutoFormat command or as you type. When you use the AutoFormat command, you can review AutoFormat's choices and accept or reject them. Using AutoFormat can save you time because Word assigns styles for you. The formatting may not be exactly what you want, but you can still change fonts, styles, sizes, and so on after using AutoFormat.

You can use AutoFormat with unformatted text, or you can begin formatting (by creating and applying a few styles) and then let AutoFormat complete the process. AutoFormat finds similar text and assigns the same styles. If you choose the latter method, you have more control over which styles AutoFormat uses. Experiment with both methods and see which you prefer.

Formatting Text as You Type

If you want to use the AutoFormat feature as you type text, choose the **Tools** menu, select **Options**, click the **AutoFormat** tab, and select the **AutoFormat as You Type** option. You can check as many of the dialog box options (see Table 6.2) as you want.

TABLE 6.2 **AutoFormat as you type options**	
Option	**How to Make It Work**
Headings	Type a short line of text and press Enter twice for Heading 1 style. After two Enters, type Tab, type a short line of text and press Enter twice for Heading 2.

continues…

Caution: To close or not to close

After you choose **OK** from the Modify Style dialog box, the formatting of the style changes throughout your document. If you choose **Apply** in the Style dialog box, the selected text or text at the insertion point is the only text changed, even if this text originally was not formatted with that style. If you want to change all the text formatted with the changed style, make sure that you choose **Close** in the Style dialog box at step 8.

AutoFormat saves time

Use AutoFormat to remove unnecessary spacing, change asterisk bullets to round bullets, and headings to styles.

Save time using the keyboard

For those of you who may not like using the mouse to add bullets, numbers, or symbols, the options listed in Table 6.2 can save time.

TABLE 6.2 **Continued**

Option	How to Make It Work
Bo_r_ders	Type three or more hyphens (-) and press Enter for a thin border or equal signs (=) for a double border.
Automatic _B_ulleted Lists	Start a list with an asterisk (*), lowercase o, greater than symbol (>), or a hyphen (-) followed by a space or tab. When you press Enter, each new item will be bulleted with a corresponding bullet. An * or o will produce a ●, a > will produce a ➤, and a - will produce a ■. To end the list, press Enter twice.
Automatic _N_umbered Lists	Start a list with a number, a letter (uppercase or lowercase), or a lowercase i for Roman numerals, followed by a period (.) and a space. When you press Enter, each new item will be numbered accordingly. To end the list, press Enter twice.
Straight _Q_uotes with Smart Quotes	When you type 'single' or "double" quotes, Word automatically changes them to 'smart quotes' or "smart quotes."
_O_rdinals (1st) with Superscript	Type **1st** or **2nd** to get 1st, 2nd, and so on.
_F_ractions (1/2) with fraction character (½)	Type **1/2** and **3/4** to get ½ and ¾.
Symbol Characters with Symbols	Type **(c)** for ©, **(r)** for ®, **(tm)** for ™. Type **:)**, **:I**, and **:(**, for ☺, ☻, and ☹ faces; **<-, ->** for thin arrows; **<=, =>** for thick arrows.

Formatting Text Automatically

To start AutoFormat, choose the **F_o_rmat** menu and select **AutoFormat**. A message box—the first AutoFormat dialog box—appears. Choose **OK** to begin formatting. You can also use the AutoFormat button 📄 on the Standard toolbar to apply all formatting without being prompted.

Accepting or Rejecting Changes

After AutoFormat completes the formatting, another dialog box appears. Choose **_A_ccept** to accept all changes. If you choose

Accept too hastily, you can reverse your decision by clicking the Undo button on the Standard toolbar. If you do not like the changes you see behind the AutoFormat dialog box, choose **Reject All**. Alternatively, choose **Review Changes** or **Style Gallery**.

Reviewing Changes

If you choose to **Review Changes**, Word shows you each change to the formatting by highlighting the change and displaying a dialog box with a description of the change. You can choose to accept or reject individual changes. If you choose the **Style Gallery** button, you can apply different templates and styles to the document to see what they look like.

The Review AutoFormat Changes dialog box enables you to accept or reject changes. To accept a change, choose one of the Find buttons. **Find** with a left arrow moves to the previous change; **Find** with a right arrow moves to the next change. If you do not like the formatting, choose the **Reject** button. Word changes the current selection back to its original formatting.

If you don't reject any changes, you see a **Cancel** button that enables you to return to the AutoFormat dialog box. If you reject any changes, the Cancel button changes to **Close**. Choose **Close** after reviewing the changes, or at any time, and Word displays the initial AutoFormat dialog box again. You can choose to accept or reject all changes.

As you go through reviewing changes, AutoFormat shows items in red that have been deleted (such as paragraph marks) and items in blue that have been added. If you don't want to see the marks where changes have been made, choose the **Hide Marks** button. If you want Word to automatically go to the next change after you choose the **Reject** button, check the **Find Next after Reject** check box. If you make a mistake and don't want to reject a change after you choose the **Reject** button, choose the **Undo Last** button.

> **Edit your document while you review changes**
>
> You can click the mouse outside the Review AutoFormat Changes dialog box to work in your document. The dialog box remains onscreen. This way, you can scroll through the document to compare changes, format text, and add or edit text.

Using the Style Gallery

Style Gallery is a special dialog box that contains Word's various templates. Each template contains preset page formatting and preset styles. You can use Style Gallery to apply various templates and styles to your document and view an example in the dialog box before choosing to accept the style.

You can use the Style Gallery with or without AutoFormat. When you use AutoFormat, Word automatically applies a template and style sheet. If you do not like Word's choice, you can choose the **Style Gallery** command button and select a different template and style for your document. On the other hand, you can format your document yourself by applying styles to text and paragraphs, and then decide to look at the document with various templates applied. Style Gallery gives a formatted document a different look using various styles of fonts, indents, type sizes, and so on.

To open the Style Gallery from the menu, choose the **Fo̲rmat** menu and select **Style G̲allery**. To open Style Gallery from the AutoFormat dialog box, choose the **Style Gallery** button. (Figure 6.9 shows the Style Gallery dialog box with the Professional Report template displayed.)

FIGURE 6.9

Apply any of the templates and styles to your document or choose to preview examples of the template.

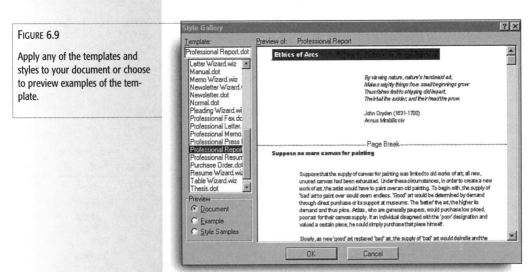

Use the Style Gallery

1. From the second AutoFormat dialog box, choose **Style Gallery**. To use Style Gallery directly, choose the **Fo̲rmat**

menu and select **Style Gallery**. The Style Gallery dialog box appears.

2. Select a template from the **Template** list.

3. To change what displays in the **Preview of** box, choose one of the options in the Preview section. The default choice, **Document**, shows your document with styles applied from the selected template. To see an example document with many of the styles for the template, choose **Example**. To see a list of styles in the template and how they are formatted, choose **Style Samples** in the Preview section.

4. If you find a template and style you like, choose **OK**. If you do not find a template you like, choose **Cancel**. Word returns to the AutoFormat dialog box or to your document.

5. If you started from AutoFormat, choose to **Accept** or **Reject All** changes. The dialog box closes, and you are returned to the document.

Adding Headers and Footers

Headers and footers contain repeated information at the top and bottom of documents. Headers and footers are typically used in long documents and may include one or more of the following: page number, date, company name, author name, or chapter title. You can edit and format headers and footers like any other part of a Word document.

Inserting a Header or Footer

When you add a header or footer, Word switches to Page Layout view, opens up the Header pane, and displays a Header and Footer toolbar. To add a header or footer, choose the **View** menu and select **Header and Footer**. The Header and Footer toolbar appears along with a dotted area surrounding the header area (see Figure 6.10). Type in the header pane or use the Switch Between Header and Footer button 🖫 to go to the footer.

In the header or footer pane, you can do any of the following:

■ Type and format text as you do in a normal document.

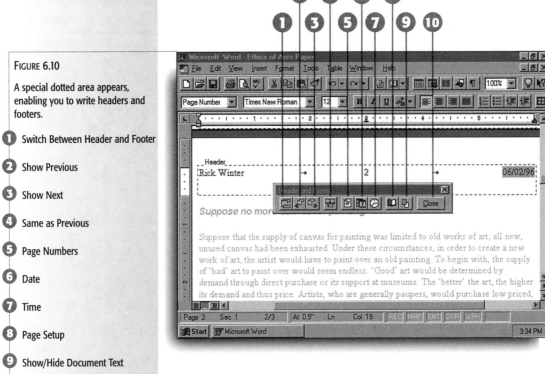

FIGURE 6.10

A special dotted area appears, enabling you to write headers and footers.

1 Switch Between Header and Footer

2 Show Previous

3 Show Next

4 Same as Previous

5 Page Numbers

6 Date

7 Time

8 Page Setup

9 Show/Hide Document Text

10 Close header/footer pane

- Press Tab to get to the center tab, and press Tab again to get to the right-alignment tab. You can also change the tab settings if you want.

- Click the Page Numbers button to add a page number for each page.

- Click the Date button to add a field that shows today's date. To have this field updated when printing, make sure that the **Tools**, **Options**, **Print** Tab shows that **Update Fields** is checked.

- Click the Time button to add a field that shows the current time.

- If you want headers and footers on the first page to appear different from those on other pages or if you want different headers and footers for odd and even pages, click the Page Setup button. In the Headers and Footers section of the

Layout tab, you can check the **Different Odd and Even** check box to have headers and footers change on facing pages. You can check the **Different First Page** option to have headers and footers that are different for the first page (this is usually done for report title pages and long business letters). If you have different sections in your document, you can choose **This Section** or **Whole Document** in the **Apply To** pull-down list. When finished with the Page Setup dialog box, choose **OK** to return to the Header and Footer pane.

When you are finished entering information for the headers and footers, click the **Close** button to return to the document.

Inserting Fields in the Header or Footer

You can add field codes to the document or in the header or footer—the procedure is the same. To add a code to the header or footer while you are in the header or footer pane, choose the **Insert** menu and select **Field**. You can choose any of the field codes from the Field dialog box shown in Figure 6.11.

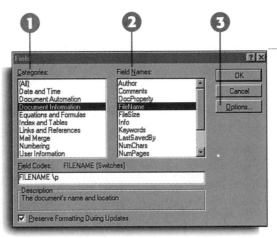

FIGURE 6.11

The FileName code with the \p switch adds a file name with the file location, including the drive and folder.

1 Choose one of the **Categories**

2 Choose an item in the **Field Names** list

3 The **Options** button lists more choices

Table 6.3 shows some useful fields for headers and footers.

TABLE 6.3.   **Useful field codes**

Result	Categories	Field Names
Document name (include the \p switch for the \path name)	Document Information	FileName \p
Total number of pages	Document Information	NumPages
Author Information	Document Information	Author
User Information	User Information	UserName
Section numbering	Numbering	Section
Save Date	Date and Time	SaveDate

Inserting Section Breaks

You may determine that you need more options for headers and footers than **Different First Page** or **Different Odd and Even Pages**. If you need multiple headers and footers in your document, you first need to break your document into different sections.

Insert section breaks in your document

1. Position the insertion point where you want the new section.
2. Choose the **Insert** menu and select **Break**. The Break dialog box appears (shown in Figure 6.12).

FIGURE 6.12

Use the Break dialog box to add new sections to your document.

3. In the Section Breaks area of the dialog box, select **Next Page** for a section beginning on a new page.
4. Choose **OK** to insert the new break and close the dialog box.

5. Repeat steps 1 through 4 for all the section breaks you need in the document.

6. When you are adding headers and footers, click the Show Next button on the Header and Footer toolbar to go to the next header or footer pane (see Figure 6.13).

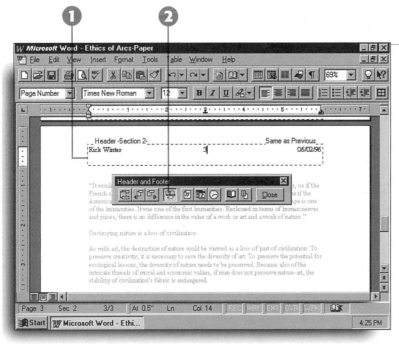

FIGURE 6.13

Notice Same as Previous on the top right corner of the header or footer pane.

① Header pane for Section 2

② Click Same as Previous to turn option off

7. To change the header or footer for this section, first click the Same as Previous button on the Header and Footer toolbar to turn this option off.

8. Type the new header or footer information.

9. Repeat steps 6 through 8 for each section of the document.

10. Click the **Close** button when you finish adding or editing your headers and footers.

Editing or Deleting a Header or Footer

To edit the header or footer, you can double-click the header or footer in Page Layout view or choose the **View** menu and select

Double-click shortcut

Double-click a header or footer in Page Layout view to open the pane for editing.

Header and Footer. Edit the header or footer as you would regular document text. If you want to delete the header or footer, select the text (press Ctrl+A to select the entire header or footer) and press Delete. Click the **Close** button on the Header and Footer toolbar to return to the document.

Using Footnotes and Endnotes

When you write a report or want to identify the source of your text, you can use footnotes (which go on the bottom of each page) or endnotes (which appear at the end of the document). To create an endnote or footnote, first position the insertion point at your reference in the document and then choose the **Insert** menu and select **Footnote**. The Footnote and Endnote dialog box appears (shown in Figure 6.14).

FIGURE 6.14

Choose the **Footnote** option to add notes at the bottom of the current page. Choose the **Endnote** option to add notes at the end of the document.

In the Insert section of the dialog box, select **Footnote** or **Endnote** and choose **OK**. The bottom portion of the screen opens up to enable you to type the reference (see Figure 6.15). When finished, click the **Close** button. A superscript number appears next to your text in the document referring to the footnote numbers at the bottom of your page or the endnote numbers at the end of your document. To delete a footnote or endnote, highlight the superscript number and press Delete.

Changing the Footnote or Endnote Reference Mark

When creating footnotes or endnotes, you have display options. After you choose the **Insert** menu, select **Footnote** to go to the Footnote and Endnote dialog box. **AutoNumber** is the default choice, which means that each new note is incremented by one. You can change the mark to appear as a letter, a number, or another character by choosing the **Custom Mark** option and typing in your choice. The **Symbol** command button enables you to choose symbols for your custom mark from the Symbol dialog box. The **Options** command button leads to another dialog box, which enables you to change the location of the footnotes and endnotes, the number format (numbers, letters, symbols), which number to start with, and when to restart numbering.

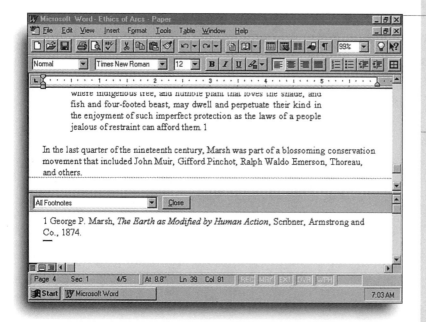

FIGURE 6.15

A new pane opens up to enable you to add a footnote or endnote. Choose **Close** to get out of the pane or click your document to continue working.

Annotating Your Work

Annotations are similar to endnotes except that they are usually used when more than one person works on a document (annotations help identify the reviewer). To create an annotation, choose the **Insert** menu and select **Annotation**. A window opens on the lower part of the document for your annotation (see Figure 6.16). When finished writing your comment, click the **Close** button. The reviewer's initials appear in superscript in the document, followed by a number. This number references the annotations at the end of the document.

FIGURE 6.16

A pane is also created for annotations.

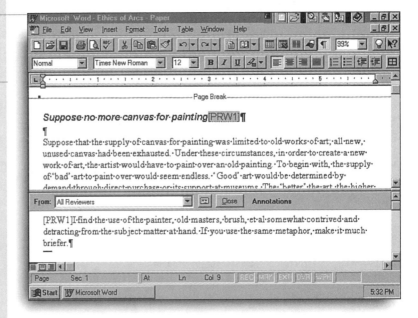

To edit an annotation, double-click the annotation reference. To delete the annotation, select the superscript reference and press Delete. To print annotations, choose the **File** menu, select **Print,** and choose **Annotations** from the **Print What** pull-down list.

Reviewer's initials are automatic

The reviewer's initials are based on the user information from the reviewer's computer. To view or change the initials, choose the **Tools** menu, select **Options**, select the User Info tab, view or change the **Initials** text box, and choose **OK**.

Using Bookmarks and Cross-References

You can use bookmarks to create easy jump-to sections in your document or for cross-references. To create a bookmark, move to or select the text that you want to mark as the bookmark. Choose the **Edit** menu, select **Bookmark**, type the name of the

bookmark in the Bookmark dialog box (see Figure 6.17), and
choose **Add**.

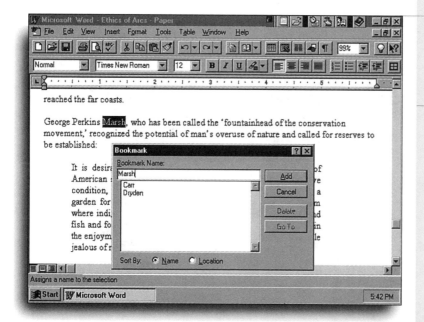

FIGURE 6.17

To add a bookmark, type the
name in the **Bookmark
Name** text box and choose
Add.

After you have a bookmark, you can press F5 to display the Go
To dialog box (see Figure 6.18). Choose **Bookmark** from the
Go to What list and type or choose the bookmark name from
the **Enter Bookmark Name** section.

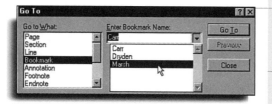

FIGURE 6.18

The Go To dialog box shows a list
of all the bookmarks.

To add a cross-reference to the bookmark in your document (for
example, *see page 25* where *25* is the page on which the bookmark appears), first position your insertion point where you want
the cross-reference to go, choose the **Insert** menu, and select
Cross-Reference. The Cross-Reference dialog box appears

(shown in Figure 6.19). Choose Bookmark from the **Reference Type** list. From the **Insert Reference To** list, choose **Page Number** and then choose the appropriate bookmark in the **For Which Bookmark** list box. The reference goes into the document as a field.

FIGURE 6.19

You can use a cross-reference to refer the reader to the page number on which the bookmark is located.

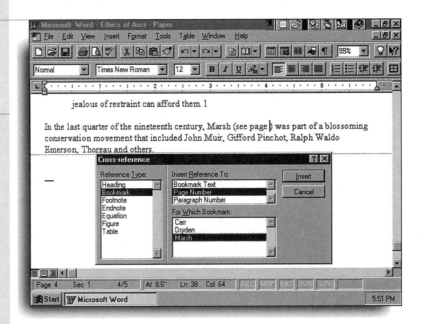

Working with Tables and Borders

Working with Tables

You can enhance documents by adding tables to organize information. Using tables rather than aligning data with tabs enables you to apply enhancements that liven up the information you are presenting and make it more noticeable.

Word enables you to enter and format text in a table, create calculations in the table, and format the table itself. You can add rows and columns, adjust spacing, perform calculations, add borders, adjust row height, and much more.

Word also enables you to add graphics such as lines, borders, and shading to illustrate your documents and to add interest.

A table is a convenient way to organize text. You can use a table to create forms, reports, simple spreadsheets, and columns of numbers. You even can use tables to produce side-by-side paragraphs, such as those in a resume or an agenda.

Tables consist of columns and rows. *Columns* are the vertical divisions of a table; *rows* are the horizontal divisions. The box formed by the intersection of a column and a row is called a *cell*. Cells can be filled with both text and graphics. When you type information into a cell, the text wraps from one line to the next, enlarging the cell as you enter more text.

When you insert a table, you enter the number of columns and rows you want the table to contain. After the table is inserted, you can modify the table and its contents by adding borders and shading, formatting the text, adjusting column width and row height, and so on. Word provides the following two options for creating a table automatically:

- Using the **Insert Table** command in the **Table** menu
- Using the Insert Table button

SEE ALSO

➤ *For information about adding borders and shading to a table, see page 179*

Inserting a Table Using the Menu Command

Using the **Table** menu to insert a table displays dialog box options for the number of columns, the number of rows, and the

---

Use a Word table instead of an Excel spreadsheet

In a Word table, you can display numbers in rows and columns and can perform mathematical functions on these numbers. This is not as powerful as an Excel spreadsheet, but if you have a situation in which you need a small table with text and numbers that require calculations, Word can handle it quite well.

column width. You also can let Word create and format the table for you using the Wizard and AutoFormat buttons.

Insert a table

1. Position the insertion point where you want to insert the table.

2. Choose the **Table** menu and select **Insert Table**. The Insert Table dialog box opens (see Figure 7.1).

3. Enter values for the **Number of Columns** and the **Number of Rows**. You also have the option to enter a value in the **Column Width** box.

4. If you prefer, you can choose **Wizard** or **AutoFormat** and answer these queries in the dialog boxes.

5. Choose **OK** to insert the table and to close the Insert Table dialog box.

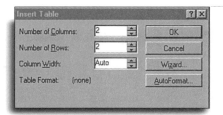

FIGURE 7.1

You can specify the number of columns and rows in the Insert Table dialog box.

The following list describes the options in the Insert Table dialog box:

- **Number of Columns**. Enter the number of columns for the table.

- **Number of Rows**. Enter the number of rows for the table.

- **Column Width**. Set a specific column width for all columns or leave the option set to Auto. Auto column width divides the space equally between the left and right margins. You can adjust the width of any column at any time.

- **Table Format**. If you use AutoFormat to format the table, this option displays the predefined format.

- **Wizard**. Starts the Table Wizard. You answer the wizard's questions and choose options for formatting the table.

Inserting and deleting rows and columns

You can always add rows and columns by choosing the **Table** menu and selecting **Insert Rows** (if a row is selected) or **Insert Columns** (if a column is selected). You can delete rows and columns by choosing the **Table** menu and selecting **Delete Rows** or **Delete Columns**.

Displaying table gridlines

When you insert a table, Word usually displays table gridlines. If you do not see gridlines, choose the **Table** menu and select **Gridlines** to display the nonprinting guides.

- **AutoFormat**. Displays the Table AutoFormat dialog box, in which you can choose styles, borders, fonts, and more from a list of predefined table formats. AutoFormat is similar to the Style Gallery.

SEE ALSO

➤ *For more information about letting Word do your document formatting, see page 157*

➤ *For more information about adding and deleting columns in Word tables, see page 176*

Inserting a Table Using the Insert Table Button

If you want to create a free-form table, use the Insert Table button 🔳 on the Standard toolbar. To insert the table, click the Insert Table button and drag the mouse pointer across the grid to specify the number of columns; drag down the grid to specify the number of rows. When you release the mouse button, Word inserts a table with the specified number of columns and rows at the position of the insertion point.

Entering Text into a Table

After you insert the table, you can add text in much the same way as you enter text in any document. Moving around in a table, however, is a bit different. You also can edit text in a table as you edit any text. After entering the text, you can select it to apply various types of formatting, such as type sizes and alignments.

Some basic principles to remember when working with a Word table include:

- To enter text in a table, position the insertion point in a cell and then type the text.
- To move to another cell in the table, use the arrow keys. The arrow keys help you move from cell to cell, from column to column, and from row to row. If a cell contains text, the arrow key first moves one character or line at a time, and then moves from cell to cell.

- Press the Tab key to move the insertion point to the right one cell, highlighting any text in the cell.

- Press Shift+Tab to move one cell to the left. To insert a tab into a cell, press Ctrl+Tab and then set the tab as usual.

SEE ALSO

➤ *To learn more about applying text and paragraph formats, see pages 78 and 84*

Selecting Text in a Table

Selecting text in a table is similar to selecting text in any document. You can drag the I-beam pointer over text to select it, or you can click the selection bar to select an entire row. You also can use the following techniques, which are specific to selecting text in a table:

- To select one cell, triple-click that cell or click the left inside edge of the cell.

- To select an entire column, drag the mouse down the column. Alternatively, you can place the mouse pointer at the top of the column; the pointer changes to a black down arrow. Click the column to select it; click and drag across columns to select more than one column.

- To select an entire row, click the selection bar to the left of the table. Drag the mouse up or down to select more than one row.

- To select the entire table, position the cursor anywhere in the table and press Shift+Alt+5 (on the numeric keypad with Num Lock on). Alternatively, you can place the insertion point in the table and choose the **Table** menu, and then **Select Table**.

SEE ALSO

➤ *For more information about using the ruler to indent text, see page 90*

After selecting text in the table, you can format it as you would any other text by applying various fonts, font sizes, alignment, and so on. Figure 7.2 shows a column that was selected using the black down arrow. The first row of text is centered with bold headings, and the columns of numbers are right-aligned.

FIGURE 7.2

You can select text in a table to format it.

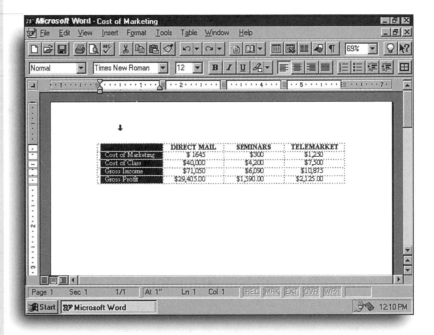

The interactive Table menu

The **Table** menu's commands change depending on the object you select. If you select a column, the **Table** menu contains the **Insert Columns** and **Delete Columns** commands. If you select a cell, the commands are **Insert Cells** and **Delete Cells**.

Adding rows to the end of your table

To add a row at the end of a table, position the insertion point in the bottom-right cell and press Tab. Every time you are in the last cell of a table and press Tab, you create a new row in the table.

Inserting and Deleting Columns and Rows

You can use the commands in the **Table** menu to insert or delete rows and columns, to change cell height and width, and to make other modifications. Use the methods described in the preceding section to select a row or column.

Insert or delete a column or row

1. Select the column or row to be deleted, or select the column or row to the right of or below the point at which you want to add a column or row.

2. Point the mouse at the selected column or row and press the right mouse button to display the shortcut menu.

3. Select **Insert Columns/Rows** or **Delete Columns/Rows**. The selected columns and rows are deleted, or columns and rows are inserted before the selected columns or rows in your table.

Insert a column at the end of a table

1. Turn on the nonprinting characters with the Show/Hide button ¶ in the Standard toolbar.

2. Place the mouse pointer above the end-of-row markers to the right of the table. When you see the black down arrow, click to select the column of end-of-row markers.

3. Place the mouse pointer in the selected column and right-click to display the shortcut menu.

4. Select **I**nsert Column to insert a column at the end of the table.

Adjusting Cell and Row Height

Adjusting cell and row height in Word tables is a simple process. Choose the **T**able menu and select **Cell Height and Width**. Select the **Row** or **Column** tab of the Cell Height and Width dialog box, depending on which area of the table you want to adjust (see Figure 7.3).

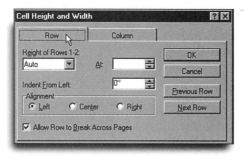

FIGURE 7.3

In the Row tab, you can adjust the height of the rows and can indent or align one row

To adjust the height of the row, select one of the following options in the **H**eight of Row 1-2 drop-down list:

- **Auto**. Word adjusts the height of the row to accommodate the tallest font or graphic.

- **At Least**. Enter the minimum row height in the **A**t box. Word still adjusts the height of the rows to the contents of the cells.

- **Exactly**. Enter a row height in the **A**t box. If a cell's contents exceed the height you entered, Word prints only what fits in the cell.

Creating a form that needs to have exact dimensions

If you want information on a form to stay within certain dimensions, use the **Exactly** option to limit what can be entered in the cell. This option restricts the number of characters that can be displayed or printed. In some cases, this is "exactly" what you want to happen.

178

To indent selected rows or the entire table from the left margin, type a number in the **Indent From Left** box or use the scroll arrows to select a number.

To change the horizontal alignment of selected rows or the entire table, choose **Center** or **Right** in the **Alignment** options.

To allow the text in a row to split across pages, choose the **Allow Row to Break Across Pages** option.

When you make changes in the Cell Height and Width dialog box, you change all rows of the table by default unless you selected certain rows first. To adjust one row at a time, click either the **Previous Row** or **Next Row** button to display the row number you want to change in the **Height of Rows** option at the top of the dialog box (refer to Figure 7.3). Choose either of these buttons to move from row to row as you adjust the height of the rows.

Click **OK** when you finish adjusting the rows or proceed with adjusting columns (discussed in the next section).

Adjusting Column and Cell Width

You also can adjust column and cell width in the Cell Height and Width dialog box. Choose the **Table** menu select **Cell Height and Width,** and then select the **Column** tab (see Figure 7.4).

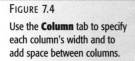

FIGURE 7.4

Use the **Column** tab to specify each column's width and to add space between columns.

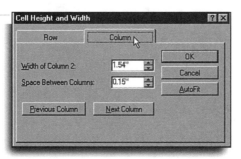

To adjust column width, enter a new width in the **Width of Column** text box. In the **Space Between Columns** text box, you can specify the amount of blank space between column boundaries and the contents of the cell.

If you select the **AutoFit** button, Word automatically resizes all columns in the table to fit the contents of the cells. Click the **Previous Column** or **Next Column** button to change other columns in your table.

Splitting a Table

Sometimes you might start a table at the top of a page, and then decide you want a paragraph of text above the table. In this situation, you can split the table in its first row to create a blank line above the table. You also might decide to insert a paragraph of text somewhere in the middle of a table. In this case, you also can split the table to insert a blank line wherever the insertion point is located.

Split a table to create a blank line or paragraph

1. Position the insertion point where you want the split to occur. Use the first row of the table if you want to add a blank line above the table.

2. Press Ctrl+Shift+Enter to split the table. The row containing the insertion point moves down, and a blank line is inserted at the location of the insertion point.

Adding Lines, Borders, and Shading

Word includes many graphical elements you can add to your documents including lines, borders, and shading. Use these elements to attract attention to your document, break the monotony of straight text, emphasize text, and pique the reader's interest. You can add a line above headings to make them stand out, and you can add lines to a table to help divide data. You can create a shaded border to attract attention to text or add clip art to a newsletter to make it more interesting.

Word enables you to add graphical lines and borders using the Borders toolbar or menu commands. The toolbar method, however, is much easier. You can add borders and shading to text, tables, charts, and other elements using the Borders toolbar.

Remember Undo

If you adjust cell height or width and don't like the results, click the Undo ⟲▾ button in the Standard toolbar to remove your changes.

Displaying the Borders Toolbar

To display the Borders toolbar, place the mouse pointer over any toolbar currently onscreen and click the right mouse button. This displays the Toolbar shortcut menu. Click **Borders** and the Borders toolbar displays; repeat the process and the toolbar disappears.

You also can click the Borders tool 📧 on the Formatting toolbar to turn the Borders toolbar on or off. Figure 7.5 shows the Borders toolbar. Drop-down lists contain options for line thickness (the **Line Style** drop-down list) and various fills and patterns (the **Shading** drop-down list). The other buttons in the Borders toolbar help you specify the border's location.

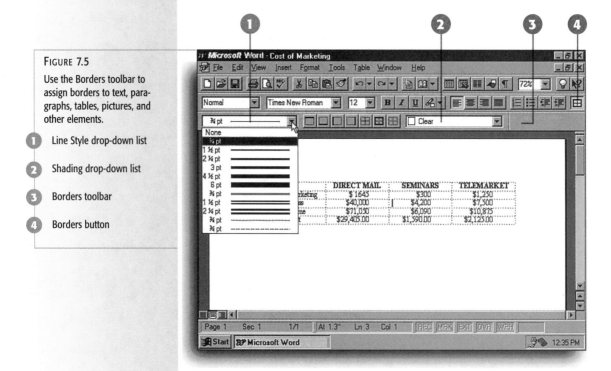

FIGURE 7.5

Use the Borders toolbar to assign borders to text, paragraphs, tables, pictures, and other elements.

1 Line Style drop-down list

2 Shading drop-down list

3 Borders toolbar

4 Borders button

Applying a Border

To apply a border, place the insertion point in the cell where you want the line or border to appear, or select the table, row, column, cell, picture, frame, or text. Choose the Line Style drop-down list from the Borders toolbar and select a line style. Then, on the Borders toolbar, click the border button you want to use (see Table 7.1). When you click a border button, Word inserts the border from left indent marker to right indent marker or from side to side (for objects). If you click the same border button again, Word removes the border.

TABLE 7.1 **The border buttons**

Button	Button Name	Description
	Top Border	Inserts a border along the top of a table, row, column, cell, frame, or picture, or above a paragraph of text.
	Bottom Border	Inserts a border along the bottom of a table, row, column, cell, frame, or picture, or below a paragraph of text.
	Left Border	Inserts a border along the left side of the object or paragraph.
	Right Border	Inserts a border along the right side of the object or paragraph.
	Inside Border	Inserts a border along the inside lines of a table or between selected paragraphs.
	Outside Border	Applies a border to the outside of an object or frame or around selected paragraphs.
	No Border	Removes a border. Before using this button, select the bordered paragraph, table, or object.

You can apply more than one border to an object or text. For example, you can apply a 3/4-point top border and a 6-point bottom border. You can add 3-point left and right borders, creating a somewhat strange box around the object or text. You also can apply shading to the same text or object to which you have applied one or more borders.

You can apply shading and patterns by selecting the object or text or by positioning the insertion point. Choose shading from the Shading drop-down list in the Borders toolbar. The list provides shading in percentages from 5 percent to 100 percent (or solid). Word also displays a variety of patterns you can apply to text or objects. The available pattern follow the shading percentages in the Shading drop-down list.

Adjusting border lengths

Adjust the length of a border line by selecting it and moving the indent markers in the ruler.

Colors for borders and shading

For additional shading or color options, open the **Format** menu and select **Borders and Shading** to see many other choices.

Figure 7.6 shows a table with a double 3/4-point outside border, a single 3/4-point inside border, and 20-percent shading in the heading row.

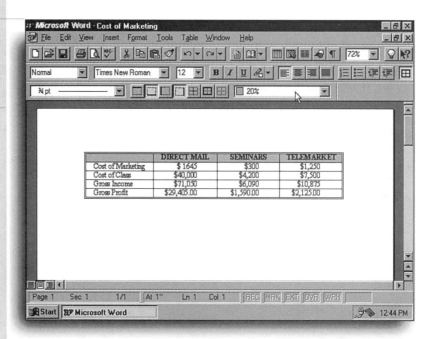

Summing Up in Tables

 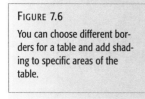
You might have a table that requires numbers in a column or row to be calculated. Word enables you to create formulas and perform spreadsheet-type calculations in Word tables. If your table has a simple calculation, if you don't want to use Excel or a spreadsheet application, or if you want to keep everything in the same application, you can choose the **Table** menu and select **Formula** to add formulas to your tables.

SEE ALSO

➤ *For more information about using the formulas built into Office, see page 259*

Inserting a Formula into a Cell

Inserting a formula into a cell in Word is similar to performing the same action in a spreadsheet application. If you know how to use spreadsheet programs, you can use what you already know. If you aren't familiar with spreadsheet programs, however, you can still use formulas in Word. Figure 7.7 shows the Formula dialog box, which displays when you choose the **Table** menu, and then select **Formula**.

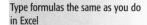

Type formulas the same as you do in Excel

Spreadsheet-type references similar to **=SUM(A2:A9)** are valid in the Word formula field.

FIGURE 7.7
This formula calculates gross profit in the Direct Mail column.

Cell references in Word tables are the same as cell references in spreadsheet applications, except for one major difference— you don't have row or column headings telling you which cell you are using (see Figure 7.8). To determine the cell reference, you need to keep track of headings on your own. Columns are lettered beginning with A. Rows are numbered beginning with 1. The intersection of the column and row is the cell reference.

Insert a formula into a cell

1. Position the insertion point in the cell to receive the formula.

2. Choose the **Table** menu and select **Formula**.

3. Either accept the default formula of the column or row, or delete the default formula and type a new formula beginning with = (an equal sign) and followed by a mathematical calculation using cell references in place of actual numbers where necessary.

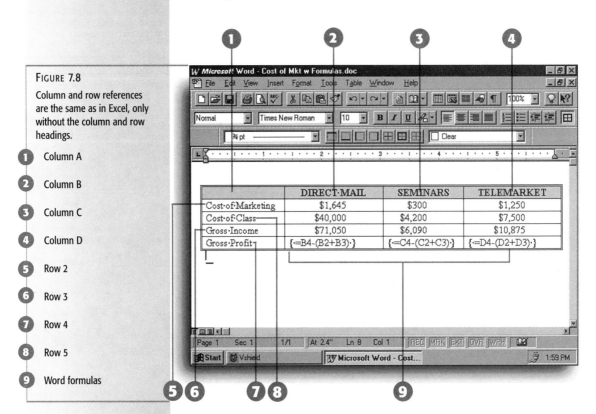

FIGURE 7.8

Column and row references are the same as in Excel, only without the column and row headings.

1 Column A

2 Column B

3 Column C

4 Column D

5 Row 2

6 Row 3

7 Row 4

8 Row 5

9 Word formulas

You also can use the functions that come with Word. Instead of typing a formula in the preceding step, you can click the **Paste Function** drop-down list to display the functions in Word's formula field. Common functions include the following:

- Average(). Calculates the average of the arguments. Arguments are cell references inside parentheses.

- Count(). Counts the numeric items within the arguments, including the beginning and ending reference.

- MAX(). Finds the highest number within the arguments, including the beginning and ending reference.

- MIN(). Finds the lowest number within the arguments, including the beginning and ending reference.

4. Choose the **Number Format** you want to use. You can select from the following number formats:

- *#,##0.* Displays numbers with commas and no decimal places.
- *#,##0.00.* Displays numbers with commas and two decimal places.
- *$#,##0.00;($#,##0.00).* Displays numbers with dollar signs, commas, two decimal places, and negative numbers in parentheses.
- *0.* Displays whole numbers rounding up, with no commas and no decimal places.
- *0%.* Displays numbers as a percentage, rounded up.
- *0.00.* Displays numbers with two decimal places.
- *0.00%.* Displays numbers as a percentage with two decimal places.

5. Choose **OK**.

Recalculating a Formula

One of the best reasons to use formulas in a table is the ease with which you can recalculate the formula when one of the values changes. You can enter a new value in the table, and Word performs the recalculation for you. If you have more than one formula to calculate, you can update all the formulas at once.

Recalculate formulas in a table

1. Enter the new value or values in your table.

2. Do one of the following:
   - Move to the cell containing the formula.
   - Select the row or column containing all the formulas.
   - Select the entire table.

3. Press **F9**, the calculation key.

Using Excel

Creating Worksheets

Learn to navigate in your worksheets with the mouse, keyboard, and scrollbars

Understand how to enter text, numbers, dates, times, and formulas

Learn selection techniques using the mouse and keyboard

Learn how to automatically enter and format series of data using the AutoFill feature or menu commands

Save your workbooks in Excel or other file formats

Defining Excel Terms

When you start Excel, a blank workbook is displayed in the document window. The *workbook* is the main document used in Excel for storing and manipulating data. A workbook consists of individual *worksheets*, each of which can contain data. Initially, each new workbook you create contains 16 worksheets; Excel will allow you to add more worksheets later. In addition to worksheets, you can create charts, macros, visual basic modules, and dialog sheets.

Each worksheet is made up of 256 columns and 16,384 rows. The columns are lettered across the top of the document window, beginning with A through Z and continuing with AA through AZ, BA through BZ, and so on through column IV. The rows are numbered from 1 to 16,384 down the left side of the document window.

The intersections of rows and columns form *cells*, which are the basic units for storing data. Each cell takes its name from this intersection, which is referred to as a *cell reference*. For example, the address of the cell at the intersection of column C and row 5 is referred to as cell C5.

At the bottom of each worksheet is a series of *sheet tabs*, which enable you to identify each worksheet in the workbook. The tabs initially are labeled Sheet1, Sheet2, and so on, as shown at the bottom of the screen in Figure 8.1.

Moving Around in a Worksheet

In a new worksheet, the cell at the intersection of column A and row 1 is highlighted, indicating that cell A1 is the active cell. When you start typing, the data appears in the active cell. To enter data in another cell, make that cell active by moving the mouse pointer to it using either the mouse or keyboard. You can view another area of your worksheet but you cannot move the active cell by using the scrollbars.

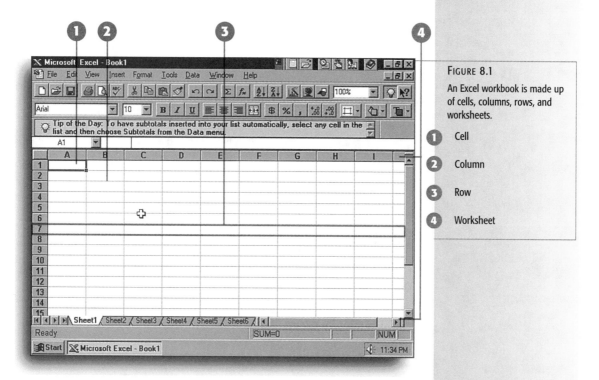

FIGURE 8.1

An Excel workbook is made up of cells, columns, rows, and worksheets.

1 Cell

2 Column

3 Row

4 Worksheet

Mouse Movements

Using the mouse, you can activate a cell quickly by placing the mouse pointer on the cell and clicking the left mouse button. Figure 8.2 shows the mouse pointer highlighting the active cell.

Keyboard Movements

You can use the arrow, Page Up, and Page Down keys, or various key combinations, on your keyboard to move to another cell (see Table 8.1).

TABLE 8.1. **Using the keyboard to move among cells**	
Keys	**Description**
←, →, ↑, ↓	Moves one cell to the left, right, up, or down, respectively.

continues…

TABLE 8.1.   Continued

Keys	Description
Ctrl+←, →, ↑, ↓	Moves to the edge of the current data region in the direction indicated. If already at edge of data region, moves to next data region or edge of worksheet.
End+←, →, ↑, ↓	Moves to the edge of the current data region in the direction indicated. If already at edge of data region, moves to next data region or edge of worksheet.
Tab	Moves one cell to the right.
Enter	Moves one cell down.
Shift+Tab	Moves one cell to the left.
Shift+Enter	Moves one cell up.
Home	Moves to column A of the active row.
Ctrl+Home	Moves to cell A1 of the worksheet.
Ctrl+End	Moves to the cell intersecting the rightmost column and last row used in the worksheet.
Page Up	Moves up one screen.
Page Down	Moves down one screen.
Alt+Page Up	Moves one screen width to the left.
Alt+Page Down	Moves one screen width to the right.
Ctrl+Page Up	Moves to the following worksheet.
Ctrl+Page Down	Moves to the preceding worksheet.

Use the name box to move to a specific cell

You also can move to a specific cell by using the *name box*, located at the left end of the formula bar. Click the box, type the address of the cell to which you want to move, and then press Enter. (The formula bar is discussed in "Entering Data" later in this chapter.)

Use the **Go To** command to move to a specific cell. Choose the **Edit** menu, and then select **Go To**, or press Ctrl+G or the F5 key to display the Go To dialog box (see Figure 8.3).

When the Go To dialog box appears, type the reference of the cell, the range name, or the range of cells you want to move to in the **Reference** text box, and then press Enter. To move to cell D5, for example, type D5 and then press Enter or click the **OK** button. The mouse pointer moves to cell D5, which now becomes the active cell. To select cells A1:C5, type that range in the **Reference** text box.

SEE ALSO

➤ *To find out how to manipulate range names, see page 259*

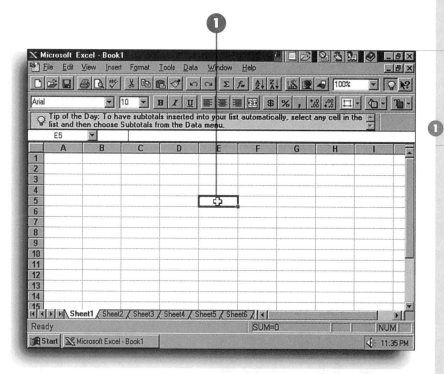

FIGURE 8.2

To activate a cell, place the mouse pointer on that cell and click the mouse.

1   Mouse pointer

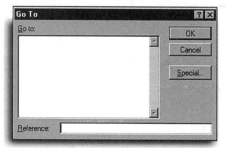

FIGURE 8.3

The Go To dialog box enables you to move to a specific cell.

Moving Around by Scrolling

To view another section of the worksheet without moving the active cell, use the vertical and horizontal scrollbars to reposition the screen. Using the mouse, click the up or down scroll arrow to scroll line by line. You also can scroll the screen by dragging the scroll box up and down the scrollbar. (As you drag the scroll box, the row number or column heading is displayed for your reference.) If you click the scrollbar above the scroll box, the

View the active cell and don't undo your selection

To see the active cell when it's not visible in the current window, press Ctrl+Backspace. The window scrolls to display the active cell; selected ranges remain selected.

screen scrolls up one page. If you click the scrollbar below the scroll box, the screen scrolls down one page.

To scroll through a worksheet using the keyboard, press the Scroll Lock key on your keyboard and use the arrow keys to scroll to the section of the worksheet you want to view. Scrolling moves the screen but does not change the active cell.

Entering Data

After you activate the cell in which you want to enter data, you can type text, numbers, dates, times, or formulas in the cell. As you type, the data appears in the active cell and in the area above the worksheet called the *formula bar* (see Figure 8.4). The formula bar displays the *insertion point*, a blinking bar that indicates where the next character you type will appear.

FIGURE 8.4

When you enter data in a cell, the data is displayed in the cell and in the formula bar.

1. Name box

2. Click here to reject data

3. Click here to accept data

4. Click here to activate Function Wizard

5. Formula bar

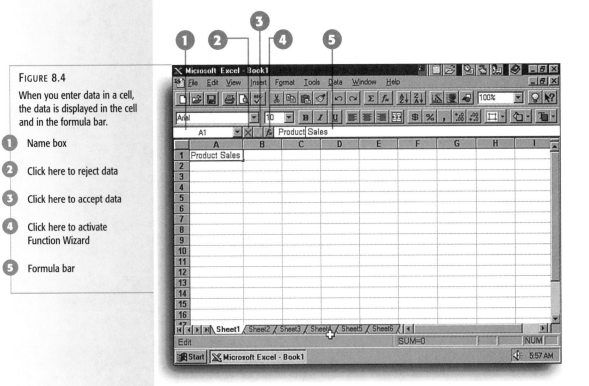

Three small boxes appear between the name box and the insertion point in the formula bar. The first two boxes enable you to reject or accept the data you entered. To reject your entry, click the x box or press Esc. To accept your entry, click the checkbox or press Enter. The third box in the formula bar activates the Function Wizard, a dialog box that enables you to build formulas using Excel's built-in functions.

Entering Text

Text entries consist of alphanumeric characters such as letters, numbers, and symbols. You can enter up to 255 characters in a single cell, although Excel might not be able to display all the characters if the cell is not wide enough or an entry is in the cell to its right. When you enter text in a cell, Excel stores that entry as text and aligns it to the left edge of the cell.

When you enter anything that consists of numbers and text, Excel evaluates the entry to determine its value. If you type an entry such as 1098 Adams Street, for example, Excel automatically determines that it is a text entry because of the letters.

If you want to enter a number as text, such as a zip code, precede the entry with an apostrophe. For example, 46254 would be read as a number, but '46254 would be read as a text entry. You can use the apostrophe when you want to enter a number but do not want Excel to interpret it as a value to be used in calculations.

Entering Numbers

Numeric entries are constant values and consist only of numeric values. You can enter integers (such as 124), decimal fractions (14.426), integer fractions (1 1/5), and values in scientific notation (1.23E+08). If your number is too long to display, you might see the scientific notation or #####.

SEE ALSO

➤ *To change column width, see page 237*

➤ *If you want to change the way the number is displayed in the cell, see page 230*

Are you a former Lotus 1-2-3 user?

The apostrophe is an old Lotus 1-2-3 trick that was required even for entries such as 1098 Adams Street. If you used Lotus, see notes about converting from the slash (/) commands by choosing **Help** and selecting **Lotus 1-2-3 Help**. Also, see Lotus navigation and formula options by selecting **Tools**, choosing **Options**, and choosing the **Transition** tab. However, I would recommend keeping the default Excel options to learn Excel because it is used in most places.

Don't panic if you see ##### in a cell

If you enter a long number in a cell and the cell displays as ##### or the number displays in scientific notation (1.23E+08), the current column width is too small to display the number in its entirety. To widen it, double-click the right edge of the column.

Entering Dates and Times

Use keyboard shortcuts to enter the date and time

To enter the current date in a cell quickly, press Ctrl+; (semicolon). To enter the current time, press Ctrl+: (colon).

In addition to entering text and numbers, you can enter dates and times in a worksheet cell. When you enter a date or time, Excel converts the entry to a serial date number, so that it can perform calculations based on these dates and times. The information in the cell is displayed in a regular date or time format, however.

Because Excel converts dates and times to serial numbers, you can perform calculations on these values as you would with any number. For example, you can determine the number of days that have passed between two dates.

You can enter a date using any of these formats:

8/12/96
12-Aug-96
12-Aug
Aug-12

You can enter a time using any of these formats:

14:25
14:25:09
2:25 PM
2:25:09 PM

SEE ALSO
➤ *To enter formulas in cells, see page 259*

Selecting Cells and Ranges

Many commands in Excel require that you select a cell or range of cells. You have already learned how to select a single cell. You also can select several cells at the same time. A *range* is a group of cells that can be acted upon with Excel commands.

You can use the keyboard or the mouse to select a range.

Select a range with the mouse

1. Click a corner of the range you want to select.

2. Drag the mouse over the range.

Dimmed commands: What it means

Some Excel commands require a specific action before you can use the command. If you do not cut or copy something to the Clipboard, for example, you cannot choose the **Edit** menu and then select **Paste** (it appears grayed or dimmed). If an object is not selected, the commands that are relevant only to that object are dimmed and unavailable.

3. When you reach the end of the selection range, release the mouse button.

Select a range with the keyboard

1. Move to a cell at a corner of the range you want to select.

2. Press and hold down the Shift key and then press the arrow keys to select the range.

Figure 8.5 shows a selected range.

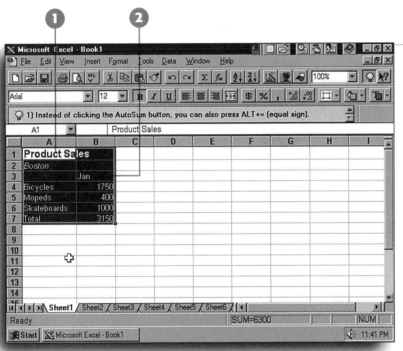

Is the fast scrolling driving you batty?

Me too—until I learned this technique for large ranges: Click the first cell. Use the scroll bars (not the keyboard) to view the last cell in the range. Hold your Shift key down and then click the last cell.

FIGURE 8.5

The first cell of the selected range is the active cell and has a white background.

❶ Active cell

❷ Selected range

With Excel, you can select more than one range of cells at a time as easily as selecting a single range.

Select multiple ranges with the mouse

1. Click and drag the mouse over the first range you want to select.

2. Press and hold down the Ctrl key and continue selecting other ranges.

Selecting noncontiguous cells is important later

Mastering the skills in this section will become important later when you are learning how to select noncontiguous cells for use in your Excel charts or for formatting worksheets. See Chapter 14, "Creating and Printing Excel Charts" and Chapter 10, "Formatting Worksheets" for more information.

Select multiple ranges with the keyboard

1. Press and hold down the Shift key and use the arrow keys to select the first range.

2. Press Shift+F8. The indicator ADD appears in the status bar at the bottom of the screen, showing that you can extend a selection.

3. Move to a cell at a corner of the next range you want to select.

4. Press Shift and an arrow key to select the range. ADD disappears from the status bar. To add another range, press Shift+F8 to go back to Add mode and repeat steps 3 and 4.

To select the entire worksheet, press Ctrl+A. To deselect a range, click any cell.

To select an entire row, click the heading of the row you want to select. You also can position the pointer in the row you want to select and press Shift+Spacebar. Figure 8.6 shows two ranges selected in a worksheet.

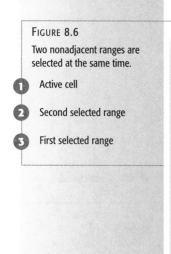

Caution: Be careful if you select the whole worksheet

When you select an entire worksheet, any command or action you perform affects the worksheet as a whole. If you press Delete while an entire worksheet is selected, for example, you delete all the data in the worksheet.

FIGURE 8.6

Two nonadjacent ranges are selected at the same time.

1 Active cell

2 Second selected range

3 First selected range

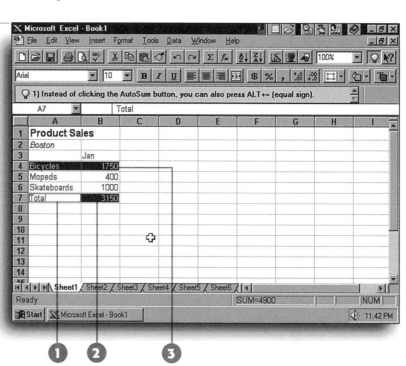

To select an entire column, click the heading of the column you want to select. You also can position the pointer in the column you want to select and press Ctrl+Spacebar (see Figure 8.7).

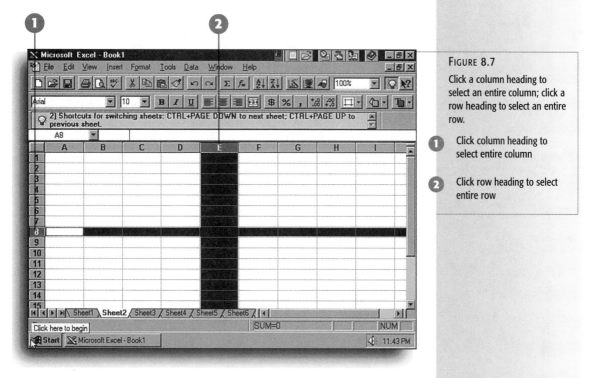

Entering a Series of Text, Numbers, and Dates

When creating budgets and forecasts, you often need to include a series of dates, numbers, or text. Excel relieves you of this tedious task by offering the AutoFill feature, which enables you to create a worksheet quickly by filling a range of cells with a sequence of entries. For example, you can fill a range of cells with consecutive dates or create a series of column titles.

You can create a series of entries in three ways:

- Use the mouse to drag the AutoFill handle (the small square at the bottom-right corner of the active cell).

- Use the right button on the mouse to drag the AutoFill handle. When you release the mouse button, a shortcut menu asks you whether to copy the value or fill the series, formats, or values. If the original cell is a date, the menu gives you options for days, weekdays, months, and years.

- Choose the **E**dit menu, select **Fi**ll, and then select **Series**.

Another feature useful in creating a series is AutoComplete. As you enter data in a list, Excel memorizes each entry. If you begin to make an entry that matches a previous entry, Excel automatically completes it for you. You can accept the entry or continue typing new data. For example, if you type San Francisco in cell A3 and then enter the letter s in cell A4, Excel automatically enters San Francisco in A4. This helps cut down on the time it takes to enter data as well as prevent errors.

Creating a Series of Text Entries

Excel recognizes common text entries, such as days, months, and quarterly abbreviations.

Fill a range of cells with text entries

1. Select the first cell that contains the data.

2. Drag the AutoFill handle over the range of adjacent cells that you want to fill (see Figure 8.8).

3. Release the mouse button. Excel fills the range of selected cells with the appropriate text entries (see Figure 8.9).

Excel's AutoFill feature recognizes numbers, dates, times, and key words, such as days of the week, month names, and quarterly abbreviations. Excel knows how these series run and extends the series to repeat correctly. Table 8.2 shows examples of series that Excel can use with AutoFill.

TABLE 12.2 **Fill sequences**

Data You Enter	Sequence Returned
10:00 am	11:00 AM, 12:00 PM, 1:00 PM
Qtr 1	Qtr 2, Qtr 3, Qtr 4
Product 1	Product 2, Product 3, Product 4

Data You Enter	Sequence Returned
1993	1994, 1995, 1996, 1997
Jan	Feb, Mar, Apr
Jan 93	Jan 94, Jan 95, Jan 96, Jan 97
Jan 96, Apr 96	Jul 96, Oct 96, Jan 97
Mon	Tue, Wed, Thu
North	South, East, West
2, 4	6, 8, 10

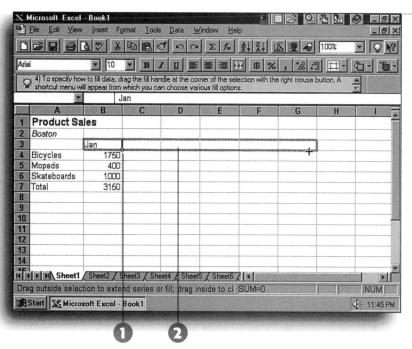

FIGURE 8.8

The AutoFill handle is dragged to the right to create a series of column titles.

1 AutoFill handle of the cell containing data

2 Range to fill

Creating a Series of Numbers

You can enter a series of numbers that increase incrementally by 1 or by values you specify.

Fill a range of cells with a series of numbers

1. Enter the starting number in the first cell of the range. If you want to increment the numbers by a value you specify, enter at least the first two values in adjacent cells.

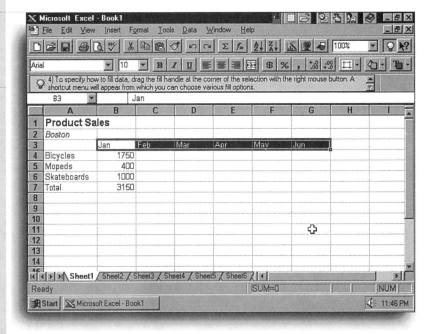

2. Select the range containing the numbers.

3. Drag the AutoFill handle over the range of adjacent cells you want to fill.

4. Release the mouse button. Excel fills the range of selected cells with the appropriate numeric entries (see Figure 8.10).

Creating a Series of Dates

You can fill a range of cells with a series of consecutive dates that increment by a specific value, similar to filling a series of numbers.

Fill a range of cells with dates

1. Enter the starting date in the first cell in the range. If you want to increment the date by a specific value, enter the appropriate date in the next cell in the range.

2. Select the range containing the dates.

3. Drag the AutoFill handle over the range of adjacent cells you want to fill.

4. Release the mouse button. Excel fills the range of selected cells with the appropriate dates (see Figure 8.11).

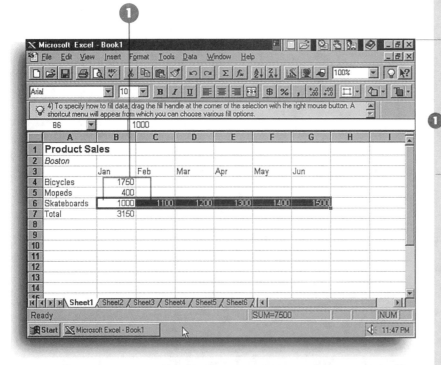

FIGURE 8.10

The AutoFill handle created this series of numbers in increments of 100.

1 To increment by a value other than 1, enter desired values in the first two cells of the range

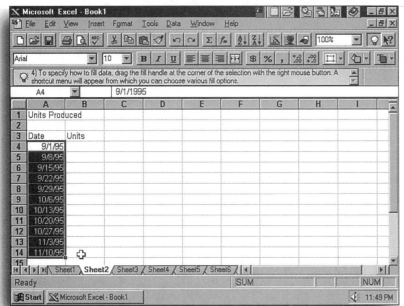

FIGURE 8.11

The AutoFill handle created this series of dates in increments of one week.

Entering a Series with the Edit Fill Series Command

Choosing the **Edit** menu, then **Fill**, and selecting **Series** enables you to fill a range of cells with greater precision than you can with the AutoFill handle. For example, when you choose **Edit**, select **Fill**, and then select **Series**, you can specify a stop value as well as a start value.

Fill a range of cells by choosing the **Edit** menu, then selecting **Fill**, and selecting **Series**

1. Enter the starting number or date in the first cell of the range you want to fill.

2. Select the range of cells you want to fill.

3. Choose the **Edit** menu, select **Fill**, and then select **Series**. The Series dialog box is displayed (see Figure 8.12).

FIGURE 8.12

In the Series dialog box, select the type of series and the step and stop values.

4. Indicate whether you want to fill your series in **Rows** or **Columns**.

5. Specify the **Type** of series you want to create.

6. If you are creating a series of dates, specify the **Date Unit**.

7. Enter the **Step Value**. This value represents the amount by which the series changes from cell to cell.

8. Enter the **Stop Value**. This value represents the last value in the series.

9. Choose **OK**.

Repeating and Undoing a Command

Excel has a built-in safety net that enables you to reverse many commands or actions. The **Undo** command reverses the last command you selected or the last action you performed. To undo a command or action, choose the **Edit** menu and then select **Undo**, or press Ctrl+Z ⟲.

Undo is not available for all commands. If you choose the **Edit** menu and then select **Delete Sheet** to delete a worksheet from a workbook, for example, the **Edit** menu shows `Can't Undo` as a dimmed command. Although **Undo** can reverse many actions, you still must use certain commands with caution.

To reverse the **Undo** command, choose the **Edit** menu and then select **Undo** again, or press Ctrl+Z.

Excel also enables you to repeat the last command or action you performed. To repeat a command or action, choose the **Edit** menu and then select **Repeat**, or press Ctrl+Y ↻.

<aside>
Be aware: Undo works only on the last action or command

Excel, unlike Word, retains only the last action or command. You must choose the Undo command immediately after the command or action.
</aside>

Saving Workbooks

When you create a new workbook, Excel assigns to it the name `Book1` if it is the first workbook created and `Book2` if it is the second, and continues to increment in this pattern. You must save the file to disk to make the workbook permanent.

Save a file in Excel

1. Press Ctrl+S 🖫.
2. If desired, change the location by selecting the **Save in** drop down.
3. Type a name in the **File name** text box and choose **OK**.

SEE ALSO
➤ *For more detailed help on saving your files, see page 38*

In addition to saving new workbooks, you can also save files to other file formats, such as previous versions of Excel, Lotus 1-2-3, or delimited text. Excel also enables you to save workbook settings in a workspace file.

Saving Files to Other File Formats

When you save a file, Excel automatically assigns an extension to the file. If you are saving a workbook, the extension is .XLS; the extension for a template is .XLT; and the extension for a workspace is .XLW.

You can use the **Save as Type** drop-down list to save an Excel file in another file format. To save an Excel file for use in Lotus 1-2-3, for example, drop down the **Save as Type** list and then select the Lotus 1-2-3 file format you want (see Figure 8.13). Excel supports 1-2-3 Releases 1 (WKS), 2 (WK1), 3 (WK3), and 4 (WK4).

FIGURE **8.13**

You can save an Excel file in a 1-2-3 file format.

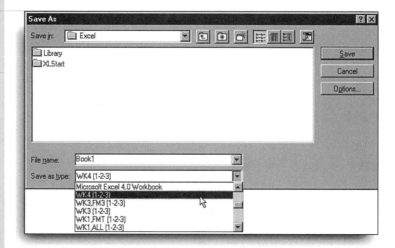

If you use a worksheet feature that is not supported by earlier versions of Excel or other spreadsheets, the value result of that feature is calculated and saved with the worksheet.

Saving a Workspace File

If you work with the same set of workbooks on a daily basis, you might find it useful to save information about what workbooks are open and how they are arranged onscreen. With Excel, the next time you want to work with these workbooks, you only need to open the workspace file, and all the workbooks are opened and arranged as they were when you saved the file.

The **Save workspace** command creates a workspace file that contains the name and location of each workbook in the workspace and the position of each workbook when the workspace was saved.

Create a workspace file

1. Open and arrange the workbooks as you want them to be saved in the workspace.

2. Choose the **File** menu and then select **Save Workspace**. Figure 8.14 shows the Save Workspace dialog box that is displayed.

3. Type a name for the workspace file in the **File name** text box.

4. Choose **OK**.

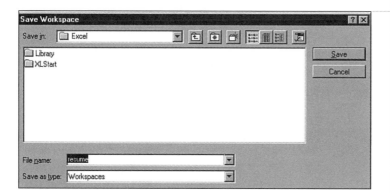

Caution: Do not move workbook files

When you create a workspace file, do not move any of the workbook files to a new location. If you do, Excel will not be able to locate the files when you open the workspace file.

FIGURE 8.14

Type a name for the workspace file in the Save Workspace dialog box.

You can open a workspace file just as you would any other Excel file. After you have opened the file, you can save and close the individual workbooks in the workspace as you normally would. When you make changes to a workbook in the workspace, you must save the file by choosing the **File** menu and then selecting **Save**. The **Save Workspace** command saves only information on which workbooks are open and how they are arranged onscreen.

Editing Worksheets

Copy data in the worksheet

Move worksheet data with drag and drop or cut and paste

Insert and delete rows, columns, and cells

Insert, delete, move, copy, and rename worksheets

Use find and replace to edit worksheets

Check for spelling errors

Editing Worksheet Data

After you enter data in a cell, you can edit the contents of the cell by using the formula bar. Or you can use the in-cell editing feature of Excel to edit the contents directly in the cell.

Editing an Existing Cell Entry

Make sure the in-cell editing feature is turned on

To use the in-cell editing feature of Excel, you must make sure that the feature has been enabled. To double-check, choose the **Tools** menu; then select **Options** and select the Edit tab. The **Edit Directly in Cell** option should be selected. If it isn't, click the checkbox to the left of the option. Choose OK when you finish.

To edit the contents of a cell, first select the cell that you want to edit and then click the formula bar or press F2. The contents of the cell are displayed in the formula bar. You can also edit the contents of a cell directly in the cell by double-clicking it.

SEE ALSO

➤ *To change the way numbers display in a cell, see page 230*

To edit the entry, use the left- and right-arrow keys to reposition the insertion point in the cell, or move the mouse and use the I-beam pointer to reposition the insertion point in the cell or formula bar. A vertical blinking bar displays where the I-beam is positioned when you click the mouse (see Figure 9.1). Then press Delete or Backspace to delete characters to the right or left of the insertion point, respectively.

When editing a cell, you can reposition the insertion point by using the mouse or the keyboard. Table 9.1 lists the editing keys on the keyboard.

TABLE 9.1 **Editing keys**

Key	Action
←	Moves one character to the left
→	Moves one character to the right
Ctrl+→	Moves to the next word
Ctrl+←	Moves to the preceding word
End	Moves to the end of the cell entry
Home	Moves to the beginning of the cell entry
Shift	When used with any one of the previously mentioned keys, selects multiple characters for editing

Key	Action
Delete	Deletes next character to the right
Ctrl+Delete	Deletes next word to the right
Backspace	Deletes preceding character

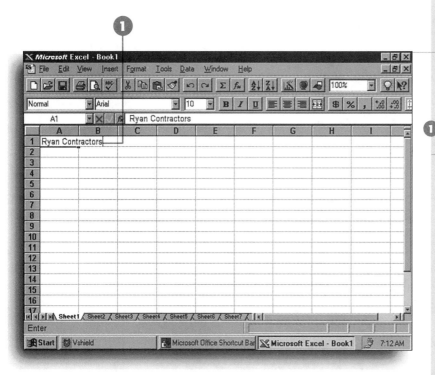

1

FIGURE 9.1

The insertion point shows where the next character you type will display.

1 Insertion point

Deleting Worksheet Data

In addition to editing the contents of a cell, you can delete the data in a cell. To replace an existing cell entry, select the cell and type the new entry. The new entry replaces the current contents of the cell. To delete the contents of a cell or range altogether, it is easiest to select the cell or range of cells and then press the Delete key. Excel clears the contents of the cell or range.

Clearing Cell Contents

When you use the Delete key to clear a cell, Excel clears all data from the cell but does not change cell formatting. The **Clear**

Clear Cell Contents and Formatting

To clear the contents of a cell or range quickly, highlight the range, click the right mouse button, and choose **Clear Contents** from the shortcut menu.

command on the **Edit** menu, on the other hand, enables you to choose what you want to clear from the cell.

Clear the contents of a cell or range

1. Select the cell or range.
2. Choose the **Edit** menu and select **Clear**.
3. From the cascading menu, choose one of the following:
   - Choose **All** to clear everything from the cell, including cell formatting and cell notes.
   - Choose **Formats** to clear only cell formatting from the cell.
   - Choose **Contents** to clear the contents of a cell but leave formatting and cell notes intact.
   - Choose **Notes** to remove only notes from a selected range of cells.

SEE ALSO
➤ *To apply formatting, page 244*
➤ *To create notes, see page 275*

Copying Worksheet Data

The quickest way to copy worksheet data is to use the drag-and-drop method. As its name implies, you simply drag the data you want to copy to another area of the worksheet.

Copy or Move data with drag and drop

1. Select the range of cells you want to copy.
2. Position the mouse pointer on the border of the selected data (the mouse pointer will change to a white arrow).
3. Drag the selection with the right mouse button to the new location.

   As you move the mouse pointer, Excel displays an outline indicating the size and location of the copied data (see Figure 9.2).

Caution: A space is not a blank cell

A common error many new users make when clearing cells is selecting the cell and then pressing the Spacebar. Although the cell might appear to be blank, Excel actually stores the space in the cell. This can cause problems in worksheet calculations. Do not press the Spacebar to clear a cell. Instead, use the methods outlined in this section.

Another drag and drop will give you warnings

If you use this method, Excel will automatically overwrite existing data. If you do not use the right mouse button, Excel will display a prompt asking you if you really want to overwrite data. Dragging with the left mouse button moves the range. Hold down Ctrl and drag to copy the range.

4. Release the mouse button and choose whether to **Copy** or **Move** the data to this new location.

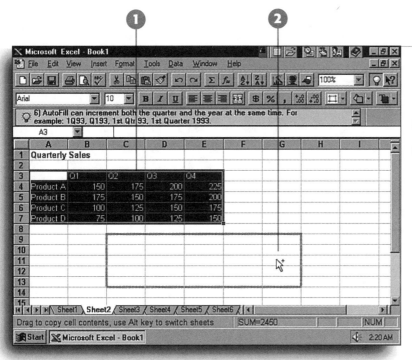

Copying Data with Copy and Paste

When you need to make multiple copies of worksheet data, it's easiest to use the **Copy** and **Paste** commands. When you choose the **Edit** menu and then select **Copy**, a copy of the selected data is stored on the Clipboard. You then can paste as many copies in the worksheet as you need.

Copy data

1. Select the range of data you want to copy.

2. Press Ctrl+C or click the Copy button .

A marquee (also known by some as "marching ants") surrounds the selection you copied, and the status bar at the bottom of the screen prompts you to select the location where you want to copy the data (see Figure 9.3).

The marquee means you can paste again

As long as the marquee surrounds the copied data, you can continue to choose Ctrl+V or **Edit** and then **Paste** to paste copies of the data in the worksheet. If you press Enter to paste a copy of the data in the worksheet, Excel clears the copied data from the Clipboard.

FIGURE 9.3

A marquee surrounds the copied data.

1 Marquee

2 Status bar

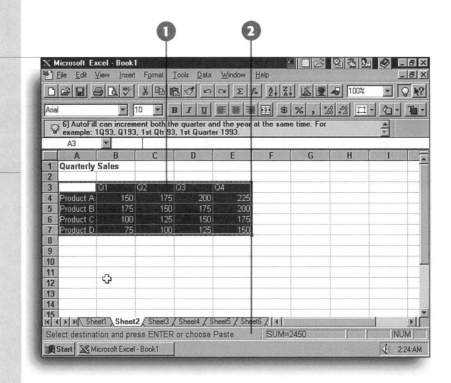

3. Select the cell in which you want to paste a copy of the data.

4. Press Ctrl+V or click the Paste button 🔳. If you want to paste a single copy of the selection, press Enter.

Copying Data with AutoFill

The AutoFill command enables you to copy cell contents to adjacent cells quickly. As a bonus, if the entry consists of a date, day of the week, or alphanumeric item such as Product 1, Excel automatically extends the series in the selected cells (see Figure 9.4).

SEE ALSO

➤ For a more detailed description of AutoFill, see page 199

Use the AutoFill command to copy data

1. Select the cell that contains the data you want to copy.

2. Position the mouse pointer on the AutoFill handle that appears in the lower-right corner of the cell. The mouse pointer changes to a thin black plus.

3. Drag the fill handle over the adjacent cells in which the copied data will be displayed and release the mouse button.

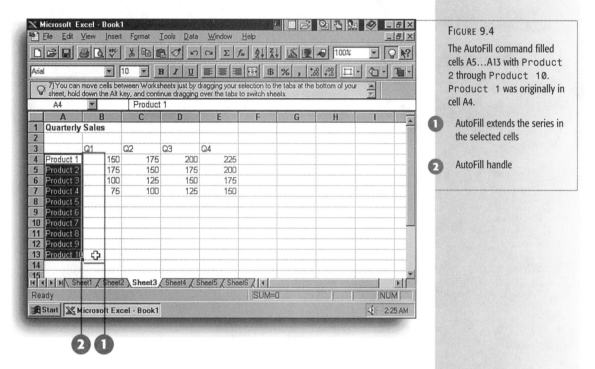

FIGURE 9.4

The AutoFill command filled cells A5…A13 with Product 2 through Product 10. Product 1 was originally in cell A4.

1 AutoFill extends the series in the selected cells

2 AutoFill handle

Copying and Applying Formats

Another option for copying data in your worksheet is to copy cell formatting from one range to another. This feature is handy if you want to apply formatting to a range of cells but don't want to create a style.

Copy formatting from one range to another

1. Select the range of cells that contains the formatting you want to copy.

2. Click the Format Painter button or double-click the button if you want to apply the formatting to more than one range. Figure 9.5 shows the result of using the Format Painter.

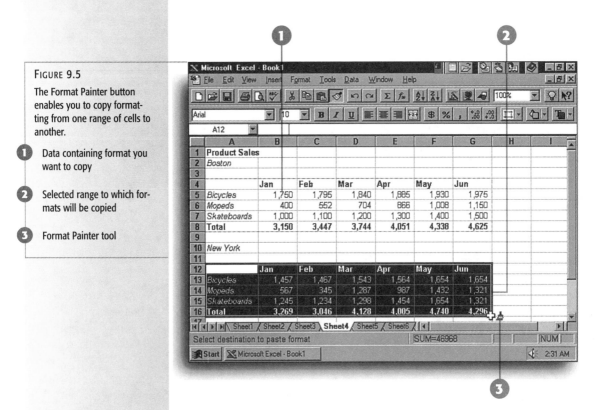

FIGURE 9.5

The Format Painter button enables you to copy formatting from one range of cells to another.

1 Data containing format you want to copy

2 Selected range to which formats will be copied

3 Format Painter tool

3. Select the cell or range of cells where you want to apply the formatting. When you release the mouse button, Excel applies the formatting.

4. Continue selecting each additional range of cells. If you double-clicked the Format Painter button, click the button again to turn off the feature or press Esc.

SEE ALSO

➤ To save and use multiple formats, see page 250

Moving Worksheet Data

As with copying, you can move worksheet data from one area of the worksheet to another. You can use the drag-and-drop method to move a range of data quickly, or you can choose **Edit** and then select the **C**ut and **P**aste commands to cut a range of data and paste it in another location.

SEE ALSO

➤ *The drag-and-drop method is described earlier in this chapter; see page 212*

Moving Data with Cut and Paste

When using the **C**ut command to move worksheet data, a copy of the data is stored on the Windows Clipboard. You then can paste the data in another area of the worksheet.

Move data

1. Select the range of data you want to move.

2. Press Ctrl+X or click the Cut button ![scissors icon].

   A marquee surrounds the selection you cut, and the status bar at the bottom of the screen prompts you to select the location where you want to paste the data.

3. Select the cell in which you want the data to display and press Ctrl+V ![clipboard icon].

SEE ALSO

➤ *Formulas might or might not be affected by copying or moving cells. Make sure you look at the description of absolute and relative referencing. See page 262*

Inserting and Deleting Columns, Rows, and Cells

Another area of editing you'll perform in Excel is that of inserting and deleting columns, rows, and cells. Sometimes, restructuring a worksheet entails more than moving data to another location. For example, if you add another sales region to your sales tracking worksheet, you can insert a new column to hold the data. Likewise, if you remove a product from your product line, you can delete the rows that contain the data.

Inserting Columns, Rows, and Cells

When you need additional space in your worksheet, you can insert columns, rows, and cells in the middle of existing data.

Trick to Pasting Data

When choosing Ctrl+V or **Edit** and then **Paste** to paste data from the Clipboard, indicate a single cell rather than a range of cells in which to paste the data. If you select a range of cells, the range you select must be the same size as the range you placed on the Clipboard.

Copying or moving formulas: What happens to cell references

When copying and moving formulas, keep in mind that Excel might adjust cell references in the formula to reflect the new location. When you copy a formula, Excel adjusts the cell references. When you move a formula, Excel does not adjust cell references.

When you insert columns, rows, and cells, existing data shifts to accommodate the insertion.

Insert a column

1. Right-click the column header.

2. Choose **Insert** from the shortcut menu. Excel inserts a new column, and existing columns shift to the right.

Insert a row

1. Right-click the row header.

2. Choose **Insert** from the shortcut menu. Excel inserts a new row, and existing rows move down.

Insert a cell or range

1. Select the cell or range where the new cells should appear.

2. Right-click the selection and choose **Insert** from the shortcut menu. The Insert dialog box appears (see Figure 9.6).

FIGURE 9.6

The Insert dialog box prompts you to specify the direction in which the existing cells should move.

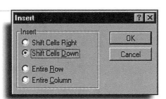

3. Select **Shift Cells Right** to insert the new cells to the left of the selection. Select **Shift Cells Down** to insert the new cells above the selection.

4. Choose **OK**. The selected cells move in the direction you specified.

Deleting Columns, Rows, and Cells

You can delete columns, rows, and cells from your worksheet when they contain data that is no longer needed. When you delete columns, rows, and cells, existing data moves to close the space.

Delete a column

1. Click the heading letter of the column you want to delete. To delete multiple columns, highlight each additional column heading.

2. Right-click in the selection and choose **Delete** from the shortcut menu. The selected column is removed from the worksheet, and existing columns move to the left.

Delete a row

1. Click the number of the row you want to delete. To delete multiple rows, highlight each additional row.

2. Choose the **Edit** menu and then select **Delete**, or click the right mouse button in the selection and then choose **Delete** from the shortcut menu. The selected row is removed from the worksheet, and existing rows move up.

Delete a cell or range of cells

1. Select the range of cells that you want to delete.

2. Right-click in the selection and then choose **Delete** from the shortcut menu. The Delete dialog box appears (see Figure 9.7).

3. Select **Shift Cells Left**; the existing data moves to the left. Choose **Shift Cells Up**; the existing data moves up.

4. Choose **OK** after you make your selection.

Inserting and Deleting Sheets

Excel enables you to create workbooks that contain multiple sheets of data. Each new workbook you create contains 16 worksheets, but you can add more worksheets and delete worksheets that you no longer need.

Caution: Formulas might need to be changed

Use care when choosing **Edit** and then **Insert** and **Delete** in your worksheets. When you use these commands (or the right-mouse button equivalents), the entire worksheet is affected by your action. If a formula refers to a cell that is deleted, for example, the cell containing the formula returns the #REF! error value. If this occurs, choose **Edit** and then select **Undo** immediately after making a deletion.

FIGURE 9.7

In the Delete dialog box, specify the direction in which the existing cells should move.

You can change the default number of worksheets

To change the number of worksheets that appear in new workbooks, choose the **Tools** menu, select **Options**, and change the number in **Sheets in New Workbook**.

Caution: Shortcut menu is relative to what you are pointing at

Be sure to position the mouse pointer over the sheet tab before trying to use the shortcut menu (the menu that appears when you right-click the mouse) to insert a new worksheet; if you don't, Excel might only provide options for inserting a new row or column. This also applies when using this feature to delete, rename, move, or copy a worksheet.

Inserting Sheets

When you insert a worksheet, Excel inserts the sheet before the current worksheet.

Insert a worksheet

1. Right-click on a worksheet tab and choose **Insert**. The Insert dialog box appears (see Figure 9.8).

2. Double-click on the Worksheet icon from the General tab. Excel inserts a sheet after the tab originally selected and assigns a name to the new sheet.

FIGURE 9.8

Select the Worksheet icon in the Insert dialog box to add a new worksheet to your workbook.

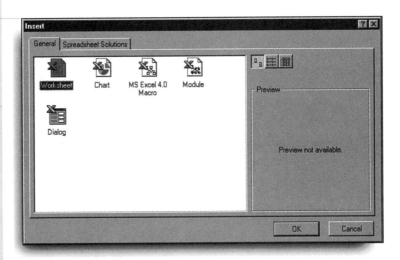

Deleting Sheets

Delete a sheet

1. Right-click on the sheet you want to delete and choose **Delete**.

2. Choose **OK** to confirm the deletion.

Moving Sheets

In addition to inserting and deleting sheets, you can rearrange worksheets in the workbook by moving them to a new location.

Excel employs the drag-and-drop method for moving sheets. To move a sheet, click the tab of the sheet you want to move. Hold down the mouse button and drag the sheet to the new position in the workbook. When you release the mouse button, the sheet is dropped in its new location.

Alternatively, position the mouse pointer over an existing sheet tab, right-click the mouse, and choose **Move** or **Copy** from the shortcut menu. The Move or Copy dialog box appears (see Figure 9.9). Select the book to which you want to move your worksheet in the **To book** drop-down list. Choose where to place the worksheet in the **Before sheet** drop-down list. You can also select the **Create a copy** box to copy your worksheet. Click **OK** to finish.

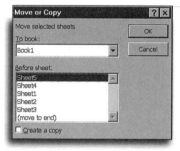

FIGURE 9.9

Use this dialog box to move or copy Excel worksheets.

Naming Sheets

Initially, Excel names each worksheet in the workbook Sheet1, Sheet2, and so on incrementally. You can, however, easily rename a sheet to reflect the data it contains. In a Monthly Sales worksheet, for example, you can use a separate sheet for each sales region. You then could name each sheet North, South, East, and West. Thereafter, anyone else who uses the worksheet will be able to tell what the worksheet contains just by looking at the name.

Rename a worksheet

1. Double-click the sheet tab of the worksheet you want to rename.

2. The worksheet name is highlighted. Type a new name for the sheet and then choose **OK** (or press Enter).

Finding and Replacing Worksheet Data

Excel provides the capability to find and (optionally) replace specific data in your worksheet. You can, for example, search for all occurrences of the value 1995 and replace it with 1996.

Finding Worksheet Data

You can search the entire workbook, or you can search only a selected worksheet range. To search the entire workbook, select a single cell. To search a specified range, select the range that you want to search.

Search for specific data

1. Press Ctrl+F. The Find dialog box is displayed, as shown in Figure 9.10.

FIGURE 9.10

The Find command enables you to locate specific data in your worksheets.

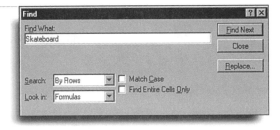

2. In the **Fi_n_d What** text box, type the data you want to find. Then specify the search options, described in Table 9.2.

3. Choose **Find Next** to begin the search. When Excel locates the characters, choose **Find Next** to find the next occurrence or choose **Replace** to access the Replace dialog box. (This option is discussed in the next section, "Replacing Worksheet Data").

4. Choose **Close** to end the search and close the dialog box.

Moving the dialog box

If the Find dialog box is obstructing your view of the worksheet, click and drag the title bar of the dialog box until you can see the active cell in the worksheet.

If you already closed the Search dialog box

Press Shift+F4 to go to the next occurrence of the search text.

TABLE 9.2	**Find options**
Option	**Action**
Search	Specifies whether to search across rows or down columns.

Option	Action
Look in	Selects the location of the data: cell formulas, cell values, or cell notes.
Match **C**ase	Finds only characters that match the case of the characters you specified.
Find Entire Cells **O**nly	Searches for an exact match of the characters you specified. It does not find partial occurrences.
Find Next	Finds the next occurrence of the search string.
Close	Ends the search and returns to the worksheet.
Replace	Opens the Replace dialog box (discussed in the next section, "Replacing Worksheet Data").

Replacing Worksheet Data

The **Replace** command (Ctrl+H) is similar to the **Find** command in that you can use it to locate specific characters in your worksheet. The **Replace** command then enables you to replace the characters with new data.

Replace worksheet data

1. To search the entire workbook, select a single cell. To search a specified range, select the range you want to search.

2. Choose the **Edit** menu and then select **Replace**. The Replace dialog box appears (see Figure 9.11).

FIGURE 9.11

You can use the **Replace** command to replace formulas, text, or values.

3. In the **Find What** text box, type the data you want to replace. In the **Replace with** text box, type the data with which you want to replace the current data.

4. Specify the replace options, as described in Table 9.3.

Use wildcards in your search

If you're not sure of the specific string you are looking for, you can specify wildcard characters in the search string to locate data that contains some or all of the characters. You can use an asterisk (*) to search for any group of characters and a question mark (?) to search for any single character.

5. Choose **Find Next** to begin the search. When Excel locates the first occurrence of the characters, choose the appropriate replace option (see Table 9.3).

6. Choose **Close** to close the dialog box.

TABLE 9.3   Replace options

Option	Action
Search	Specifies whether to search across rows or down columns.
Match Case	Finds only characters that match the case of the characters you specified.
Find Entire Cells Only	Searches for an exact match of the characters you specified. It does not find partial occurrences.
Find Next	Finds the next occurrence.
Close	Closes the Replace dialog box.
Replace	Replaces the characters in the active cell with those specified in the **Replace with** text box.
Replace All	Replaces all occurrences of the characters with those specified in the **Replace with** text box.

Spell-Checking the Worksheet

Excel's Spelling command enables you to check worksheets, macro sheets, and charts for misspellings and to correct the errors quickly. The spelling feature offers a standard dictionary and also enables you to create an alternate customized dictionary to store frequently used words not found in the standard dictionary. When you check spelling, Excel looks in the standard dictionary and the custom dictionary for the correct spelling.

In addition to finding spelling errors, Excel finds repeating words and words that might not be properly capitalized. You can check spelling in the entire workbook, a single cell, or a selected range.

Check the spelling of data in your worksheet

1. Specify the worksheet range you want to check. To check the entire worksheet, select cell **A1**. Excel starts checking from the active cell and moves forward to the end of the worksheet. To check a specific word or range, select the cell containing the word or select the range.

2. Press F7 or click the Spelling button 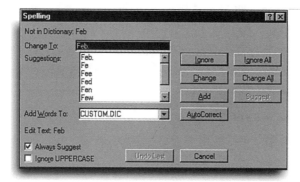. When Excel finds a spelling error, the Spelling dialog box appears (see Figure 9.12).

The options in Table 9.4 are available to correct a spelling error.

TABLE 9.4 Spelling dialog box options

Option	Action
Change **T**o	Allows you to type a replacement for the word.
Suggestio**n**s	Gives you options for replacing the word from a list.
Add **W**ords To	Selects the dictionary to which you want to add words that are spelled correctly but are not found in the standard dictionary.
Ignore	Ignores the word and continue the spell check.
Ignore All	Ignores all occurrences of the word.
Change	Changes the selected word to the word displayed in the Change To box.
Change A**l**l	Changes all occurrences of the word to the word displayed in the Change To box.
Add	Adds the selected word to the custom dictionary.
A**u**toCorrect	Adds misspelling and correct entry to AutoCorrect list.

continues…

TABLE 9.4 **Continued**	
Option	**Action**
Suggest	Displays a list of additional suggestions based on a selection from the **Suggestio**n**s** list.
Alwa**y**s Suggest	Automatically displays a list of proposed suggestions whenever a word is not found in the dictionary.
Ignore UPPERCASE	Skips words that are all uppercase.
Undo Last	Undoes the last spelling change.
Cancel/Close	Closes the dialog box. (The Cancel button changes to Close when you change a word or add a word to the dictionary.)

SEE ALSO

➤ *For information on using AutoCorrect in Word, see page 102*

The *AutoCorrect* feature allows Excel to correct common typing errors as you make them. For example, many people accidentally type two initial capital letters while holding down the Shift key or routinely transpose letters in certain words such as adn for and.

Set up AutoCorrect

1. Choose the **T**ools menu and then select **A**utoCorrect. The AutoCorrect dialog box opens, as shown in Figure 9.13.

FIGURE 9.13

AutoCorrect corrects your mistakes as soon as you make them.

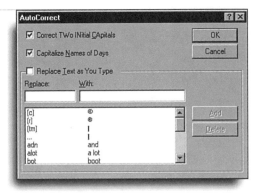

2. Check the appropriate boxes to activate any of the following options: **Correct TWo INitial CApitals**, **Capitalize Names of Days**, or **Replace Text As You Type**.

3. To add a common error to the AutoCorrect list, enter the incorrectly typed word in the **Re̲place** box and the correct version in the **W̲ith** box. Then click the **A̲dd** button to add this entry to AutoCorrect.

4. Choose **OK** to return to your worksheet.

Be careful changing options

Deselecting the **Replace T̲ext as You Type** box deactivates AutoCorrect.

Deleting unwanted AutoCorrect entries

To remove an AutoCorrect entry, select it and click **Delete**.

Formatting Worksheets

Learn options for formatting cell data

Format numbers to appear as currency, dates, percentages, and more

Change column and row height

Learn how to align data

Learn how to create formatting styles and apply them to worksheet cells

Create, edit, move, and modify graphic objects

Formatting Numbers

When you enter numbers in a worksheet, don't be concerned with the way they look. You can change the appearance of numbers by applying a numeric format later after you enter your data.

Excel provides many common numeric formats; you can create your own as well. For example, you can apply a predefined currency format that uses two decimal places or create a currency format that uses an international currency symbol.

Apply a numeric format

1. Select the cells containing the numbers you want to format.

2. Choose the **Format** menu and select **Cells**; or press Ctrl+1. Alternatively, click the right mouse button and choose the **Format Cells** command from the resulting shortcut menu. The Format Cells dialog box appears (see Figure 10.1).

FIGURE 10.1

The Format Cells dialog box displays a list of predefined number formats.

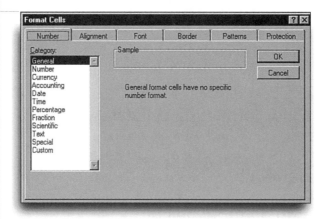

3. Select the type of number format you want to apply from the **Category** list. A list of sample formats displays in a **Type** list box for the Date, Time, Fraction, Special, and Custom categories. The Number, Currency, Accounting, Percentage, and Scientific categories include options for setting decimal places, and in some cases, for negative numbers. General and Text categories include no further options.

4. Select the number format you want to use from the choices displayed. A sample of the selected format appears in the **Sample** area of the dialog box.

5. Choose **OK**. Excel applies the selected number format to the selected cells in your worksheet.

SEE ALSO

➤ *For more information about using toolbars, see page 18*

Applying Number Formats Using the Toolbar

When you enter numbers into cells, they might display with the numeric appearance you need. You can quickly apply commonly used number formats—such as Currency, Comma, and Percentage—by using the Formatting toolbar (see Figure 10.2). Use either the number format buttons that appear in the toolbar by default or the Style menu that you manually add to the toolbar (see the following section, "Formatting Numbers Using the Style Menu").

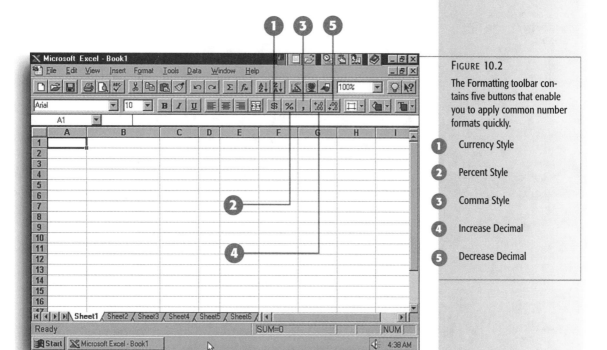

FIGURE 10.2

The Formatting toolbar contains five buttons that enable you to apply common number formats quickly.

❶ Currency Style

❷ Percent Style

❸ Comma Style

❹ Increase Decimal

❺ Decrease Decimal

To apply a number format by using the Formatting toolbar, select the cells containing the numbers you want to format and then click the appropriate button (refer to Figure 10.2) in the toolbar.

Formatting Numbers Using the Style Menu

Although the formatting toolbar gives you five buttons for common number formats, you can use styles to format your numbers. Using one of the six default styles enables you to control the display of decimals at the same time you define the format. To apply one of the predefined number formats listed as a style, select the cells containing the numbers you want to format and choose the **Format** menu; then select **Style**. The Style dialog box appears (see Figure 10.3). Select the desired style in the **Style Name** drop-down list and then choose **OK**. Table 10.1 describes the predefined formatting choices.

FIGURE 10.3

Format numbers using the predefined styles in the Style dialog box.

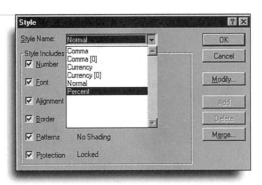

TABLE 10.1   Number formats available in the Style dialog box

Format	Description
Comma	Adds two decimal places to the number and adds commas to numbers that contain four or more digits. A number entered as 1000 is formatted as **1,000.00**.
Comma (0)	Rounds decimals and adds commas to numbers that contain four or more digits. A number entered as 1000.55 is formatted as **1,001**.
Currency	Adds a dollar sign and two decimal places to the number. Also adds a comma to numbers that contain four or more digits. A number entered as 1000 is formatted as **$1,000.00**.

Format	Description
Currency (0)	Adds a dollar sign to the number and rounds decimals. Also adds a comma to numbers that contain four or more digits. A number entered as `1000.55` is formatted as **$1,001**.
Normal	Applies the style that defines normal or default character formatting. A number entered as `1000` is formatted as **1000**.
Percent	Multiplies the number by 100 and adds a percentage symbol to the number. A number entered as `.15` is formatted as **15%**.

You also can use the following shortcut keys to format numbers:

Key	Format
Ctrl+Shift+~	General format (No specific number format, displays number as accurately as Excel can determine)
Ctrl+Shift+!	Comma format with two decimal places
Ctrl+Shift+$	Currency format with two decimal places
Ctrl+Shift+%	Percent format
Ctrl+Shift+^	Scientific notation format

Creating a Custom Number Format

Although Excel provides most of the common number formats, at times you might need a specific number format that the program does not provide. For example, you might want to create additional numeric formats that use various international currency symbols. Excel enables you to create custom number formats. In most cases, you can base your custom format on one of Excel's predefined formats.

Create a custom number format

1. Choose the **Format** menu and select **Cells**; or press Ctrl+1. Alternatively, click the right mouse button and choose **Format Cells** from the resulting shortcut menu. If necessary, select the **Number** tab in the Format Cells dialog box.

Make using styles easier

To add the Style box to the Formatting toolbar, choose the **View** menu, select **Toolbars**, and then choose **Customize**. Select **Formatting** from the **Categories** list. In the **Buttons** section of the dialog box, drag the Style box to the Formatting toolbar and choose **Close**.

Select the format closest to what you want

If you select a category and type closest to what you need first, the Custom Type will begin with that format selected. You can then make changes in the **Type** text box for the custom format you are creating.

2. Select **Custom** in the **Category** list box. Then select the predefined format in the **Type** list. Some common symbols used in these formats are listed in Table 10.2. The formatting symbols appear in the **Type** text box, and a sample appears above the text box (see Figure 10.4).

3. Edit the selected format in the **Type** text box.

TABLE 10.2   Numeric formatting codes

Code	Description
#	Placeholder for digits.
0	Placeholder for digits. This is the same as #, except that zeros on either side of the decimal point force the numbers to match the selected format.
$	Currency symbol appears with the number.
,	Placeholder for thousands separator.
.	Placeholder for decimal point.
%	Multiplies number by 100 and displays number with a percent sign.

FIGURE 10.4

You can define your custom format in the **Type** text box.

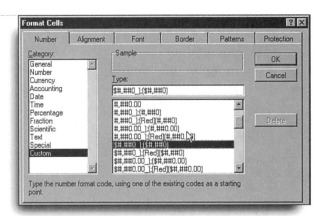

4. Choose **OK**. The custom format appears at the end of the list.

Changing Date and Time Formats

Excel recognizes most dates and times entered in a worksheet cell. If you enter 9-1-96 in a cell, for example, Excel assumes that you are entering a date and displays the number in a date format. (The default date format is 9/1/96.) If you enter 9:45, Excel assumes that you are referring to a time and displays the entry in a time format. If you need to display the date or time format differently, you can change to another date or time format.

SEE ALSO
➤ *For more information about entering dates and times, see page 196*

Apply a date or time format

1. Select the cell or range containing the data you want to format.

2. Choose the **Fo̲rmat** menu and select **Cells**; or press Ctrl+1. Alternatively, click the right mouse button and choose **Format Cells** from the resulting shortcut menu.

3. Select **Date** from the **C̲ategory** list to display the list of date formats (see Figure 10.5). To apply a time format, select **Time** from the **C̲ategory** list.

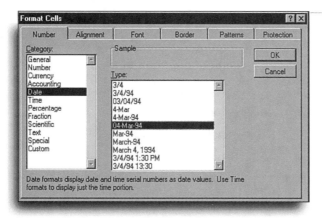

Caution: If your dates don't look right

If you enter a date and it displays as a number, you might have accidentally entered an equal sign (=) in the beginning of the cell. Simply re-enter the date or edit the cell and delete the equal sign.

FIGURE 10.5
A list of predefined date formats appears in the Date section of the Format Cells dialog box.

4. Select the format you want to use from the **T̲ype** list box.

5. Choose **OK**. Excel applies the format to the data.

You also can use the following shortcut keys to enter and format the current date and time:

Key	**Format**
Ctrl+;	Current date (entering)
Ctrl+:	Current time (entering)
Ctrl+#	Date Format d-mmm-yy (formatting)
Ctrl+@	Time format h:mm AM/PM (formatting)

Use the same procedure to create custom date and time formats as custom number formats; the only difference is that you use date and time format codes. Table 10.3 lists these codes.

TABLE 10.3   Date and time format codes

Code	Description
m	Month as a number with no leading zero
mm	Month as a number with leading zero
mmm	Month as a three-letter abbreviation
mmmm	Month as a full name
d	Day of month with no leading zero
dd	Day of month with leading zero
ddd	Day of week as a three-letter abbreviation
dddd	Day of week as a full name
yy	Year as a two-digit number
yyyy	Year as a four-digit number
h	Hour with no leading zero
hh	Hour with leading zero
m	Minute with no leading zero
mm	Minute with leading zero
AM/PM	AM or PM indicator

Changing Column Width and Row Height

When you enter data in a cell, the data often appears truncated (or shortened) because the column is not wide enough to display the entire entry. If a cell cannot display an entire number or date, Excel fills the cell with pound signs or displays the value in scientific notation (for example, **4.51E+08**). After you adjust the width of the cell, the entire number or date appears.

You can change the column width by using the mouse or menu commands. When you use the mouse to change the column width, you drag the column border to reflect the approximate size of the column. When you choose the **Format** menu, select **Column**, and choose **Width**, you can specify an exact column width.

Using the Mouse to Change Column Width

Change the column width by using the mouse

1. Position the mouse pointer on the right border of the heading of the column whose width you want to change. The mouse pointer changes to a double-headed horizontal arrow when positioned properly. To change the width of multiple columns, select the columns by dragging the mouse over the additional column headings.

2. Drag the arrow to the right or left to increase or decrease the column width, respectively. A dotted line indicates the column width (see Figure 10.6).

3. Release the mouse button when the column is the width you want.

Using the Column Width Command to Change Column Width

Change the column width by using the Column Width command

1. Click the heading of the column whose width you want to change. To change the width of multiple columns, drag the mouse pointer over each additional column.

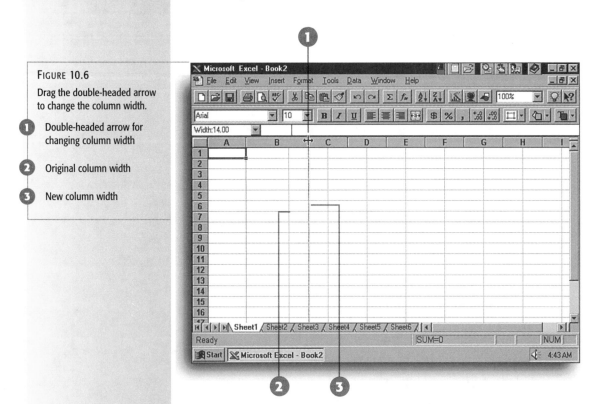

2. Choose the **Format** menu, select **Column**, and choose **Width**. Alternatively, click the right mouse button and choose **Column Width** from the shortcut menu. The Column Width dialog box appears (see Figure 10.7).

3. Enter the column width in the **Column Width** text box.

4. Choose **OK**. Excel adjusts the width of the selected columns.

Adjusting Column Width Automatically

In addition to changing column width manually, Excel enables you to adjust the column width to accommodate the widest cell entry in a column.

To adjust the column width to the widest entry, select the cell containing the widest entry and then choose the **Format** menu. Select **Column** and choose **AutoFit Selection**. Excel adjusts the width of the column.

Adjusting the Row Height

You might decide you need more whitespace for column headings, row headings, or rows with subtotals and totals. Excel automatically adjusts the row height based on the font you use, but you can change the row height to accommodate additional whitespace or to minimize the row height in your worksheet. You can use both the mouse and Excel commands to change the row height.

Adjust the row height by using the mouse

1. Position the mouse pointer on the bottom border of the heading of the row whose height you want to change. The mouse pointer changes to a double-headed vertical arrow when positioned properly. To change the height of multiple rows, drag over the additional row headings.

2. Drag the arrow down or up to increase or decrease the row height, respectively. A dotted line indicates the row height (see Figure 10.8).

3. Release the mouse button when the row is the height you want.

Adjust the row height by using the Row Height command

1. Click the heading of the row whose height you want to change. To change the width of multiple rows, drag the mouse pointer over each additional row.

2. Choose the **Format** menu, select **Row**, and choose **Height**. Alternatively, click the right mouse button and choose **Row Height** from the shortcut menu. The Row Height dialog box appears (see Figure 10.9).

Quickly AutoFitting column data

To quickly change the column width to fit the widest entry, position the mouse pointer on the right border of the column heading and double-click the mouse.

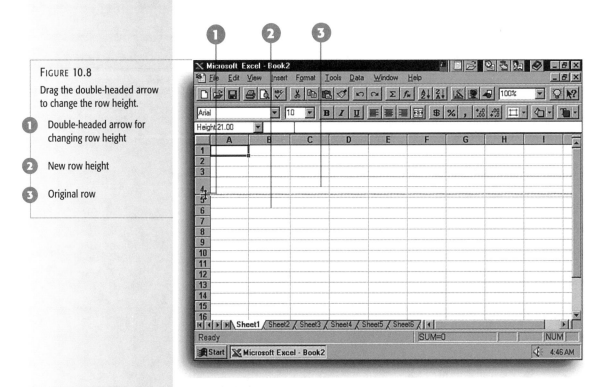

FIGURE 10.8

Drag the double-headed arrow to change the row height.

1 Double-headed arrow for changing row height

2 New row height

3 Original row

FIGURE 10.9

Enter a specific row height in the Row Height dialog box.

3. Enter the row height in the **Row Height** text box.

4. Choose **OK**. Excel adjusts the height of the selected rows.

Aligning Data

Excel provides several formatting options for changing the appearance of data in the worksheet. Using the buttons shown in the following list, you can change the alignment of text or numbers within a cell:

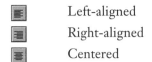

Left-aligned

Right-aligned

Centered

You also can format lengthy text to wrap within a cell, center text across a range of columns, or align text vertically within a cell.

Align data in a cell or range of cells

1. Select the cell or range that contains the data you want to align.

2. Choose the **Format** menu and select **Cells**; or press Ctrl+1. Alternatively, click the right mouse button and choose the **Format Cells** command from the resulting shortcut menu. The Format Cells dialog box appears (see Figure 10.10).

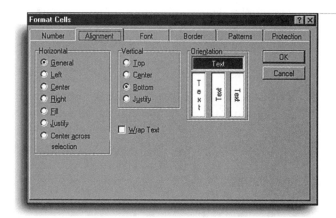

FIGURE 10.10
Change the alignment of data in the **Alignment** tab of the Format Cells dialog box.

3. Select the **Alignment** tab and specify the alignment you want to use in the **Horizontal** and **Vertical** drop-down lists. See Table 10.4 for descriptions of alignment options.

4. Choose **OK**.

TABLE 10.4 **Alignment options**

Option	Description
General	Aligns text to the left and numbers to the right
Left	Aligns text and numbers to the left edge of the cell
Center	Centers text and numbers within a cell

continues...

TABLE 10.4 **Continued**	
Right	Aligns text and numbers to the right edge of the cell
Fill	Repeats the contents until the cell is full
Justify	When text is wrapped within a cell, aligns text evenly between the cell borders
Center **a**cross selection	Centers text across multiple columns

Wrapping Text Within a Cell

You might find that the data entered in a cell or group of cells needs to wrap down to the next line so your column width can remain the same and you can see everything in the cells. You can align text entries to wrap within a single cell or a range of cells. To wrap text within a cell or range, select the cell or range of cells containing the entry, choose the **Fo**rmat menu, and select **C**ells; or press Ctrl+1. You also can click the right mouse button and choose the **Format Cells** command from the shortcut menu. In the Format Cells dialog box, select the **Alignment** tab. Then select **W**rap Text and choose **OK**. Excel wraps the text (see Figure 10.11).

Centering Text Across Columns

Many instances occur where you want to center text across multiple columns. For instance, you might have a spreadsheet that lists monthly sales in columns and you want to center the quarter headings over the related columns.

Center text across columns

1. Select the cell that contains the text and the range of cells across which you want to center the text. Selected cells defining the range of columns must be blank.

2. Choose the Center Across Columns button 🞖 on the Formatting toolbar. Excel centers the text across the specified columns (see Figure 10.12).

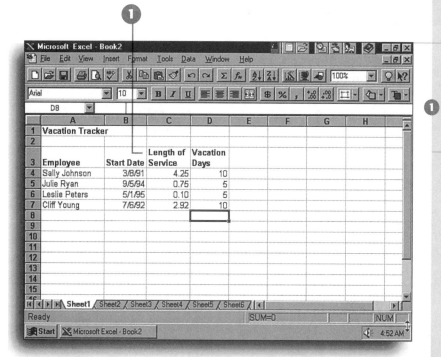

FIGURE 10.11

Column titles are wrapped within each cell.

❶ Excel automatically adjusts row heights for rows with wrapped text in cells.

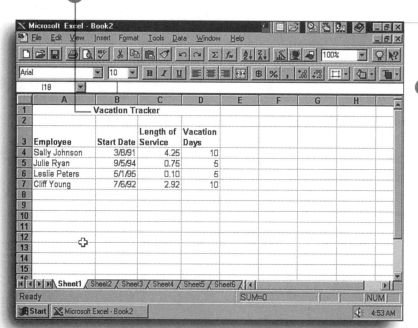

FIGURE 10.12

Text is centered across the selected columns.

❶ The text is centered across columns A–D.

Aligning Text Vertically or Horizontally

Excel enables you to align text either vertically or horizontally in a cell. To draw attention to specific text, you can change the alignment of the text vertically or horizontally. You can also change the orientation of the text. If your spreadsheet has narrow columns, for example, you might want to display the column headings vertically so the columns retain a narrow width. You might also want to center the text vertically within the cell. You might have another situation where the text is horizontal in the cell but you want it to be positioned on the top of the cell to create more whitespace before the first row of information.

Format text vertically or horizontally

Quick format options

When aligning text, use Excel's **Format**, **Column**, **AutoFit Selection** and **Format**, **Row**, **AutoFit** commands to adjust the column width or row height quickly.

1. Select the cell or range of cells containing the text you want to format.

2. Choose the **Format** menu and select **Cells**; or press Ctrl+1. Alternatively, click the right mouse button and choose **Format Cells** from the shortcut menu. The Format Cells dialog box appears. Select the **Alignment** tab.

3. In the **Orientation** section, select the vertical or horizontal orientation. If you select a vertical orientation, you also must select a specific vertical alignment (**T**op, **C**enter, **B**ottom, or **J**ustify) in the **Vertical** section of the dialog box. **B**ottom is the default.

4. Choose **OK**. Excel aligns the text (see Figure 10.13).

Changing Fonts, Sizes, and Styles

You can change the appearance of data in your spreadsheet to draw attention to titles, headings, subtotals, or totals, or to break up the monotony of information. Excel provides several formatting options for changing the appearance of text in your spreadsheets. You can, for example, choose a different font, change the size of the selected font, and apply a font style to cells in your worksheet.

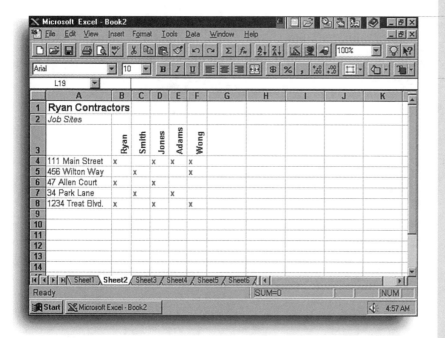

FIGURE 10.13
Text is aligned vertically in row 3.

Changing Fonts

You can use a wide variety of fonts to define titles on spreadsheets and charts, emphasize column and row headings, and make text more readable. You can quickly change the font and font size using the font and font size boxes on the Formatting toolbar.

Change a font in the Format Cells dialog box

1. Select the cell or range of cells that you want to change.

2. Choose the **Format** menu and select **Cells**; or press Ctrl+1. In the Format Cells dialog box, select the **Font** tab.

3. In the **Font** list box, select the font you want to use; to change the text size, select a size in the **Size** list or type any size in the **Size** text box (see Figure 10.14).

4. Choose **OK**.

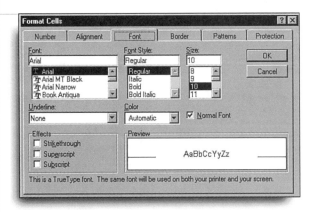

Applying Text Formats

You might want to enhance your text by applying attributes that distinguish the text from the body of the worksheet. This works well for subtotals and totals and for any information you want to draw to the attention of the reader. In addition to changing the font and size of data in your worksheets, you can apply text attributes to the data. For example, you can assign attributes such as bold, italic, and underline, and change the color of text.

To quickly apply one of these basic formatting attributes, select one of the following buttons from the Formatting toolbar:

B   Bold

I   Italic

U   Underline

Font Color

Excel also enables you to use the Format Cells dialog box to apply bold, italic, underline, and color formats, as well as several other text formatting options.

Apply text formats in the Format Cells dialog box

1. Select the cell or range of cells you want to format.

2. Choose the **Format** menu and select **Cells**; or press Ctrl+1. In the Format Cells dialog box, select the **Font** tab.

3. Select the style you want to apply in the **Font Style** list box. Use the **Underline** drop-down list to select an underline style. To change the color of the data, click the **Color** drop-down list and select a color. Select **Strikethrough**, **Superscript**, or **Subscript**, if you want.

4. When you finish, choose **OK**.

Formatting Characters in a Cell

You can apply formatting to individual characters in a text entry. This can be useful for emphasizing specific words in titles, or in cells containing wrapped text. For example, you can assign the **Bold** format to a single character in a cell.

Format characters in a cell

1. Double-click the cell containing the data you want to format; or select the cell and then press F2.

2. In the cell or formula bar, select the characters you want to format.

3. Choose the **Format** menu and select **Cells**; or press Ctrl+1. The **Font** tab appears.

4. Select the attributes you want and then choose **OK**.

Applying Patterns and Borders

In addition to formatting numbers or text, you can format cells. For example, you can add a border to a cell or range of cells and fill a cell with a color or pattern.

Applying a Border

Borders enhance a worksheet's appearance by providing visual separations between areas of the worksheet. Borders also improve the appearance of printed reports. Using borders enables you to dress up your worksheets or reports by making important information stand out.

Use the Preview box to see your selections

As you make changes in the dialog box, Excel applies the selections to the text in the **Preview** box. The changes aren't made to the selected cells until you choose **OK**.

Don't forget the tools on the Formatting toolbar

When formatting characters in a cell, you also can use the buttons in the Formatting toolbar to change the appearance of text.

Apply a border

1. Select the cell or range you want to format.

2. Choose the **Format** menu and select **Cells** 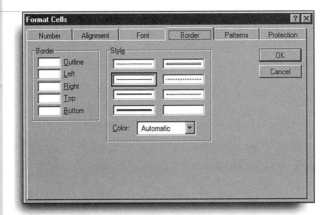; or press Ctrl+1. Alternatively, click the right mouse button and choose the **Format Cells** command from the shortcut menu. In the Format Cells dialog box, select the **Border** tab (see Figure 10.15).

FIGURE 10.15

In the Format Cells dialog box, select a border to add to a cell.

Use the Borders button for quick formatting

To apply borders quickly, select the cell or range you want to format and then click the arrow next to the Borders button to display the Border buttons.

3. Choose the placement of the border by selecting **Outline**, **Left**, **Right**, **Top**, or **Bottom** in the **Border** box. The **Outline** option puts a border around the outer edges of the selection. The **Left**, **Right**, **Top**, and **Bottom** options place a border along the specified edges of each cell in the selection.

4. In the **Style** area, select the type of border you want. To change the color of the border, select the color from the **Color** drop-down list.

5. When you finish, choose **OK**.

Applying Patterns

As with borders, you create an impression of polished work with the use of patterns. You can enhance a cell with patterns and colors. The Format Cells Patterns command enables you to choose foreground and background colors as well as a pattern.

Format a cell with colors and patterns

1. Select the cell or range you want to format.

2. Choose the **F<u>o</u>rmat** menu and select **C<u>e</u>lls**; or press Ctrl+1. Alternatively, click the right mouse button and choose the **Format Cells** command from the shortcut menu. In the Format Cells dialog box, select the **Patterns** tab (see Figure 10.16).

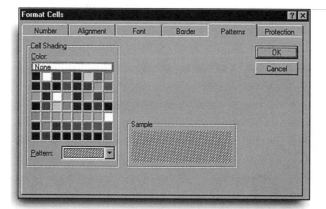

Repeat formatting quickly

To apply the same formatting to a different area, select the new area and then click the Repeat button 🔲 or press F4 immediately after you apply the formatting.

FIGURE 10.16

Apply patterns and colors to a cell with the Format Cells dialog box.

3. Select a background color for the cell in the **Color** section. The Sample box in the bottom-right corner of the dialog box shows you what the color looks like.

4. Select a pattern in the **Pattern** drop-down list by clicking the down arrow. To specify a background color for the pattern, select a pattern color from the **Pattern** drop-down list. If the foreground and background colors are the same, the cell displays a solid color. The **Sample** box shows you what the formatting looks like.

5. Choose **OK**.

Use colors in place of percent shading

If you have a black-and-white printer, you can choose to use a color background to produce a better shade of gray than a percent shading option. For instance, try yellow to see the difference on the printed black and white page to a 25-percent shading.

Using Automatic Range Formatting

If you aren't sure which colors and formats work well together, Excel's AutoFormat feature can eliminate much of the guesswork. AutoFormat enables you to select choices from a list of predefined formatting templates. These formats are a combination of number formats, cell alignments, column widths, row heights, fonts, borders, and other formatting options.

Use the AutoFormat feature

1. Select the range you want to format.
2. Choose the **F**ormat menu and select **A**uto**F**ormat. The AutoFormat dialog box appears (see Figure 10.17).
3. Select one of the format types in the **T**able Format list box. Excel displays the selected format in the Sample box.
4. Choose **OK** to apply the format.

Copy formats to another area of the worksheet

To copy the formats from a range of cells to another range in the worksheet, select the range of cells containing the formats and click the Format Painter button 🖉 in the Standard toolbar. Then, using the mouse, highlight the range of cells to which you want to copy the formats. When you release the mouse button, Excel applies the formats to the selected range.

FIGURE 10.17

The AutoFormat dialog box displays formatting templates.

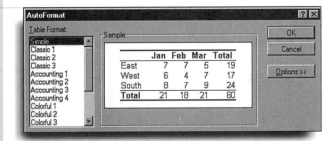

Creating and Applying a Style

When you find yourself applying the same worksheet formats over and over, you can save some time by saving the formats in a *style*. Then when you want to use the formats, you can apply all of them with a single command.

You can create a style based on cell formats that already appear in the worksheet, or you can create a new style by using the options in the Style dialog box.

Creating a Style by Example

When you spend the time to apply formats to your worksheet, you might decide you particularly like an area of the worksheet. Instead of remembering the formats you used, you can define a style based on the existing formats. When you create a style by example, Excel uses the formats of the selected cell to create the style.

Create a style by example

1. Select the cell that contains the formats you want to name as a style.

2. Choose the **Format** menu and select **Style**. The Style dialog box appears (see Figure 10.18).

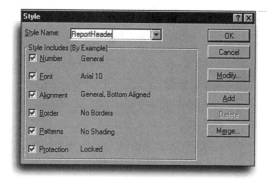

3. Type a name for your new style in the **Style Name** text box and then choose **Add**. The style appears in the **Style Name** drop-down list.

4. Choose **OK**.

Defining a Style

If the style doesn't exist in the worksheet, you can create a new style by selecting formats as you do from the Format commands.

Create a new style

1. Choose the **Format** menu and select **Style** to display the Style dialog box.

2. Type a name for the style in the **Style Name** text box. (**Normal** is the default style.) The current format appears in the **Style Includes** box.

3. Choose the **Modify** button. The Format Cells dialog box appears.

4. Select the tab for the attribute you want to change. The dialog box for the selected attribute appears.

5. Enter the changes you want to make. Choose **OK** to return to the Style dialog box.

6. After you make all the necessary style changes, choose **OK**. The dialog box closes, and Excel applies the style to any selected cells in the worksheet.

Applying a Style

After you define styles, you can easily apply them anywhere in any worksheet, as many times as you like.

Apply a style

1. Select the cell or range to which you want to apply the style.

2. Choose the **Format** menu and select **Style** to display the Style dialog box.

3. Select the name of the style you want to apply in the **Style Name** list.

4. Choose **OK**. Excel applies the style to the selected cell or range.

Creating and Working with Graphic Objects

Excel makes it easy to enhance your worksheets with graphic objects by providing a full set of Drawing tools. You can create such objects as circles, squares, and rectangles and add them to your worksheet.

Creating an Object

To add more emphasis to your worksheet, you can create objects such as rectangles, circles, squares, arrows, and text boxes. You can use the objects to draw attention to a specific area of the worksheet.

To create a drawn object, click the Drawing button in the Standard toolbar to display the Drawing toolbar. Select the Drawing tool that represents the object you want to create.

Position the mouse pointer in the area of the worksheet where you want to start drawing. (The mouse pointer changes to a small cross when you position it in the worksheet area.) Click and hold down the left mouse button and drag the mouse until the object is the size you want. Then release the mouse button. Excel adds the drawing to the worksheet (see Figure 10.19).

Create a perfect circle or square

If you need to create a square or circle, while you drag the mouse to define the size of the object, hold down the Shift key. This forces the rectangle or oval object to be a square or circle.

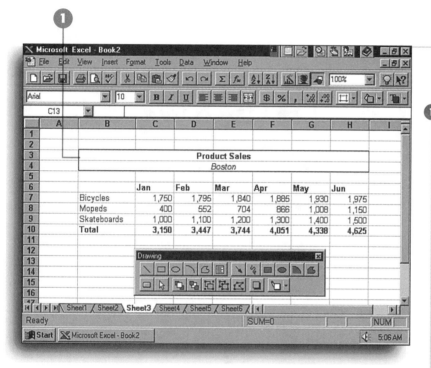

FIGURE 10.19

A rectangle is added to the worksheet.

1 Rectangle, not a border

Selecting an Object

After placing an object in the worksheet, you might want to move that object to a new location or resize it.

Before you can move or resize an object, first select it by placing the mouse pointer next to the object and clicking the left mouse button. The mouse pointer becomes an arrow when positioned on the border of the object. Handles appear around the object, indicating that it is selected (see Figure 10.20).

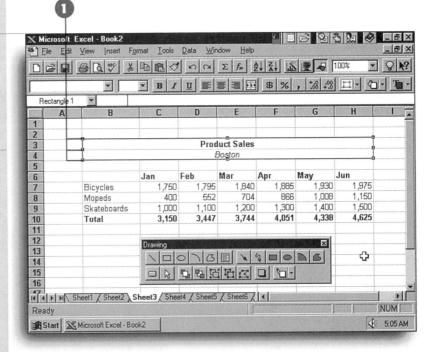

FIGURE 10.20
Handles appear around this
object, indicating that it is
selected and can be moved
or resized.

1 Handles

Moving an Object

Select the object you want to move and then position the mouse
pointer inside and close to a boundary of the object. When the
mouse pointer becomes an arrow, click and hold down the left
mouse button; drag the selected object to the desired location
and release the mouse button.

Resizing an Object

Select the object you want to resize. Handles appear around the
object; these handles enable you to resize the selected object.

Position the mouse pointer on one of the handles. The mouse
pointer changes to a double-headed arrow when properly positioned. To make the object wider or longer, position the mouse
pointer on one of the middle handles. To resize the object proportionally, position the mouse pointer on one of the corner
handles.

Click and hold down the left mouse button; drag the handle
until the object is the size you want (see Figure 10.21) and then
release the mouse button.

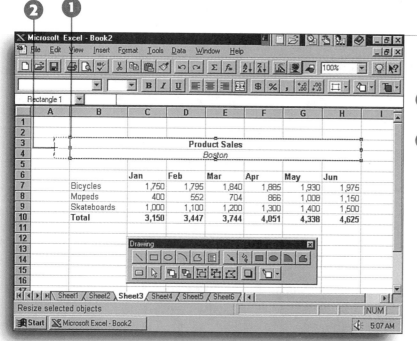

Formatting Objects

As you can with text, you can add color, patterns, and borders to drawn objects in your worksheet.

Format an object

1. Select the object you want to format.

2. Choose the **Format** menu and select **Object**; or press Ctrl+1. Alternatively, click the right mouse button and choose the **Format Object** command. The Format Object dialog box appears (see Figure 10.22).

3. Select a border style in the **Border** section of the dialog box. Select a color and pattern in the **Fill** section of the dialog box. The **Sample** area in the bottom-right corner of the dialog box shows what the formatting will look like.

4. Choose **OK** to close the dialog box and apply the selected formats.

Quick formatting for objects

To format an object quickly, position the mouse pointer on the object you want to format. When the pointer changes to an arrow, double-click the object to display the Format AutoShape dialog box.

FIGURE 10.22

Change the appearance of a drawn object with the Format Object dialog box.

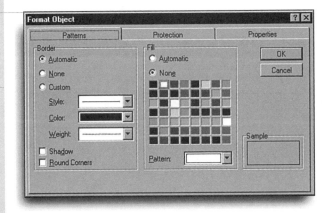

Grouping Objects

In creating a graphic or picture, you might draw several separate objects. If you want to work with multiple objects at the same time—for example, if you want to move the object to another area in the worksheet or want to create a copy of the drawing—you can group the objects to form a single object.

To group objects, first select the objects. (You can use the Select Objects button 🔄 in the Drawing toolbar or hold down the Shift key as you click each object.) Choose the **Format** menu, select **Placement**, and choose **Group** to group the objects together. A single set of selection handles appears around the grouped object (see Figure 10.23).

To break a grouped object back into multiple objects, select the grouped object, choose the **Format** menu, select **Placement**, and choose **UnGroup**. Individual objects appear, with handles surrounding each object.

Creating a Text Box

Excel enables you to create text boxes in your worksheets for adding paragraphs of text.

To create a *text box*, select the Text Box button 🔲 on the Drawing toolbar and position the mouse pointer in the worksheet. (The mouse pointer becomes a small cross.) Click the left mouse button and drag the pointer in the worksheet area. After you release the mouse button, the insertion point appears in the top-left corner of the text box, ready to accept the text you type. The text wraps according to the size of the box (see Figure 10.24).

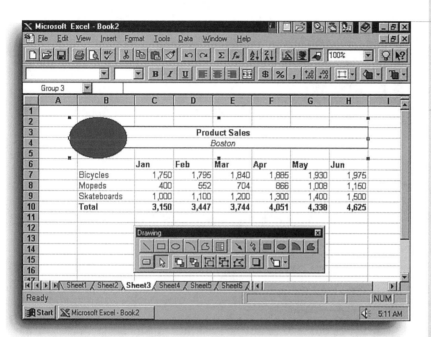

FIGURE 10.23

All selected objects appear as one object, with handles outlining the area of the single grouped object.

You can format, move, and resize a text box as you can any other object in a worksheet. When you resize a text box, the text automatically wraps to fit the new size of the box. You can apply formats to all the text in the text box or only to individual words. To make the entire text bold, for example, select the text box and click the Bold button **B** in the Formatting toolbar. To make a single word of the text bold, place the mouse pointer inside the text box. The mouse pointer changes to an I-beam. Select the text you want to format by clicking and dragging the I-beam over the text. Then use standard formatting commands, tools, or shortcuts to format the selected text. As long as the insertion point appears inside the text box, you can use normal formatting and editing procedures.

SEE ALSO

➤ *For information on formatting, see pages 230 and 244*

FIGURE 10.24

Text wraps within this text box.

1 Text box

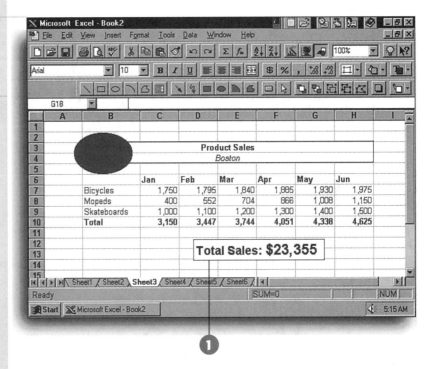

1

Check your spelling in text boxes

When you use text boxes, remember to use the **Spelling** command to check your work. F7 is the keyboard shortcut, or you can use the Spelling button ![spelling] in the Standard toolbar.

To select and move a text box, position the mouse pointer (arrow) on the border of the text box and then click the left mouse button.

Using Formulas

Create formulas

Use operators

Debug or fix formulas

Use range names

Creating Formulas

The greatest benefit in using a spreadsheet application such as Excel is the program's power to calculate formulas based on values in the worksheet. You can, for example, create a formula that calculates the difference between sales figures on a quarterly basis or another formula that totals the commissions received by each sales representative. Excel includes several tools to simplify creating formulas. Excel also can help you resolve problems with your formulas.

You can create formulas in Excel in two ways: Type the formula directly in the cell, or point to the cells you want the formula to compute.

Creating a Formula by Typing

You can enter a formula by typing the cell references and operators in the cell and the *Formula bar*. If you think better while you are typing, this might be the easiest method for you.

Create a formula by entering the cell addresses and numeric operators in a cell

1. Select the cell in which you want to enter a formula.

2. Type = (equal sign) to start the formula.

3. Type the cell references containing the values to be computed, entering the appropriate operator. To find the difference between the two values in cells B5 and B11, for example, enter =B5-B11 in another cell, such as cell B14.

4. Click the check box in the Formula bar. Excel displays the result of the formula in the active cell, and the formula appears in the Formula bar. You can also press Enter to accept a formula entry. (This moves the active cell down to the next row, not showing you the formula in the Formula bar.)

SEE ALSO
➤ *To enter worksheet data, see page 194*

Using Lotus' Input method

You can enter a plus sign (+) or minus sign (–) to begin a formula; Excel converts the formula to the appropriate format. If you enter +B4+B5, for example, Excel converts the formula to =+B4+B5.

Creating a Formula by Pointing

You can, unfortunately, make errors when typing cell references in a formula. To minimize errors that occur when you use cell references in formulas, build a formula by pointing to cells rather than by typing the cell references.

Suppose that you want to enter, in cell B14, a formula that subtracts the total in cell B11 from the total in cell B5.

Build a formula by pointing to cells with the mouse

1. Select the cell in which you want to enter a formula.
2. Type = (equal sign) to start the formula. For this example, type = in cell B14.
3. Click the cell whose reference you want to add to the formula. For this example, click cell B5 to add the cell address in the Formula bar.
4. Type – (minus sign).
5. Click the next cell you want to add to the formula. For this example, click cell B11.
6. Click the check box in the Formula bar to complete the formula entry. You can also press Enter to accept a formula entry. Figure 11.1 displays another example of a completed formula entry.

SEE ALSO
➤ *To move around a worksheet, see page 190*
➤ *For more information about using AutoSum, see page 287*

Entering Cell References with the Keyboard

Suppose that in cell D9 you want to build a formula that finds the difference between the totals in cells B9 and C9.

Enter cell references with the keyboard

1. Select the cell in which you want to enter a formula.
2. Type = (equal sign) to start the formula. For this example, type = in cell D9.

Using the AutoSum feature

To automatically sum a list of numbers, as in Figure 11.1 (Total Sales and Total Expenses), you can select the cell where you want to place your summed amount and click the AutoSum button on the toolbar to automatically sum the numbers.

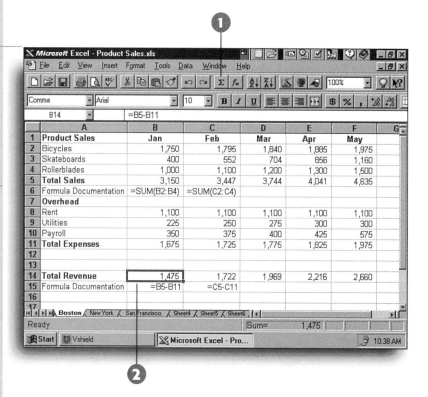

FIGURE 11.1

The result of the formula appears in cell B14. The formula appears in the Formula bar.

1   AutoSum button

2   Result of AutoSum Function

Displaying formulas in the worksheet

To display formulas in a worksheet instead of their calculated values, select any cell in the worksheet and press Ctrl+` (accent grave). Press Ctrl+` a second time to display the formula result; this works as a toggle key. The accent grave key generally is located just under the Esc key.

3. Use the arrow keys to highlight the cell that contains the data you want to use. For this example, press ← twice to select cell B9. Notice that the marquee is positioned in cell B9. Cell B9 is added to the formula.

4. Type – (minus sign).

5. Use the arrow keys to highlight the next cell you want to use. For this example, press ← to select cell C9. Cell C9 is added to the formula.

6. Press Enter to complete the entry. Or click the check box in the Formula bar to complete the entry.

Referencing Cells in Formulas

You often refer to other cells in creating your formulas. Excel provides several options for referring to these cells; you can refer to cells that change for each row or column location, cells that remain absolute in every location, or cells that are located in other worksheets or even other workbooks.

Using Relative References

In most instances, you will use a *relative reference* when referring to other cells in a formula. By default, when you copy a formula that contains cell references, the cell references adjust to their new location. For example, if you create a formula based on the data in column B, copying that formula to column F references the data in that column, rather than the original data (see Figure 11.2).

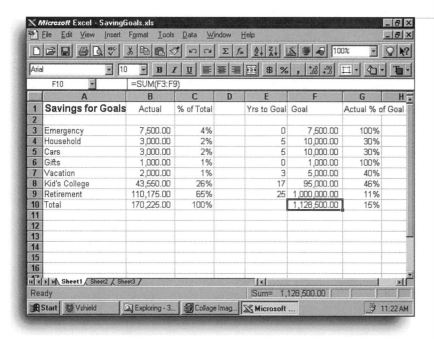

FIGURE 11.2

Using relative reference, copying the formula in cell B10 to cell F10 changes the cell references to the data in column F.

Using Absolute References

Absolute references are useful when you want your formula to refer to data in a specific cell, rather than allowing the reference to change based on the column or row. For example, say that the current commission rate for your sales staff is displayed in cell A3. Your worksheet also contains columns for sales representative, total sales, and commissions. To calculate the commission each representative receives based on his sales, you divide total sales by the commission rate. The sales figure changes in each row, but the commission rate remains the same, or absolute. You can make a column, row, or cell reference absolute by placing a dollar sign ($) before the reference. A1, B7, AB8 are all examples of absolute references.

Enter an absolute reference in a formula

1. In the Formula bar or the cell, type the equal sign (=) and the cell you want to make absolute.

2. Press F4 to activate the absolute reference key.

3. Continue pressing F4 until the appropriate combination of letters and dollar signs appear.

4. Enter the remainder of your formula and press Enter.

Figure 11.3 illustrates the use of an absolute reference.

FIGURE 11.3

The absolute reference in cell C3 remains the same when copied to C4 through C10. The first part of the calculation changes, and the second part appears as B10 (an absolute) all the way down.

1 Relative reference

2 Absolute reference

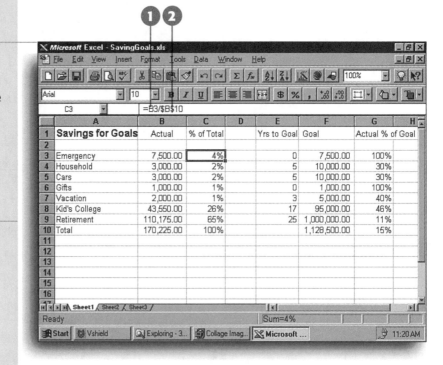

Using Mixed References

You can also combine the use of relative and absolute references into a mixed reference. For instance, you might want the column to remain absolute but not the row, or vice versa. Entering $A1 allows the row to change if you copy data, but not the column. Use the absolute reference key, F4, to enter the appropriate mixed reference by scrolling through its options.

Editing Absolute and Relative References

If you have a relative or absolute reference in a cell and need to edit it, you can either manually type the changes or use the F4 toggle key to change the reference. Sometimes it is easier to figure out what you need if you cycle through the options. To edit an existing reference, place the insertion point on the Formula bar within the formula you want to change. Press F4 until the desired change takes place and then press Enter. Each time you press F4, you cycle through the absolute references and back to the relative reference.

Entering References to Other Sheets

You can also include references to data in other worksheets in your workbook. To do so, enter the name of the sheet, an exclamation mark, and the cell reference. For example, typing Sheet1!A1 would refer to cell A1 in Sheet1. If you renamed your sheet, indicate the name you have given it.

Enter a formula referencing a cell on another sheet

1. Select the cell in which you want to enter a formula.

2. Type = (equal sign) to start the formula. For this example, on a new sheet type = in cell B2.

3. Click the sheet where the first cell reference you want to add is located. For this example, click the Boston sheet tab.

4. Click the cell reference on this sheet that you want to include in the formula. For this example, click cell B2 to add the cell address from the Boston sheet in the Formula bar.

5. Type [+] (plus sign).

Type the absolute reference instead of using F4

You can also enter or edit absolute references by entering the appropriate reference manually in the Formula bar, typing the $ (dollar sign) where it needs to be.

Caution—You might need to use single quotation marks

If your new sheet name includes spaces, you must surround the sheet name with single quotation marks—for example, 'Budget 1997'!A1.

6. Click the next sheet and cell you want to add to the formula. For this example, click sheet New York and cell B2.

7. Repeat steps 3, 4, and 5 until all the cell references are included in the formula.

8. Click the check box in the Formula bar to complete the formula entry. You can also press Enter to accept a formula entry. Figure 11.4 displays a completed formula using sheet references.

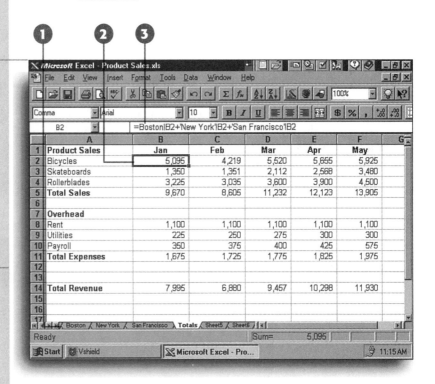

FIGURE 11.4

The sheet references in cell B2 refer to the sheets named: Boston, New York, and San Francisco. The calculation shows Total Bicycle Sales for all locations.

1 Sheet tabs

2 Result of formula

3 Formula with Sheet references

Referencing Other Files

Sometimes you might want to refer to data located in another workbook. Suppose you created separate workbooks containing sales information for each of your company's regions. You might want to refer to data in each of those workbooks when you create a new workbook that summarizes sales information for the entire corporation. To refer to cell C10 in the Sales 1997 sheet in the Western workbook, enter the following reference:

```
='[WESTERN.XLS]SALES 1997'!$C$10
```

Using Operators in Formulas

Excel's operators enable you to perform arithmetic calculations with formulas, manipulate text, perform comparisons, and refer to several different ranges in the worksheet with references.

Arithmetic Operators

In addition to using Excel's built-in functions to perform calculations, you can use arithmetic operators to perform a calculation on worksheet data. Table 11.1 lists the arithmetic operators used in basic calculations.

TABLE 11.1 Arithmetic operators

Operator	Purpose
+	Addition
–	Subtraction
*	Multiplication
/	Division
%	Percentage
^	Exponentiation

Text Operators

There might be instances where you want to display more than just a number or calculation. By using text operators, you can concatenate (or join) text contained in quotation marks or text in other cells. For example, entering the formula `="Total Sales: "&B5` returns `Total Sales: 3,150` when cell B5 contains the value 3,150.

Comparative Operators

Sometimes you need to find out if something is greater than something else. For example, if your sales in cell C3 are greater than 100,000, you get a big fat raise; if they are less than 10,000, you are fired. To compare results, you can create formulas with comparative operators, which return TRUE or FALSE, depending on how the formula evaluates the condition. For example, the formula =C3>100,000 returns TRUE if the value in cell C3 is greater than 100,000; otherwise, it returns FALSE.

Table 11.2 shows the comparative operators you can use in a formula.

TABLE 11.2 Comparative operators

Operator	Purpose
=	Equal to
<	Less than
>	Greater than
<=	Less than or equal to
>=	Greater than or equal to
<>	Not equal to

Reference Operators

Whenever you use functions in formulas, you usually need to use multiple cell references to receive with your answer. Reference operators enable you to define the location of different cells. They control how a formula groups cells and ranges of cells when calculating the formula. *Reference operators* enable you to refer to several different cells in a single formula. The most common reference operator is : (colon). For example, entering the formula SUM(A4:A24) sums the values located in cells A4 through A24.

TABLE 11.3 Reference operators

Operator	Example	Type	Result
: (colon)	SUM(B5:B45)	Range	Evaluates all the cells between and including the two references as a single reference.
, (comma)	SUM(B5:B45,B50)	Union	Evaluates the two references as a single reference.

Operator	Example	Type	Result
space	SUM(B5:B45 B25:B40)	Intersection	Evaluates the cells common to the two references. If no cells are common to both, #NULL is the result.
Space	=Yr98 Sales	Intersection	Evaluates the cell contents at the intersection of the column named Yr98 and the row named Sales.

SEE ALSO

➤ *For more information about working with ranges, see page 277*

Order of Operators

Most formula errors occur when the arithmetic operators are not entered in the proper *order of precedence* the order in which Excel performs mathematical operations. Table 11.4 displays is the order of precedence for arithmetic operations in a formula.

TABLE 11.4 **Order of operators**

Operator/Precedence	Purpose
^	Exponentiation
*, /	Multiplication, division
+, −	Addition, subtraction

Exponentiation occurs before multiplication or division in a formula, and multiplication and division occur before addition or subtraction. For example, Excel calculates the formula =4+10*2 by first multiplying 10 by 2 and then adding the product to 4, which returns 24. That order remains constant whether the formula is written as =4+10*2 or 10*2+4.

Please Excuse My Dear Aunt Sally

For some of us, the easiest way to remember the order of precedence is to use the mnemonic device we learned in high school. **P**arentheses, **E**xponential, **M**ultiplication, **D**ivision, **A**ddition, **S**ubtraction. Try it; it might help.

Same level arithmetic operator precedence

If a formula includes arithmetic operators at the same level, the calculations are evaluated sequentially from left to right.

You can change the order of precedence by enclosing segments of the formula in parentheses. Excel first performs all operations within the parentheses and then performs the rest of the operations in the appropriate order. Notice the difference between these results (see Table 11.5).

TABLE 11.5   Example of order of precedence

Formula	Result	Order of Precedence
=4+10*2	24	Multiplication then Addition; 10*2=20+4=24
=(4+10)*2	28	Parentheses then Multiplication; 4+10=14*2=28

By adding parentheses, you force Excel to add first and then multiply changing the resulting value.

Entering Dates and Times in Formulas

You also can create formulas to calculate values by using dates and times. When you use a date or time in a formula, you must enter the date or time in a format that Excel recognizes, and you must enclose the entry in double quotation marks. Excel then converts the entry to its appropriate value. To find the number of days that elapsed between two dates, for example, you enter a formula such as =`"4/2/97"-"3/27/97"`. In this example, Excel returns 6, the number of days between March 27, 1997 and April 2, 1997.

If Excel does not recognize a date or time, it stores the entry as text and displays the #VALUE! error value.

SEE ALSO
➤ *For more information on entering dates and times, see page 196*

Converting Formulas to Values

Think before converting formulas to values

Before you convert formulas to values, make certain that the values you use to calculate the formula result will not change at a later time. It can be extremely time-consuming to go back and change values back to formulas.

In many cases, after you create the formula, you need only the result rather than the formula itself. After you calculate your monthly mortgage payment, for example, you no longer need the formula. In such a situation, you can convert the formula to its actual value.

Convert a single formula to a value

1. Select the cell that contains the formula.

2. Press the F2 function key or double-click the cell.

3. Press the F9 function key. Excel replaces the formula with the value.

Convert a range of formulas to values

1. Select the range that contains the formulas you want to convert.

2. Choose the **Edit** menu and select **Copy** or click the right mouse button and choose **Copy** from the shortcut menu. A marquee surrounds the selected range.

3. Choose the **Edit** menu and select **Paste Special**. The Paste Special dialog box appears (see Figure 11.5).

FIGURE 11.5
Use the Paste Special dialog box to convert formulas to values.

4. Select the **Values** option.

5. Choose **OK**. Excel replaces the formulas in the selected range with their values.

Debugging Formulas

Excel formulas can be great time-savers, enabling you to quickly create worksheets that include calculations and references to the contents of other cells. On occasion, though, your formulas can produce errors when you enter them incorrectly or refer to cells that are invalid. Fortunately, Excel offers several ways to locate and solve errors within your formulas.

Several errors can occur when you enter formulas in Excel. In many cases, Excel displays an error value that enables you to

Look at partial results using the F9 shortcut

If you want to check a formula, you can select part of the formula in the Formula bar and press F9 to see the value associated with the reference. For instance, if you have the formula =A4+(B4-C4), you can select the reference in parentheses, press F9 to see the value, and visually check your work. It is extremely important to remember to press Esc or click the red **X** on the Formula bar so you don't make this value part of the formula, instead of the cell references.

debug or fix your formulas based on that value. Table 11.6 shows the error values and their possible causes.

TABLE 11.6   **Error values**

Error	Meaning
#DIV/0!	The formula is trying to divide by zero.
#N/A	The formula refers to a value that is not available.
#NAME?	The formula uses a name that Excel does not recognize.
#NUL!	The formula contains a reference that specifies an invalid intersection of cells.
#NUM!	The formula uses a number incorrectly.
#REF!	The formula refers to a cell that is not valid.
#VALUE!	The formula uses an incorrect argument or operator.

Effective use of TipWizard

When an error value appears in the worksheet, click the TipWizard button 💡 to see a description of the error value.

To access Excel's error values' help screens, click the Help button �help, select the **Index** tab in the Help Topics dialog box, type cell contents and error values, and then click the **Display** button to show the help options for error values.

Finding Formula Errors

Using the **Special** command button on the Go To dialog box provides an easy way to locate cells with errors.

Use Edit, Go To, Special

1. Choose the **Edit** menu, select **Go To**, and choose the **Special** button. The Go To Special dialog box appears (see Figure 11.6).

2. Select **Formulas**, **Errors**. Be sure all other options are deselected.

3. Choose **OK** to go to cells that contain errors.

Using Auditing Features

Auditing is another useful feature that helps you trace errors, locate cells that refer to your current cell, and attach notes to your cells. You can use auditing to troubleshoot errors as well as prevent errors by reviewing and commenting on your work.

FIGURE 11.6

The Go To Special dialog box assists in troubleshooting formula problems.

Definition of Terms

Excel's auditing tools enable you to accomplish three tasks:

- *Trace precedents.* In a cell that contains a formula, tracing precedents point to cells included in that formula. For example, if cell B10 refers to the SUM of cell B3 through cell B9, cell B10 points to its precedents, cell B3 through cell B9.

- *Trace dependents.* Tracing dependents point to any cells that include a formula reference to the current cell. For example, cell B10 is referred to in the formula for cells C3 through C10 and cell G10, therefore they are dependents of cell B10.

- *Trace errors.* In a cell that contains an error, tracing errors point to cells included in the formula. For example, if cell B10 displayed #VALUE!, when you choose trace errors you see what cell or cells should not be included in the formula.

Figure 11.7 illustrates both precedents and dependents.

Choosing from the Menu or Auditing Toolbar

You can access Excel's auditing feature from either the menu or toolbar. To access from the menu, choose the **Tools** menu, select **Auditing**, and select your option from the menu that displays. Options include **T**race Precedents, **T**race **D**ependents, **T**race **E**rror, Remove **A**ll Arrows, or **S**how Auditing Toolbar.

To display the Auditing toolbar, choose the **T**ools menu, select **A**udi**t**ing, and choose **S**how Auditing Toolbar. Table 11.7 illustrates each button on this toolbar.

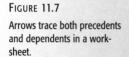

FIGURE 11.7

Arrows trace both precedents and dependents in a worksheet.

1   Precedents

2   Dependents

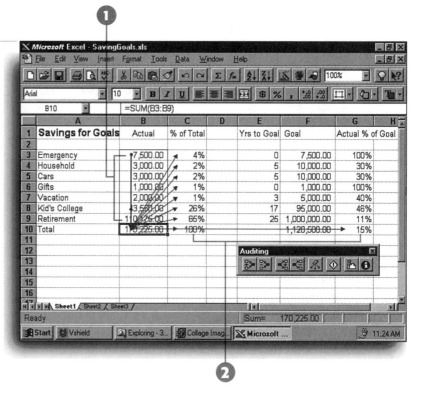

TABLE 11.7   **Auditing toolbar**

Button	Name
	Trace Precedents
	Remove Precedent Arrows
	Trace Dependents

Button	Name
	Remove Dependent Arrows
	Remove All Arrows
	Trace Error
	Attach Note
	Show Info Window

Auditing an Error

Audit an error

1. Select the cell you want to audit.

2. Click the Trace Error button from the Auditing toolbar or choose the **Tools** menu, select **Auditing**, and choose **Trace Error** from the menu.

3. View the precedents of the problem formula to help you determine a solution.

Annotating Your Worksheet Formulas

Annotating or adding notes to your worksheet can become very important if you create complex, sophisticated formulas. They can help you determine both the sources of and the reasoning behind any formula, months or even years after you created it. Good notes can save time and energy spent auditing and tracing errors in your formulas. Excel offers the option of adding either text or voice notes to your cells.

Add a note

1. Select the cell you want to annotate.

2. Click the Attach Note button on the Auditing toolbar or choose the **Insert** menu and select **Note** to display the Cell Note dialog box (see Figure 11.8).

Turn on Tool options if auditing features don't work

Be sure that the **Show All** or **Show Placeholders** option is selected in the **View** tab of the Options dialog box, or you won't be able to use the auditing features. (The toolbar will beep or the menu options will be dimmed.) To access this tab, choose the **Tools** menu and select **Options**.

FIGURE 11.8

Excel lets you add extensive notes to each cell.

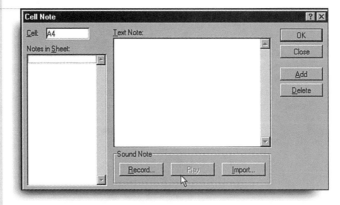

3. Enter a note in the **Text Note** area, if desired. This note appears in the **Notes in Sheet** list.

4. Click **OK** to return to the worksheet or **Add** to add another note.

5. To add another note to a different cell, enter that cell name in the **Cell box** and repeat steps 3 and 4.

6. To attach a recorded sound note to the cell, click **Record** to open the Record dialog box (see Figure 11.9).

FIGURE 11.9

You can attach recorded voice notes to your worksheet in the Record dialog box.

7. Click the **Record** button and begin speaking. The scale shows you how much time you have remaining, up to a total of 1:11 minutes.

8. When you finish speaking, click **Stop** and then **OK** to return to the Cell Note dialog box.

9. Choose **Close** to return to your worksheet.

After you finish annotating your worksheet, you notice that all the cells with notes have a small red dot in the upper-right corner. You can position the mouse pointer over any annotated cell to display the contents of the note. To edit the note, press

Shift+F2. After you create a text or sound note, you can delete it in the Cell Note dialog box by selecting it in the **Notes in Sheet** list and clicking the **Delete** button.

Working with Range Names

As you become more proficient in writing formulas, you will find that cell references are sorely lacking in describing the data that is being calculated. If you saw the formula =B9–C9 in a worksheet, it wouldn't be clear as to which data is being used.

By assigning a name to a cell or range of cells, you can describe the data in your worksheets. For example, the formula +Total_Sales–Total_Expenses instantly tells you what data the formula uses.

Creating a Range Name

Create a range name

1. Select the cell or range of cells you want to name.

2. Click the **Name** box located at the left end of the Formula bar.

3. Enter the name you want to assign to the selected range.

4. Press Enter.

Create a range name using the menu commands

1. After selecting cells, choose the **Insert** menu, select **Name**, and choose **Define**. The Define Name dialog box appears.

2. Type a name in the **Names in Workbook** text box.

3. Choose **OK**.

Keep the following rules in mind when choosing a range name:

- The first character of a range name must be either a letter or underline.

- The remaining characters can be letters, numbers, underlines, or periods.

- Spaces aren't allowed in range names.

- Don't name a range like a cell reference (such as B1 or C4, for example).

See where a formula is coming from

To display the cells to which a formula refers, select the formula in the worksheet and then click the Trace Precedents button in the Auditing toolbar, as detailed in the previous section, "Using Auditing Features."

To display a list of range names in the active workbook, click the arrow next to the **Name** box in the Formula bar. The drop-down list displays all range names in the workbook (see Figure 11.10).

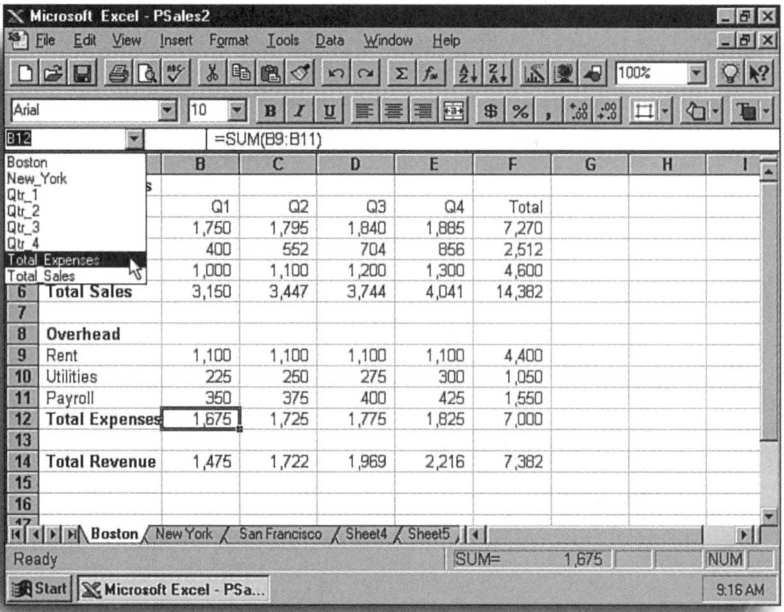

FIGURE 11.10

This drop-down list displays all range names in the workbook.

Use the Name box to insert a range name into a formula

You also can use the **Name** box to insert a name into a formula. Click the drop-down arrow next to the **Name** box and select the range name you want to use.

Inserting Names

After you assign a range name, you can refer to that range name the way you refer to cell references.

Insert a name into a formula

1. To create a formula that uses range names, type = (equal sign) to start the formula.

2. Choose the **Insert** menu, select **Name**, and choose **Paste**. The Paste Name dialog box appears (see Figure 11.11).

3. In the **Paste Name** list, select the name you want to insert.

4. Choose **OK** to close the dialog box.

5. Type the rest of the formula, and press Enter or click the check box in the formula bar when you finish (see Figure 11.12).

FIGURE 11.11

Insert a name into a formula in the Paste Name dialog box.

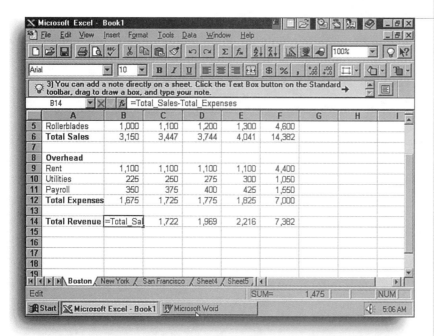

FIGURE 11.12

This formula refers to two range names in the worksheet, Total_Sales and Total_Expenses.

Deleting Range Names

If you change the contents of a range, you might want to delete the range name if it no longer applies.

Delete a range name

1. Choose the **Insert** menu, select **Name**, and choose **Define**. The Define Name dialog box appears (see Figure 11.13).

2. In the **Names in Workbook** drop-down list, select the range name you want to delete.

3. Click the **Delete** button.

4. Choose **OK**.

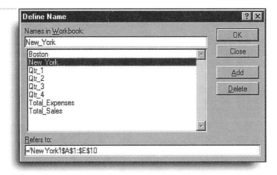

Creating Range Names from Existing Text

Excel enables you to create range names by using existing text
from a worksheet. You can, for example, use text that appears in
a column to name the cells to the immediate right. Naming cells
from existing data enables you to create many range names at
one time.

Create range names from existing text

1. Select the range of cells that contains the text and the cells
   to be named.

2. Choose the **Insert** menu, select **Name**, and choose **Create**.
   The Create Names dialog box appears (see Figure 11.14).

3. Select the check box that shows the location of the cells containing the text you want to use for range names. Options
   include **Top Row**, **Left Column**, **Bottom Row**, or **Right
   Column**.

4. Choose **OK**.

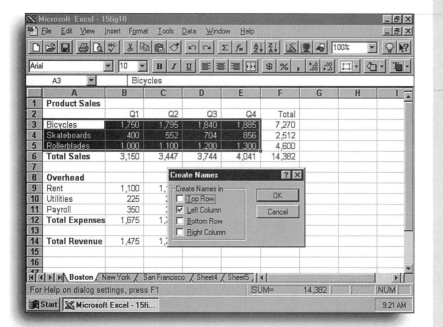

Using Functions

Create and edit sophisticated calculations

Use the Function Wizard to enter functions

Use the Help feature to get help with understanding functions

Examine some of the most common Excel functions

Understanding Functions

Excel's *functions* are built-in calculation tools that perform complex financial, statistical, or analytical calculations; assist in decision-making; and create or manipulate text. Although you can enter many of these functions manually as a formula, using a built-in function can help reduce errors. To make creating a function even easier, Excel offers additional guidance with the Function Wizard.

If you could not calculate complex formulas in Excel, creating worksheets would be quite difficult. Fortunately, Excel provides more than 200 built-in functions, or predefined formulas, that enable you to create formulas easily for a wide range of applications, including business, scientific, and engineering applications.

Excel comes with a large number of built-in worksheet functions, including mathematical, database, financial, and statistical functions. Excel also includes date, time, information, logical, lookup, reference, text, and trigonometric functions.

Formula versus function

Functions allow you to speed up your calculation compared to writing a formula. For example, you can create a formula to find the average number in a group of numbers such as =(C5+C6+C7+C8+C9+C10+C11+C12+C13)/9 or you can use the function =AVERAGE (C5:C13) to do the same thing.

Using Arguments

Each function consists of the equal sign (=), the function name, and the *argument(s)* (cells used for carrying out the calculation). Arguments give the information needed to solve a calculation. The SUM function, for example, adds the numbers in a specified range of cells (see Figure 12.1). The addresses of the specified cells make up the argument portion of the function. The active cell shows the result of the function. The most common argument type is numeric, but arguments can also include text, values, dates, times, or arrays.

Functions can include both mandatory and optional arguments. Mandatory arguments are indicated in bold italic type; optional arguments are in italic type. Mandatory arguments are required to perform the calculation. Optional arguments can be included to perform the calculation but don't have to be included for the calculation to be carried out. For example, the format for the payment function is PMT (***rate***,***nper***,***pv***,*fv*,*type*). This indicates that in order to calculate a payment, you *must* include the rate, number of periods, and present value; but the future value and type are not required. Functions such as PMT() are explained in more detail later in this chapter.

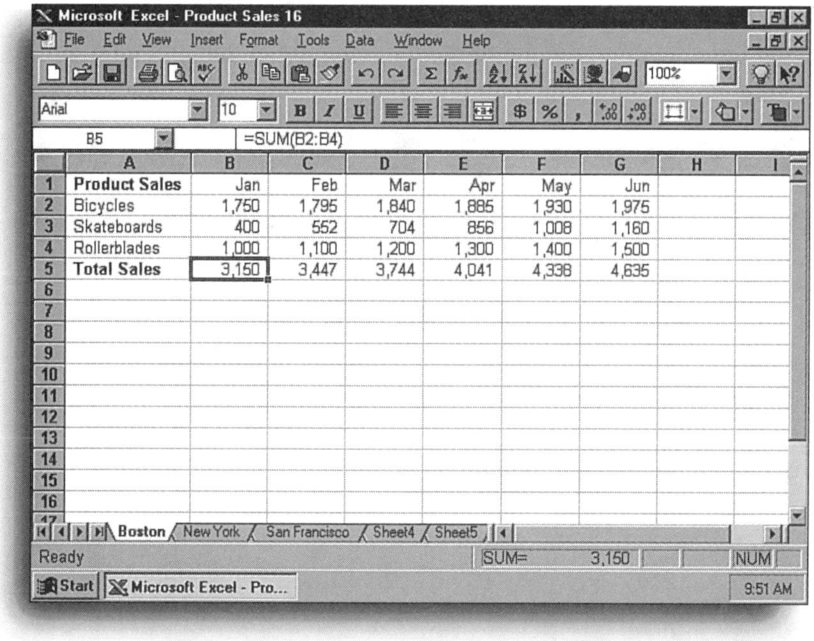

FIGURE 12.1

This formula uses the SUM function to total the entries in cells B2, B3, and B4.

SEE ALSO

➤ *To create formulas, see page 260*

Viewing Parts of the Screen That Help Create Functions

Two toolbars contain buttons or boxes that assist in the creation of functions: the Standard toolbar and the Formula bar. The Standard toolbar is the default toolbar; the Formula bar appears when you enter data into a cell. Figure 12.2 shows a typical Excel spreadsheet with descriptions of the toolbars and buttons discussed here.

When you begin to enter a function into a cell, what you enter displays in the Entry area. To accept the function data, you can press Enter or click the Enter button on the Formula bar. To cancel your entry, click the Cancel (x) button. The Formula bar also shows you the cell reference or name of the active cell in the Name box and the list of named cells or ranges in the Range Name drop-down list. For more automated function creation, you can use the AutoSum button to automatically total a range. The Function Wizard button is also available on both the Standard toolbar and the Formula bar to help you build a function.

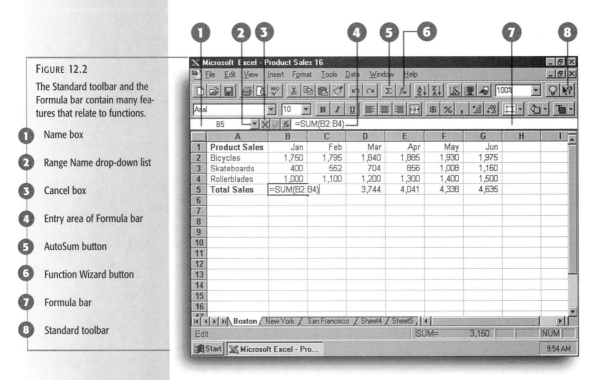

FIGURE 12.2

The Standard toolbar and the Formula bar contain many features that relate to functions.

① Name box

② Range Name drop-down list

③ Cancel box

④ Entry area of Formula bar

⑤ AutoSum button

⑥ Function Wizard button

⑦ Formula bar

⑧ Standard toolbar

SEE ALSO

➤ *For more information about using toolbars, see page 18*

➤ *For more information about using the Function Wizard, see page 288*

Entering Functions

You can use several ways to enter a function in Excel:

- Type the function in yourself.
- Use the AutoSum button to sum ranges of data.

- Use the Function Wizard to guide you in entering the function you need.

Typing Functions

To enter a function in the active cell, type = (equal sign), followed by the function name (for example, SUM), followed by an open parenthesis. Then specify the cell or range of cells you want the function to use, followed by a closed parenthesis. When you press Enter to enter the function in the cell, Excel displays the result of the formula in the cell.

SEE ALSO

➤ *For more information about entering data, see page 194*

➤ *For more information about creating formulas, see page 260*

Using the AutoSum Button to Sum Ranges

You can use the AutoSum button Σ located in the Standard toolbar to sum a range of cells quickly. You can, for example, use the AutoSum button to total the values in adjacent columns or rows. To do so, select a cell adjacent to the range you want to sum, and then click the AutoSum button. Excel inserts the SUM function and selects the cells in the column above the selected cell or in the row to the left of the selected cell.

A running marquee appears around the range of cells that Excel determines should be in the calculation. To determine the range, Excel includes all cells with numbers up to or over to the first cell that is blank or contains data other than a number.

If this is not the range you want included in the calculation, you can select the range you want to sum. To do so, select the range of cells (including blank cells) above or to the left of the cell containing the formula.

You also can highlight the range of cells you want to sum before you click the AutoSum button. To do so, select the range of cells (including blank cells) to the right of or below the range, and then click the AutoSum button. Excel fills in the totals.

Excel converts Lotus 1-2-3 entries

If you're a Lotus 1-2-3 user, you can enter a 1-2-3 function, such as @SUM(A1..A4), and Excel converts it to the appropriate Excel function.

Shortcut when entering formulas

You do not need to enter the last parenthesis if you are creating a formula with Excel's built-in functions. Excel automatically adds the last parenthesis when you press Enter.

Using the Function Wizard

If you're not sure how a particular function works, the Function Wizard can guide you through the process of entering the function.

To display the Function Wizard, choose the **Insert** menu and select **Function**. The Function Wizard dialog box appears (see Figure 12.3) or simply click the Function Wizard button 🔢 on the Standard toolbar.

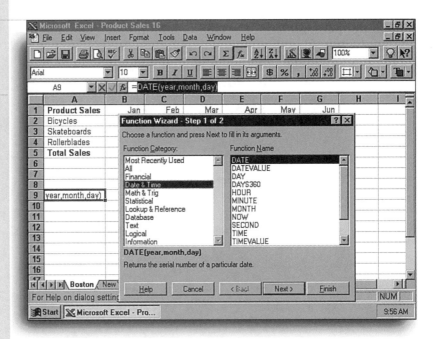

The **Function Category** list displays Excel's built-in functions, and the **Function Name** list shows an alphabetized list of functions available for the highlighted category. To access the DATE function, for example, select **Date & Time** in the **Function Category** list and then select **DATE** in the **Function Name** list. When you select a function, the function appears in the Formula bar, and the Formula bar is activated.

After you select the function you want, click **Next** or press Enter to display the next Function Wizard dialog box. The Step 2 dialog box prompts you to enter the arguments required for the function (see Figure 12.4). An argument can be a single cell reference, a group of cells, a number, or another function. Some functions require a single argument; others require multiple arguments. Function arguments are enclosed in parentheses, and arguments are separated by commas.

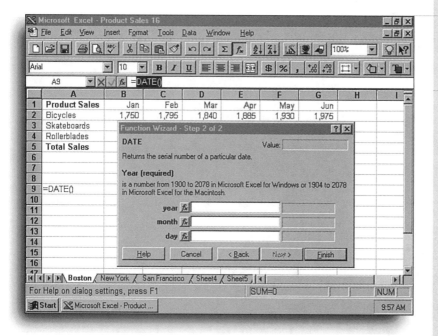

Each of the argument text boxes must contain a cell reference or data. If an argument is required, the label to the left of the text box is bold.

To enter argument data, click the mouse or press Tab to position the insertion point in the first argument text box. The Function Wizard displays a description of the argument in the display area above the text boxes. Enter the values to be used for the arguments, use the mouse to select the cell(s) in the worksheet to be used for the argument, or use the keyboard to enter the cell reference(s) or name(s). The Function Wizard displays the value to the right of the text box (see Figure 12.5).

To enter the first argument for the function, select the cell that contains the data you want to use. To indicate a range of cells, select the range you want to use in the formula. You can also enter the cell references from the keyboard. If, for example, you want to sum the numbers in cells B1, B2, and B3, enter B1:B3 or B1,B2,B3 in the argument text box. Each argument appears between the parentheses in the Formula bar.

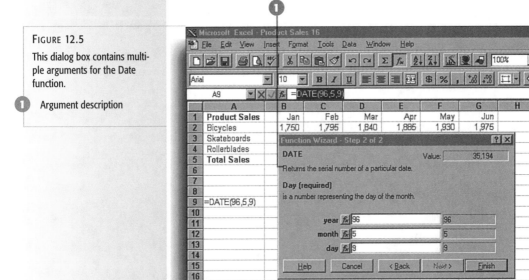

FIGURE 12.5

This dialog box contains multiple arguments for the Date function.

1 Argument description

Move the dialog box to see more of the worksheet

If the Function Wizard dialog box is in the way, move the dialog box by dragging its title bar.

When you finish entering the arguments required by the function, the result of the formula appears in the **Value** box in the top-right corner of the Function Wizard dialog box. Click **Finish** to enter the function in the cell. The dialog box disappears, and the result of the formula appears in the cell. If the formula contains an error or is incomplete, either an alert box appears (see Figure 12.6) or an error value, such as #NAME? or #NUM!, appears in the cell.

FIGURE 12.6

This alert box appears if your formula contains an error.

In some cases, Excel highlights the part of the function that contains the error. Edit the function in the Formula bar, and when the formula is corrected or complete, click the Enter (check mark) button or press Enter.

SEE ALSO

➤ *For more information about error messages, see page 271*

➤ *For more information about fixing formulas, see page 271*

Editing Functions

After entering a function, you can use the Function Wizard to edit it, or you can edit the formula and function directly in the cell.

Use the Function Wizard to edit a formula

1. Select the cell that contains the function you want to edit.

2. Choose the **Insert** menu and select **Function** f_x. The Function Wizard appears, displaying the function used in the formula.

3. Change any of the arguments as necessary.

4. Click **Finish** when you complete the function. If the formula contains another function, click **Next**.

5. Repeat steps 3 and 4 for each function you want to edit.

Edit a function manually

1. Select the cell that contains the function you want to edit.

2. Double-click the cell or click the Formula bar.

3. Select the argument you want to change.

4. Enter the new argument.

5. Press Enter or click the Enter (check mark) button in the Formula bar.

SEE ALSO

➤ *For more information about editing worksheets, see page 210*

Getting Help with Functions

More in-depth instructions on functions

For more details on using functions, read *Special Edition Using Excel for Windows 95*, published by Que.

As you use Excel's functions, you can use Excel's context-sensitive help system for assistance. To access Excel's online help for functions, choose the Help button 🔍 (double-click the button) on the toolbar. Double-click **Reference Information** in the **Contents** tab and then double-click **Worksheet Functions**. This section includes a help topic for each function with detailed information and examples (see Figure 12.7). For more information about debugging or fixing formulas, read Que's *Special Edition Using Microsoft Excel for Windows 95*.

FIGURE 12.7

Excel's Help feature offers detailed information on many types of worksheet functions.

SEE ALSO

➤ *For more information about editing worksheets, see page 210*

Examining Some Sample Functions

The easiest way to learn to create functions in your worksheets is to see some examples of functions in action. The following section details some of the most common Excel functions and gives real-life examples of how you can use them.

Financial

Financial functions are one of the most common functions used in Excel. With financial functions, you can calculate annuities, cash flow, depreciation, interest, and internal rate of return, among other things. Once again remember, arguments that are **_bold italic_** are required to perform the calculation; the others are optional. Some common financial functions include:

- DDB(**_cost,salvage,life,period_**,*factor*). Returns the depreciation of an asset for a specified period using the double-declining balance method.

- FV(**_rate,nper,pmt_**,*pv,type*). Returns the future value of an investment.

- IPMT(**_rate,per,nper,pv_**,*fv,type*). Returns the interest payment for an investment for a given period.

- IRR(**_values_**,*guess*). Returns the internal rate of return for a series of cash flows.

- NPER(**_rate,pmt,pv_**,*fv,type*). Returns the number of periods for an investment.

- NPV(**_rate,value1_**,*value2,...*). Returns the net present value of an investment based on a series of periodic cash flows and a discount rate.

- PMT(**_rate,nper,pv_**,*fv,type*). Returns the periodic payment for an annuity.

- RATE(**_nper,pmt,pv_**,*fv,type,guess*). Returns the interest rate per period of an annuity.

- SLN(**_cost,salvage,life_**). Returns the straight-line depreciation of an asset for one period.

To intelligently use these functions, you first need to understand the arguments they contain. Table 12.1 explains some of the arguments used in the common functions previously listed whose definitions might not be readily apparent. Remember that the Function Wizard and online help also explain these arguments as they are used for each function.

TABLE 12.1   **Arguments in common functions**

Argument	Description
Nper	Total number of payment periods in an annuity
Pv	Present value—the total amount that a series of future payments is currently worth
Fv	Future value—the amount of cash you want to attain after the last payment

To see a real-life example of a financial function, examine the PMT function. You can use PMT to determine a potential monthly mortgage rate if you already know the loan amount, term of the loan, and interest rate. For example, if you want to purchase a house with a loan amount of $200,000 at 8 percent for 30 years, you can use the PMT function to learn that this house requires monthly payments of $1,467.53 (see Figure 12.8).

FIGURE 12.8

The PMT function helps you determine a monthly mortgage.

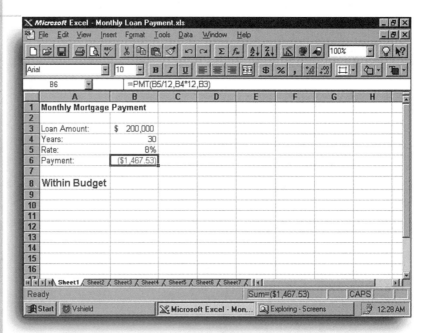

Date and Time

Date and time functions are also very common. Here are some of the ones you see most often:

- DATE(*year,month,day*). Returns the serial number of a particular date.
- NOW( ). Returns the serial number of the current date and time.
- TODAY( ). Returns the serial number of today's date.

Common examples of these functions include using TODAY( ) to enter a date such as 9/15/95 or NOW( ) to enter 9/15/95 8:43.

Math and Trigonometry

Math and trigonometry functions vary from simple formulas that perform basic calculations to complex ones that are more in the realm of the mathematician than the general spreadsheet user. Here are some examples:

- ABS(*number*). Returns the absolute value of a number.
- COS(*number*). Returns the cosine of a number.
- INT(*number*). Rounds a number down to the closest integer.
- LOG(*number,base*). Returns the logarithm of a number to a specified base.
- ROUND(*number,num_digits*). Rounds a number to a specified number of digits.
- SUM(*number1,number2...*). Adds the arguments.

SUM( ) is probably the most common function you will use in Excel, and one you are already familiar with. You can also summarize cells by using the AutoSum button Σ on the toolbar, which automatically creates a formula using the SUM( ) function. This was discussed in more detail in the "Using the AutoSum Button to Sum Ranges" earlier in this chapter.

Statistical

Statistical functions include ways to average and count as well as to determine the minimum and maximum in a range. Excel also offers more sophisticated statistical functions such as absolute and standard deviations, negative binomial distribution, and the inverse of the lognormal distribution. Here are some examples:

- AVERAGE(***number1***,*number2*...). Averages the arguments.
- COUNT(***value1***,*value2*...). Counts how many numbers are in the argument list.
- MAX(***number1***,*number2*...). Returns the maximum value in a list of arguments.
- MIN(***number1***,*number2*...). Returns the minimum value in a list of arguments.
- STDEV(***number1***,*number2*...). Estimates the standard deviation based on a sample.

A frequently used statistical function is AVERAGE. Suppose that you want to average the sales made in each of your company's regions. The sales totals for each region are listed in cells D4 through D10. You can enter the function AVERAGE(D4:D10) in cell D11 to find out the average sales per region.

Text

Text functions can be used to change case, trim text, or perform searches. Here are some common examples:

- CONCATENATE(***text1***,***text2***,...,*text30*). Joins up to 30 text arguments.
- LOWER(***text***). Converts text to lowercase.
- PROPER(***text***). Capitalizes the first letter of each word in a string of text.
- REPLACE(***old_text***,***start_num***,***num_chars***,*nex_text*). Replaces characters within text.
- SEARCH(***find_text***,***within_text***,*start_num*). Locates one text value within another.
- TRIM(***text***). Removes spaces from text.
- UPPER(***text***). Converts text to uppercase.

For example, you might want to title a sales report Monthly Sales = $1,500,000. "Monthly Sales =" is a text field, but the $1,500,000 is based on a formula located in cell B40. To create your title as described, you can use the CONCATENATE function—CONCATENATE("Monthly Payment=",B40).

Quick calculations

If you have a list of numbers and want to get a quick sum of them, select the list and look at the right side of the status bar. You will see the Sum=[number]. If you right-click on the Sum=, you can select another function, such as Average, Count, Count Nums, Max, or Min. Click one of the functions to see the result based on your selected cells.

Logical

Logical functions are useful for testing and decision-making:

- AND(*logical1*,*logical2*...). Returns TRUE if all the arguments are true.

- IF(*logical_test*,*value_if_true*,*value_if_false*). Returns one value if true, another value if false.

- OR(*logical1*,*logical2*...). Returns TRUE if one or more of the arguments is true, FALSE if all are false.

You also can use a combination of logical functions to assist in decision making. For instance, in the mortgage example you looked at earlier, you can set up a function that displays Within Budget or Beyond Budget, depending on what your maximum budgeted house payment is (see Figure 12.9). The following function sets a budget limit at $1,500:

```
=IF (B6<1500,"Within Budget","Beyond Budget")
```

Anything more than $1,500 results in a text field that tells you this particular loan is beyond your means.

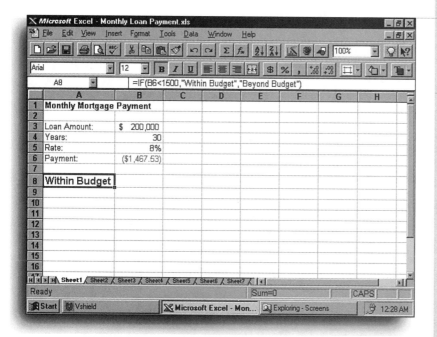

FIGURE 12.9

The IF function can assist you in making decisions based on the result.

Other Functions

Other functions include lookup and reference functions that manipulate references, cells, or ranges; database functions that return information about a database; and information functions that provide information about the Excel environment:

- DGET(*database,field,criteria*). Extracts the record that matches the criteria from the database and returns TRUE if all the arguments are true.
- ISBLANK(*value*). Returns TRUE if the value is blank.
- ISNUMBER(*value*). Returns TRUE if the value is a number.
- LOOKUP(*lookup_value,array*). Looks up values in an array.

Creating and Printing Reports

Learn options for defining print areas, page settings, previewing, and printing worksheet data

Create custom views using multiple print ranges

Create reports using named views and scenarios

Printing a Particular Area of a Worksheet

You can print the entire workbook, a selected range of data, or a specific worksheet in the workbook. By default, Excel automatically selects and prints the current worksheet. You can, however, define a portion of the worksheet to print.

SEE ALSO

➤ *For more information about printing worksheets, see page 40*

Printing a Specific Range

You might have a very large worksheet in which you need to print only certain sections. By specifying a range to print, you can pick and choose what parts of the worksheet you want to print.

Print a specific range in the worksheet

1. Select the range to be printed, using the mouse or the keyboard.

2. Choose the **File** menu and select **Print** or press Ctrl+P. The Print dialog box appears, as shown in Figure 13.1.

FIGURE 13.1

The Print dialog box enables you to specify the data you want to print.

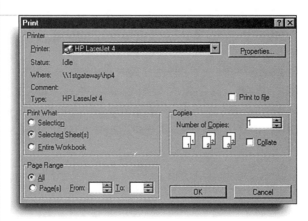

3. In the **Print What** section of the dialog box, select the **Selection** option.

4. Choose **OK**. Excel prints the selected worksheet range.

SEE ALSO

➤ *For more information about using ranges, see page 277*

Defining a Print Area

If you are printing the same range in a worksheet over and over, you can define that range as the print area so that you no longer need to specify the range each time you print the worksheet.

Define the print area

1. Select your specified area, either with the keyboard or the mouse.
2. Choose the **File** menu and select **Print Area**.
3. Select **Set Print Area** from the menu.

Removing a Defined Print Area

You might need to remove a print area if you decide to print the entire worksheet.

To remove a defined print area, choose the **File** menu, select **Print Area**, and select **Clear Print Area** from the menu.

Use Page Setup to clear a print area

1. Choose the **File** menu and select **Page Setup** to display the Page Setup dialog box.
2. Click the **Sheet** tab.
3. Delete the reference in the **Print Area** text box and choose **OK**.

Inserting and Removing Page Breaks

When you define a print area, Excel inserts automatic page breaks into the worksheet. Automatic page breaks, which appear as dashed lines in the worksheet, control the data that appears on each printed page. Excel also inserts automatic page breaks when a selected print range cannot fit on a single page. If you aren't satisfied with the location of the automatic page breaks, you can insert manual page breaks.

Use Page Setup to define print area

You can also set the print area in the **Sheet** tab of the Page Setup dialog box. (Choose the **File** menu and select **Page Setup**.)

Adding the Set Print Area button to the toolbar

If you find you are setting print areas often, you might want to add the Set Print Area button to the toolbar. Right-click on any visible toolbar and select **Customize** from the shortcut menu. Select **File** from the **Categories** list and point to the fifth button on the top row of buttons; drag it to one of the toolbars. Now you can select your print area and click this button.

You can insert two types of page breaks:

- *Vertical page breaks*. Break the print range at the current column.

- *Horizontal page breaks*. Break the page at the current row.

Inserting a Vertical Page Break

Insert a vertical page break

1. Click the heading of the column to the right of where the page break should occur.

2. Choose the **Insert** menu and select **Page Break**. A dashed line appears in the worksheet, indicating the page break.

Inserting a Horizontal Page Break

Your worksheet might have many rows, in which case Excel determines where the worksheet breaks for a new page. If you don't like the page breaks Excel defines, you can insert your own page breaks. Horizontal page breaks enable you to control what rows are forced to the next page.

Insert a horizontal page break

1. Click the heading of the row below where the page break should occur.

2. Choose the **Insert** menu and select **Page Break**. Excel adds the page break.

Figure 13.2 shows a horizontal page break added to a worksheet.

Removing Page Breaks

Remove all manual page breaks

To remove all manual page breaks from the worksheet, click the Select All button in the top-left corner of the worksheet frame (the rectangular button next to cell A1), choose the **Insert** menu, and select **Remove Page Break**.

If you have inserted page breaks, you might decide at some point that you want to see where the automatic page breaks would be. Sometimes after many changes to the worksheet, your manual page breaks don't work as well as they did. You can remove page breaks to allow Excel to add the automatic breaks again.

To remove a page break, position the cell pointer below or to the right of the page-break intersection, choose the **Insert** menu, and select **Remove Page Break**.

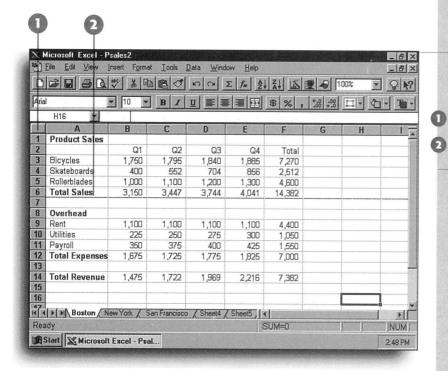

FIGURE 13.2

A horizontal page break has been added to this worksheet.

1 Select All button

2 Horizontal page break

Fitting the Print Range to a Single Page

If the specified print range is a few lines too long to print on a single page, you can fit the worksheet to the page. When you use this method, Excel scales the worksheet so that it fits on a single page.

Fit the print range on a single page

1. Choose the **File** menu and select **Page Setup**.

2. If necessary, select the **Page** tab.

3. Select the **Fit To** option. By default, the **Fit To** option is one page wide by one page tall.

4. Choose **OK**. When you print, Excel scales the worksheet range to a single page.

Modifying the Page Setup

The **Page Setup** command enables you to define the page settings for the printed output. You can change the orientation of the page, change the margins and text alignment, and set print titles. You can also define header and footer information that is covered following this section.

Changing the Worksheet Page Orientation

The default setting for printed output arranges the data in *portrait orientation*—that is, the data is arranged vertically on the page. You might, however, want the data to print in *landscape orientation*—arranged horizontally on the page. If the data range is wide, for example, you can print it in landscape orientation, across the width of the page.

Change the page orientation

1. Choose the **File** menu and select **Page Setup**.
2. Select the **Page** tab.
3. Select the **Landscape** option to print the range across the width of the page.
4. Choose **OK**.

Changing Worksheet Page Margins

The margins define the distance between the printed output and the edge of the page. Excel enables you to change the top, bottom, left, and right margin settings. In addition, you can specify margins for the headers and footers, as well as center the print range between the margins, either horizontally or vertically.

Change the margins

1. Choose the **File** menu and select **Page Setup**.
2. Select the **Margins** tab.
3. Enter the measurements, in inches, in the appropriate text boxes. You also can click the up and down arrows to change the margin settings by increments. Figure 13.3 shows the margins for the current print range.
4. To indicate the header and footer margins, specify the measurement in the **Header** and **Footer** boxes.

Changing margins in Print Preview

You also can change the margins from within **Print Preview** by dragging the margin borders. For more information, see "Changing Worksheet Page Margins and Other Settings in Print Preview" later in this chapter.

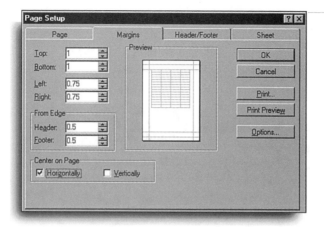

FIGURE 13.3
Use the **Margins** tab of the Page Setup dialog box to change the margins and the alignment of data on a page.

5. To center the data between the top and bottom margins on the page, select the **Vertically** option in the **Center on Page** section of the dialog box. To center the data between the left and right margins, select the **Horizontally** option. To center the text both horizontally and vertically on the page, select both options.

6. Choose **OK**.

Setting and Removing Print Titles

When you print large worksheets, you can set print titles so that information such as worksheet titles, column headings, and row headings appear on each page in the printout.

Create print titles

1. Choose the **File** menu and select **Page Setup**.

2. Select the **Sheet** tab, if necessary.

3. If you want to define titles across the top of each page, select the **Rows to Repeat at Top** box. If you want to define titles down the left side of each page, select the **Columns to Repeat at Left** box (see Figure 13.4).

4. If you are defining titles to appear across the top of each page, select the row headings containing the data you want to use as titles or enter the row references.

Titles might appear twice

When you print a worksheet that contains print titles, do not select the range containing the titles when you define the print area. Otherwise, the titles will appear twice on the first page of the printout.

If you are defining titles to appear down the left side of the page, select the column headings containing the data you want to use as titles or enter the column references.

5. Choose **OK**.

FIGURE 13.4

In the **Sheet** tab of the Page Setup dialog box, define the area to be used as the print titles.

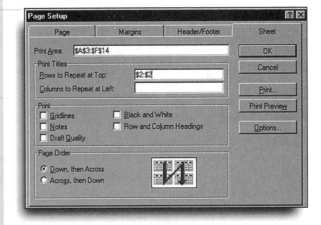

Remove print titles

1. Choose the **File** menu and select **Page Setup**.

2. Select the **Sheet** tab, if necessary.

3. Delete the cell references in the **Print Titles** section of the dialog box.

4. Choose **OK**.

Setting Other Print Options

You can define additional print settings in the Page Setup dialog box. You can include the worksheet gridlines in the printout; print notes that have been added to cells; print the data in black and white, even if color has been applied to the worksheet; and include the row and column headings.

Choose the **File** menu, select **Page Setup**, and select the **Sheet** tab. In the **Print** section of the dialog box, select or deselect the check box adjacent to the appropriate print option. Figure 13.5 shows the **Sheet** tab of the Page Setup dialog box.

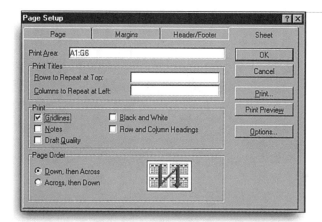

FIGURE 13.5
Select the appropriate print options in the **Sheet** tab of the Page Setup dialog box.

Creating Headers and Footers

Headers and footers enable you to add text—such as the current date, page number, and filename—to the top and/or bottom of the printed page. Excel provides default header and footer information. (The name of the current sheet is centered in the header, and the current page number is centered in the footer.) You also can select additional options and define your own header and footer information.

Using Predefined Headers and Footers

Excel provides many predefined headers and footers. This makes it easy to include header and footer information on your worksheets. Headers and footers help you document information on your worksheets, such as titles, page number, date information, or a filename.

By default, Excel uses the **Sheet** name as the header and the word **Page** and the page number as the footer. You can delete or change either one of these defaults. The next section, "Creating Custom Headers and Footers," tells you how to do this.

Select one of Excel's predefined header and footer options

1. Choose the **File** menu and select **Page Setup**.

2. Select the **Header/Footer** tab (see Figure 13.6).

FIGURE 13.6

Select the text you want to use
in the header and footer area
of the printed page.

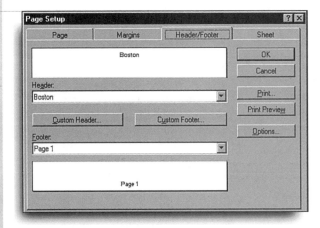

Remove a header or footer

To remove a header or footer, select
None from the appropriate list.

3. Click the arrow next to the **Header** box, and select a header
   from the drop-down list.

4. Select the predefined footer you want to use from the
   Footer list.

5. Choose **OK**.

Creating Custom Headers and Footers

You might decide that you want to personalize your header and
footer information. The predefined choices are a great start but
might not include exactly what you want. You can create your
own header and footers, using a predefined option, or start completely from scratch.

Define your own custom header and footer

1. Choose the **File** menu and select **Page Setup**.

2. Select the **Header/Footer** tab, if necessary.

3. If appropriate, select an existing header or footer that
   resembles the header or footer you want to create.

4. Select the **Custom Header** or **Custom Footer** option to
   display a new dialog box. Figure 13.7 shows the Header
   dialog box.

   Each text box that appears in the dialog box controls the
   alignment of the text in the header or footer. Data can be
   left-aligned, centered, or right-aligned. Excel uses codes to

create certain types of text in the headers and footers. The Page Number code, for example, is used to insert page numbering. The buttons that appear above the text boxes are used to insert the codes. Table 13.1, which follows these steps, describes the code buttons you can use in the header and footer.

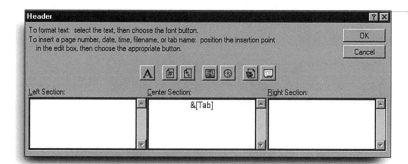

FIGURE 13.7

Create custom headers and footers by using the text boxes and buttons that appear in this dialog box.

5. Select one of the three text boxes and type the header or footer text or choose a button to enter a header or footer code. To apply text formatting to the header or footer information, click the Font button **A** to display the Font dialog box and select the appropriate options.

6. Choose **OK**.

TABLE 13.1   Header and footer codes

Button	Name	Code	Description
A	Font	None	Displays the Font dialog box
	Page Number	&[Page]	Inserts the page number
	Total Pages	&[Pages]	Inserts the total number of pages
	Date	&[Date]	Inserts the current date
	Time	&[Time]	Inserts the current time

continues…

Put your company logo on the worksheet

Even though you can't insert graphics in the **Header** box, you can put your logo on the spreadsheet. Insert the graphic in a repeating title row on the worksheet. Choose the **Insert** menu and select **Picture**. From the Picture dialog box, navigate to the folder that stores the Company logo and select it; then choose **OK**. If the logo isn't placed correctly on the worksheet, select it and move it to the correct position.

Keyboard shortcuts to move in Print Preview

In Print Preview, press **Page Up** and **Page Down** to display each page in the document. Press **Home** to move to the first page; press **End** to move to the last page.

TABLE 13.1   Continued

Button	Name	Code	Description
	Filename	&[File]	Inserts the filename
	Sheet Name	&[Tab]	Inserts the name of the active sheet

SEE ALSO

➤ *To work with graphic objects on a worksheet, see page 252*

➤ *For more information about setting print titles, see page 305*

Previewing a Worksheet

You can preview the data before you print the worksheet to make sure that the it appears the way you want. You also can change the margin settings and column widths, if necessary.

Preview the data

1. Choose the **File** menu and select **Print Preview**. Excel switches to Print Preview and displays the print range, as shown in Figure 13.8.

2. Click the **Next** and **Previous** buttons to move from page to page. Notice that these buttons appear dimmed if the data you are previewing fits on a single page.

Zooming In and Out on the Worksheet

For a closer look at data, you can zoom in and view an enlarged display; when you want to see more of the data, you can zoom out.

To zoom in on the worksheet, click the **Zoom** button or position the mouse pointer over the section you want to view and click the left mouse button. The mouse pointer changes to a magnifying glass when positioned over the page. To view other areas of the page, use the vertical and horizontal scrollbars. To zoom out, click the **Zoom** button again, or click the left mouse button.

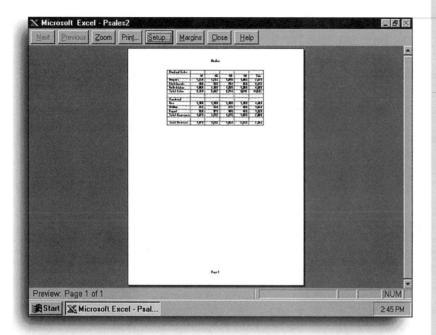

FIGURE 13.8
Print Preview shows what the worksheet will look like when printed.

Changing Worksheet Page Margins and Other Settings in Print Preview

If, while previewing the worksheet, you find that the current margins or column widths are not adequate, you can change them in Print Preview. When you click the **Margins** button, light-gray boundaries indicating the margins appear around the page. Black handles also appear to indicate the top, bottom, left, and right margins. Square handles appear along the top of the page, with lines indicating the width of each column. Figure 13.9 shows margin and column markers in Print Preview.

To adjust the margins, click to drag the handle that represents the margin you want to change. When you do, the mouse pointer changes to a crossbar, and the status bar shows the actual margin setting. Drag the handle to the appropriate location. When you release the mouse button, the margin adjusts, and the data is repositioned on the page.

To change a column width, click to drag the square handle that indicates the column width you want to change. The status bar displays the current column width. Drag the marker to increase or decrease the column width. When you release the mouse button, the column width and data adjust to fit the new size.

FIGURE 13.9

You can change the margins and column widths by dragging the markers.

① Margin markers

② Column marker

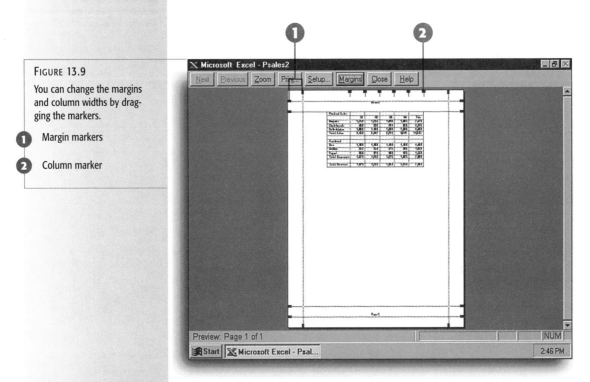

SEE ALSO

➤ *To change column width and row height, see page 237*

When you're satisfied with the way the data appears, click the **Print** button to print the worksheet. To return to the worksheet, click the **Close** button.

Printing the Worksheet

After you define the print settings and preview the data, you're ready to print the worksheet. The **File Print** command enables you to specify the number of copies you want to print, as well as the number of pages (if the print range spans multiple pages). You also can specify the data you want to print, if you have not already defined a print area.

Use the Print button

Click the Print button 🖨 in the Standard toolbar to bypass the Print dialog box and send the output directly to the printer with the default print settings. To save paper, before you do this, use the Print Preview option 🔍 to see if the worksheet will print the way you expect it to.

Print the worksheet

1. Choose the **File** menu and select **Print** or press Ctrl+P. The Print dialog box appears.

2. If you have not defined a print area, you can specify the data you want to print by selecting options in the **Print What** section of the dialog box (refer to Figure 13.1).

3. Select the **Selection** option to print the selected range of cells. Select the **Selected Sheet(s)** option to print the selected worksheets in the workbook or select the **Entire Workbook** option to print every worksheet in the current workbook.

4. To specify the number of copies to be printed, enter the amount in the **Number of copies** box.

5. To specify a specific range of pages to be printed, enter the range in the **Print Range** section of the dialog box.

6. When you're ready to print, choose **OK**.

> **Change printer properties**
>
> The Print dialog box also includes a button that enables you to access the Printer Properties box. To change any of these settings, click the **Properties** button and make the necessary selections.

Using Views and Reports

Excel provides two add-ins that enable you to create and generate printed reports:

- *View Manager add-in*. Enables you to assign names to worksheet ranges and to include the print settings and display options for the ranges.

- *Report Manager add-in*. Enables you to create a report consisting of named views and scenarios.

Installing the View and Report Manager Add-Ins

Before you can define a named view or create a report, you must install the View Manager and Report Manager add-ins. You probably installed this option during setup. If you do not see the View Manager and Report Manager options on the Add-Ins dialog box, run Setup again to install the options.

Install the add-ins

1. Choose the **Tools** menu and select **Add-Ins**. The Add-Ins dialog box appears (see Figure 13.10).

FIGURE 13.10

Use the Add-Ins dialog box to install Excel add-ins.

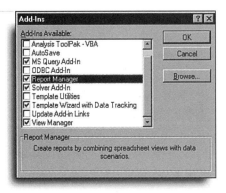

FIGURE 13.10

Use the Add-Ins dialog box to install Excel add-ins.

2. Select **Report Manager** and **View Manager** from the **Add-Ins Available** list.

3. Choose **OK**. The **Report Manager** and **View Manager** commands are added to the **View** menu.

Creating a View

Choosing the **View** menu and selecting **View Manager** enables you to define multiple print ranges, with different display and page-setup characteristics, in a single worksheet. Normally, every print area of a worksheet must contain the same display characteristics. By using named views, however, you can print multiple ranges with different print settings at the same time.

Create a view

1. Select the range of cells you want to define as a view.

2. Choose the **View** menu and select **View Manager**. The View Manager dialog box appears (see Figure 13.11).

3. Click the **Add** button. The Add View dialog box appears (see Figure 13.12).

4. Enter a name for the view in the **Name** text box.

5. Choose **OK**.

Creating a Report

If your worksheet consists of multiple views of your worksheet, or scenarios of data, you can print those different views and scenarios as a report.

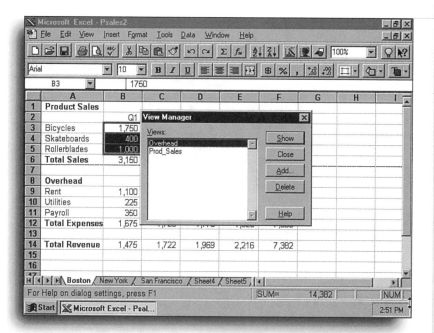

FIGURE 13.11

Create multiple views of worksheet data in the View Manager dialog box.

FIGURE 13.12

Enter a name for the view in the Add View dialog box.

Create a report

1. Choose the **View** menu and select **Report Manager**. The Report Manager dialog box appears.

2. Click the **Add** button to create the report. The Add Report dialog box appears (see Figure 13.13).

3. Enter a name for the report in the **Report Name** text box.

4. Select the view you want to add to the report from the **View** drop-down list and click **Add**. The view you added appears in the **Sections in this Report** list.

5. Select the scenario you want to add to the report from the **Scenario** drop-down list and then click **Add**. The scenario you added appears in the **Sections in this Report** list.

Use Excel data in Access

You can also create a report in Access using Excel data (if you have this option installed). To do so, choose the **Data** menu and select **Access Report**. To create an Access form with your data, choose the **Data** menu and select **Access Form**; to export the data to Access, use the **Data**, **Convert to Access** command.

6. To change the order of the views and scenarios in the
   Se̲ctions in this Report list, select a view or scenario
   and then choose the **Move U̲p** or **Move D̲own** button
   to rearrange the order.

7. Repeat steps 4 through 6 until you finish adding views and
   scenarios to the report.

8. Select **Use C̲ontinuous Page Numbers** to number the
   pages consecutively.

9. Choose **OK**. You return to the Report Manager dialog box.

10. Choose **P̲rint** to print the report or **C̲lose** to close the dia-
    log box without printing the report.

SEE ALSO

➤ *To create reports in Access, see page 582*

Editing and Printing a Report

If you want to change the contents of a report or print a report,
you can use the **V̲iew**, **Report M̲anager** command to do so.

Edit a report

1. Choose the **V̲iew** menu and select **Report Manager**.
   The Report Manager dialog box appears.

2. Select the name of the report you want to edit from the
   Reports list and choose **E̲dit**.

3. Change the views and scenarios, as outlined in the preceding section.

4. Choose **OK**.

Print a report

1. Choose the **View** menu and select **Report Manager**. The Report Manager dialog box appears.

2. Select the report you want to print from the **Reports** list.

3. Click the **Print** button. The Print dialog box appears.

4. Specify the number of copies to be printed.

5. Choose **OK** to print the report.

CHAPTER 1

Creating and Printing Excel Charts

Create a chart following a series of prompts from the ChartWizard

Arrange a chart's placement

Determine the type of chart you should use

Modify the character and appearance of the chart

Use page setup options to chart precisely the way you want

Creating a Chart with the ChartWizard

A chart is a graphic representation of worksheet data. Excel offers 15 types and more than 70 subtypes of charts. By selecting from these chart types and subtypes, you can create charts that accurately depict nearly any situation.

You can create charts on an existing worksheet or as a separate sheet within a workbook. If you change data represented by the chart, Excel updates the chart automatically. After creating a chart, you can add elements such as trend lines and modify existing elements such as titles and gridlines.

The *ChartWizard* provides an automated, step-by-step approach to creating charts from worksheet data. You can create the chart on the current worksheet, or you can place it on a new sheet in the current workbook. The following sections describe each step in the ChartWizard process.

Selecting Worksheet Data for the Chart

The first step in creating a chart is to select the data on the worksheet. Although you can select data to be charted before, during, or after the ChartWizard runs, it's typical to select the data first. Use these guidelines when selecting data for a chart:

- On the worksheet, place the data for the chart in columns and rows, though not necessarily in adjacent columns and rows.
- Position labels to be used on a chart in the top row and leftmost column of the data range.
- Select the labels along with the chart data.
- Select nonadjacent cells by holding down the Ctrl key.

Figure 14.1 illustrates sales data for three products over four quarters in a layout suitable for charting.

Create a chart using the ChartWizard button

1. When the data is selected, click the ChartWizard button ![ChartWizard icon] in the Standard toolbar. The mouse pointer changes to a plus sign with a chart object as a subscript of the plus sign.

Create a chart on a separate worksheet

You can create a chart on a separate sheet by choosing the **Insert** menu, selecting **Chart**, and then choosing **As New Sheet**.

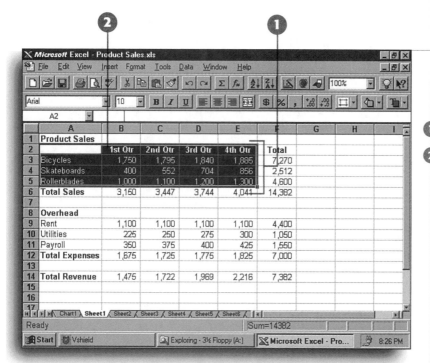

FIGURE 14.1

Labels in row 2 and column A are selected along with chart data.

1 Data

2 Headings

2. Click and drag a box on the worksheet to indicate the position and size of the chart. You can also just click to place the top-left corner; Excel will automatically size the chart. Step 1 of the ChartWizard and the Chart toolbar are displayed, as shown in Figure 14.2.

3. The Step 1 dialog box indicates which cell range or ranges will be charted. If the desired range is not indicated, you can enter or select a new range at this time by dragging in the worksheet. ChartWizard displays the range coordinates.

   If the data range indicated in the Step 1 dialog box is correct, click the **Next** button to move to the Step 2 dialog box.

4. In Step 2, choose the chart type that will best represent your data. See "Selecting the Chart Type" later in this chapter for more information on choosing the correct chart type.

5. Depending on your Chart Type choice in Step 2, you will have a number of subtypes (or formats) in Step 3. Choose one of the Chart Formats, which give you options for labels, data points, and other layouts. For more information on

When data changes, the chart is updated

The chart is linked to the cell range indicated in Step 1 of the ChartWizard. If data in this cell range changes, the chart is updated automatically.

selecting the best chart format, see "Selecting the Chart Format" later in this chapter.

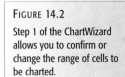

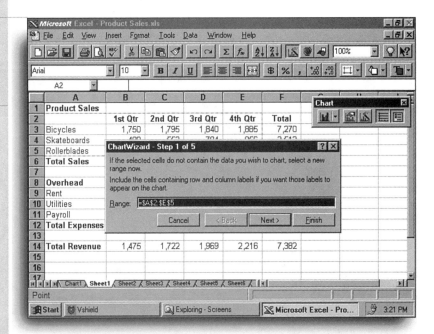

6. In Step 4 of the ChartWizard, choose whether your data is oriented in rows or columns and whether you have labels for your data (and how many rows define the labels). For more information on ways to choose data series, see "Identifying the Data Series" later in this chapter.

7. In Step 5 of the ChartWizard, create identifying parts of your chart such as a legend and titles for the top of the chart and any axis. For more information on when you would add titles and legends, see "Adding the Titles and Legend" later in this chapter.

8. If you make a mistake at any point during the ChartWizard, click the **Back** button. When you are finished, click the **Finish** button.

9. If you need to change the location or size of the chart, drag the chart or the edges. For more information, see "Moving and Sizing a Chart Object" later in this chapter.

Selecting the Chart Type

Step 2 in the ChartWizard allows you to select a basic chart type (see Figure 14.3).

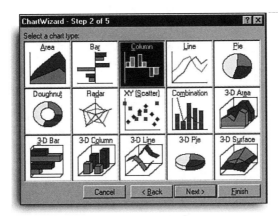

FIGURE 14.3

Use the ChartWizard–Step 2 of 5 dialog box to select the desired chart type.

Some chart types work better for particular types of data. For example, a pie chart might be the best choice to view the percentage of total revenue produced by each department in a company. In the Department Sales example, a line or column chart is used to compare departmental performance over time. Click the desired chart type from the 15 options. There are many new chart types, so make sure your readers understand what the chart represents. In my opinion, the best chart types to use are the old standards: column, line, and pie. Table 14.1 describes when you might use each chart type.

TABLE 14.1 Excel chart types

Chart Type on ChartWizard	Illustrates
Area	Relative importance of data over a period of time. Area charts show the data in terms of the volume or the area it consumes. Each set of data is stacked on top of the other sets of data. The stacked format shows relationships to the total.
Bar	Shows horizontal bars for each period of time or category. It is easy to see the difference between two categories. Use a bar chart to de-emphasize the continuity of the category or time and emphasize the comparison of data in each category.

continues…

TABLE 14.1 **Continued**	
Chart Type on ChartWizard	**Illustrates**
Column	More common than the bar chart. This chart type shows vertical bars for each time or category. The column chart emphasizes the amount of change between each category or time period. Use a column chart when the x-axis labels represent categories and noncontinuous data.
Line	Shows trends or changes in data and emphasizes the passage of time. Use a line chart when the x-axis labels represent continuous data (such as days, months, or years). The lines connecting these data points help the reader estimate what the value was between two periods. A line chart also gives clues about the data before and after the time covered in the chart.
Pie	Used to show the relationship or proportion of parts to a whole. A pie chart always contains only one data series.
Doughnut	A cross between a pie chart and bar chart. You can see the relationship to the whole and the amount of change between each category. Be careful when using this chart type; people are not used to this chart type, and it will take longer for your audience to digest what it conveys.
Rad**ar**	A series of lines that shows changes of data relative to a center point and to each other. Each category has its own value axis extending from the center point. Lines connect all the data markers in the same series. Unless your audience is familiar with this kind of chart, avoid it. Radar charts are difficult to understand.
XY (S**catter)**	Used when one variable is dependent on another. For example, use the XY chart to see the effect of weather on ice cream or battery sales.
Comb**ination**	Used when you want to use more than one chart type for different data series. The most common would be a column and line chart mix. This would show the comparisons of data but also show the trend.
3-D	Used more often in slide show or overhead presentations. The 2D alternatives make it easier to read the actual values but are more boring during a presentation. Use 3D charts for the general idea and 2D charts when the audience needs to know the actual data more exactly. Use 3D area, 3D bar, 3D column, 3D line, and 3D pie charts generally for the same reasons you use the 2D alternatives mentioned previously.
3-D Su**rface**	Picture a 3-D Surface chart as a sheet of cellophane stretched over a 3-D Column chart. The color indicates areas that have

Chart Type on ChartWizard	Illustrates
	the same height (value) but does not mark the data series. I would avoid the 3-D Surface chart as well unless your audience has experience with it.

You can change the chart type after you're finished with the ChartWizard. The Chart toolbar is the quickest way to choose a chart type, but the menu option gives you more choices.

Change the chart type

1. Select the chart.

2. Click the arrow next to the Chart Type button 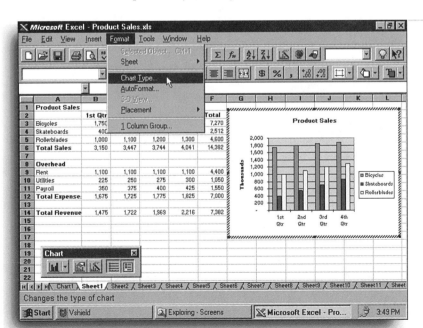 on the Chart toolbar.

3. Select the type of chart you want from the displayed palette (refer to Figure 14.3).

Change the chart type using menu choices

1. Double-click the chart to activate it. You should see a dashed border around the chart rather than the selection handles discussed previously (see Figure 14.4).

Remember the shortcut menu

To edit the chart, right-click the chart and choose **Edit Object** from the shortcut menu.

FIGURE 14.4
The heavy dashed border indicates that the chart has been activated.

2. If you want to change the type for only one series, click on the bar or line representing the series.

3. Choose the **Format** menu; then select **Chart Type** to display the dialog box shown in Figure 14.5.

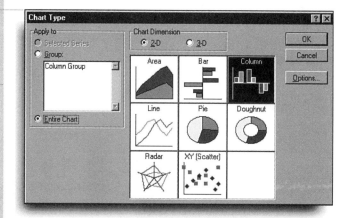

4. Select either **2-D** or **3-D** in the Chart Dimension area.

5. In the **Apply to** section, choose **Entire Chart**. If you chose a series in step 2, choose **Selected Series**. If you already have multiple chart types, you can also choose which chart type you want in the **Group** list box.

6. Choose a chart type by clicking on one of the sample charts.

7. Choose **OK**.

Selecting the Chart Format

Step 3 in the ChartWizard lets you select a specific format for the chosen chart type (see Figure 14.6). This dialog box offers different options depending on which chart type you selected in the previous step of the ChartWizard. Generally, it is best to go with the default option displayed in Step 3 of the ChartWizard. However, depending on your circumstances, you might want to change the option. There are 4–10 options for each of the 15 chart types. I'll cover only some of the options for the most common chart types. Some of these options (gridlines, data labels) are discussed individually in later sections. The following guidelines might be helpful in choosing a chart format:

- Generally, use gridlines on 2D charts when you want to make it easier to locate the value for a bar, column, or line. 3D charts are busy enough, so don't use gridline options.

- Line charts also allow you to see symbols for data points to help the reader locate the value on the axes.

- Option 9 for a line chart format is a special case for stock values. It allows you to plot a high, low, open, and close for the time period.

- Choose data labels when you have one or two data series in lines or bars if you need to emphasize the actual values.

- Pie charts can show the labels for each pie slice. Use this instead of a legend so the categories appear close to the slice.

- Pie charts can also show the percentage of each piece to emphasize its relationship to the whole.

- Bar charts and column charts (2D and 3D) have stacked options (choices 3 and 9 in Figure 14.7). Use this option to show how much each category represents as a proportion of the total for the time period and to see what the total is for the time period. The 100% options (choices 5 and 10 in Figure 14.7), on the other hand, emphasize the proportion for each category in a time period and do not show the total value (all stacked bars are the same height).

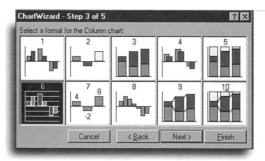

FIGURE **14.6**

Select chart formatting on the ChartWizard–Step 3 of 5 dialog box.

If you want to change the format of a chart after you've created it, you can use the AutoFormat feature to see all chart types and formats for each chart type.

Change format for a chart

1. Double-click the chart you want to format.

2. Click the right mouse button in the chart background and then choose **AutoFormat** from the shortcut menu. The AutoFormat dialog box is displayed (see Figure 14.7).

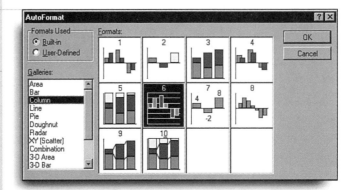

FIGURE 14.7
Select a built-in AutoFormat to apply to a chart.

3. Choose the **Built-In** option to use one of Excel's built-in AutoFormats.

4. Select the type of chart you want from the **Galleries** list box.

5. Select the format you want to use from the **Formats** area, which gives you a sample of the appearance of formats available for the chart type selected in the **Galleries** list box.

6. Choose **OK**. Excel applies the AutoFormat to the chart.

You can also create your own format based on a chart that you've already customized.

Create a custom chart format

1. Double-click the chart that contains the formats you want to define as a custom chart format, or activate the chart sheet.

2. Click the right mouse button in the chart background and then choose **AutoFormat** from the shortcut menu. The AutoFormat dialog box is displayed (refer to Figure 14.7).

3. Select the **User-Defined** option. After you select that option, the buttons in the dialog box change.

4. Choose the **Customize** button. The User-Defined AutoFormats dialog box is displayed (see Figure 14.8).

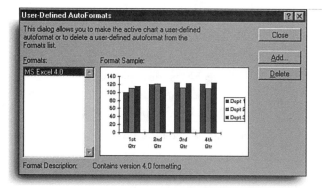

FIGURE 14.8

Customized chart formats are in the Format Sample area.

5. Click the **Add** button. The Add Custom AutoFormat dialog box is displayed, as shown in Figure 14.9.

FIGURE 14.9

Enter a name and description for the custom AutoFormat.

6. Enter a name for the AutoFormat in the **Format Name** text box and a description in the **Description** text box.

7. Choose **OK**. You return to the User-Defined AutoFormats dialog box, where the custom AutoFormat now is displayed in the **Formats** list (see Figure 14.10).

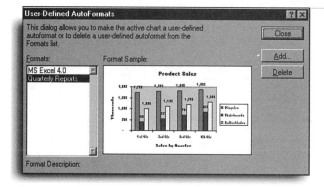

FIGURE 14.10

The custom AutoFormat has been added to the **Formats** list.

8. Choose **Close**.

Apply a custom AutoFormat

1. Double-click the chart you want to format, or activate the chart sheet.

2. Click the right mouse button on the chart background and then choose **AutoFormat** from the shortcut menu. The AutoFormat dialog box is displayed.

3. Select the **User-Defined** option.

4. Select the format you want to use from the **Formats** list.

5. Choose **Close**.

Identifying the Data Series

Step 4 of the ChartWizard shows a sample of the chart you are creating and allows you to select additional charting options.

The **Data Series In** options allow you to choose the location of the data in the chart—that is, whether the data series (information that is represented on the chart as columns, lines, data points, and so on) comes from rows or columns. Figure 14.11 shows the worksheet data charted using the **Data Series In Columns** option. Compare this figure with the sample chart in Figure 14.12, which shows the appearance of the chart with the **Data Series In Rows** option selected. Notice that the data series names are in the legend for each figure. If the x-axis and y-axis don't look right, just choose the other option.

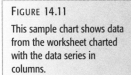

FIGURE 14.11

This sample chart shows data from the worksheet charted with the data series in columns.

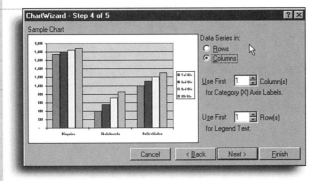

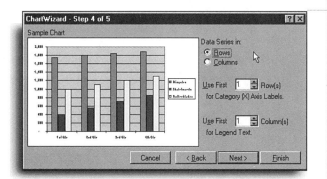

If you chose the wrong data series during the ChartWizard, you can change it after you've built the chart.

Change the data series

1. Select the chart.

2. Click the ChartWizard button ![button] on the Chart or Standard toolbar. The ChartWizard—Step 1 of 2 dialog box displays, and a marquee displays around the current data series.

3. Type a new range in the Range text box or drag over the range you want on the worksheet. To select noncontiguous ranges, select the first range, hold down Ctrl, and select the next range. Choose **Next**.

4. If necessary, change whether you want the data series in rows or columns and how many rows to use for the labels and legend. When you edit a chart with the ChartWizard button, this is Step 2 of 2 of the ChartWizard. This is the same as Step 4 or 5 when you create a chart from scratch with the ChartWizard.

5. Choose **OK**.

Using Axis and Legend Labels

Step 4 of the ChartWizard also allows you to specify two other ways data should be used in the chart: for axis labels and legend text (for pie and doughnut charts, the chart title and slice labels). In Figure 14.11, ChartWizard used the first column for the axis labels and the first row for legend text; therefore, the settings in the dialog box are as follows:

- **Use First 1 Column(s) for Category (X) Axis Labels**
- **Use First 1 Row(s) for Legend Text**

If the worksheet data you selected does not include axis labels or legend text, the corresponding option should be set to **0**. When you specify **0** for one of these options, the first row or column is displayed as a data series or data point. You can enter numbers for these options by typing or by using the up and down arrows to the right of each number.

You can also have more than one row for axis labels or legend text. Type a number or use the spinner buttons to increase the number of rows in the text boxes. To change the options after you've created the chart, follow the steps in the "Identifying the Data Series" section.

Adding the Titles and Legend

You can add titles to the chart and each of the axes, and you can add a legend in Step 5 of the ChartWizard (see Figure 14.13).

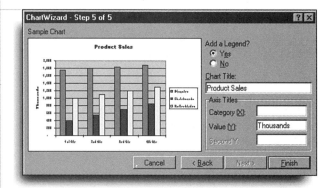

Choose the desired legend option, enter a chart title and axis titles if desired, and then click the **Finish** button to end the ChartWizard and create the chart. Figure 14.14 shows the completed chart embedded in the Excel worksheet.

You usually include a legend or chart titles describing the chart. However, if you print the worksheet and chart together, text within the worksheet might be sufficient, making chart titles unnecessary. Another trick is to color-code the data ranges corresponding to the slices, bars, columns, or pie slices instead of a legend. Select each range, click on the Color button 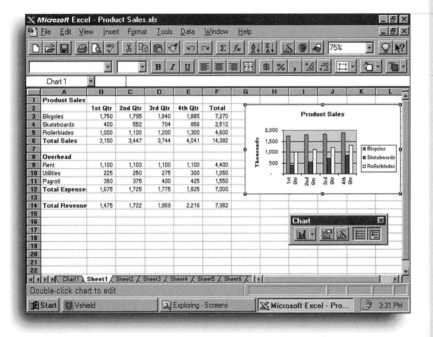, and select a color matching the chart item.

FIGURE 14.14

ChartWizard places the finished chart in the worksheet.

Turn legend on or off

   1. Click to select the chart. A solid line surrounds the chart, and the Chart toolbar is displayed.

   2. Click the Legend button on the Chart toolbar to turn the legend on or off.

If you do not add chart titles during Step 5 of the Wizard, you can add or change them after you create your chart.

Add titles to a chart

   1. Double-click the chart to which you want to add titles, or activate the chart sheet. A hatched line surrounds the chart.

2. Click the right mouse button in the chart background and then choose **Insert Titles** from the shortcut menu. The Titles dialog box is displayed (see Figure 14.15).

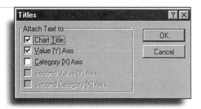

3. Select the chart and axis titles you want to add and then choose **OK**. The dialog box closes, and you return to the chart, in which the title objects now appear.

4. Select each object to type the title text, and then click outside the text box. The titles are displayed in the chart (see Figure 14.16).

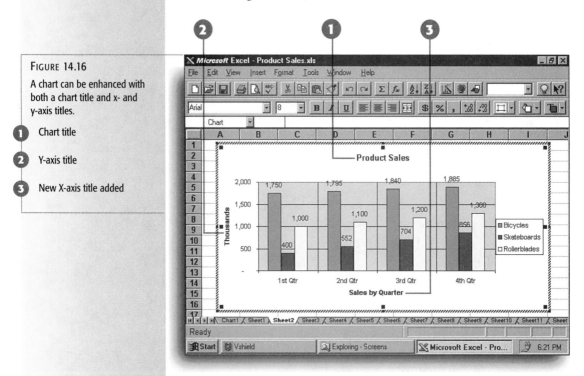

5. Press **Esc** to deselect the title objects.

Moving and Sizing a Chart Object

The initial size and shape of a completed chart is determined by the size of the area dragged after clicking the ChartWizard. After a chart is created, you can make it larger or smaller or move it to a new location on the worksheet.

Size a chart

1. Select the chart by clicking it. Selection handles appear as small black handles around the chart.

2. Position the mouse pointer over a handle. The mouse pointer becomes a double-headed arrow.

3. Click and drag the handle to make the chart larger or smaller. To proportionally size the chart, hold down the Shift key while dragging one of the corner handles.

Figure 14.17 shows the dotted lines that display to indicate the increase or decrease as a chart is being resized. While you are resizing the chart, the pointer changes to a crosshair.

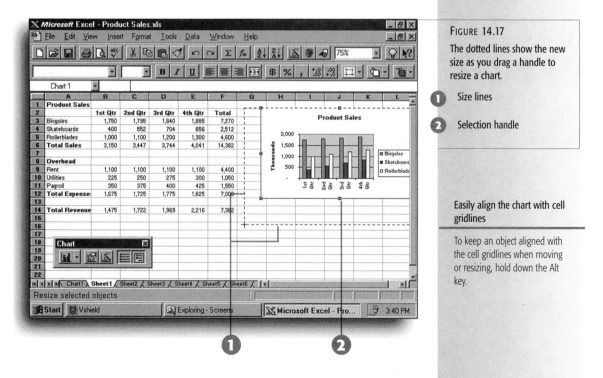

FIGURE 14.17

The dotted lines show the new size as you drag a handle to resize a chart.

① Size lines

② Selection handle

Easily align the chart with cell gridlines

To keep an object aligned with the cell gridlines when moving or resizing, hold down the Alt key.

Move a chart to a new location on the worksheet

1. Select the chart.

2. Click inside the chart boundary (not on one of the handles) and drag the chart to a new position.

Changing Chart Type Options

You can see additional options for chart types by clicking the **Options** button in the Chart Type dialog box. The Format [Column Group] dialog box shown in Figure 14.18 is displayed. (The exact name of the dialog box varies depending on your selection in the Chart Type dialog box.)

Change chart options

1. Double-click the chart to select it. A hatched outline appears around the chart.

2. Choose **F̲ormat** and select **Chart T̲ype**.

3. On the Chart Type dialog box, click the **Options** button. The dialog box is similar to the one shown in Figure 14.18. The specific options depend on the chart type.

FIGURE 14.18

Use the Format Column Group dialog box to choose a chart subtype for the column chart type.

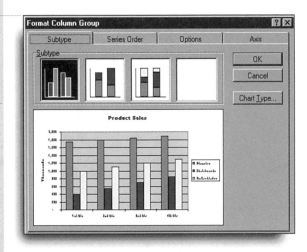

4. Make choices on each of the tabs as follows:

- *Subtype tab.* Here you can choose the desired chart sub-type. Different subtypes are available depending on the selected chart type. The subtypes for a column chart, as shown in Figure 14.18, include regular column, stacked column, and percentage stacked column. These subtypes are a subset of the possibilities for chart formats described in the "Selecting the Chart Format" section.

- *Series Order tab.* Select this tab at the top of the dialog box to change the order in which the chart series is plotted.

- *Options tab.* This tab displays varying controls dependent on the chart type. In the Product Sales example, column overlap and gaps between column groups can be changed using this tab.

- *Axis tab.* Select this tab to specify which axis the column group is using in a multiple-axis chart.

5. Choose **OK** when you have finished making changes in all tabs. Excel applies the changes to your chart.

3-D View Options

When working with a 3D chart type, you can use additional controls for chart appearance by choosing the **Format** menu and selecting **Excel,** and then **3-D View**. The dialog box shown in Figure 14.19 opens.

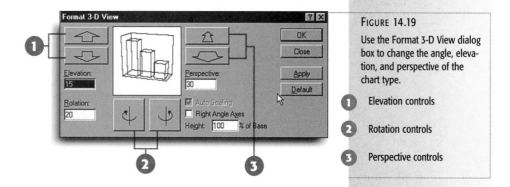

FIGURE 14.19

Use the Format 3-D View dialog box to change the angle, elevation, and perspective of the chart type.

1. Elevation controls

2. Rotation controls

3. Perspective controls

Elevation controls the relative level at which the chart is viewed. Enter a value or use the arrow buttons to adjust the value.

Rotation controls the view angle of the chart around the vertical axis. Enter a rotation value in degrees or click the rotation arrows to change the view angle.

Perspective sets the amount of depth in the chart view. Select the **Right Angle A<u>x</u>es** option to remove all perspective from the chart view.

To return to the standard 3D view, click the **<u>D</u>efault** button.

Enhancing a Chart

Nearly every part of an Excel chart can be formatted. This flexibility gives you complete control over the appearance of your chart. Before an individual chart item can be formatted, it must be selected. Chart items in an active chart can be easily selected with the mouse. Table 14.2 lists mouse procedures for selecting various items on an active chart.

Activate the chart to select a chart object

Don't forget: You need to activate the chart by double-clicking it before you can select individual chart objects.

TABLE 14.2 **Selection options**

To	Do This
Select an item	Click the chart item. Black handles appear around the edges or at the ends of the item.
Select a data series	Click any marker in the chart data series. Handles appear on each marker in the series.
Select a single marker	Select the entire series and then click again on the desired data marker. Handles appear around the edges of the item. The top (larger) handle can be dragged to change the value of a single marker.
Select gridlines	Click a gridline. Make sure the tip of the mouse pointer is exactly on the gridline.
Select an axis	Click the axis or the area containing the axis labels.
Select the legend	Click the legend. Click again to select an individual legend entry or legend key.
Select the entire plot area	Click any area in the plot area not occupied by another item, including gridlines.
Select the entire chart	Click anywhere outside the plot area not containing another item.

Don't forget the right mouse button

You can also use the right mouse button to select an item on the chart and display a shortcut menu allowing you to change items on the chart.

You can format each component of an Excel chart individually to change its appearance or add annotations. To display the formatting options available for a specific chart item, select the chart item and then choose the **Format** menu; then select **Selected [Object]** (where [Object] is the name of the selected item). You can also double-click the desired chart item. Either of these methods will open a formatting dialog box with options relating to the selected chart item. Figure 14.20 shows an example of this dialog box. Note the tabs for various formatting options.

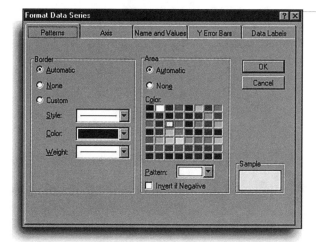

Definition of a marker

A marker is an object that represents a data point in a chart. Bars, columns, pie wedges, and symbols are examples of markers. All the markers that belong to the same data series appear as the same shape, symbol, and color.

FIGURE 14.20

The Format Data Series dialog box enables you to change the appearance of each data series.

The following sections describe additional enhancement options available for various chart components.

Adding Data Labels

You can add data labels to a chart to annotate the chart elements.

Add data labels to a chart

1. Double-click the chart you want to enhance, or activate the chart sheet.

2. If you want to add labels for only one data series, click on the marker to select the series. If you want only one marker, click again to choose just the single bar.

3. Choose the **Insert** menu; then select **Data Labels** or click the right mouse button on a bar or line and then choose

Insert Data Labels from the shortcut menu. The Data
Labels dialog box is displayed (see Figure 14.21).

FIGURE 14.21
Use the options in the Data
Labels dialog box to annotate
the chart elements.

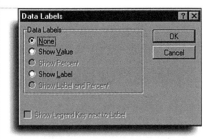

3. Select the type of data labels you want to display.

4. Choose **OK**. Excel adds the data labels to each data series
in the chart (see Figure 14.22).

FIGURE 14.22
The actual data values are displayed above each marker.

1 Data label

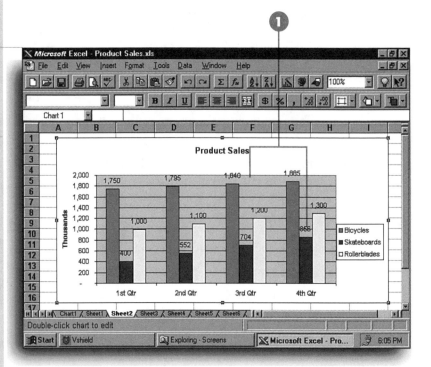

If the data markers seem crowded, you can resize the chart. Or,
you can change the font size or alignment of the data labels by
double-clicking them and making changes in the Format Data
Labels dialog box.

Creating Custom Labels

You can also create an individual custom label anywhere on the chart. Select the chart and just start typing.

Add a custom label

1. Double-click on the chart. A hatched pattern surrounds the chart.

2. Type a label and press Enter.

3. Drag the label to where you want it displayed.

Adding Gridlines

Gridlines are horizontal and vertical lines that overlay a chart. These lines help you follow a point from the x- or y-axis to identify a data point's exact value. Gridlines are useful in large charts, charts that contain many data points, and charts in which data points are close together. Depending on the format option you choose in Step 3 of the ChartWizard, you might or might not have gridlines on your chart. (Gridlines are not possible for a pie chart.) You can turn gridlines on or off by clicking on the Gridlines button ![icon] on the Chart toolbar. Follow the procedure described next for more options.

Add gridlines to a chart

1. Double-click the chart you want to enhance, or activate the chart sheet.

2. Click the right mouse button in the chart background and then choose **Insert Gridlines** from the shortcut menu. The Gridlines dialog box is displayed (see Figure 14.23).

Need to show geographic data?

Data Map is a new feature of Excel. This feature allows you to see colors, shading, or symbols for values on a map of the United States, world, or other geographic area. To use the map feature, highlight the range in your worksheet that includes place names and values and click on the Map button on the standard toolbar. For instructions on how to use this feature, see *Special Edition, Using Microsoft Excel 95* or look up Microsoft Data Map in Help.

FIGURE 14.23

Use the Gridlines dialog box to add major and minor gridlines to a chart.

3. Select the type of gridlines you want to display.

   Major Gridlines occur at the major intervals on the axis.

Use **Minor Gridlines** if you also want gridlines between the major intervals on the axis.

4. Choose **OK**. Excel adds the gridlines to the chart (see Figure 14.24).

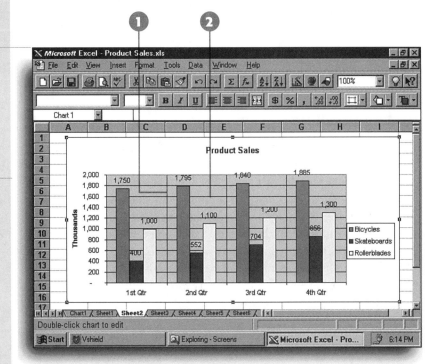

FIGURE 14.24

Major gridlines have been added to both the x- and y-axes.

1 Major gridlines x-axis

2 Major gridlines y-axis

Editing a Chart

When you use the ChartWizard to create charts, Excel plots the data according to the selected worksheet range. You can use several commands to edit an existing chart. For example, you can delete a data series from a chart, add a new data series to a chart, and change the order in which the data series appear.

To delete a data series from a chart, select the data series you want to remove and then press the Delete key. Excel removes the data series and redraws the chart to reflect the deletion.

Add a data series

1. Double-click the chart to which you want to add new data or switch to the chart sheet that contains the chart.

2. Choose the **Insert** menu; then select **New Data**. The New Data dialog box is displayed.

3. Enter or select the range in the worksheet that contains the data you want to add.

4. Choose **OK**. Excel adds the data series to the chart.

Change the order of the data series

1. Double-click the chart you want to modify, or switch to the chart sheet.

2. Click the right mouse button in the chart background and then choose **Chart Type** from the shortcut menu. The Chart Type dialog box is displayed.

3. Choose the **Options** button.

4. Select the Series Order tab.

5. Select the series you want to change and then choose the **Move Up** or **Move Down** button until the series is listed in the order you want.

6. Choose **OK**.

Printing Charts

When you print a worksheet that contains an embedded chart, the chart prints along with the other worksheet data, just as it is displayed on the screen. You can also print only the chart, without other worksheet data. To print just the worksheet and the embedded chart or the chart sheet, click on the sheet tab and then select the Print ⎙ button on the Standard toolbar.

SEE ALSO

➤ *For more information about printing worksheets, see page 312*

Printing charts in Excel is no different from printing any worksheet range. You can specify print options for charts in much the same way that you do for data in the worksheet. You can, for example, specify the size of the chart and the printing quality, and preview the chart before printing.

Specify the chart print settings

1. Double-click the chart you want to print, or move to the chart sheet that contains the chart you want to print.

2. Choose the **File** menu; then select **Page Setup**.

3. Select the Chart tab to view special options for printing charts. Figure 14.25 shows the printing options that are available for a chart.

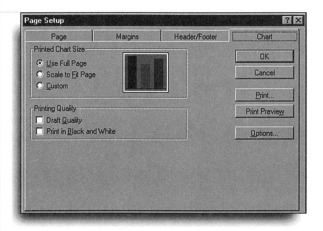

4. Select the appropriate chart size in the **Printed Chart Size** area of the dialog box.

5. To print the chart in black and white, select the **Print in Black and White** option in the **Printing Quality** area.

6. When you finish specifying the print settings, you can print the chart. Choose **Print** in the Page Setup dialog box. The Print dialog box is displayed.

7. Choose **OK** to accept the print settings and begin printing the chart.

PART

III

Using PowerPoint

Getting Acquainted
with PowerPoint

Create attractive presentations using templates and the AutoContent Wizard

Use PowerPoint's window elements, toolbars, and menu commands to perform common functions

Use PowerPoint's components to work on slides and to generate speaker notes and audience handouts

Organize presentation contents with outlines

Use masters, templates, objects, and layouts

Add visuals—from a simple drawing to an animated video clip—to PowerPoint slides

Starting and Exiting PowerPoint

PowerPoint is the component of Microsoft Office used to create professional-quality overhead transparency, paper, 35mm slide, photoprint, or onscreen presentations. This chapter discusses the layout of the PowerPoint window, its tools, and its capabilities.

Like other applications in Microsoft Office, PowerPoint can be started in more than one way. You can use whichever method is most convenient. The following are the ways in which PowerPoint can be started:

- Click the Start button and choose the PowerPoint shortcut, usually found in the Programs menu.
- Double-click the PowerPoint icon in the Microsoft Office folder (found in your hard disk window).

After a few seconds, the PowerPoint window opens. Like other Microsoft Office applications, PowerPoint displays a Tip of the Day dialog box, which contains a new tip each time you start PowerPoint. If you don't want to see these tips when you start PowerPoint, deselect the **Show Tips at Startup** check box and click **OK**. (You can display tips at any time by choosing the **Help** menu and selecting **Tip of the Day**.)

When you're ready to exit PowerPoint, click on the x (close) button in the upper-right corner of the title bar or choose the **File** menu and select **Exit**. If the current file has not been saved, PowerPoint displays a dialog box asking whether you want to save the changes to the current file. Choose **Yes** if you want to save before exiting, **No** if you don't want to save before exiting, or **Cancel** to return to your file without saving.

Create a PowerPoint shortcut on the desktop

You can create a shortcut to PowerPoint by dragging the PowerPoint icon from the Power-Point folder to the desktop. You then can just double-click the shortcut to open the program.

Becoming Familiar with the PowerPoint Window

When you first open PowerPoint, it automatically displays the dialog box in Figure 15.1. This dialog box enables you to choose how you want to create a presentation. PowerPoint offers a variety of options, including using an existing presentation, opening

a blank presentation, using a template, or running the
AutoContent Wizard.

SEE ALSO

➤ *For more information about creating a new presentation, see page 366*

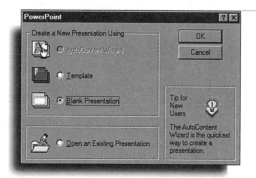

FIGURE 15.1
You can choose which method to
use to create your presentation.

Figure 15.2 shows a typical PowerPoint presentation screen.
PowerPoint's menu bar, Standard toolbar, and Formatting toolbar are shown below the window's title bar. The Drawing toolbar is displayed down the left side of the window. Surrounded by
a gray background, the white area in the middle of the screen
represents the first slide in the presentation. Slides are the individual "pages" in a presentation that become overheads, 35mm
slides, or an onscreen slide show. Note that vertical and horizontal scrollbars are now visible onscreen. To the left of the horizontal scrollbar are view buttons, which are used to display
different views of your presentation.

**Maximize the PowerPoint window
for easier use**

If your presentation window is
smaller than the one in Figure
15.2, click the Maximize button
to enlarge the window.

SEE ALSO

➤ *For more information about creating, saving, and opening presentations, see page 365*

Understanding the PowerPoint Window Elements

PowerPoint menus are similar to menus in other Microsoft
Office applications. Menus such as **File**, **Window**, and **Help** are
standard in all Office applications. PowerPoint's menus are most
similar to Word's, but the **Draw** menu is unique to PowerPoint.
Table 15.1 describes the types of commands found on each
PowerPoint menu.

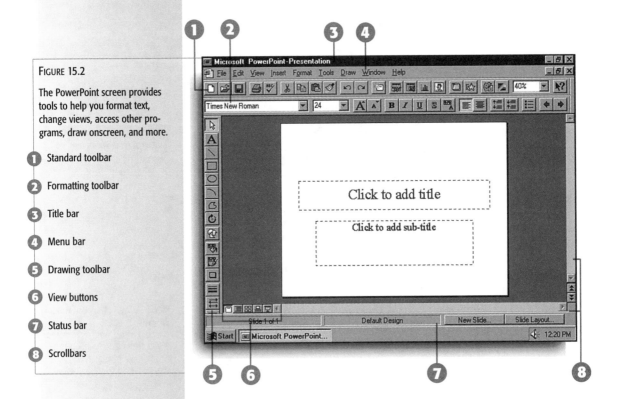

FIGURE 15.2

The PowerPoint screen provides tools to help you format text, change views, access other programs, draw onscreen, and more.

1 Standard toolbar

2 Formatting toolbar

3 Title bar

4 Menu bar

5 Drawing toolbar

6 View buttons

7 Status bar

8 Scrollbars

TABLE 15.1   **PowerPoint menus**

Menu	Description
File	Contains the standard Microsoft Office application **File** options as well as commands specific to PowerPoint such as **Pack and Go** and **Send to Genigraphics**. If you're using the version of Microsoft Exchange installed with Windows 95, an extra section adds mail commands such as **Send** and **Add Routing Slip**.
Edit	Contains **Undo**, **Cut**, **Copy**, and **Paste** commands. **Duplicate** (Ctrl+D) and **Delete Slide** also are found on this menu, along with commands to create **Links** to other files, to **Find** or **Replace**, and to edit an **Object**.
View	Contains commands to help you choose the presentation view you want to display onscreen or to display masters. This menu also contains commands for displaying and removing toolbars, rulers, and guides. (Rulers and guides are discussed in the "Displaying Rulers and Guides" section of this chapter.) This menu also enables you to control the zoom percentage used in a particular view.

Menu	Description
Insert	Contains commands that enable you to insert a variety of elements into a presentation, from a simple date or time to clip art, graphs, and other objects.
Format	Contains commands for changing how text and objects look in a presentation (font, alignment, spacing, color, shadow, and so on). Also contains commands for selecting templates, color schemes, and layouts.
Tools	Contains the usual Microsoft Office tools (such as **Spelling**) as well as some tools unique to PowerPoint. Use the commands on this menu to create transitions between slides, to hide slides, or to recolor or crop a picture. You'll also find commands for customizing toolbars, setting PowerPoint options, setting animation, reminding you of meetings, interactive settings, and so on.
Draw	Contains commands for manipulating objects in a presentation. You can group several objects as one, rearrange the "stacking order" (or layers) of objects, and rotate, flip, and change the scale of objects.
Window	Contains the standard Microsoft Office application **Window** options—such as **New Window** and **Arrange All**—and includes a **Fit to Page** command.
Help	Contains the standard Microsoft Office application **Help** options, plus an **Answer Wizard** and a **Tip of the Day**.

SEE ALSO

➤ For more information about creating a new presentation, see page 366

➤ For more information about enhancing text in a presentation, see page 405

➤ For more information about working with templates in PowerPoint, see page 400

The status bar is located near the bottom of the PowerPoint window, just above the taskbar. The left side of the status bar displays the number of the current slide or other element you're working on (Slide Master, Outline Master, Handout Master, or Notes Master). The center of the status bar tells you which design template currently is in use; you can double-click this area to apply a new design template. The right side of the status bar contains two buttons. The **New Slide** button enables you to add a new slide to your presentation without choosing the **Insert** menu and selecting **New Slide**. Clicking the **Slide Layout** button opens the Slide Layout dialog box, from which you can choose a specially designed slide layout.

Directly above the status bar is the horizontal scrollbar. To the left of the scrollbar are five view buttons. Each button displays a different view of the current presentation. These view buttons are described in the section "Examining the Components of a PowerPoint Presentation" later in this chapter.

PowerPoint's Standard Toolbar

Additional toolbars you can use

Right-click any toolbar to display a list of other available toolbars. You can select a toolbar to display or to hide from the list.

Table 15.2 describes the buttons on PowerPoint's Standard toolbar. Each button represents a PowerPoint menu command. You'll learn how to use most of these buttons while performing common tasks in subsequent chapters.

TABLE 15.2   Buttons on PowerPoint's Standard toolbar

Button	Description
	Creates a new presentation and displays the New Presentation dialog box.
	Displays the File Open dialog box, from which you can choose a presentation file to open (or a design template or an outline).
	Saves the current presentation under the current name and file type. If the presentation has not yet been saved, the File Save dialog box opens.
	Prints the active presentation.
	Checks spelling in the current presentation. Displays the Spelling dialog box if errors are found.
	Removes the selected text or object from the slide and places it on the Windows Clipboard.
	Places a copy of the selected text or object on the Windows Clipboard but leaves the original text or object unchanged.
	Pastes the contents of the Clipboard into the current slide.
	Records all formatting attributes (color, font, shadow, pattern, and so on) of the selected object or text selection so you can copy these attributes to another object or text selection.
	Reverses the most recent action taken. Note that not all actions (commands) can be reversed.

Button	Description
	Redoes or repeats the most recent action taken (depending on the action). Not all actions can be redone or repeated.
	Opens the New Slide dialog box, from which you can choose an AutoLayout for the new slide.
	Embeds a Microsoft Word table of a specified size (rows and columns) in your presentation.
	Embeds an Excel worksheet of a specified size (rows and columns) in your presentation.
	Embeds a graph in your presentation using specified data.
	Enables you to insert clip art into your presentation using Microsoft's ClipArt Gallery.
	Applies a selected design template to the slide show.
	Displays or removes the Animation Effects toolbar, which provides access to special moving effects for the text and body of the slide.
	Transfers the content of the current presentation to Microsoft Word.
	Displays the presentation in black and white rather than in color. Clicking the button again toggles the view back to color.
49%	Enables you to zoom in and out of your presentation.
	The mouse pointer changes to a question mark, which you can click on any PowerPoint menu command, button, or toolbar to receive help. You also can double-click the icon to open Help Topics.

Table 15.3 describes the buttons on the Formatting toolbar.

TABLE 15.3   Buttons on PowerPoint's Formatting toolbar

Button	Description
Times New Roman	Shows the current font and displays a drop-down list of other available fonts.
24	Shows the current font size and displays a list of other available font sizes.
A	Increases font size of the selected text to the next larger available size.
A	Decreases font size of the selected text to the next smaller available size.

continues…

TABLE 15.3   Continued

Button	Description
B	Adds or removes boldface to or from selected text. (This button toggles on and off with each click.)
I	Adds or removes italic to or from selected text. (This button toggles on and off with each click.)
U	Adds or removes underlining to or from selected text. (This button toggles on and off with each click.)
S	Adds or removes text shadow to or from selected text. (This button toggles on and off with each click.)
A	Displays eight colors for text in a palette. To choose a different color, click the **Other Color** option to display the Other Color dialog box.
≡	Left-aligns selected text.
≡	Centers selected text.
≡	Right-aligns selected text.
↕	Increases line spacing between paragraphs for the selected text.
↕	Decreases line spacing between paragraphs for the selected text.
☰	Adds bullets to selected text. (This button toggles on and off with each click.)
⇦	Promotes selected text to next higher level in an outline.
⇨	Demotes selected text to next lower level in an outline.

Displaying Rulers and Guides

When working with text documents in Word, it's helpful to display horizontal and vertical rulers in the Word window. Because some slides contain text, rulers also can be useful in PowerPoint. Rulers provide a reference point within a slide so you can see at what point on a page (in inches) a text or drawn object is located. They also can help you plan the use of space on a slide by providing guides for object and text placement.

To display rulers in the PowerPoint window, choose the **View** menu and select **Ruler**. Rulers appear in one of two states— drawing or text—depending on the item currently selected in the slide. Figure 15.3 shows rulers in the drawing state, in which the zero point is placed at the center of each ruler. This enables you to position objects from the center point to the outer edges of a slide. The mouse position is indicated on each ruler by a dashed line.

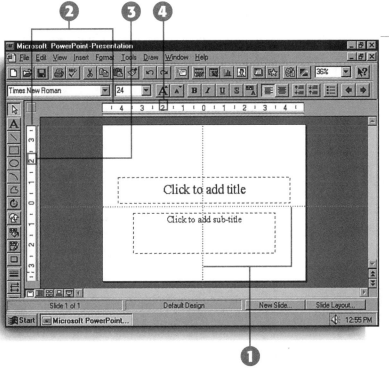

FIGURE 15.3.
Rulers and guides assist in the layout and alignment of slide components.

1 Guides

2 Rulers

3 Vertical position of the mouse

4 Horizontal position of the mouse

When it's important to position slide elements precisely or to align certain elements vertically or horizontally, you can choose the **View** menu and select **Guides**. This command displays dotted lines that intersect vertically and horizontally through a specific point on a slide. You can use guides to help you visually align elements. Guides are shown in Figure 15.3.

Repositioning guides

You can reposition a guide by dragging it to a new location. Guides do not appear on printed copies of your slide; they appear onscreen only while you are working in PowerPoint.

Examining the Components of a PowerPoint Presentation

Although you might think PowerPoint is used only to create slides for a presentation, PowerPoint offers much more. It helps you plan, create, and deliver a presentation in a practical way. Think about how a speaker gives a presentation. First, the speaker outlines the presentation, then she completes the "look" and contents of the slides, and finally she prints them. During the presentation, the speaker might refer to printed copies of the slides that contain handwritten notes. She also might provide copies of the slides to the audience so it can follow along or take notes.

Key components of a PowerPoint presentation include the following:

- Slides
- Outlines
- Speaker's notes
- Audience handouts

After you create content, you can use any combination of these four components, depending on your particular requirements. PowerPoint simplifies the task by automatically generating the following:

- Slide content in the Slide view when you enter text in the Outline view
- Content in the Outline view when you enter text directly on slides
- An audience handout page for each slide you create, ready for notes that can be used by the speaker

Use the view buttons on the horizontal scrollbar

You can quickly display a presentation component by clicking one of the view buttons to the left of the horizontal scrollbar. Click the Slide View 🔲, Outline View 📄, or Notes Pages View 📄 button to display the desired element.

You can view any components onscreen, or you can print copies. PowerPoint displays slides by default, as previously shown in Figure 15.2. Outline pages look like a typical outline; main headings are aligned at the left margin, and lower-level headings are indented (see Figure 15.4). Pages for the speaker's notes contain a reduced version of the slide at the top of the page and space for notes at the bottom (see Figure 15.5). Audience handouts can contain two, three, or six slides per printed page, as shown in Figure 15.6. Note that you can't view audience handouts onscreen. The Handout Master shows dotted outlines of potential slide locations on the page.

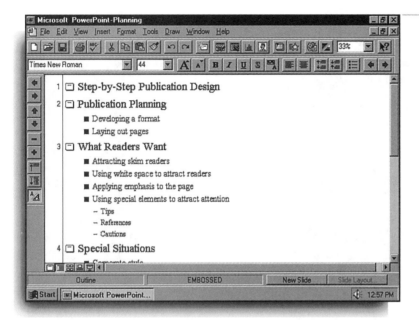

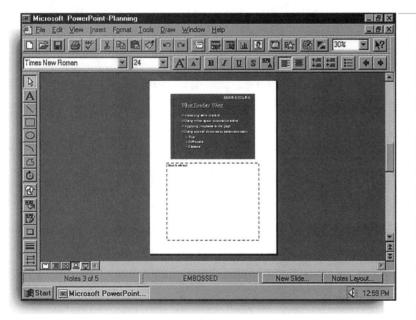

FIGURE 15.6

The Handout Master shows layout options for audience handout pages.

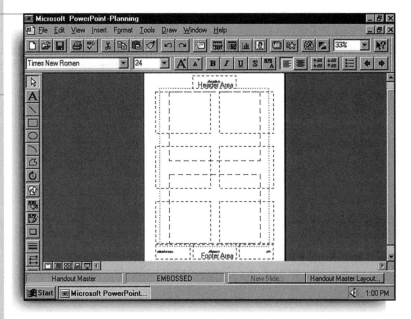

FIGURE 15.6

The Handout Master shows layout options for audience handout pages.

To view slides, outlines, or note pages, choose the **View** menu and select either **Slides**, **Outline**, or **Notes Pages**. To view handout pages, choose the **View** menu and select **Master**, and then choose **Handout Master** from the submenu. After you choose a view, the status bar indicates which view is displayed.

SEE ALSO

➤ *For more information about creating an outline in Word, see page 146*

Understanding Templates and Masters

PowerPoint provides design templates and masters to help you create attractive, eye-catching slides. Design templates are built-in designs containing color schemes and design elements that provide a background for a slide. A particular design's color scheme employs matching colors for text, lines, background, and so on. Design elements include lines, shapes, and pictures added to a background to enhance the text and graphics in a slide.

A design template also includes masters with preformatted fonts and styles that complement the "look" of the template. The EMBOSSED template, for example, looks formal and sophisticated. The use of Times New Roman font and the bullet styles add to the look.

Slide Masters enable you to control the global font styles, formatting, and placement of text on a slide. A Slide Master, for example, might place titles in a 48-point Univers font at the top center of your slides. Text formatting and placement also are included on the Slide Master. You can select one design template to maintain an overall look for all your slides, and then you can modify the Slide Master to change a particular element of that template. You might, for example, want to reconfigure where titles are located on your slides after you've applied a template.

Using Slide Masters and design templates creates consistency within a presentation. When you choose a design template, the same color scheme, layout, and formatting are applied to all slides in the presentation. The elements and formatting of the master slide also apply to all slides in the presentation. For added flexibility, PowerPoint enables you to change any element of a design template—text formatting, color scheme, layout, master elements, and so on. You even can create your own templates and use them again and again.

Using Masters

For every presentation you create, PowerPoint makes a set of masters available—a Slide Master, a Title Master, a Notes Master, and a Handout Master. Masters correspond directly to the slides, speaker's notes, and handouts of a presentation. Masters contain the elements (text or pictures) that you want to appear on every component page. If you want your company logo to appear on each slide, for example, it isn't necessary to manually insert the logo on each individual slide. You can just add the logo to the Slide Master, and it automatically appears on every slide. Other elements you might add to a master include pictures or clip art, page numbers, the date, the title of the presentation, and reminders such as "Company Confidential."

The Slide Master is in control

Slide Masters control formatting on all slides except title slides, which are controlled by a Title Master.

Use the view buttons with Shift to display masters

You can quickly display a master using the view buttons to the left of the horizontal scrollbar. Press and hold down the Shift key, and then click one of the view buttons. Hold down the Shift key, for example, and click the Slide View 🔲 button for a Slide Master. To return to the Slide, Outline, Slide Sorter, or Notes view, choose the appropriate command from the **View** menu or click the appropriate view button (without the Shift key) at the lower-left corner of the window.

Display a master

1. Choose the **View** menu and select **Master**, which displays a submenu.

2. From the submenu, choose **Slide Master**, **Title Master**, **Handout Master**, or **Notes Master**. The left side of the status bar indicates which master currently is displayed.

The Slide Master in Figure 15.7 includes areas for a master title, bulleted text, the date, and footer text. The company's name—Design Docs, Inc.—has been added as a header on the master slide and, therefore, on all slides in the presentation.

FIGURE 15.7

A Slide Master contains all the elements you might want to appear on a slide.

1 Elements added to the Slide Master

2 Slide Master is indicated

3 Default Slide Master elements

4 Placeholder for slide number

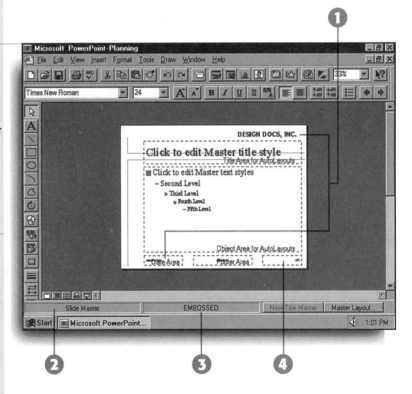

Using Design Templates

A *presentation template* is a saved presentation file containing pre-defined Slide and Title Masters, color schemes, and graphical elements. The design templates provided by Microsoft are designed by professional graphic artists who understand the use of color, space, and design. Each template is designed to convey a certain look, feel, or attitude. Figure 15.8 shows the EMBOSSED template.

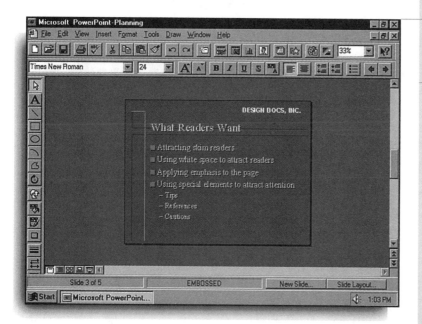

FIGURE 15.8

The EMBOSSED template conveys a formal, sophisticated image.

Select a design template based on the look you want for your presentation, then apply the template to your new or existing presentation file. The template applies to all slides in the presentation. You can apply a new template to a presentation at any time. If you want selected slides in a presentation to look different from the template, you can change any aspect of any slide on an individual basis.

SEE ALSO

➤ *For more information about working with templates, see page 400*

➤ *For more information about working with different color schemes, see page 417*

When creating a new blank presentation, use PowerPoint's default template called Default Design. It doesn't seem like a template because it contains no color (except black and white), no graphical elements, and no stylistic formatting. (Refer to Figure 15.3 to see the Default Design template.) Use this template if you want complete control over your presentation's design, color scheme, and graphical elements; it enables you to start from scratch as much as possible. You can, however, modify aspects of any template, not just the Default Design template.

Understanding Objects and Layouts

PowerPoint slides are made up of objects—the key elements in any slide. Anytime you add text, a graph, a drawing, an organization chart, clip art, a Word table, an Excel spreadsheet, or any other inserted element into a slide, it becomes an *object*. To work with an object, just select it. Then you can change its content, or you can size, move, copy, or delete it. You also can change *attributes* of an object, such as its color, shadow, border, and so on.

If you don't feel confident positioning or arranging objects on a slide, PowerPoint can do the work for you using AutoLayouts. AutoLayouts save you the time and trouble of creating new objects for a new slide, and they can arrange, position, and align the objects for you. Each AutoLayout contains placeholders for various types of objects such as text, clip art, organization charts, and so on. Placeholders appear as faint dotted lines on the slide and contain identifying text such as "double-click to add clip art" or "click to add text."

Each AutoLayout contains different object placeholders in different arrangements. The AutoLayout for a presentation title page, for example, contains two text placeholders: one for a slide title and one for a subtitle. (The title page AutoLayout was shown in Figure 15.3.) The AutoLayout in Figure 15.9 shows three placeholders: one for a slide title, one for text, and one for clip art.

Whenever you add a new slide to a presentation, PowerPoint automatically displays the New Slide dialog box (see Figure 15.10). Use this dialog box to select the desired AutoLayout. If you want to change the AutoLayout for an existing slide, click the **Slide Layout** button on the status bar.

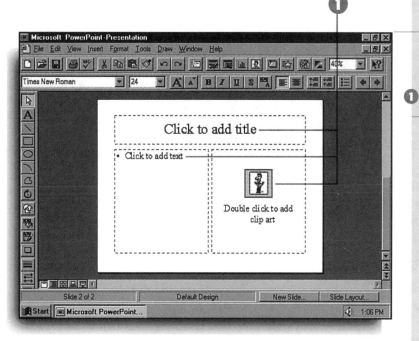

FIGURE 15.9
AutoLayouts ease the tedium of arranging objects on a slide.

❶   Object placeholders

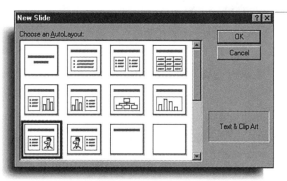

FIGURE 15.10
The New Slide dialog box displays a variety of AutoLayouts.

Adding Objects to PowerPoint Slides

There's no reason for a PowerPoint presentation to contain dull slides full of text. PowerPoint enables you to add many different types of objects to your slides to grab an audience's attention, to add interest or humor, or to illustrate a particular point. Some objects can be created within PowerPoint; others need to be imported from other applications.

To insert an object from another application, choose an option on the **Insert** menu or use one of the buttons on the Standard toolbar. Table 15.4 summarizes the options available on the **Insert** menu.

More information about inserting objects

See Chapter 17, "Entering Slide Content," for more information about inserting objects in a presentation.

TABLE 15.4   Insert menu commands for inserting objects into PowerPoint slides

Object Type	Description
Clip Art	Provides access to a collection of prepared illustrations depicting a wide variety of items and topics. Clip art is an excellent choice if you don't feel confident in your drawing abilities.
Picture	If you have access to other prepared artwork, such as bitmap files, you can insert it into a PowerPoint slide. (PowerPoint recognizes many different picture file formats.)
Movie	If you have access to movie files, such as Microsoft AVI or Quicktime for Windows, you can insert them into a slide.
So**u**nd	Enables you to insert sound files into a slide.
Microsoft **G**raph	An embedded application that enables you to create a chart or graph from tabular data. You create the graph similar to how you create a graph from spreadsheet data in Excel.
Microsoft **W**ord Table	Because Microsoft Word is part of Microsoft Office, you have quick and easy access to Word if you want to insert a table into a slide. The Word table can contain up to 26 columns and up to five rows.
Object	Provides access to a wide variety of object types, such as Microsoft Excel spreadsheets and charts, Word documents, Paintbrush pictures, and Microsoft WordArt.

Creating, Saving, and Opening Presentations

Use templates and the AutoContent Wizard to create polished presentations

Learn to manage your presentations using PowerPoint's views

Create multiple presentations by adding and deleting slides

Understand the different file types for your presentation medium

Creating a New Presentation

To provide maximum flexibility, PowerPoint offers a variety of ways to create a new presentation. You can create a "blank" presentation that contains no color or style enhancements, you can copy the appearance of an existing presentation, or you can get step-by-step help in creating a presentation by using a wizard. (Wizards are described in the following section, "Creating a Presentation Using a Wizard.")

When you open the PowerPoint application, it automatically displays the dialog box in Figure 16.1. This dialog box enables you to choose a method for creating your presentation. You see this dialog box only when you first open PowerPoint.

FIGURE 16.1

Use this dialog box to choose a method for creating a presentation.

The following sections discuss the possible methods you can use to create a presentation.

SEE ALSO

➤ For more information about starting and exiting PowerPoint, see page 348

Creating a Presentation Using a Wizard

Locating the AutoContent Wizard

If you are already in PowerPoint, you can locate the AutoContent Wizard by choosing the **File** menu, selecting **New**, then choosing the **Presentations** tab in the New Presentation dialog box. Double-click the AutoContent Wizard icon.

In PowerPoint, you can create the framework for a new presentation by responding to questions presented by a wizard.

The AutoContent Wizard asks questions about the content of the presentation and, based on your answers, creates an outline. The wizard's outline uses each slide's title as the main heading; the heading appears next to a slide number and a slide icon. You then can enter body text for the slide—using up to five levels if necessary. The wizard helps you rearrange points and slides within the outline. Editing also is easier using the wizard's outline.

Creating a Presentation Using a Template

At times, you might just want to apply a design template to a presentation and leave the topics for you to complete. In such a case, select the **File** menu, select **New**, and then choose the presentation design template option you want to use in the New Presentation dialog box.

SEE ALSO

➤ *For more information about masters and templates, see pages 358 and 400*

To use a template when creating a presentation, select **Template** from the PowerPoint dialog box in Figure 16.1 or from anywhere else in PowerPoint.

Use a design presentation template to create a presentation

1. Choose the **File** menu and select **New**. PowerPoint displays the New Presentation dialog box.

2. Select the **Presentation Designs** tab (see Figure 16.2). The presentation design names are shown in Large Icons view. The other possible views are List and Details. You can select one of these views by clicking the appropriate button in the dialog box, as labeled in the figure.

3. Click any presentation template to see a preview of that design in the lower-right corner of the dialog box. You can scroll the window to view more designs.

4. When you decide on a design, select its icon and choose **OK** to apply it to the presentation.

Creating a Blank Presentation

When creating a blank presentation, PowerPoint uses the DEFAULT.PPT template. The default template uses no colors (only black and white) and includes no styles or enhancements. Creating a blank presentation puts you in complete control of

List view shows more filenames at one time

Use List view to see more presentation designs at a time. You can choose any filename to preview.

Create your own presentation template

To create your own template, you can add colors, lines, and objects to a blank presentation and then save it as a presentation template file type.

the color scheme, the layout, and the style characteristics of your slides. You can leave the presentation blank, or you can add a template, colors, and other enhancements at any time using menu or toolbar commands. Use the blank presentation method when you want maximum flexibility.

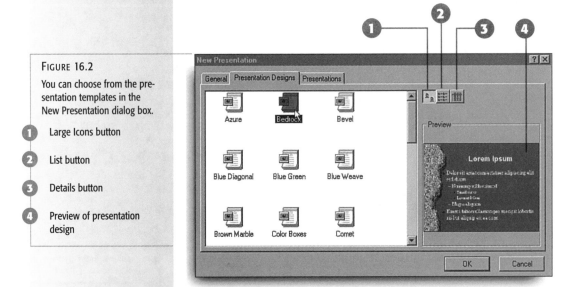

FIGURE 16.2

You can choose from the presentation templates in the New Presentation dialog box.

1 Large Icons button

2 List button

3 Details button

4 Preview of presentation design

Applying existing templates to a presentation

You can use a template from another presentation; it doesn't matter whether the template is PowerPoint's or your own. (If the template is your own, make sure to save the presentation as a presentation template in the **Save as Type** list box of the Save As dialog box.) To apply an existing template to a presentation, choose **Format** and select **Apply Design Template**. Choose the folder containing the template and select the template from the **Name** list. Click **Apply** to close the dialog box and apply the template to the existing presentation.

SEE ALSO

➤ *For more information about working with colors and lines, see page 411*

➤ *For more information about working with color schemes, see page 417*

Create a blank presentation

1. Choose **Blank Presentation** from the choices in the PowerPoint dialog box (refer to Figure 16.1). From elsewhere in PowerPoint, you can select the **File** menu and select **New** or simply press **Ctrl+N**. PowerPoint displays the New Presentation dialog box (refer to Figure 16.2).

2. Select the **General** tab and choose the Blank Presentation icon.

3. Choose **OK**. PowerPoint displays the New Slide dialog box (see Figure 16.3).

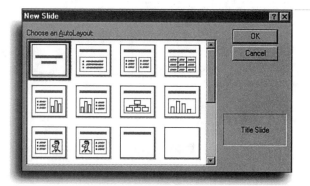

FIGURE 16.3
Choose the layout for the first slide in a blank presentation.

4. Select the layout you want to use for the first slide and click **OK**. PowerPoint displays the first slide in your new presentation, using the layout you specify.

SEE ALSO

➤ *For more information about working with templates, see page 400*

Navigating in a Presentation

When a presentation contains more than one slide, you must be able to easily display the slide you want. The left end of the status bar displays the number of the current slide. To move from one slide to another in Slide view or in Notes Pages view, use the vertical scrollbar. To display the preceding slide, click the Previous Slide button. Click the Next Slide button to display the following slide. The Next Slide and Previous Slide buttons are located at the bottom of the vertical scrollbar (see Figure 16.4).

When a presentation contains a large number of slides, the Previous Slide and Next Slide buttons are not efficient for moving from a slide near the beginning to a slide near the end of the presentation. You can move to a specific slide more quickly by dragging the scroll box in the vertical scrollbar. As you drag the box up or down, PowerPoint displays a slide number and, if you've entered title text, a title to the left of the scrollbar (see Figure 16.5). When you see the number of the slide you want, release the mouse button. PowerPoint goes directly to the slide you specify without moving through all the slides in between.

Use the keyboard to move from slide to slide

If you prefer, you can use the Page Up and Page Down keys to move from one slide to another.

FIGURE 16.4

You can move from slide to slide using the Next Slide and Previous Slide buttons.

 Next Slide button

 Previous Slide button

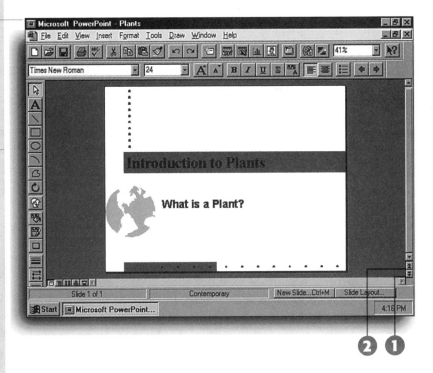

FIGURE 16.5

Dragging the scroll box enables you to move to a specific slide more quickly.

Scrollbar

Slide number and title

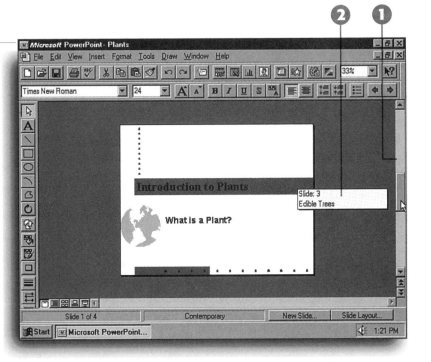

Adding, Inserting, and Deleting Slides

After your presentation file is created, you can add, insert, or delete slides whenever necessary.

Add a slide

1. Click the Insert New Slide button [icon] on the Standard toolbar or the New Slide button on the right side of the status bar. You also can add a new slide by choosing the **Insert** menu and selecting **New Slide** or by pressing **Ctrl+M**. The New Slide dialog box opens (refer to Figure 16.3).

SEE ALSO
➤ *To insert clip art pictures, see page 388*
➤ *To insert other objects, see page 395*

2. Choose an AutoLayout for the new slide.

3. Click **OK**.

The new slide is inserted after the slide currently displayed in Slide view or after the selected slide in Slide Sorter view.

You can delete a slide at any time. Simply display the slide you want to delete, choose the **Edit** menu, and then select **Delete Slide**. You also can select the slide in Slide Sorter view, and then press the Delete key to delete the slide.

Viewing a Presentation

As you work on your presentation, you can view one slide at a time or many slides at once. If you choose to view one slide at a time, you can adjust the individual details of each slide by entering text, formatting, adding pictures, changing colors, and so on. When several slides are completed, you can view them onscreen at the same time as small pictures, or thumbnails, so you can organize them.

PowerPoint offers several ways to view your presentation. Each view has a particular purpose and its own advantages. The five views are summarized in Table 16.1 and are described in detail in the sections that follow.

Try Slide Sorter view

Another way to quickly move from slide to slide is to switch to Slide Sorter view, then double-click the slide you want to view. PowerPoint automatically switches back to Slide view and displays the slide you selected. For more information, see the section "Viewing a Presentation" later in this chapter.

Choose Cancel if you make a mistake

When creating a new presentation, you can use the keystroke combination **Ctrl+N**. This easily can be mistaken for **Ctrl+M**, which is used to create a new slide. If you make this mistake, simply choose Cancel to close the New Presentation dialog box.

Add your own objects to a slide

If you want to add your own objects and text blocks to a slide, choose the blank slide AutoLayout in the New Slide dialog box.

TABLE 16.1   **PowerPoint views**

View		Description
	Slide	Displays an individual slide in full view, which enables you to see the slide in detail.
	Outline	Displays only the text from all slides in the presentation, giving you an overview of the content and the order of the presentation.
	Slide Sorter	Displays a miniature version of every slide in the presentation in proper order, providing an overview of the look and flow of the presentation.
	Notes Page	Displays a miniature version of an individual slide at the top of the screen and a space for speaker's notes below the slide. This enables you to review your notes while viewing the slide.
	Slide Show	Uses the entire screen area to display slides as they would appear during an onscreen slide show. Press Page Down or Page Up to switch from slide to slide. Press Esc to exit Slide Show view.

The quickest way to switch views is to click the view buttons pictured in Table 16.1. These buttons are found in the bottom-left corner of the PowerPoint window. To change the view of the current presentation, just click the button for the view you want to use.

Zooming In and Out

No matter which view you choose, PowerPoint displays your presentation at a preset percentage of its full size. The display percentage is the zoom setting used by PowerPoint. The percentage PowerPoint uses varies, depending on your video driver, the screen resolution you use, and the size of your monitor.

PowerPoint uses a different zoom percentage in each view. The default percentages are designed to provide an optimized view within the window. If you zoom in closer by setting a higher zoom percentage, you reduce the portion of the page you are able to view.

To change the zoom percentage in any view, select an option from the Zoom Control drop-down list 49% in the

See all of the slide on the page

Select **Fit** from the **Zoom Control** drop-down list to make the slide fit completely on the page.

Standard toolbar (see Figure 16.6) or type a new percentage in the Zoom Percentage text box.

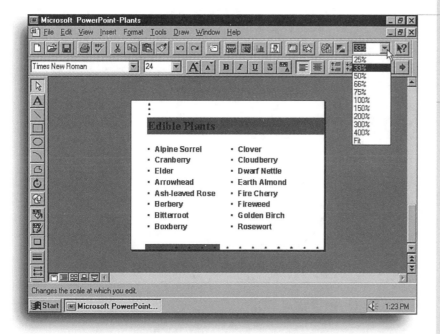

FIGURE 16.6

Choose a percentage from the Zoom Control drop-down list or type a percentage in the Zoom Control text box.

To change the percentage using a menu command, choose the **View** menu and select **Zoom** to display the Zoom dialog box. Select a zoom option or type a custom percentage in the Percent box, and then click **OK**.

Using Slide View

Slide view displays individual slides in the current PowerPoint window. Figure 16.7 shows a presentation displayed in Slide view. This view is the best way to get a detailed picture of each slide. Slide view also is useful when you are entering or changing slide content. To switch from one slide to another, press the Page Up and Page Down keys or use the scrollbar, as described in the "Moving Through a Presentation" section earlier in this chapter.

FIGURE 16.7

Use Slide view to enter and edit text in individual slides.

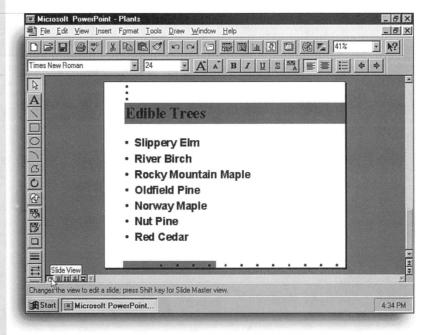

Using Outline View

Outline view displays only the text of multiple slides in outline form, as shown in Figure 16.8. A special set of tools is located to the left of your presentation text in Outline view. To the left of each slide's title is a numbered slide icon. When a slide contains no pictures or graphics, the icon is empty except for a narrow line near the top representing the title. When a slide contains a picture or other object, the icon also contains a graphical representation. This helps you identify at a glance which slides contain objects and which slides contain only text.

To view only the titles of each slide, click the Show Titles button; to view all titles and text, click the Show All button.

Using Slide Sorter View

Slide Sorter view provides an overall perspective of your presentation by displaying a miniature version of each slide on a single screen. The number of slides you can view at one time depends on the video card, driver, monitor, and zoom percentage used.

Rearranging slides

You can move slides and their contents around in Outline view by clicking and dragging the slide icon to the left of each slide's title. To make sure a slide's entire contents move with the title, first collapse the outline to just the titles. To collapse an outline, click the Show Titles button on the toolbar.

The lower the zoom percentage, the more slides you can view at one time.

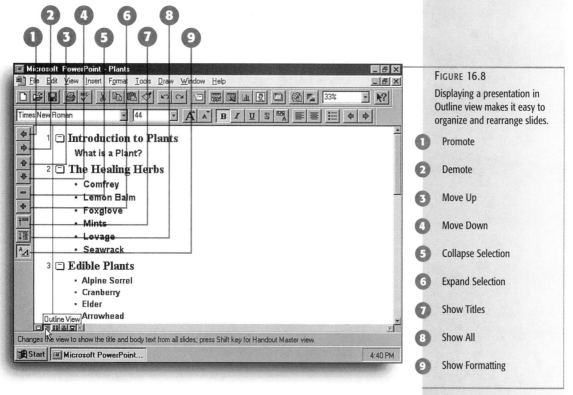

FIGURE 16.8

Displaying a presentation in Outline view makes it easy to organize and rearrange slides.

1. Promote
2. Demote
3. Move Up
4. Move Down
5. Collapse Selection
6. Expand Selection
7. Show Titles
8. Show All
9. Show Formatting

In Slide Sorter view, the slide number appears beneath the bottom-right corner of each slide (see Figure 16.9). When your presentation output is intended to be a slide show, you can rehearse the presentation to determine the display duration for each slide. The amount of time each slide should be displayed during the slide show appears beneath the bottom left corner of each slide.

You also can change the order of slides or copy slides in Slide Sorter view. First, you must select a slide.

To select a slide in Slide Sorter view, either click the slide you want to select or use the arrow keys to highlight a slide. A bold outline surrounds the selected slide. To select multiple slides, press and hold down the Shift key while clicking all the slides you want to select. You also can select multiple slides by clicking and holding down the left mouse button as you drag an outline around the slides you want to include. To cancel a selection, click any blank area of the Slide Sorter view window.

FIGURE 16.9

The slides in this view have been assigned a display duration in Rehearse mode.

1 Timing

2 Slide number

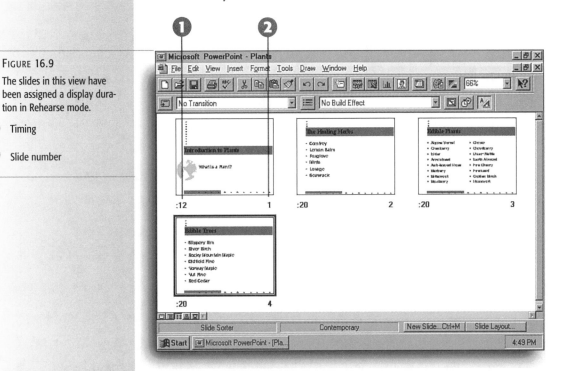

In Slide Sorter view, you can rearrange slides by selecting a slide and dragging it to a new location. As you drag the mouse, the mouse pointer changes to a miniature slide with an up arrow. When you move the pointer between two slides, a vertical bar appears to mark the current insertion point if you release the mouse button. You also can select multiple slides and move them all at once using this method. PowerPoint automatically renumbers the rearranged slides.

Slide Sorter view is the best view for copying slides. Select the slide (or slides) you want to copy, then press and hold down the Ctrl key as you drag the slide to the copy location. The mouse pointer changes to a miniature slide with a plus symbol (+), and a vertical bar appears between slides to mark the insertion point. When you release the mouse button, a copy of the selected slide is inserted in the new location. The slide copy retains any timing assigned to the original. This can be changed by choosing **Slide**

Transition from the shortcut menu, and then changing the **Automatically after** option at the bottom of the dialog box.

Using Notes Pages View

PowerPoint provides notes pages on which you can type notes to use as you make the presentation. The top half of the page displays a smaller version of the slide; the bottom half contains a text object in which you can type your notes (see Figure 16.10).

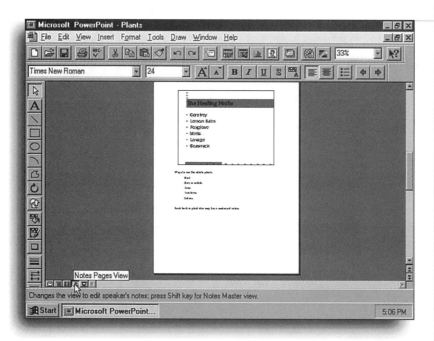

FIGURE 16.10

A slide presentation can be shown in Notes Pages view. To better see the notes onscreen, zoom to 75–100%.

At PowerPoint's default zoom percentage, Notes Pages view displays an entire page onscreen. When typing or editing speaker's notes, it's difficult to read the text at the default percentage. If you use a larger percentage (such as 66–75%), the text is more readable, and you still can view part of the slide content as you type. Another option is to select the text and use the Increase Font Size tool ▣ or the Font Size drop-down list ▣ to make the text more legible.

To change the view to Notes Pages, click the Notes Pages View button ▣ on the horizontal scroll bar or choose the **View** menu and select **Notes Pages**.

Using Slide Show View

Slide Show view enables you to see each slide in your presentation at maximum size. When you use this view, the PowerPoint window is not visible; each slide occupies the complete screen area (see Figure 16.11). If your final output is intended to be an onscreen slide show, Slide Show view can be used to preview your slides to see how they will look during the slide show.

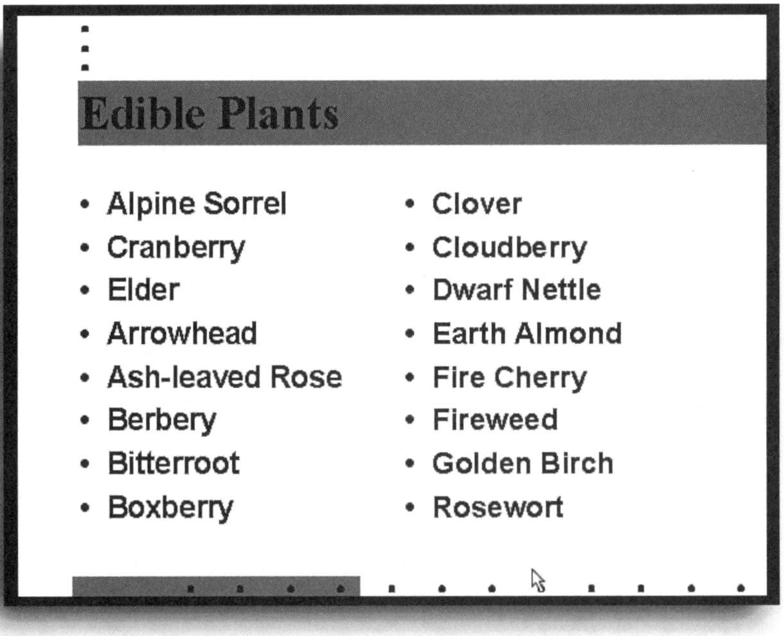

FIGURE 16.11

A presentation in Slide Show view can be run onscreen for customers to see.

Edible Plants

- Alpine Sorrel
- Cranberry
- Elder
- Arrowhead
- Ash-leaved Rose
- Berbery
- Bitterroot
- Boxberry

- Clover
- Cloudberry
- Dwarf Nettle
- Earth Almond
- Fire Cherry
- Fireweed
- Golden Birch
- Rosewort

Begin slide show at slide 1

Slide Show view displays your slides starting with whichever slide is displayed before you switch views. If you want the slide show to begin at slide 1, make sure to select slide 1 before switching to Slide Show view. You also can press Home to move to the first slide and End to move to the last slide in a presentation.

SEE ALSO

➤ *For more information about running a slide show, see page 433*

Saving a Presentation

When you save a presentation, PowerPoint saves all components of the presentation (slides, outline, speaker's notes, and handout pages) in one file.

You can save a file in PowerPoint the same way you save a file in any other Microsoft Office application. The first time you save a file, PowerPoint displays the Save As dialog box whether you choose the **File** menu and select **Save** or choose the **File** menu and select **Save As**. If you want to save an existing file with a different name, on a different disk or directory, or as a different file type, choose the **File** menu and select **Save As**. If you simply want to save changes to an existing file, choose the **File** menu and select **Save** or click the Save button ▦.

You can name the file with a long filename as you would in any other Windows 95 application.

Opening an Existing Presentation

You can open a PowerPoint presentation using the same method you would use in any other Microsoft Office application.

As in many applications, you can open several files at the same time. The active presentation appears on top of other files and its title bar is highlighted. As with all Windows applications, the names of all open presentation files are listed in the **Window** menu and appear on the taskbar.

SEE ALSO

➤ *For more information about finding and opening files, see page 26*

Closing a Presentation

To close an existing presentation, choose the **File** menu and select **Close** or click the x (close) button in the top-right corner of the document window. If you have made changes in the file since you last saved it, PowerPoint asks whether you want to save those changes. Choose **Yes** to save the changes, choose **No** to ignore the changes, or choose **Cancel** to return to the presentation without saving the file.

Entering Slide Content

Work with AutoLayout

Enter and edit text

Insert clip art, tables, and worksheets

Insert graphs, organization charts, and other objects

Reviewing AutoLayout

PowerPoint slides can contain more than just text. You can insert clip art, pictures, tables, worksheets, graphs, organization charts, and other object types into your slides. This chapter teaches you how to choose a slide layout and how to enter and edit slide text. You also learn how to enter information other than text (such as pictures, tables, and graphs).

Chapter 15, "Getting Acquainted with PowerPoint," briefly introduced you to AutoLayout, a PowerPoint feature with 24 prepared slide layouts that contain different object placeholders and arrangements. Using AutoLayout, you can choose a slide layout that contains the object placeholders you need for your current slide. A title slide, for example, contains two text-object placeholders: one for a title and one for a subtitle. After you select a slide layout, you can insert the actual content of your presentation—text, pictures, and graphs—into the placeholders on the slide.

Whenever you add a new slide to a presentation, PowerPoint automatically displays either the Slide Layout or New Slide dialog box, both of which contain 24 AutoLayouts (see Figure 17.1)

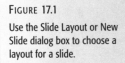

FIGURE 17.1

Use the Slide Layout or New Slide dialog box to choose a layout for a slide.

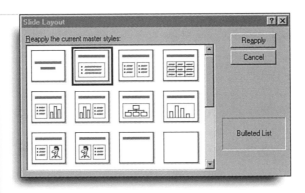

The dialog box in Figure 17.1 is titled Slide Layout. Depending on the method you use to display this dialog box, it also might be titled New Slide. The contents of the dialog box are always the same no matter what name is shown in the title bar. To avoid confusion, this chapter refers to the dialog box as the Slide Layout dialog box.

As you highlight the different AutoLayouts, a description of the currently selected layout appears in the bottom-right corner of the dialog box. This description lists the types of objects included in the layout, such as a title slide, a table, a bulleted list, an organization chart, and so on.

The solid gray line at the top of each slide layout represents the slide's title. Other text in a slide layout is represented by faint gray lines. Text nearly always is formatted with bullets. Placeholders with vertical bars represent graphs; those with a picture represent clip art or pictures. Empty boxes represent placeholders for other objects, which usually are imported from other applications such as Excel.

Apply a new layout to an existing slide

1. Select the slide you want to change. Click the Slide Layout button on the right side of the status bar.

2. Select the layout you want to use for your new slide.

3. Choose the **Apply** button. PowerPoint automatically applies the selected layout to the slide, complete with placeholders for objects.

4. Now you can replace the sample in each placeholder with actual text or another object such as a graph or a table.

SEE ALSO

➤ *For more information about typing and editing, see page 54*

➤ *For more information about using Undo, see page 62*

Be careful when changing the slide layout

Objects that contain information remain in the slide while placeholders for the new layout are added. PowerPoint tries to rearrange the objects so all will fit, but this isn't always possible. The slide can become cluttered with overlapping objects and placeholders, and sometimes an object is deleted. Remember, you can always use the Undo button 🔄 on the Standard toolbar.

Entering and Editing Text

Almost every slide in a presentation contains text of some kind, even if it's just a title. Entering and editing text in PowerPoint is similar to entering and editing text in any other Office application. The following sections describe how to enter text in your slides and how to edit the text when necessary.

Typing the Content for Your Slides

One method of entering slide text involves replacing the sample text in a slide placeholder with your own text. The slide shown in Figure 17.2, for example, includes two placeholders for text:

one that contains a sample title and one that contains a bulleted list. The third placeholder is for clip art. A faint dotted line appears around each placeholder.

FIGURE 17.2

This slide layout contains two placeholders for text and one placeholder for clip art.

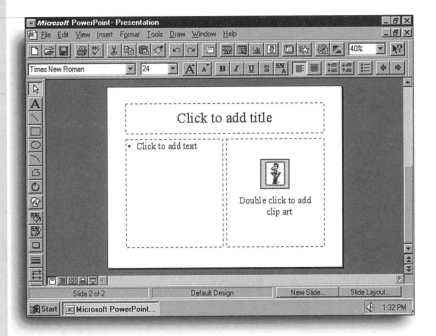

Type content on your slide

1. Click anywhere within a placeholder to select it. The faint outline is replaced by a wide-hashed border, as shown in Figure 17.3.

   • In a title or subtitle placeholder, the insertion point can be centered or left-aligned.

   • In a bulleted-list placeholder, the sample text disappears and the bullet remains. The insertion point is positioned where the text begins.

2. Type the replacement text for your slide inside the selected placeholder.

   • When entering titles and subtitles, press Enter only when you want to begin a new centered line of text.

   • When entering bulleted lists, press Enter only when you want to begin a new bulleted item. If your bulleted text is longer than one line, PowerPoint automatically wraps the text to the next line and aligns it appropriately.

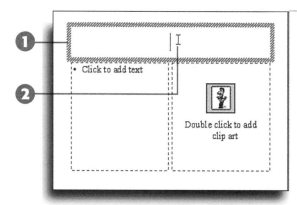

FIGURE 17.3

A wide-hashed border indicates which text placeholder is selected.

1 This border indicates the selected placeholder.

2 An insertion point replaces the sample text inside the placeholder, indicating that you can enter new text.

3. When you finish entering text, deselect the object by clicking either a blank area of the slide or the gray border around the slide.

The object no longer is defined by the faint dotted line (see Figure 17.4). The absence of the dotted line gives you a more realistic idea of how the completed slide will look.

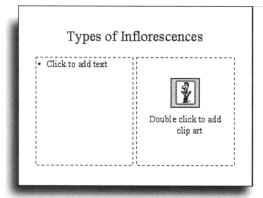

FIGURE 17.4

When the sample text of a placeholder is replaced, the dotted border is removed.

Creating New Text Objects

You might need to add a label or other text that is not part of a standard placeholder. Suppose your slide contains a title and a bulleted list like the one in Figure 17.5. If you want to add a note that is not formatted like the bulleted list, you must add the note as a separate object.

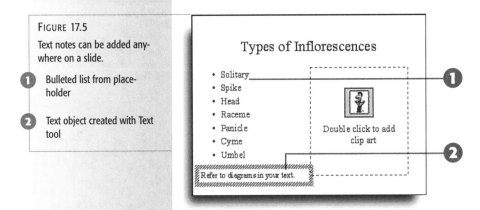

Create a text object

1. Click the Text Tool button **A** in the Drawing toolbar.
2. Position the pointer (now a vertical bar) where you want the text box to be.
3. Click the mouse button. A text box the size of one character appears. An insertion point is visible in the text box.
4. Type the desired text. The text box expands to accommodate the text you enter. If you want to type on a new line, press Enter.

SEE ALSO
➤ *For more information about selecting text, see page 58*

Changing Text and Correcting Errors

Change text in an object

1. Click the object you want to change. An insertion point appears, indicating that you are able to edit the text.
2. Use standard editing conventions to change text, as summa-rized in Table 17.1.
3. To deselect the text box, click any blank area of the slide or the gray area surrounding the slide.

TABLE 17.1   Editing conventions for text objects

Action	Result
Arrow keys	Move the insertion point right, left, up, or down within the text.
Backspace or Delete	Erases characters (to the left and right, respectively) at the insertion point. Also clears any selected text from the object without placing it in the Clipboard.
Click and drag the mouse	Selects a string of characters.
Double-click a word	Selects the entire word.
Triple-click a line or paragraph	Selects the entire line (title) or paragraph (bullet item).
Ctrl+A	Selects all text in a selected text object.
Ctrl+click	Selects an entire sentence.
Ctrl+X	Cuts the selected text and places it in the Clipboard.
Ctrl+C	Copies the selected text to the Clipboard.
Ctrl+V	Pastes the text from the Clipboard.

Checking Your Spelling in PowerPoint

The spelling checker in PowerPoint compares every word in your document with a dictionary file, much the way any other Microsoft Office application does. When the spelling checker finds a word that's not in the dictionary file, it highlights the word in your slide and displays the word in the Spelling dialog box, as shown in Figure 17.6.

The spelling checker moves through your presentation one slide at a time. It then checks the speaker's notes (if there are any) before closing the Spelling dialog box. You can exit the spelling checker at any time by clicking the **Close** button in the Spelling dialog box.

Check the spelling in a presentation file

1. Click the Spelling button 🔤 on the Standard toolbar to display the Spelling dialog box. The spelling checker highlights

---

Additional editing tools

In addition to the keyboard shortcuts listed in Table 17.1, you can use the **Cut**, **Copy**, **Paste**, **Clear**, and **Select All** commands (on the **Edit** menu) to edit text. When text is selected on a slide, the **Cut**, **Copy**, and **Paste** commands also appear on the shortcut menu when you click the right mouse button.

Spelling checker does not catch everything

The spelling checker checks text in all objects in a presentation file except those objects that contain text imported from other applications.

the first unrecognized word in the presentation file and displays the word in the **Not in Dictionary** box.

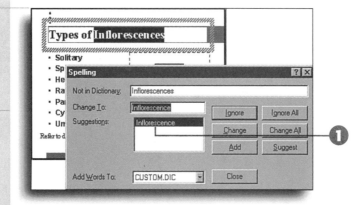

2. Choose the appropriate command button (**Ignore**, **Ignore All**, **Change**, **Change All**, or **Add**). The spelling checker takes the indicated action, and then highlights the next unrecognized word.

3. Repeat step 2 until the spelling checker displays a message that the entire presentation has been checked.

4. Choose **OK**.

SEE ALSO
➤ For more information about checking spelling, see page 100
➤ For more information about AutoCorrect, see page 102

Inserting Clip-Art Pictures

One of the best ways to spice up a slide show is to insert a clip-art drawing. The ClipArt Gallery contains many drawings covering a wide range of topics.

You can insert clip art into a slide in several ways. If you select a slide layout with a clip-art placeholder, simply double-click the placeholder to choose a clip-art file to insert.

You can use the Insert Clip Art button on the Standard toolbar to insert clip art onto a slide that doesn't have a clip-art placeholder. No matter which method you use to access clip art,

AutoCorrect fixes common errors

You can use PowerPoint's Auto-Correct feature to automatically correct common typing errors. (To open AutoCorrect, choose the **Tools** menu and select **AutoCorrect**.) If you constantly type "wrod" rather than "word," for example, you can add this to the AutoCorrect list. Anytime you type the wrong letters and press the spacebar, PowerPoint automatically corrects your typing.

Using clip art from Microsoft Office

The first time you attempt to access clip art, PowerPoint asks whether you want to add clip-art files from Microsoft Office. Responding **Yes** makes the clip-art files available for you to insert into your slides.

the next step is to select a file in the ClipArt Gallery 2.0 dialog box (see Figure 17.7).

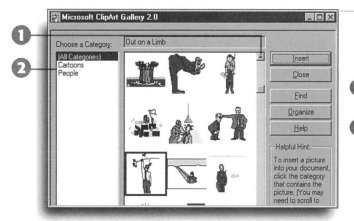

FIGURE 17.7

The ClipArt Gallery 2.0 dialog box enables you to choose from a variety of pictures.

1 Use the scrollbar to see each picture in a category

2 Click a category to see the pictures in that category

Add a clip-art drawing to your slide

1. Display the slide into which you want to insert clip art.

2. Click the Clip Art button 🖼 on the Standard toolbar; if your slide contains a clip-art placeholder, double-click it. The Microsoft ClipArt Gallery 2.0 dialog box opens.

3. Select a category in the **Categories** list.

4. Select a picture and then click **OK**. PowerPoint closes the Microsoft ClipArt Gallery 2.0 dialog box and inserts the picture into your slide. Figure 17.8 shows a slide with a clip-art picture.

Add clip art to the Slide Master

If you want a piece of clip art to appear on every slide in the presentation, insert it on the Slide Master.

FIGURE 17.8

Adding clip art to a slide makes a presentation more interesting and more professional-looking.

Letting PowerPoint Choose Art for You

Have PowerPoint pick the art for you

1. Choose the **Tools** menu and select **AutoClipArt**. PowerPoint takes a while to analyze your presentation, and then goes to the AutoClipArt dialog box shown in Figure 17.9.

FIGURE 17.9

Click **View Clip Art** to see which clip-art figures PowerPoint found that match words in your presentation.

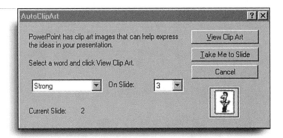

2. Select the word that brings up the clip art in the pull-down box.
3. Click on the **Take Me to Slide** button to go to the slide in the presentation. If necessary, drag the title bar of the dialog box so you can view the slide.
4. To add the art, click on the **View Clip Art** button and choose one of the objects in the ClipArt Gallery, as shown in Figure 17.10. Choose the **Insert** button if you want to insert the picture. If you don't want to insert the picture, choose the **Close** button.

FIGURE 17.10

Choose an object in the **Pictures** box; then choose **Insert** to add the object to the slide.

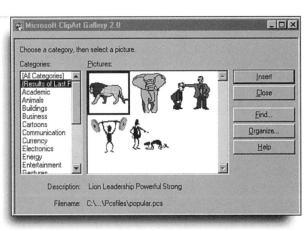

5. To add another picture, repeat steps 2 through 4. Choose
   Cancel or click on the x (close) button in the upper-right
   corner when finished.

6. Move or resize the pictures as necessary when you return to
   the presentation.

Inserting a Word Table or an Excel Worksheet

A table of data can convey useful information on a slide.
Although PowerPoint's text-editing tools don't provide the
means to create a table, PowerPoint enables you to use Word
or Excel to create any tables you need.

Create a worksheet or table

1. Click either the Insert Microsoft Excel Worksheet button
   [icon] or the Insert Microsoft Word Table button [icon] in the
   Standard toolbar. You'll see a drop-down grid of cells. This
   grid enables you to define the size of your table or worksheet (see Figure 17.11).

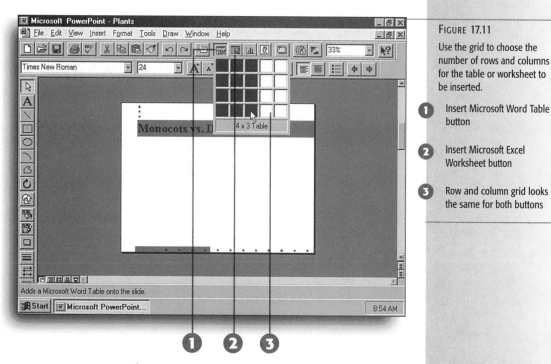

FIGURE 17.11

Use the grid to choose the
number of rows and columns
for the table or worksheet to
be inserted.

① Insert Microsoft Word Table
button

② Insert Microsoft Excel
Worksheet button

③ Row and column grid looks
the same for both buttons

2. Click and drag the mouse pointer across the cells in the grid to indicate how many rows and columns you want in the table or worksheet. The cells you select are highlighted, and the dimensions are listed below the grid.

When you release the mouse button, PowerPoint inserts a special object into your slide. If you're inserting a Microsoft Word table, the object looks like the one in Figure 17.12.

FIGURE 17.12

Inserting a Word table provides Word's formatting flexibility.

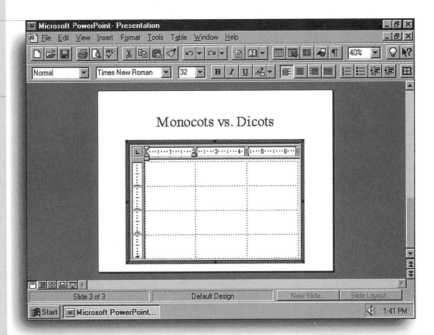

PowerPoint's Standard toolbar and menu bar temporarily are replaced by the Word menus and toolbar. All Word features and commands are available to you while you create your table. In effect, you are using Word inside a PowerPoint window.

SEE ALSO

➤ *For more information about creating Word tables, see page 172*

➤ *For more information about creating a worksheet, see pages 194 and 199*

Create the content of your table

1. Click the area in which you want to add text or press Tab to move the insertion point from left to right across the cells in the table.

Press the up- and down-arrow keys to move the insertion point from one row to another. Use standard editing conventions to enter and edit text in the table.

2. Enter text as you would in Word or Excel.

3. When the table is complete, deselect it by clicking any blank area outside the table or the gray area surrounding the slide.

When the table no longer is the selected object, the PowerPoint menus and toolbar return. You can make changes in the table at any time by double-clicking anywhere inside it. Whenever the table is selected, the Word menus and toolbar automatically return.

The same principles that govern Word tables hold true for Excel worksheets. When you insert a worksheet, you enter, edit, and format the data in Excel. Click anywhere outside the worksheet to return to PowerPoint. When you click the Insert Excel Worksheet button 🔳 in the PowerPoint toolbar, a drop-down grid appears. Click and drag the mouse pointer across the cells in the grid to indicate the number of rows and columns you want in the worksheet. PowerPoint inserts a special worksheet object into your slide, and PowerPoint's menus and toolbar are replaced by the Excel menus and toolbar.

Use Excel's commands and tools to create and edit your worksheet. When the worksheet is complete, deselect it by clicking any blank area on the slide or the border of the slide. The standard PowerPoint menus and toolbar return.

SEE ALSO

➤ *For more information about formatting text, see pages 79 and 81*

➤ *For more information about editing worksheet data, see page 210*

➤ *For more information about formatting numbers, see page 230*

Inserting an Organization Chart

Organization charts can be added to PowerPoint presentations. An organization chart can convey information about new management, a group or department reorganization, or people to contact for specific types of information.

Resize the table object

You can resize the table by dragging one of the corner or side handles.

Format text as you would in Word

You can select text in the table and change the typeface, size, attributes, alignment, and so on, just as you can in Word.

Copy a chart from Excel

Charts are graphical representations of data in worksheets. In a presentation, a bar, pie, or area chart often can depict data more clearly than words can. In PowerPoint, you can insert a chart into a slide by copying a chart from Microsoft Excel.

Insert an organization chart into a PowerPoint slide

1. Select a slide layout that includes a placeholder for an organization chart. Click the Slide Layout button at the bottom right of the PowerPoint window to display the Slide Layout dialog box (see Figure 17.13).

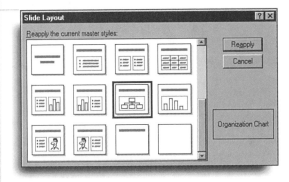

2. In the Slide Layout dialog box, highlight the layout that includes an organization chart and choose **Reapply**. PowerPoint applies the layout to the current slide, inserting an organization-chart placeholder.

3. To access the Microsoft Organization Chart, double-click the placeholder. After a few seconds, the Microsoft Organization Chart window displays. Figure 17.14 shows a completed organization chart.

4. Enter the appropriate information in the sample organization chart, using Microsoft Organization Chart commands. Because Microsoft Organization Chart is a separate application, it contains its own help files. If you are not familiar with this application, select any of the topics listed in the **Help** menu, or press **F1**.

5. To save the organization chart information, choose the **File** menu and select **Update [filename]**.

6. To return to your presentation document, choose the **File** menu and select **Exit and Return to [filename]**. The organization chart is inserted into the current slide. To deselect the organization chart, click any blank area of the slide or the gray area surrounding the slide.

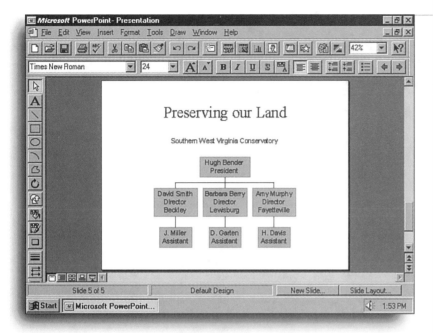

FIGURE 17.14
The Microsoft Organization Chart enables you to create simple or complex charts for your presentation.

Inserting Other Objects

This chapter has shown you how to insert clip art, a Word table, an Excel worksheet, and an organization chart into a PowerPoint slide. You can insert many other types of objects by choosing the **Insert** menu and selecting **Object**. This command opens another application on top of your PowerPoint window, enabling you to create a new file or to open an existing file within that application.

Insert a new file from another application

1. Display the PowerPoint slide into which you want to insert an object.

2. Choose the **Insert** menu and select **Object**. PowerPoint displays the Insert Object dialog box (see Figure 17.15). The **Object Type** list box displays the types of files you can insert into a PowerPoint slide.

3. Select the **Create New** option.

4. Select the **Display As Icon** option if you want to display the object as an icon. (This is optional.)

Objects related to applications you have installed

The Insert Object feature of PowerPoint works by opening another application; that application must be installed on your computer.

FIGURE 17.15

The Insert Object dialog box lists the types of objects that can be inserted onto a slide.

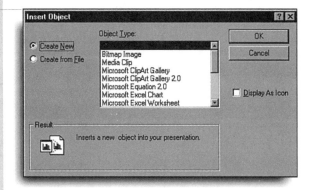

5. Select the object you want to insert from the **Object Type** list, and then click **OK**. The Insert Object dialog box closes, and the window for the appropriate application opens on top of the PowerPoint window.

6. Use the application as you normally would. You can create a new file if necessary or simply select an item (such as an equation or a clip-art file). If you select an item, PowerPoint inserts the item and closes the application. If you create a new file, return to PowerPoint by choosing the **Exit and Return to [filename]** command from the open application's **File** menu. The application window closes, and the file you created is inserted into the current PowerPoint slide.

7. To deselect the object, click any blank area on the slide or the gray area surrounding the slide.

If you want to insert an existing file onto your slide that was created in another application, select the **Create from File** option in the Insert Object dialog box. When you insert an existing file from another application, the file is inserted onto the PowerPoint slide directly. PowerPoint does not open the application used to create the file. If you want to modify the file, you must open the application by double-clicking the object after it is inserted into your PowerPoint slide.

Insert an existing file from another application

1. Display the PowerPoint slide into which you want to insert an object.

2. Choose the **Insert** menu and select **Object**. PowerPoint
displays the Insert Object dialog box.

3. Select the **Create from File** option. PowerPoint modifies
the Insert Object dialog box to match the one in Figure
17.16.

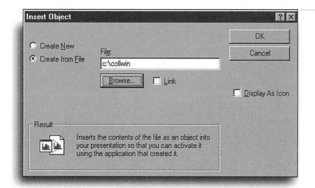

FIGURE 17.16

The Insert Object dialog box
changes if you create from a
file instead of creating a new
object.

4. If you know the name of the file, type the complete path-
name in the **File** text box.

If you don't know the name of the file, click the **Browse**
button to display the Browse dialog box with a directory
tree. Select the correct filename, and then click **OK**. The
Browse dialog box closes, and you return to the Insert
Object dialog box. The filename you selected now appears
in the **File** text box.

5. Select the **Display As Icon** option if you want to display the
object as an icon. (This is optional.)

6. Click **OK** in the Insert Object dialog box. The file you specified is inserted into your PowerPoint slide without opening
the application used to create the file.

7. To deselect the inserted object, click any blank area on the
slide or the gray area surrounding the slide.

Enhancing a Presentation

Customize a template to make your presentation shine

Master the art of enhancing text

Use PowerPoint tools to adjust spacing and alignment

Emphasize points using customized bullets

Add visual impact

Enhance objects using border styles, fill patterns, and shadows

Learn to create custom color schemes

Working with Templates

In this chapter, you see the many different techniques you can use to give your slides a powerful presence. You don't have to be a graphic arts expert; even the simplest touches can make a world of difference in the appearance and impact of a presentation.

In Chapter 15, "Getting Acquainted with PowerPoint," you learned that templates are saved presentation files for which special graphic elements, colors, font sizes, font styles, slide backgrounds, and other special effects have been defined. PowerPoint includes templates designed for black-and-white overheads, color overheads, and onscreen slide shows.

Using a template is the quickest and easiest way to create professional-looking presentations because it takes the guesswork and experimentation out of designing a presentation. PowerPoint templates are designed by graphic arts professionals who understand the elements required to achieve a certain effect and convey a particular attitude.

SEE ALSO

➤ *For more information about masters and templates, see page 358*

Choosing a Template

To specify a template when you create a new presentation, select the **Template** option in the PowerPoint dialog box that displays automatically when you start the program.

Figure 18.1 shows a preview of a presentation using the Blue Weave presentation design.

In the New Presentation dialog box, you can choose one of the following tabs:

- *General*. Contains the blank presentation or default format. Using this basic black-and-white presentation template, you can set your own format by making changes to the master template.

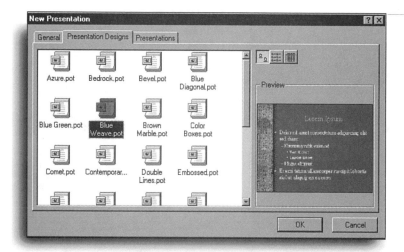

FIGURE 18.1
The Blue Weave presentation design creates a simple grid and design element border template.

- *Presentation Designs*. Contains professionally designed templates on which you can base a presentation. Each presentation design includes a color scheme, graphics such as lines or art, and a master with complete text formatting.

- *Presentations*. Contains many specific preset presentation templates (see Figure 18.2) that include color schemes and font formatting in addition to slide layouts with suggestions for slide content. For example, one presentation is titled "Training" another "Selling a Product." The Presentations tab also includes the AutoContent Wizard, which steps you through the process of creating your own presentation. Select the presentation that best suits your needs.

If you choose one of the presentation designs—such as Azure, Bevel, Blue Diagonal, Embossed, and so on—PowerPoint displays the New Slide dialog box from which you choose an AutoLayout. When you choose the layout, PowerPoint applies it to the slide template. Figure 18.3 illustrates the Blue Weave template used with a Title slide.

SEE ALSO

➤ *For more information about AutoLayout, see page 382*

FIGURE 18.2

Click the Presentations tab to
show a list of preset templates
with suggested content.

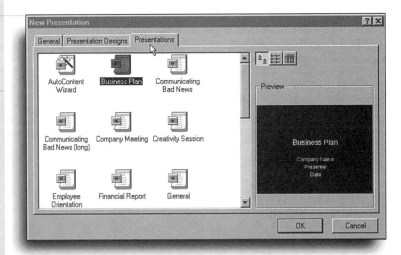

FIGURE 18.3

Use a template when you
already have an idea of the
content of your presentation.

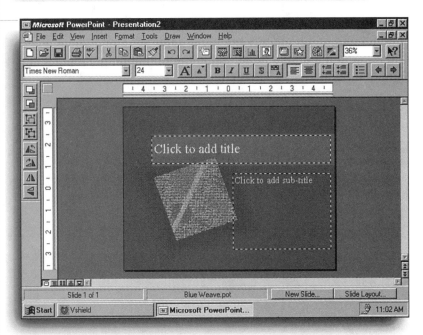

Figure 18.4 illustrates the preset slide presentation Reporting
Progress. Notice the second slide suggests that you define the
subject as a title for the slide and then break the subject into
smaller topics and list them with the bullets. Other slides in this
presentation suggest overall status, background information, key
issues, and future steps.

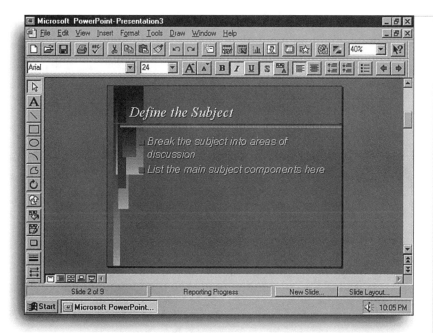

FIGURE 18.4
PowerPoint's preformatted presentations guide you by suggesting slide content and
format.

To enter text into any of the Presentation text blocks, click the
text block, delete the text, and then enter your own. You also can
add new slides, objects, and other enhancements to the presentation.

SEE ALSO

➤ *For more information about inserting clip-art pictures, see page 388*

Altering a Template

After you select a template for your presentation, you might
want to change its characteristics. You might decide to use a different font and larger point size for your slide titles or to add a
graphic element to the template. You can choose to change items
on just one slide or on all slides. You might change, for example,
the font on just one slide's title to set it apart from the other
slides. On the other hand, you can make changes to all slides for
consistency by changing the Slide Master.

To make changes that affect all slides in the presentation quickly
and easily, change the Slide Master. To access the Slide Master,

**Slide Master changes affect entire
presentation**

The Slide Master looks very
much like a presentation slide,
but any changes made here
affect all slides in the presentation.

choose the **View** menu, then select **Master**, and choose **Slide Master** from the resulting menu.

You can change the text in a slide by modifying the font, style, color, and so on. In addition, you can change fill and line colors of objects or entire color schemes. (See the sections "Enhancing Text" and "Working with Colors and Line Styles" later in this chapter.)

Applying a Different Template

One major change you can make to a slide presentation is to change the template, or presentation design, you're using. When you change the template, you change color schemes, some graphic elements, and the master template. Changing templates does not change "Click here" box contents; added objects such as text blocks, charts, or drawings; slide layouts; or the number of slides in the presentation.

Change the template of the active presentation

1. Choose the **Format** menu; then select **Apply Design Template** to open the dialog box shown in Figure 18.5.

Caution: Double-check your presentation for content

Sometimes, when changing from one template to another, you might gain an extra "Click here" box or lose a title or subtitle because of individual designs. Check all slides carefully after changing templates to make sure all of your slide contents are there. If you're missing something, you can either go back to the original template or add the missing text.

FIGURE 18.5

Choose the desired template from the Name list in the Apply Design Template dialog box.

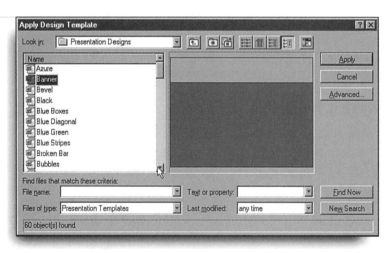

2. Choose **Presentation Designs** in the **Look in** box, if it is not already selected.

3. Select a template name; then click **Apply** or press Enter to select the highlighted template. The dialog box closes, and PowerPoint applies the new template to the active presentation.

Figure 18.6 illustrates how a template can create an overall impression for your slide presentation. PowerPoint includes more than 50 templates for you to try.

Preview templates

To preview templates, click each template in the Name list. A sample of the highlighted template is displayed to the right in the dialog box.

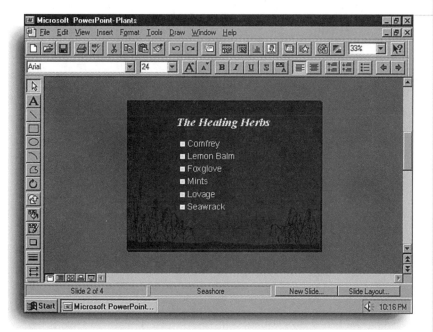

FIGURE 18.6
Use a template that best suits the contents of your presentation.

SEE ALSO
➤ *For more information about masters and templates, see page 358*

Enhancing Text

When you enter text in a slide, the font, style (regular, bold, or italic), size, color, and special effects (underline, shadow, and so on) of the text conform to the settings specified in the master assigned to the current template. The International template, for example, uses the 44-point Times New Roman font in gray for slide titles and the 32-point Arial font in white shadowed for slide text. If you want to use a different font, style, size, color, or effect, you can change these settings (collectively called *font set-tings*) for all slides in a presentation by altering the slide master, or you can change font settings only for selected text objects.

Choosing a Font, Style, and Color for Text

To change font settings, select the text you want to change; then choose the **Format** menu and select **Font**, or select the **Font** command on the shortcut menu, to display the Font dialog box (see Figure 18.7). The **Font**, **Font Style**, **Size**, and **Color** settings are self-explanatory; these options are available in most word processing, spreadsheet, and graphics programs.

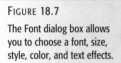

FIGURE 18.7

The Font dialog box allows you to choose a font, size, style, color, and text effects.

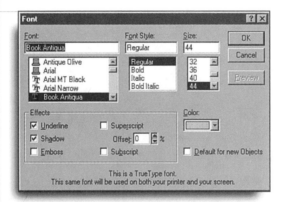

The **Effects** area, however, contains some options with which you might not be familiar. The **Shadow** option adds a shadow at the bottom and the right side of each character. The **Emboss** option gives the text the appearance of raised letters by using a light color for the characters and a faint shadow behind each character. The **Subscript** option drops a selected character slightly below the normal line level, as in H_2O, whereas the **Superscript** option raises a selected character, as in 10^5. When you choose either of these options, you can specify the **Offset** percentage.

Choose the desired formatting and click **OK**.

You also can change specific format settings by clicking the Formatting toolbar buttons listed in Table 18.1.

TABLE 18.1 Font formatting options

Button	Button Name	Description
Times New Roman	Font Face	Changes the font of selected text
24	Font Size	Changes the font size of selected text
A	Increase Font Size	Increases the font size
A	Decrease Font Size	Decreases the font size
B	Bold	Makes selected text bold
I	Italic	Makes selected text italic
U	Underline	Underlines selected text
S	Text Shadow	Adds a drop shadow to selected text
A	Text Color	Changes the color of selected text

SEE ALSO

➤ *For more information about formatting documents, see page 73*

Changing Line and Paragraph Spacing

Just as the template defines color schemes, graphics, and other characteristics for a presentation, the master attached to the template defines the line spacing for text in a text object. PowerPoint enables you to set the spacing between lines, as well as the amount of space before and after paragraphs. In most templates, the default spacing is 1 line, the space after paragraphs is 0, and the space before paragraphs is 0.2 or 0.

You might want to change line or paragraph spacing, depending on the content of your slides.

Change line and paragraph spacing

1. Select the text for which you want to adjust line or paragraph spacing, either in the master or on an individual slide.

2. Choose the **Format** menu; then select **Line Spacing**. PowerPoint displays the Line Spacing dialog box, as shown in Figure 18.8.

FIGURE **18.8**

Use the Line Spacing dialog box to set line and paragraph spacing.

3. In the **Line Spacing**, **Before Paragraph**, and **After Paragraph** boxes, enter the number of lines or points to be used. If you prefer to use points rather than lines, be sure to choose the Points setting in each drop-down list.

4. Click **OK**. PowerPoint returns to your slide and reformats the selected text.

You also can change the line spacing by clicking the Formatting toolbar buttons listed in Table 18.2.

TABLE 18.2   **Line spacing and paragraph formatting options**

Button	Button Name	Description
![button]	Increase Paragraph Spacing	Increases the line spacing for the selected text
![button]	Decrease Paragraph Spacing	Decreases the line spacing for the selected text

Use either before or after paragraph spacing– not both

When setting paragraph spacing, specify a setting for **Before Paragraph** or **After Paragraph**, but not both. If you set both options, the actual space between paragraphs will be the sum of the two settings.

Aligning Text

Alignment refers to the horizontal positioning of text within a text object. In presentation slides, text generally is left-aligned for paragraphs or bullets and centered for titles. However, you can also justify or right-align text. Table 18.3 describes the alignment options.

TABLE 18.3   Alignment options

Button	Alignment	Result
	Left	Aligns text along the left edge of a text object
	Right	Aligns text along the right edge of a text object
	Center	Aligns text at the center point of the text object so that an equal number of characters are to the right and left of the center point
	Justify	Aligns text along both the right and left edges so that the characters in a line cover the entire width of a text object

Because alignment involves horizontal positioning of text at margins or at the center point of a text object, alignment affects entire paragraphs. In other words, you cannot align a single word or line in a paragraph.

You don't have to select any text to align a single paragraph; PowerPoint aligns the entire paragraph in which the insertion point is located. To align several paragraphs, select a portion of text in each paragraph and then choose an alignment style.

Change the alignment of text

1. Select the object that contains the text you want to align.

2. Place the insertion point anywhere in the paragraph you want to align or select a portion of each paragraph you want to align.

3. Choose the **F**o**rmat** menu; then select **A**lignment or choose Alignment from the shortcut menu. The Alignment cascading menu is displayed.

4. Choose **L**eft, **R**ight, **C**enter, or **J**ustify. PowerPoint realigns the current paragraph or selected paragraphs.

Adding Bulleted Text

In addition to assigning styles, sizes, and spacing to various fonts you use in your slides, you also can format text to include bullets. In PowerPoint, you can use the default "Click here"

Add the Right and Justify buttons to a toolbar

The Right and Justify buttons are not available in the default formatting toolbar. If you use this alignment option often, you can customize this toolbar or another toolbar to include these buttons. Click the right mouse button on any toolbar and choose **Customize**. In the **Categories** list box, choose Format. From the Buttons listed, drag the Right and Justify buttons to the desired location on any toolbar.

Alignment suggestions

Use center-aligned or right-aligned text for headings or short lists or phrases. Use left-aligned text for heads, bulleted lists, or paragraphs of text.

Bulleted versus numbered lists

Use a bulleted list to show equal importance for each item in the list. Use a numbered list to show some kind of priority or sequence for the items in the list.

bulleted lists, or you can create a list in a text block and assign a custom bullet.

When working with bullets, use the Bullet On/Off button 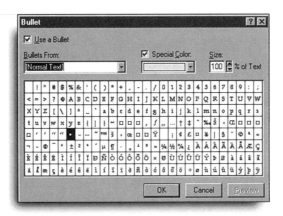 to show or hide the bullets. For example, you can turn off bullets for several items on a list or just one item, if you want to skip some text between bulleted items.

Add bullets to text or to customize the bullet used

1. Select the text to be bulleted or position the insertion point on the first line of text.

2. Choose the **Format** menu; then select **Bullet**. The Bullet dialog box is displayed (see Figure 18.9).

FIGURE 18.9

You can use any available font, such as Symbol or Wingdings, to create a bullet.

3. In **Bullets From**, choose the font you want to use for the bullet.

4. You can use the color assigned in the template (and displayed in the **Special Color** box), or you can choose a new color.

5. Size the bullet by changing the percentage in the **Size** box.

6. Choose **OK** to apply the bullet to the text.

Viewing bullets enlarged

Click any bullet in the dialog box to display an enlarged view of the bullet. To scan the symbols quickly, press the left or right arrow key on the keyboard; each symbol you move to is displayed enlarged.

SEE ALSO

➤ *For more information about inserting objects, see page 395*

Working with Colors and Line Styles

All objects that you draw in PowerPoint (except lines) have a fill color, line color, and line style. The *fill color* is the color inside an object; the *line color* is the frame that defines the boundaries of an object; and the *line style* defines the width or style of the object's frame.

For any given object, you can turn off the fill color and line color. In most templates, for example, the line that frames a text object is turned off, because text generally looks better in the slide without a frame. For other objects (such as shapes that you create with the drawing tools), the object's frame usually is visible, and the object has a fill color.

In most templates, an object's line style is a narrow solid line. You can choose any of five wider line styles or any of four double or triple lines. In addition, you can change a solid line to a dashed, dotted, or mixed line by choosing one of the four dashed-line options. If an object is a straight line or arc rather than a shape, you can add arrowheads to either end or to both ends of the line or arc.

Choosing Fill and Line Colors and Line Styles

Use the Colors and Lines dialog box (see Figure 18.10) to set line, fill, and line-style options.

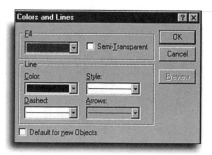

FIGURE 18.10

Use the Colors and Lines dialog box to define an object's color and frame style.

Change an object's fill color

1. Select the object.

2. Choose the **F**o**rmat** menu; then select **Colors and Li**n**es** or choose Colors and Lines from the shortcut menu. The Colors and Lines dialog box is displayed, showing the current fill color in the **F**ill box.

3. Click the arrow to open the **Fill** drop-down list and display the available fill color options. Then choose from the following options:

   * Select the **No Fill** option to remove the fill color from the object.
   * Select one of the colors (derived from the current template).
   * Choose **Background** to set the fill color of the selected object to match the slide background color.
   * Select the **Other Color** option to open the dialog box shown in Figure 18.11. Select the desired color from the palette on the Standard tab or choose another color on the Custom tab. Choose **OK** to return to the Colors and Lines dialog box.

FIGURE 18.11

The Colors dialog box displays a color palette.

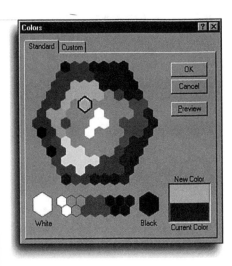

4. Click **OK** in the Colors and Lines dialog box. PowerPoint returns to your slide and changes the fill color or pattern of the selected object.

5. Click any blank area of the screen to deselect the object.

Change an object's line color or line style or add dashed lines or arrowheads

1. Select the object.

2. Choose the **F̲ormat** menu; then select **Colors and Li̲nes** or choose Colors and Lines from the shortcut menu. The Colors and Lines dialog box is displayed, showing the current line color in the Line **C̲olor** box.

3. Click the arrow to open the Line **C̲olor** drop-down list and display the available options. Then choose from the following options:

- Select the **No Line** option to remove the object's line color.
- Select one of the colors (derived from the current template).
- Select the **Other Color** option, which displays the Colors dialog box (refer to Figure 18.11). Select a color from the Standard or Custom tab and then choose **OK**.

4. To select a different line style, highlight a style in the Line **S̲tyle** list.

5. To use a dashed line, highlight a style in the **D̲ashed** list.

6. To add arrowheads to a line or arc, select an option in the **A̲rrows** list.

7. Click **OK** in the Colors and Lines dialog box. PowerPoint returns to your slide and changes the line color and style for the selected object.

8. Click any blank area of the screen to deselect the object.

A quick way to change an object's fill, line color, line style, dashed lines, or arrowheads is to use the respective tools in the Drawing toolbar. Select the object and then click any of the tools shown in Table 18.4. In each case, a drop-down list is displayed, enabling you to select a new color or style.

Use Semi-Transparent

To make the object show through to the background, choose the **Semi-T̲ransparent** check box located next to the Fill Color drop-down palette.

TABLE 18.4	**Color and line tools**
Tool	**Tool Name**
	Fill Color
	Line Color
	Line Style
	Arrowheads
	Dashed Lines

Using Shading and Patterns

Two effective variations for filled objects are shaded color and two-color pattern. A *shaded color* is a dark-to-light or light-to-dark variation of an object's color. This variation can run vertically, horizontally, diagonally, from the center outward, or from any corner. You also can adjust the intensity of the color.

Shade an object

1. Select the object you want to shade.

2. Choose the **Format** menu; then select **Colors and Lines**. The Colors and Lines dialog box is displayed. The current fill color is shown in the **Fill** box.

3. Click the down arrow to open the **Fill** drop-down list.

4. Select the **Shaded** option. The Shaded Fill dialog box is displayed, as shown in Figure 18.12.

5. Use the **Color** option in the Shaded Fill dialog box if you want to change the fill color. If you want to blend two colors for the gradient, choose the **Two Color** option. Choose the **Preset** option to display sets of predefined color gradients, such as Nightfall or Sapphire.

6. To adjust the brightness, drag the scroll box in the Dark/Light scrollbar.

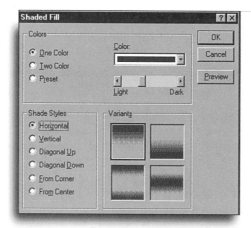

FIGURE 18.12

Use the options in the Shaded Fill dialog box to create a gradient fill pattern.

7. Select an option in the **Shade Styles** list.

8. In the **Variants** box, highlight one variant. The **Variants** box reflects the choice you make.

9. If you want, click the **Preview** button to preview the shade in the selected object.

10. Choose **OK** in the Shaded Fill dialog box. You return to the Colors and Lines dialog box.

11. Choose **OK** to close the dialog box. PowerPoint applies the shaded color to the selected object.

An alternative to shading an object is patterning. A *pattern* is a design (such as lines, dots, bricks, or checkerboard squares) that contains a foreground color and a background color.

Add a pattern to a filled object

1. Select the object to which you want to add a pattern.

2. Choose the **Format** menu; then select **Colors and Lines** or choose Colors and Lines from the shortcut menu. The Colors and Lines dialog box is displayed.

3. Click to open the **Fill** drop-down list.

4. Select the **Pattern** option. The Pattern Fill dialog box is displayed.

5. In the **Pattern** box, highlight the pattern you want to use.

6. In the **Foreground** and **Background** lists, select the colors for your pattern.

7. If you want, click the **Preview** button to preview the pattern in the selected object.

8. Click **OK** to close the Pattern Fill dialog box. You return to the Colors and Lines dialog box.

9. Click **OK** to close the dialog box. PowerPoint applies the two-color pattern to the selected object.

10. Click any blank area of the screen to deselect the object.

You can also use any of several more complex textured patterns for your objects. Select the **Textured** option rather than **Patterns** from the **Fill** drop-down list to open the Textured Fill dialog box. Choose from a variety of predesigned textured fill patterns in this dialog box.

Adding Shadows to Objects

Shadowing can enhance an object's visibility on a slide and make the object more noticeable.

Apply a shadow to an object

1. Select the object.

2. Choose the **Format** menu; then select **Shadow**. The Shadow dialog box is displayed.

3. To change the color of the shadow, select a color in the **Color** drop-down list.

4. To set a vertical shadow offset, select the **Up** or **Down** option and then enter the number of points in the **Points** box.

5. To set a horizontal shadow offset, select the **Left** or **Right** option and then enter the number of points in the **Points** box.

6. If you want, click the **Preview** button to preview the shadow on the selected object.

7. Click **OK** or press Enter to apply the shadow to the selected object.

8. Click any blank area of the screen to deselect the object.

You can quickly add or remove a shadow for an object by clicking the Shadow On/Off button ⬛ on the Drawing toolbar.

Copying Attributes from One Object to Another

Suppose that you have taken care to apply a special color, shade or pattern, line width, line style, and shadow to a particular object. You can quickly apply all these attributes to another object by using the Format Painter button ⬛ in the Standard toolbar.

Use the Format Painter button

1. Select the object that contains the desired formatting.
2. Click the **Format Painter** button ⬛. The mouse pointer changes to a paintbrush.
3. Click the object to which you want to apply the formatting. The clicked object will be reformatted to match the original object.

Using the **Format Painter** button ⬛ is equivalent to choosing the **F**ormat menu and then selecting **Pic**k Up Object Style, or choosing the **F**ormat menu and then selecting **Appl**y Object Style.

Use the menu commands to apply attributes from one object to another

1. Select the object from which you want to copy attributes.
2. Choose the **F**ormat menu; then select **Pic**k Up Object Style or choose **Pick Up Object Style** from the shortcut menu.
3. Select the object to which you want to copy the attributes.
4. Choose the **F**ormat menu; then select **Appl**y Object Style.

Working with Color Schemes

A *color scheme* is a set of colors that are chosen because they complement one another. Every template has a predefined color scheme that consists of specific colors for the slide background, title text, other text, lines, fills, shadows, and accent colors. You can use the colors defined in a template, choose a different color scheme, or change individual colors in a color scheme.

Changing Individual Colors in a Color Scheme

You can change an individual color in the current color scheme and apply the new color to the current slide or to all of the slides in the presentation.

Change individual colors

1. Choose the **Format** menu; then select **Slide Color Scheme** or choose **Slide Color Scheme** from the shortcut menu. The Color Scheme dialog box is displayed.

2. Click the Custom tab to change the dialog box options.

3. Select the color you want to change and click **Change Color**.

4. The Fill Color dialog box is displayed, looking the same as the Color palette shown in Figure 18.11. Choose the desired color and click **OK**.

5. Repeat steps 3 and 4 to change other colors in the current color scheme.

6. In the Slide Color Scheme dialog box, click the **Apply** button to apply the change to the current slide. Click **Apply to All** to apply the new color to all slides in the current presentation.

Choosing a Different Color Scheme

Suppose that a template contains all the graphic elements you want to use, but the color scheme is not appropriate for the topic you are presenting. Rather than change individual colors in the template's color scheme, you can choose a different color scheme for the current template. When you choose a new color scheme, you are choosing a new set of predefined colors. As always, you can change individual colors in the scheme later if you choose.

Use a different design template for distinct color schemes

The number of color schemes you have available in the Color Scheme dialog box (see Figure 18.16) depends on which template you are using. To change templates, choose the **Format** menu; then select **Apply Design Template** and choose a template (see "Working with Templates" earlier in this chapter).

Choose a color scheme

1. Choose the **F**ormat menu; then select **Slide C**olor Scheme or choose **Slide Color Scheme** from the shortcut menu (when no objects are selected). PowerPoint displays the Color Scheme dialog box.

2. Available color scheme options are shown in the **Color Schemes** section of this dialog box.

3. Select the desired color scheme.

4. Click **A**pply to apply the new color scheme to the current slide. Click **Apply t**o **All** to apply the new color scheme to all slides in the current presentation.

Creating Output and Doing the Show

Check slides for consistency

Build slide text

Choose a setup for presentation components

Set up your printer

Print presentation components

Create and run an onscreen slide show

Checking Slides Before the Presentation

As you learned in Chapter 15, "Getting Acquainted with PowerPoint," you can print the different components of a PowerPoint presentation such as slides (on paper or overhead transparencies), audience handouts, outlines, and speaker's notes. You also can prepare an onscreen slide show as a special kind of output.

Before you output your presentation, however, you should make sure the presentation is as good as it can be. You can check your slides by running the Style Checker. Style Checker looks for inconsistencies that you set in the Style Checker Options dialog box—inconsistencies such as case, punctuation, and the number of fonts used in the presentation.

These types of errors can be glaring when projected in front of an audience. When creating a presentation, it's easy to forget periods at the end of some sentences or to use too many fonts on a page, which makes your text hard to read and makes your slide look busy. You might miss these mistakes even in a thorough review, but Style Checker finds them all.

Run Style Checker

1. Choose the **Tools** menu and select **Style Checker**. The Style Checker dialog box appears (see Figure 19.1).

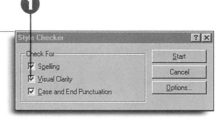

FIGURE 19.1

Choose the options that you want Style Checker to review in the Style Checker dialog box.

❶ The **Visual Clarity** option deals with font size, the number of fonts, and the number of lines in titles and bullets.

2. Click the **Options** button to change the case, punctuation, or clarity options, as described in Table 19.1 and as shown in Figures 19.2 and 19.3.

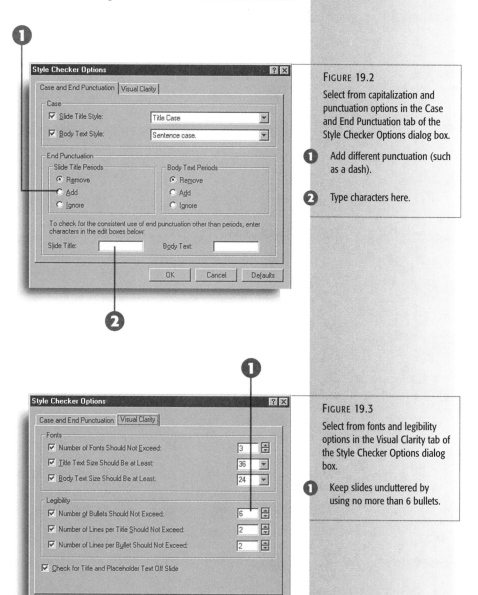

FIGURE 19.2

Select from capitalization and punctuation options in the Case and End Punctuation tab of the Style Checker Options dialog box.

1 Add different punctuation (such as a dash).

2 Type characters here.

FIGURE 19.3

Select from fonts and legibility options in the Visual Clarity tab of the Style Checker Options dialog box.

1 Keep slides uncluttered by using no more than 6 bullets.

Want to revert to the original style options?

Click the **Defaults** button in the Style Checker Options dialog box to revert to the original style options.

TABLE 19.1   **Style Checker options**

Option	Description
Case and End Punctuation Tab	
Case	
Slide Title Style	Choose to apply **Sentence case**, **Lowercase**, **Uppercase**, or **Title Case** to the titles throughout your presentation. Choose **Toggle Case** if you've accidentally typed your titles with Caps Lock on.
Body Text Style	Choose from these same cases to apply body text style.
End Punctuation	
Slide Title Periods	Choose whether to **R**emove, **A**dd, or **I**gnore periods in the slide titles.
Body Text Periods	Choose whether to **R**emove, **A**dd, or **I**gnore periods in the body text.
S**l**ide Title	Enter any other end punctuation you want to check the consistency of in slide titles.
B**o**dy Text	Enter any other end punctuation you want to check the consistency of in the body text.
Visual Clarity tab	
Fonts	
Number of Fonts Should Not **E**xceed	Choose whether to limit the number of fonts used in one presentation and enter the maximum number in the text box.
Title Text Size Should Be at Least	Enter the minimum size to be used for slide titles.
Body Text Size Should Be at Least	Enter the minimum size to be used for body text.
Legibility	
Number **o**f Bullets Should Not Exceed	Choose whether to limit the number of bullets used in body text and enter the maximum number in the text box.
Number of Lines per Title **S**hould Not Exceed	Enter the maximum number of lines to be used for slide titles.
Number of Lines per B**u**llet Should Not Exceed	Enter the maximum number of lines to be used for bullets.
Check for Title and Placeholder Text Off Slide	Check to see whether any text runs off the slide and is not visible.

3. Choose **OK** to close the Style Checker Options dialog box.

4. Click the **Start** button in the Style Checker dialog box. The Style Checker examines the slide presentation and displays a summary, as shown in Figure 19.4.

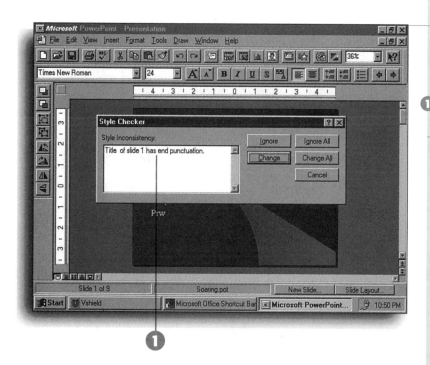

FIGURE **19.4**

The Style Checker summary reports inconsistencies; you can either change or ignore them.

❶ The Style Checker found a period at the end of a title.

5. After reading the list of inconsistencies, you can use the various **Change** and **Ignore** buttons to make adjustments. Choose **OK** to close the summary box.

Choosing a Setup for Presentation Components

Before you output a presentation, indicate the type of output you want in the Slide Setup dialog box. You can output a presentation as an onscreen slide show, as 35mm slides, as overheads,

Word not in Office dictionary?

If you left the Spelling option checked in the Style Checker dialog box, you might see a Spelling Check dialog box at this point. This dialog box enables you to correct words not found in Office's dictionary.

or as another type of printed output. You also can specify other properties of the presentation; PowerPoint then adjusts the presentation to suit your selections.

The Orientation section of the Slide Setup dialog box offers **Portrait** and **Landscape** options. When you choose **Portrait**, the slide is taller than it is wide. **Landscape** creates slides that are wider than they are tall. Slides are often printed in landscape orientation; notes, handouts, and outlines most often are printed in portrait orientation. Therefore, PowerPoint enables you to choose different orientations for slides versus notes, handouts, and outlines.

Setup for slides, notes, handouts, and outlines

   1. Choose the **File** menu and select **Slide Setup**. The Slide Setup dialog box opens (see Figure 19.5).

FIGURE 19.5

Specify output options in the Slide Setup dialog box.

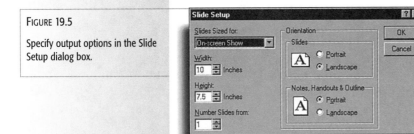

   2. Choose the appropriate option in the **Slides Sized for** drop-down list. The following options are available:
   - **On-Screen Show**. Uses an area 10 inches wide by 7.5 inches tall so the slides fill the screen.
   - **Letter Paper**. Sets the width to 11 inches and the height to 8.5 inches.
   - **A4 Paper (210mm × 297mm)**. Sets the width to 10.83 inches and the height to 7.5 inches.
   - **35mm Slides**. Sets the width to 11.25 inches and the height to 7.5 inches so the contents fill the slide area.
   - **Overhead**. Sets the width to 10 inches and the height to 7.5 inches so the contents fill a typical overhead transparency area.

- **Custom**. Enables you to choose the dimensions you want when printing on nonstandard paper. Use the **Width** and **Height** settings to enter a custom size.

3. To begin numbering slides with a number other than 1, enter a number in the **Number Slides from** box.

4. To change the print orientation for slides, choose either **Portrait** or **Landscape** in the appropriate section.

5. To change the print orientation for notes, handouts, or an outline, choose either **Portrait** or **Landscape** in the appropriate section.

6. When all settings are correct, choose **OK**.

Printing Presentation Components

Your printer probably is already set up for printing from Microsoft Office or Windows applications. If you want to use a printer you don't normally use, you can change the printer's setup using the following steps:

Change the printer setup

1. Open the presentation you want to print.

2. Choose the **File** menu and select **Print**. PowerPoint displays the Print dialog box. The current printer is displayed at the top of the dialog box.

3. Click the drop-down arrow in the **Name** list box and choose from the list of installed printing devices.

4. Finish filling out the Print dialog box.

5. Click **OK** to close the Print dialog box and print the active presentation.

Making Settings in the Print Dialog Box

After your printer is set up, PowerPoint enables you to print any component of a presentation: slides, notes pages, handouts, or an outline.

Complete slide setup before creating a new presentation

If you change slide setup after your slides are created, you might need to make adjustments to your slides, depending on the setup dimensions you choose.

Quick print

To print the current presentation using the default settings in the Print dialog box, click the Print icon 🖶.

To print any of these components, choose the **File** menu and select **Print**. The Print dialog box opens, as shown in Figure 19.6. In this dialog box, you can choose the component you want to print, the number of copies, the specific pages to print, and other printing options. Table 19.2 describes the options in the Print dialog box.

FIGURE 19.6

Use the Print dialog box to choose printing options.

① Choose to print slides, handouts, notes, or the outline.

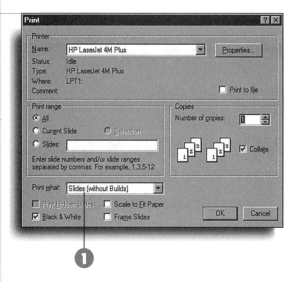

TABLE 19.2   Options in the Print dialog box

Option	Description
Name	Select which printer to send output to from this drop-down list.
Properties	Click this button to set properties specific to the printer—paper size, orientation, graphics, fonts, and so on.
Print to fi**l**e	Select this option if you want to print to a named file rather than to a printer. Slides generally are printed to file when they will be produced by a service bureau.
Print Range	This area enables you to print **All** slides, the **Current Slide**, a **Selection** of slides, or specific ranges of slides. In the **Sl**i**des** box, use a hyphen (as in 5-8) to specify a continuous range. To specify individual pages, use commas (as in 12,14,17). For multiple ranges, use a combination of the two (as in 5-8,12,17-21,25).

Option	Description
Copies	This area enables you to specify the **Number of copies** to print. Check the **Collate** option if you want PowerPoint to collate copies as they print.
Print what	This drop-down box enables you to choose whether to print slides, handouts (2, 3, or 6 slides per page), notes pages, or an outline of the presentation.
Print Hidden Slides	If some slides are hidden, select this option to include the hidden slides when printing.
Black & White	This option changes all fill colors to white and grayscale. It also adds a thin black border to any objects that are not bordered or that do not contain text.
Scale to Fit Paper	Whenever you choose a different paper size in the Slide Setup dialog box, this option scales each slide to fit the paper.
Frame Slides	This option adds a border to slides when printed.

Printing Different Kinds of Output

The **Print what** feature in the Print dialog box controls which type of output you want. Keep in mind the following variables, depending on whether you've chosen to print slides, an outline, notes, or a handout:

- When printing slides, the options in the **Print Range** section of the Print dialog box provide several different printing options. You can print all slides, just the current slide, the slides selected in the presentation, or a specified range of slides. Be sure to select the **Print Hidden Slides** check box if your presentation contains hidden slides that you want to include in the printed output.

- If you select **Notes** from the **Print what** drop-down list in the Print dialog box, a reduced-size slide prints at the top of the page with speaker's notes at the bottom (see Figure 19.7). Because notes pages print one slide per page, you follow the same steps for printing notes pages as for printing slides.

Options dimmed if unavailable

The **Print Hidden Slides** option is dimmed unless you have hidden slides in your presentation. Similarly, the **Selection** option in the Print Range section isn't available unless you have selected objects on a slide.

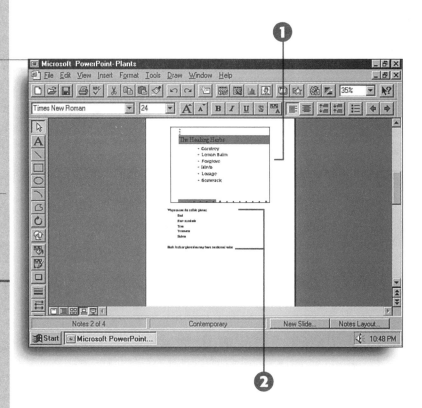

FIGURE 19.7

A notes page displays a reduced-size slide at the top of the page and speaker's notes at the bottom.

1 Slide

2 Notes

Transfer notes in a Word document

Choose the **File** menu, select **Send To**, and select **Microsoft Word**. The Write-Up dialog box opens. You can choose to link or embed the notes in the Add Slides to Microsoft Word Document area of the dialog box. When you choose **OK**, Word opens and is ready for you to create your speaker's notes. Update and exit Word using the **File** menu to return to PowerPoint.

Three slides per page enables the audience to take notes

If you choose to print three slides per page, the slides are printed on the left side of the page. The right side is lined to provide a place for audience members to take notes.

- When printing handouts, PowerPoint enables you to print with two, three, or six slides per page. To preview each of these layout options, display the Handout Master by pressing and holding the Shift key and clicking the Slide Sorter button ▦. You'll see a layout template like the one in Figure 19.8.

To print handouts, in the **Print what** drop-down list of the Print dialog box, choose **Handouts (2 Slides per Page)**, **Handouts (3 Slides per Page)**, or **Handouts (6 Slides per Page)**.

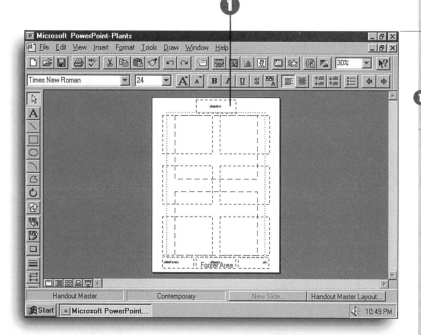

When printing selected handout pages, it's not necessary to determine on which page a slide will print. Just specify the slide numbers—which were determined in the Slide Setup dialog box—that you want to print. If, for example, you choose three slides per page and you want to print slides numbered 3, 4, 5, and 6, enter **3-6** in the **Sl<u>i</u>des** text box of the Print dialog box. PowerPoint prints the second handout page.

- When you print a presentation outline, it prints just as it last appeared in Outline view. If you click the Collapse Selection button ▬ on the Outlining toolbar, for example, PowerPoint prints only the slide titles (no body text). If you change the display scale using the Zoom Control button `49%` on the Standard toolbar, the outline prints in the current scale percentage. If you click the Show Formatting button `A` on the Outlining toolbar to display the outline text without formatting, the outline prints exactly as displayed onscreen.

Missing the Outlining toolbar?

Right-click on any toolbar and choose Outlining from the list of available toolbars.

After selecting Outline View in the **Print what** drop-down list of the Print dialog box, enter the slide numbers you want to include on the outline page. If you type 1,4,5-9, for example, PowerPoint includes only those slides on the printed outline page.

SEE ALSO

➤ *To navigate through the different views of PowerPoint, see page 371*

Setting Up and Running a Slide Show Onscreen

An effective way to present your slides is to use your computer screen as an output medium. When you use your computer for an onscreen slide show, the entire screen area is used. PowerPoint's title bar, menu bar, and toolbars are cleared from the screen.

An onscreen slide show offers several advantages over transparencies or 35mm slides:

- Saves you the expense and time involved in producing slides (and reproducing them if you make any changes to the presentation)
- Enables you to move around the presentation easily using interesting transition effects
- Enables you to utilize multimedia effects such as sound, animation, and video clips
- Makes other information available during the presentation (for example, you can open another computer program to get additional data)
- Requires no projection equipment
- Enables you to use your computer's color capabilities to their fullest

You also can annotate your slides as you give your presentation. (For more information, see the section "Annotating a Slide Show" later in this chapter.)

You can run a PowerPoint slide show manually (using the mouse or the keyboard to advance to the next slide), you can set up a slide show to advance slides automatically (by recording the amount of time each slide should display), or you can set up a slide show to run in a continuous "loop" (for demonstration purposes, such as in a kiosk display).

Running a Slide Show

You can use several methods to run a PowerPoint slide show.

Run a slide show from within PowerPoint

1. Choose the **View** menu and select **Slide Show**. The Slide Show dialog box opens, as shown in Figure 19.9.

2. In the Slides section of the dialog box, select **All** or enter a range of slides to display.

3. In the **Advance** section, select either **Manual Advance** or, for automatic slide advance, **Use Slide Timings.** Alternatively, you can choose **Rehearse New Timings** to practice your presentation speech and to set timings for each slide.

4. For a continuously looping presentation—such as at a trade show booth—check the **Loop Continuously Until 'Esc'** check box.

5. Click the **Show** button. Your slide presentation begins running.

Take notes during the presentation

You can use PowerPoint's Meeting Minder feature—choose the **Tools** menu and select **Meeting Minder**—to take notes and to record items in Slide view or during a presentation. The notes you take are added to your notes pages; recorded action items appear on the last slide of your presentation.

FIGURE 19.9

Use the options in the Slide Show dialog box to set timing, pen color, and other slide show features.

Practice makes perfect

Select **View**, select **Slide Show**, and then choose **Rehearse Timings** to practice your presentation speech along with each slide.

If you chose **Manual Advance** in step 3, you can either click the mouse, press Enter, or press Page Down when you're ready to advance to the next slide. If you chose **Use Slide Timings**, the slides advance automatically using the most recent timings set by running **Rehearse New Timings**.

Table 19.3 lists different methods for controlling your movements through a slide show.

TABLE 19.3   **Methods for controlling a slide show**

Action	Method
Show the next slide	Click the left mouse button or press the Spacebar.
Show the preceding slide	Press Backspace.
Show a specific slide	Type the slide number and press Enter.
Toggle the mouse pointer on or off	Type A.
Toggle between a black screen and the current slide	Type B.
Toggle between a white screen and the current slide	Type W.
End the slide show and return to PowerPoint	Press Esc.
Pause and resume an automatic slide show	Type S.
Toggle Pen on	Press Ctrl+P. (Press Esc to turn off pen.)

View list of all slides

If you want to see a list of all the slides during a presentation, right-click the mouse, choose **Go To**, and then select **Slide Navigator**.

Another method of running a slide show is to click the Slide Show button 🖳 on the lower-left side of the PowerPoint window. When you click this button, PowerPoint immediately runs the slide show, beginning with the currently selected slide. The slide show runs using the most recently set slide timings. If no timings are set, you must advance each slide manually.

Setting Transitions and Slide Timings

To add visual interest to your presentation, you can specify a transition style between slides. The transition style determines how one slide is removed from the screen and the next one is presented. Possible styles range from one slide simply replacing another to fancy tiling effects in which a new slide seems to rain down onto the screen. When you set up a slide show to advance automatically to the next slide, you also can set the amount of time each slide remains onscreen.

To set transitions and timings, use the Slide Transition dialog box in Figure 19.10. From any of PowerPoint's display views, you can open this dialog box by choosing the **Tools** menu and selecting **Slide Transition**. When using Slide Sorter view, you can display the Slide Transition dialog box by clicking the Transition button at the far left end of the Slide Sorter toolbar. In the Slide Sorter toolbar, you also can use the Slide Transition Effects pull-down button to choose from a list of transition effects.

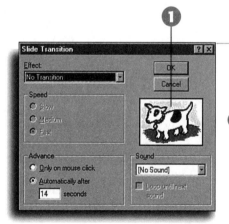

FIGURE 19.10

You can add transitions to a slide show in the Slide Transition dialog box.

① Click the dog to see the transition effect.

Set slide timings and transitions

1. Click the Slide Sorter View button 🔳 to display your presentation in Slide Sorter view.

2. Select the slide for which you want to set timing and transition options. If you want to use the same settings for multiple slides, combine the slides as a group.

3. Click the Transition button ▦ at the far left end of the toolbar. PowerPoint displays the Slide Transition dialog box.

4. Select a transition style from the **Effect** drop-down list. After you've made your selection, the transition is previewed in the box below the **Cancel** button.

5. Select the appropriate speed option (**Slow**, **Medium**, or **Fast**).

6. In the **Advance** section, choose whether you would like to advance the slide with a click of the mouse or automatically at a selected time interval.

7. You also can add sound to the transition by choosing a sound from the **Sound** drop-down list. If you want to loop the sound continuously until the next preset sound occurs, enable the **Loop until next sound** check box.

8. Click **OK** when finished.

In Figure 19.11, transition icons appear under some slides. A transition time displays under all slides in Slide Sorter view, indicating that transitions and slide times have been applied. You can click any transition icon to see a demonstration of the transition effect on the slide in Slide Sorter view.

You can repeat these steps at any time to change transitions or timing. You also can change slide timing when rehearsing a slide show, as described in the next section.

Automating a Slide Show

As discussed earlier, you can advance automatically to successive slides during your presentation if slide timings have been set to control this advancement. You can set slide timings as you rehearse a presentation.

Set slide timings as you rehearse

1. In Slide Sorter view, click the Rehearse Timings button ▣. The slide show begins, and the Rehearse Timings dialog box enables you to see the timing as you move between slides.

FIGURE 19.11

Slide Sorter view shows
the timing and transitions
for each slide.

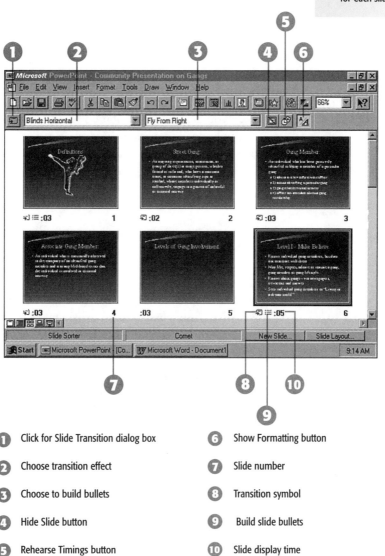

1 Click for Slide Transition dialog box

2 Choose transition effect

3 Choose to build bullets

4 Hide Slide button

5 Rehearse Timings button

6 Show Formatting button

7 Slide number

8 Transition symbol

9 Build slide bullets

10 Slide display time

2. Begin rehearsing your presentation. When you are ready to advance to the next slide, either press the arrow on the Rehearse Timings dialog box or press the Spacebar.

3. Repeat step 2 until all slides have been shown. A message appears, telling you the total time for the new slide timings.

Choose **Yes** to record the new timings. Choose **No** to ignore the new timings and retain the previous timings.

Annotating a Slide Show

When you deliver a presentation using overhead transparencies, you might need to circle or underline a specific point, or write notes on the slide in response to audience questions or comments. If you use a dry-erase marker, you can easily wipe off your annotations so the transparencies are not permanently marked.

When you run an onscreen slide show, PowerPoint gives you the capability to electronically annotate your slides in freehand form by adding comments using the mouse. You might, for example, want to draw a check mark beside an important point or underline it. As with overhead transparencies and dry-erase markers, electronic comments are not permanent. They are removed automatically when you move to the next slide in a slide show, or you can remove annotations manually as you present your slides.

Add comments to slides during a slide show

1. Start your slide show.

2. Press Ctrl+P. The pointer turns into a pen.

3. Press and hold the mouse button as you write or draw onscreen by moving the mouse. Release the mouse button to stop drawing or writing.

4. Repeat step 3 to write or draw again on the slide.

5. Press **E** to erase all comments on the current slide. You then can circle or check other areas of the slide. (This step is optional.)

6. When you have finished annotating the current slide, press Ctrl+A, right-click the mouse and choose **Arrow**, or click the annotation icon again. Choose the **Arrow** command from the pop-up menu to restore the mouse pointer.

If you don't press **E** to erase all comments on the current slide (see step 5), PowerPoint automatically erases all comments when you move to the next slide in the slide show.

Building Slide Text

You can apply an interesting animation effect called a build to a slide with a bulleted list or other objects. When using this effect, items in the list appear one at a time. Build effects can make a show more interesting and can keep viewers from reading ahead of the speaker.

Add build effects to a presentation

1. In Slide Sorter view ▦, select the slide you want.
2. In the second drop-down list on the toolbar (Text Build Effects), choose the type of build effect you want from the list or select **Off** to turn off build effects. The option appears on the drop-down button.

If you choose to advance the slide show manually, the text builds onscreen each time you click the mouse; otherwise, the build is automatic.

Animating Objects on a Slide

You also can use build and animation effects for any other object (including clip art and other text) on the slide, not just bullets.

Add an animation effect

1. In Slides view, select the object you want to animate.
2. Click the Animation Effects button ⛨ on the Formatting toolbar. A group of animation buttons display.
3. Click one of the animation buttons, which are described in Table 19.4.

TABLE 19.4   Animation buttons

Button	Name	Description (and Sound If Sound Board Installed)	Works with Graphic Objects*
	Animate Title	Title of slide flies from top (toggles on or off)	
	Build Slide Text	Each click of mouse displays new bullet item	
	Drive-In Effect	Object flies from right with car sound	Yes
	Flying Effect	Object flies from left with whoosh sound	Yes
	Camera Effect	Object starts from center outward with camera sound	Yes
	Flash Once	Flashes the object on and then off	Yes
	Laser Text Effect	Drops one letter at a time from top right with laser sound	
	Typewriter Effect	Adds one letter at a time with typewriter sound	
	Reverse Order Build	Quickly builds text from left to right; if bullets are selected, reverses order of bullets (builds from bottom to top)	
	Drop-In Text Effect	Drops down one word at a time	
2	Animation Order Order	If multiple objects are on slide, chooses order for each animation effect	Yes
	Animation Settings	Opens Animation Settings dialog box, which shows existing settings and gives more options than the Animation Effects dialog box alone	Yes

All items in this table work with text. Items that have Yes in fourth column work with pictures, clip art, and drawn objects.

If you click the Animation Settings button ![icon], the Animation Settings dialog box opens (see Figure 19.12). The following are the options in the Animation Settings dialog box:

- **Build Options**. For picture objects, you can choose **Build** or **Don't Build**. For text objects, you also can build by paragraph level.

- **In reverse order**. For bulleted items, it builds from last bullet item to first bullet item (from bottom to top).

- **Start when previous build ends**. Builds object when previous build item finishes. If this item is not checked, click the mouse or press Enter for each build item to appear.

- **Effects**. Without effects, the build item appears at once at the indicated position on the slide. With effects, the item can appear to be flying from different positions on the slide or with fades, blinds, flashing, or other options. The **Effects** option provides more choices than the Animation Effects buttons alone. In the second pull-down list, you can choose how each bullet builds (by paragraphs, words, and letters). In the third pull-down list, you can choose a sound to go with each build.

- **Build this object**. When multiple objects are on a slide, you can choose the order in which the selected item appears.

- **After Build Step**. After the build is completed, you can change the color (**Dim**) or hide the object. To keep the object onscreen unchanged, choose **Don't Dim**.

Add movement effect

To create the effect of movement on the slide, select an object and use the Flash Once button. Duplicate the object with Ctrl+D. To leave the last copy of the object onscreen, select the object and click the Animation Settings button ![icon] to display the Animation Settings dialog box. In the **Effects** tab, choose the **Don't Build in the Build Options** drop-down button.

FIGURE 19.12

The Animation Settings dialog box enables you to create visual and sound effects for objects on your slide.

1. The Build Options drop-down list changes, depending on whether text or graphics is selected on the slide.

Interacting with Objects During a Presentation

In addition to the build effects you can create for objects on slides, you can have an object react to a mouse click during a presentation.

Add mouse-click reaction

1. Select the object on the slide.

2. Choose the **Tools** menu and select **Interactive Settings**. The Interactive Settings dialog box opens, as shown in Figure 19.13.

3. Choose one of the following options in the dialog box:

   - Choose **None** for no action to occur after a mouse click.

   - Choose **Go to** and select a slide from the pull-down list to go to a specific slide in the presentation.

   - To play a sound after clicking the object in a presentation, choose **Play Sound** and choose a sound from the pull-down list.

   - To open an application, choose **Run Program** and type the name of the application in the text box or click **Browse** to locate it.

   - For an embedded file such as a Word document, a Microsoft graph, an Excel spreadsheet, or another PowerPoint presentation, choose **Object Action** and select from the options in the pull-down list.

4. Choose **OK** when finished.

FIGURE 19.13

The Action Settings dialog box enables you to choose an action to happen when you click a slide object.

1 Create graphics objects that enable you to go to specific parts in your slide show.

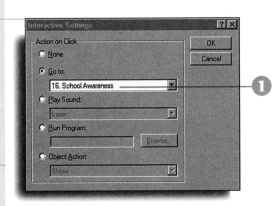

Creating a Database

Learn the basics of database management

Learn about Access database objects

Use the Database Wizard to create powerful databases

Create a database from scratch

What Is a Database?

As a consultant, one of the most noticeable things I see is that many people have spreadsheets in Excel that are more appropriate as a database in Access. Excel does have some useful database functionality (Sort, Find, PivotTables, Subtotals, and Database functions); however, when you really need database functionality, you should be using a database application.

Before you explore Access, you need to know what a database is, review some basic database concepts, and identify when to use a database. A *database* is an organized collection of information. A telephone directory is a good example of a database. In a computerized database, data appears in a *table* that looks very similar to a spreadsheet. The column headings are called *field names* and the columns are called *fields*. The rows of data are called *records*. In Figure 20.1, **First Name** is a field and **John Smith, 567-9834, 567-4433** is one of four records in a telephone table.

A computerized *database management system* (*DBMS*) is a computer application that helps you store, retrieve, sort, analyze, and print information in a database. In short, it is an application, like Access, that has the menus, toolbars, and other features that help you manage your database. Access has different objects that work on your database. Tables store information. *Queries* ask questions of tables or modify the data in them. You usually use *forms* for entering one record at a time. You use *reports* to get printed output such as subtotals and totals or mailing labels. You can use *macros* and *modules* to automate your database application.

Two types of database management systems exist:

- *File management systems.* Sometimes called *flat-file databases*, these store data in files without indexing, which means that data is processed sequentially. File management systems lack flexibility in data manipulation. Another drawback of file management systems is the user's tendency toward data redundancy (storing the same data in more than one place) to accomplish common database tasks such as reporting.

- *Relational database management systems.* Enables users to manipulate data in more sophisticated ways—without data redundancy—by defining relationships between sets of data.

Data redundancy is a bad thing

When you repeat data, you have more chance for errors, and the database gets larger and slower than it needs to be. Take, for example, a customer and order database. If you had to type the customer name and address each time you had an order for the customer, you might type the information differently each time (for example, Our Fries Inc. versus Our Fries Corp.). Data entry would take you longer, and when you totaled sales by company you would get orders spread between those two companies. If the address changed between the two orders, how would you know which address was correct? For the database to be correct, you would have to correct the address for every order. Finally, the database would be larger than necessary because of the repeated information; and the larger the database is, the slower it moves.

The *relationship* is a common element, such as a customer's ID number or Social Security number. The data stored in each set can be retrieved and updated based on data in the other set.

First Name	Last Name	Work Phone	Fax Number
Jackie	Joyner	456-2323	456-9988
John	Smith	567-9834	567-4433
Mary	Might	345-9977	345-1112
Carl	Lewis	987-4433	987-2121

FIGURE 20.1

This telephone database is organized into a table that consists of rows called records and columns called fields.

1 Field

2 Record

To further illustrate the difference between file management systems and relational database systems, consider the database used in a video rental store, which needs to maintain information on customers, rentals, and movies in stock. In a file management system (or flat file), every time a customer rents a movie, the customer's name and phone number must be entered with the movie rented. In a relational database system, the customer name and phone number would be entered in a database table only once—in a customer list. Each time a customer rents a movie, his or her name would be retrieved automatically from the related (linked) customer list and added to the rental invoice without the need for duplicate data entry and storage.

SEE ALSO

➤ *To find out how to convert an Excel spreadsheet to an Access table, see page 518*

What Are Primary and Foreign Keys?

In one of the related tables, the common element is a *primary key*, an indexed field in which data is not repeated. This primary key uniquely identifies the record. Examples of primary keys include Social Security numbers, customer IDs, and sequential numbers generated automatically.

When to use Access instead of Excel

The relational database features of Access is one of the major reasons that you choose Access over Excel for storing your data. You change your data for a customer once, and it changes for all orders. Other strengths are a database's capability to validate, find, sort, and use the same data in multiple forms and reports.

More information on Access found on the Web

Microsoft's Web site has sample files, drivers, and White Papers about many relevant topics to designing a database. For more information on relational design concepts, optimization, security, and many other topics see their Web site: http://www.microsoft.com/.

The common element in the related table is called a *foreign key*, which is not usually a primary key. For example, one customer could have many orders. In a customer table, you want each customer ID listed only once. In the order table, you (hopefully) have many orders for your customer, so the customer ID is listed many times.

Be careful when assigning primary keys. Every record has to have a unique value in the primary key and you cannot leave the value in the field blank. So, if you are not able to have everyone's Social Security number (they're too young to have one, the client forgot it, or the client doesn't want to give it out), choose another field as a primary key. To combat the problem, you can always have a field with an AutoNumber data type. Every time you add a record, the AutoNumber field changes incrementally. You do not have to show the AutoNumber field on a form or table (you can hide it).

The benefits of establishing a primary key include the following:

- *Speed*. Access creates an index based on the primary key, which enables Access to improve processing of queries and other functions.
- *Order*. Access automatically sorts and displays database records in primary-key order.
- *No duplicates*. Access does not permit users to enter data with the same primary key as an existing record.
- *Links*. Access maintains relationships between linked tables based on relating the primary key to a foreign key in another table with the same information as the primary key.

Sometimes, the unique fact about a record is a combination of the information kept in several fields. In an Invoice line item table, for example, the primary key might consist of the invoice number and the line number, because an invoice probably has more than one item on the invoice. Access enables you to key more than one field in a table to create a multi-field primary key. Another name for multi-field primary key is composite key.

SEE ALSO

➤ *To find out how to turn a field into a primary key, see page 483*

➤ *To see how to create relationships, see page 493*

Knowing When to Use a Database

Think of your computer and computer applications as tools that you use each day to accomplish your work. Microsoft Office provides a host of tools that you can use to automate daily tasks. Access is a database tool, and knowing when to use it is important.

The purpose of a database is to store, retrieve, and manage information. The following are a few common examples of information stored in databases:

- Employee data
- Product inventory
- Customer demographics
- Customer purchases and orders
- Home inventory for insurance purposes
- Exercise/workout log
- Sales contacts
- Suppliers
- Students and classes
- Video collection
- Tracking investments

Notice that the preceding examples emphasize data collection, not calculation. Although you can perform many financial and statistical calculations in a database, database applications do not calculate as quickly as spreadsheet applications. For example, a database is not the proper application to automate the calculation of a single loan; a spreadsheet application such as Excel is a better choice. If, however, you need to track, analyze, and maintain loan data for a number of clients over a period of years, a database application is more appropriate for that collection of information.

When to Use Access Versus Other Office Applications

Table 20.1 might help you with your decision to use either Access or another office application. Usually, the choice is between Access or Excel. The table is just a guideline, and many variables can influence your decision—not the least of which is knowing one application better than another.

TABLE 20.1   Applications suggested for common database tasks

Task	Application	Comments
Managing financial data	Excel	Use Excel for projects that are heavy on numbers with a lot of calculations.
	Access	Alternatively, use Access for large lists when you are searching for a lot of information and making many reports from the same set of data.
Budgets	Excel	Generally, budgets work well in Excel. You can do a lot of what-if analysis with Excel (What if inflation changes? What if we have to cut 10% of the workforce?) Excel also has PivotTables, Subtotals, Scenarios, and Views that help manage what-if conditions.
	Access	Access, however, may be better if you receive data from a lot of different sources, for many accounts, for different departments, for different years. Access manages data better than Excel.
Maintain mailing lists	Word	If the mailing list is simple (just a name and address, for example) and you do a lot of merging with different letters, labels, and envelopes.
	Access	If you have to do a lot of sorting and manipulating of your data and if the list is more complex. Do you have to ask questions like what was the total amount for each state? How many customers didn't pay on time?
	Excel	If you have Word and Access, although it works okay, generally Excel is not a good choice for mailing lists.

Task	Application	Comments
Track client contacts, log phone support, and follow up with a form letter	Access	Create a contact database with related tables for clients, phone calls, projects, letters, and correspondence. Create letter forms for data entry. Print letters directly from Access reports.
	Schedule+	Use Schedule+'s contact management features to build your contact list, schedule follow-up calls, and more. If, however, you need to customize your application, Access is a better choice.
	Word	Merge client contact data into Word and print follow-up form letters from Word (if the letters have a lot of text or formatting).

Sometimes it is better to work with multiple applications rather than to try doing everything in one. For example, if you have a large mailing list and complex text documents with a significant amount of formatting, use Word for the text documents and Access for the mailing list. If you have a lot of data from many different sources but still need a lot of calculations, use Access to manage the data and Excel to do the calculations.

Need more information about Office 95 applications?

To see the power of Word and Excel, look *at Special Edition, Using Word for Windows 95* and *Special Edition, Using Excel for Windows 95,* both by Que.

Exploring Access

Microsoft Access is a relational database management system designed for the graphical environment of Windows. With Access, you can perform the following tasks:

- Organize data into manageable related units.
- Enter, modify, and locate data.
- Extract subsets of data based on specific criteria.
- Create custom forms and reports.
- Automate common database tasks.
- Graph data relationships.
- Add clip art to forms and reports.

■ Create your own turnkey database application, complete with menus, dialog boxes, and command buttons.

In this section, you learn how to identify the components of such databases and how to start Access.

Database Objects

So what exactly is an object, anyway?

In this chapter, each document in the major divisions of Access—each table, query, report, and so on—is an *object*, and anything that you can manipulate in Access is an object—for example, a field in a table, a text box or line on a form, a toolbar or toolbar button, or the database itself.

Before you start creating databases in Access, it helps to understand the components of an Access database. In Access, the term *database* refers to a single file that contains a collection of information. Each Access database (or file) consists of the following objects: multiple tables of related information, queries, forms, reports, macros, and modules. (Table 20.2 describes the major objects in Access.)

TABLE 20.2   Database objects

Object	Description
Table	Stores data in a row-and-column format, similar to a spreadsheet.
Query	Extracts data from a table based on user-supplied criteria. Queries enable you to view fields from more than one table. You can also use queries to update tables.
Form	Displays data from a table or query based on a user-defined custom format. Forms enable you to view, enter, edit, and print data. A form can display information from more than one table.
Report	Displays and prints data from a table or query based on a user-defined custom format. You cannot edit data in a report. Reports can contain information from more than one table.
Macro	Automates common database actions based on user-specified commands and events.
Module	Automates complex operations and gives a programmer more control than macros. Modules are procedures written in the Visual Basic for Applications programming language.

Everything is in one big file

Unlike other database management programs (dBASE for example), Access includes everything (tables, forms, modules, and so on) into one file (unless you decide to link tables). By having everything in one file, it is much easier to copy and back up your database.

Starting Access

You can start Access by clicking the Windows 95 or Windows NT **Start** menu, choosing **Programs**, and then choosing

Microsoft Access; by using the Microsoft Office Shortcut Bar; clicking a desktop shortcut; or by using the Windows command prompt. Access also has many command-line options for starting Access (for a complete list, search Help for the topic Startup Command Line Options). Command-line options enable you to start Access and have Access automatically perform a task for you. For example, you can have Access run a macro for you or repair a database and then exit Access. In the following example, Access starts opening the Northwind sample database for exclusive access, and then runs the AddProducts macro:

```
C:\Access\MSAccess.exe Northwind.mdb/Excl/X AddProducts
```

SEE ALSO
➤ *To find out what "exclusive" is, see page 455*

Opening a Database

With the exception of a couple of options, saving, opening, and closing Access are the same procedures for Word and Excel. Whether you launch Access from an icon or a menu, the Microsoft Access dialog box appears (see Figure 20.2). By selecting one of the following options, you can create a new database or open an existing database:

- Select **B**lank **Database** to open a database that doesn't contain database objects such as tables, forms, or reports.

- Select **D**atabase **Wizard**, to see a list of more than available 20 database templates (such as contact management, inventory control, order processing, and video collection). Databases created with the Database Wizard contain predesigned tables, forms, and reports. You can even have the Database Wizard fill in sample data in each database object to help you get started.

SEE ALSO
➤ *For more about opening and closing documents, see page 65*
➤ *To see how saving an entire Access database is similar to saving spreadsheets, see page 205*

If Your Office Shortcut Bar does not show the Access icon

This is easy enough to fix, although I don't know why Microsoft didn't do this in the first place. Click the first icon on the Shortcut Bar (red, blue, yellow, green square) and choose **Customize**. Click the **Buttons** tab and check **Access** (you might want to do this for Word, Excel, and PowerPoint, too). Uncheck any programs or options that you don't use, and click **OK** to finish.

Create a desktop shortcut with this simple procedure

To create the same effect as a startup macro that would open a form, drag the form from the Database Window to the Windows desktop. To open a report in print preview, you can drag a report to the desktop as well.

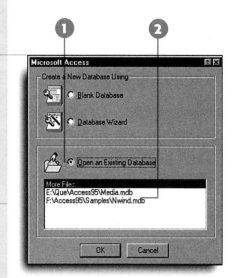

1   2

FIGURE 20.2

The Microsoft Access dialog box enables you to create a new database or open an existing database.

① Use predefined databases

② List shows last accessed databases

Don't remember your recent files?

As in Word, Excel, and PowerPoint, you can also look on the bottom of the **File** menu to see a list of the most recent files that you've worked on. You can also see the last 15 documents of all types by clicking the Windows **Start** button and choosing **Documents**.

Can't find your database?

Click the **Advanced** button on the Open dialog box. Enter the **Property** (such as File Name or Contents), type the **Value** in the text box, and then click the **Find Now** button. If you want to search your whole hard drive, place the drive letter in **Look in** and check **Search subfolders**.

- Under the **Open an Existing Database** option button, Access lists the database files that you most recently used. The **More Files** option provides access to other databases starting in the default file folder. To open an existing database, double-click the database name.

If you close the Microsoft Access dialog box without making a selection, you are left in the Access application window without any databases open. The menus available at this point include **File**, **Tools**, and **Help**. The toolbar provides buttons for creating a new database, opening an existing database, and accessing Help.

Open an existing database

1. Choose the **File** menu and select **Open Database** 📂, or press Ctrl+O. The Open dialog box appears (see Figure 20.3).
2. Specify the drive and folder in the **Look in** text box.
3. Select the desired database filename in the **File name** text box.
4. Choose **Open**.

When you create a new database or open an existing database, a database window opens (see Figure 20.4) and more menu and toolbar options become available.

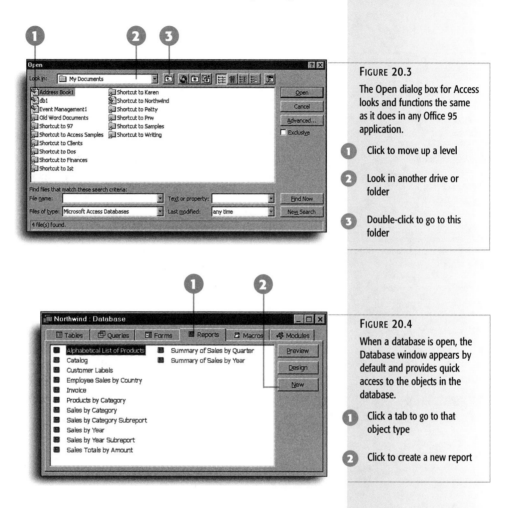

FIGURE 20.3

The Open dialog box for Access looks and functions the same as it does in any Office 95 application.

① Click to move up a level

② Look in another drive or folder

③ Double-click to go to this folder

FIGURE 20.4

When a database is open, the Database window appears by default and provides quick access to the objects in the database.

① Click a tab to go to that object type

② Click to create a new report

The Database window contains a tab for each type of database object. When you select a tab, such as Tables, Access lists the existing table names. To open a specific object, double-click the name or select it and choose the **Open** button, which is available only for tables, queries, and forms. The **Open** button becomes the **Preview** button for reports; it becomes the **Run** button for macros and modules. Use the **New** and **Design** buttons to create new database objects or to modify the design of existing database objects.

To close an open database, click the Database Window **Close** button (x) or press **Ctrl+F4**.

Allowing only one person to work on the database

Unlike Word and Excel, many people can open the same file if the file is on a network. Different people can enter data, run queries, and display reports from the same database file at the same time. If you want to prevent anyone else from working in the database, after you choose **File**, **Open Database**, check the **Exclusive** check box.

Good documentation helps you down the road

You can add comments on the objects in the Database Window. Right-click the name of an object, choose **Properties**, and add text in the **Description** text box. To see the descriptions, click the Details button ▦ on the toolbar. The other display buttons include Large Icons, Small Icons, and List. (If I'm not looking at the details, I prefer List because it's compact and more likely shows the entire list without scrolling.)

Use and modify the files that Access's Wizard creates to meet your needs

Use the Database Wizard (choose **File**, select **New**, and then click the **Databases** tab) to quickly create a complete database design.

Planning and Designing Your Database

Before you create tables, forms, and reports, take the time to plan the database. The time you invest in designing the database yields productivity gains as you create and maintain the database. Focus your design efforts on the data, the people, and the tasks. The following are some key issues to address as you design your database:

- Start by analyzing the existing database (manual or computerized). Review the current forms and reports being used. Determine the source of the data. (If computerized, could the data entry be imported or linked?) Meet with the other people who use the database information and discuss their needs. Review the database tasks performed (or to be performed), such as weekly reports, data exports, sorting, and analysis.

- From your analysis of the database, make a list of all pieces of information that you need (data elements).

- After you identify your data storage and retrieval needs, separate the data elements into groups of common subjects (for example, separate customer data from invoice data). These groups become tables. I think of each table as a noun.

- Determine the type of information to be stored in each table. What are the data elements that describe each table? (A customer table, for example, might store customer names, addresses, and phone numbers.) These categories of information in a table are called fields. Make sure that each field has only one piece of information. For example, do not include a field that says purchases and then lists multiple items purchased (you would not be able to find totals for each item purchased). Also, if you need to sort or search on fields, make sure that you break down the information into separate fields such as FirstName, LastName, Address, State, and Zip.

- Determine the type of data you will be storing in each field and any other properties that the field may have.

- Look for common elements among the tables. (A customer account number might be the common element between the customer table and the invoice table.) This common element is called the *key field*. This key field is unique and cannot be duplicated. A customer number is a good choice, but a customer name is not, because you can have many Taco Boutiques but at different addresses.

- Determine criteria for queries, and determine what questions need to be asked.

- Design forms and reports.

- Consider automating common database tasks, such as opening a form, executing a query, and printing a report.

- Review data-security issues, such as backup policies, data sharing, and network access.

SEE ALSO
➤ *For a description of data types, see page 479*
➤ *For a description of field properties, see page 483*

Naming Objects in Your Database

After you plan your database, you should be aware of the naming rules for each of the objects (fields, tables, forms, and so on). The following is a list of rules that you need to keep in mind when you create each object:

- Objects can contain up to 64 characters.

- Characters can be letters, numbers, and spaces.

- Characters can be special characters except for these: period (.), exclamation (!), accent grave (è), or brackets ([ ]).

- Objects cannot begin with a space or an ASCII control character from 0 to 31.

In general, avoid names that are too long (they're cumbersome to type and difficult to remember), cryptic names that lack meaning, or names with spaces or punctuation if you later intend to manipulate the object using Visual Basic for Applications, use them in expressions, or upload to SQL Server. For example, if you name a field First Name, when you upload Access to SQL Server, the name changes to First_Name. Any queries, forms, or reports with this field do not work, unless you edit the design to reflect this change.

Need more information on designing a database?

Data Normalization is the process of designing your database for efficient use. You find many useful descriptions on the Web. Search for "Normalized Database Design" to find much more in-depth discussions of this topic.

When I start Access, my database does not appear

The Microsoft Access dialog box does not automatically open a database. You can achieve this effect by adding *name* to the icon shortcut properties where *name* is the full directory, folder, and filename of your database.

You cannot use Edit Replace to rename objects.

I have, however, found a useful program to change the names of objects throughout your database. You can download and purchase Rick Fisher's Find and Replace to find all occurrences of a field name, for example, and replace it in all tables, queries, forms, reports and programming. See his Web site at www.RickWorld.com to download a trial version.

You may also want to use a naming convention for each of the general types of objects to make later programming easier. For example, use the prefix `tbl` for tables (tblCustomer), `qry` for queries, `frm` for forms, `rpt` for reports, `mcr` for macros, and `bas` for Visual Basic modules.

Creating a New Database

After you plan your database design, you are ready to create the database. Access provides you with many wizards to help automate the creation of the objects in the database, as well as the entire database itself. You can either use the Database Wizard to create an entire database from templates or create a blank (empty) database. If you decide to create a blank database, you can populate it later with database objects created from scratch or use an Access Wizard to create each object.

Using the Database Wizard

The Database Wizard lists over 20 databases complete with tables, defined table relationships, forms, queries, and reports ready for you to use. You can always customize the generic database objects to better meet your needs at a later time. The advantage of the Database Wizard is that you can select a wizard, create a complete database, and get right to work entering data. On the other hand, creating a database from scratch (see the section "Creating A Blank Database" later in this chapter) gives you more flexibility, control over database definition, and a better understanding of your database.

Depending on your installation, the Database Wizard templates may include the following:

Address Book	Event Management
Asset Tracking	Expenses
Book Collection	Household Inventory
Contact Management	Inventory Control
Donations	Ledger

Membership	Service Call Management
Music Collection	Students & Classes
Order Entry	Time & Billing
Picture Library	Video Collection
Recipes	Wine List
Resource Scheduling	Workout

Create a database with the Database Wizard

1. From the Microsoft Access dialog box, choose **Database
Wizard,** or if you already closed the dialog box, choose the
File menu, and select **New Database** 🗋. The New dialog
box appears (see Figure 20.5).

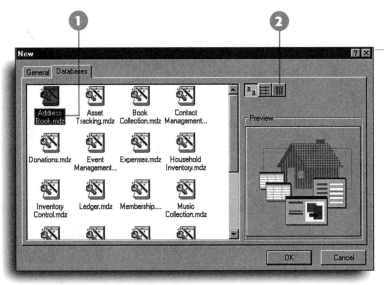

FIGURE 20.5

Choose from one of the many
built-in databases that Access
offers, such as Addresses, to
help you manage your life.

① Double-click to start the
Address Book wizard

② Click to show when wizard
was created and the size

2. On the **Databases** tab, double-click the icon for the kind of
database that you want to create.

3. When the File New Database dialog box appears, specify a
name and location for the database.

4. Click **Create** to create the new database.

5. Follow the wizard directions to customize the database
design to better meet your needs.

Creating a Blank Database

If the Database Wizard templates do not meet your database design needs, create a blank database. Or, if you have experience using Access and want to create the entire database design from scratch, you might prefer creating a blank database. The blank database is empty and doesn't contain any objects, relationships, or sample data.

Create a new blank database

1. Choose the **File** menu, select **New Database**, or choose the File New Database button 🗋 on the toolbar. The New Database dialog box appears (see Figure 20.6). In the **General** tab, choose **Blank Database** and **OK**.

2. In the **Save in** list box, select the desired drive and folder.

3. Enter a **File name** for the new database file. Access automatically assigns the MDB extension to the new database's filename.

4. Choose **OK**.

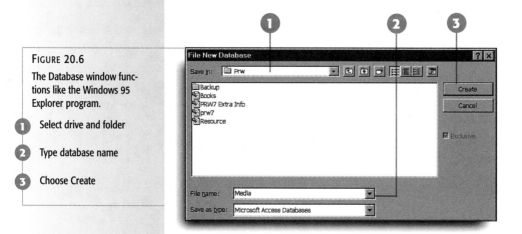

FIGURE 20.6

The Database window functions like the Windows 95 Explorer program.

1 Select drive and folder

2 Type database name

3 Choose Create

After Access creates the new database, an empty database window opens in the Access window, ready for you to create new objects (see Figure 20.7).

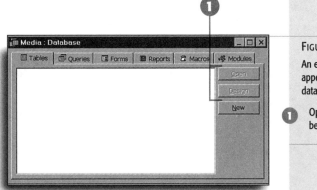

FIGURE 20.7

An empty database window appears for the newly created database.

1 Open and Design are dim because there are no tables

SEE ALSO

➤ *To create a table when starting with a blank database, see page 464*

➤ *To enter information in a table using forms, see page 528*

➤ *To create a report for lists or subtotals of your data, see page 582*

➤ *To create a query to see only certain fields or records from your table, see page 564*

Creating Tables

Create a new table, the foundation of a database

Modify table design

Set field properties to help get correct input

Set table properties

Set relationships to tie tables together

Creating a New Table

Now that you have planned and created an Access database, the next step is to create the tables that store your data. Tables are the foundation of your database. All other Access database objects, such as forms, queries, and reports, depend on the data in the tables.

If you are new to Access and used the Database Wizard to create tables from predesigned templates, you might want to skip this chapter and proceed to Chapter 22, "Viewing and Editing Data." You can always return to this chapter when you need to create a new table.

To create a new table, first display the database window. Then select the **Tables** tab and click the **New** button. Access displays the New Table dialog box. Access provides the following five methods of table creation:

- **Datasheet view**. This view enables you to create a table by entering data in a blank datasheet, similar to entering data in a spreadsheet. When you save the datasheet, Access analyzes the data entered and automatically assigns the appropriate field types and formats for you. If you are new to Access and have already organized data that you need to start entering immediately, creating tables in *Datasheet view* is a great approach.

- **Design view**. This enables you to create a table from scratch. In Table *Design view* you enter the field names, select the field data type, and set field properties such as formats and captions. If you are familiar with database design and Access, you might find that you have more control by creating a table in Design view.

- **Table Wizard**. This provides you with a list of common table designs that you can select and change to meet your needs. The Table Wizard helps you create tables quickly from numerous personal and business table types, such as mailing lists, invoices, contacts, recipes, and investments. Each predefined table comes with sample fields. Based on your responses, the Table Wizard creates the table that you request. If you are new to Access and want to see examples already created for you, use the Table Wizard.

- **Import Table Wizard**. This choice copies data stored in another Access database, or another application format, into the currently open Access database and automatically creates an Access table for the data.

- **Link Table Wizard**. This choice leaves data in its current location and enables you to view and edit the data in Access. Linking enables you to edit and view the data in Access and in the original application. In cases where the data continues to be maintained by another application and used in Access, linking is the best way to create the new table.

SEE ALSO

➤ *For a definition of databases and database terms, see page 446*

➤ *To see the similarity and differences between tables and queries (both of which have Datasheet view), see page 564*

Creating a Table Using Datasheet View

Access enables you to jump right in and start entering data into a datasheet. The datasheet appears and behaves much like an Excel worksheet. After you finish entering data, save the datasheet, and Access automatically creates the table for you. The new table has generic field names (such as Field1, Field2, and so on), which you can change to more descriptive names.

Access also looks for a *primary key* field—a unique tag for a record, such as an ID number. If Access cannot find a primary key field, it asks whether you want it to create a primary key for you. If you respond Yes, Access adds an AutoNumber field to the beginning of the table. The AutoNumber field generates a unique number for each record, called the primary key.

If you have a field that you are certain will never be duplicated and that will always be available when you first enter a record, you can create your own primary key. (For step-by-step instructions, see the section "Setting the Primary Key" later in this chapter.) If, however, you don't already have a unique field, go ahead and let Access create the primary key for you. If you don't

---

Some Wizards might not be installed

The availability and types of Wizards installed depends on your installation. You may need to rerun the Microsoft Access or Microsoft Office setup program.

Linking = Attaching

In previous versions of Access, linking was called attaching.

AutoNumber = Counter

In previous versions of Access, AutoNumber was called Counter.

think you need a primary key, you probably don't have a good design for your database or you only need one table in your database. A primary key is essential if you are going to relate tables, and if you don't relate tables, why are they in the same database? (To create relationships, see "Setting Relationships" later in this chapter.)

SEE ALSO
➤ *For a description of primary keys, see page 446*

After you create and save the table, you might want or need to edit the table design. For example, later in Figure 21.4 you can see that the Zip Code field lost the leading zero. This happened because Access automatically assigned this field a data type of number instead of text. When the data type is number, Access automatically deletes leading zeros. You can easily fix this by entering Table Design view. While in Table Design view, you can change the generic field names (Field1, Field2, and so on) to more descriptive names and set other field properties.

Create a new table in Datasheet view

1. Open the database window (press F11).

2. On the **Table** tab click the **New** button and double-click **Datasheet View**. Access displays the New Table dialog box (see Figure 21.1).

Check the design early on in Datasheet view

When using Datasheet view to create tables, save the table after entering a few rows of data. Look for and fix data type errors before entering more data.

FIGURE 21.1

You can create new tables automatically from your data either by using the Table Wizard or from scratch.

1 Click here...

2 ...to display

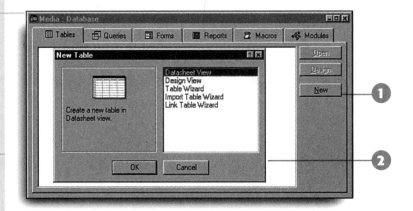

3. Type your first piece of data in the first cell under Field1. Press Tab and type the next piece of data under Field2. Continue typing data for one record in one row (see Figure 21.2).

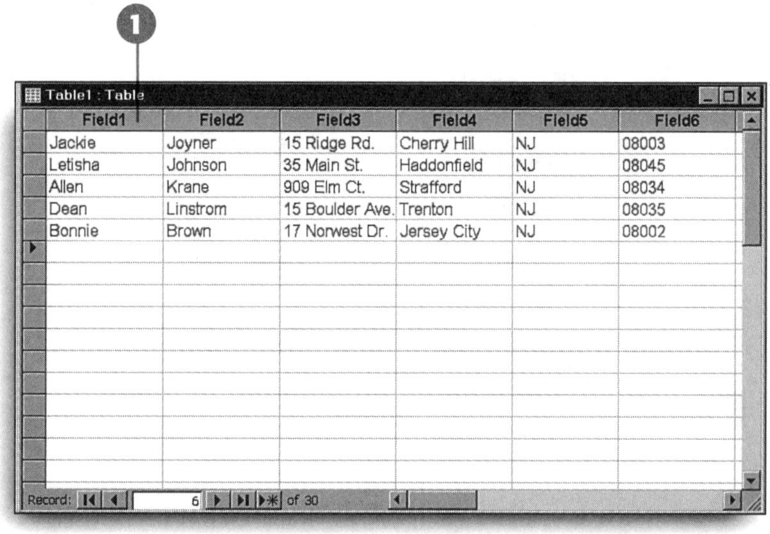

	Field1	Field2	Field3	Field4	Field5	Field6
	Jackie	Joyner	15 Ridge Rd.	Cherry Hill	NJ	08003
	Letisha	Johnson	35 Main St.	Haddonfield	NJ	08045
	Allen	Krane	909 Elm Ct.	Strafford	NJ	08034
	Dean	Linstrom	15 Boulder Ave.	Trenton	NJ	08035
	Bonnie	Brown	17 Norwest Dr.	Jersey City	NJ	08002

Record: ◄◄ ◄ 6 ► ►► ►* of 30

FIGURE 21.2
You can enter data directly into a datasheet and Access creates the table for you.

1 Double-click the heading to name the field.

4. Click the second row under Field1 to add data for your next record. Repeat step 3 for each record you want.

5. To name the columns (fields), double-click the column header (Field1, Field2, and so on), type the new field name, and press Enter.

6. Click the Save button 🖫 to save the table. When you click Save, this actually saves the table design (field names and data types) rather than the data (records). When you move to the next record, Access saves the data for you.

7. When prompted to create a primary key, choose **Yes** (see Figure 21.3). Access assigns an automatic number field for you (see Figure 21.4).

FIGURE 21.3

A primary key enables you to find unique records and create relationships between tables.

FIGURE 21.4

Access adds an AutoNumber primary key field labeled ID to the table you created.

1 Access created this AutoNumber field as a primary key.

8. If necessary, click the Design View button and change field types or modify the table design in Design view. (See "Modifying Table Design" later in the chapter.)

9. Click the Save button to save the table again.

10. Click the Datasheet View button to return to Datasheet view to continue with data entry.

SEE ALSO

➤ For rules of naming tables and other database objects, see page 457

Creating a Table with the Table Wizard

Access is no different from the other Office products with its generous sprinkling of wizards. One way to get you functioning quickly is to use a table wizard, if the table is standard (mailing list, contacts, customers, and so on).

SEE ALSO

➤ To use a wizard to create your whole database, see page 458

Using the Table Wizard

1. Click the **Tables** tab and choose the **New** button. Access displays the New Table dialog box.

2. Double-click **Table Wizard**. Access displays the Table Wizard dialog box (see Figure 21.5). **Sample Tables** are listed based on the table option button that you select—**Business** or **Personal**.

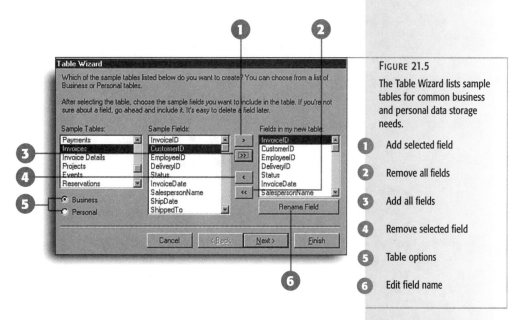

FIGURE 21.5

The Table Wizard lists sample tables for common business and personal data storage needs.

①	Add selected field
②	Remove all fields
③	Add all fields
④	Remove selected field
⑤	Table options
⑥	Edit field name

3. Click a sample table. The corresponding predefined sample fields appear in the **Sample Fields** list box.

4. Use the arrow buttons to add fields to or remove fields from your new table definition.

5. If necessary, click the **Rename Field** button to change a field name to make it more meaningful. A small Rename Field dialog box appears. Type the field new field name in the **Rename Field** text box and click **OK**.

6. After you choose all the fields in your table, click the **Next** button on the Table Wizard. The next Table Wizard dialog box appears (see Figure 21.6). The text box in this dialog box asks you for the name of your table. Type the name of the table.

Use multiple sample tables

You can use fields from more than one sample table and from Business and Personal tables for your table.

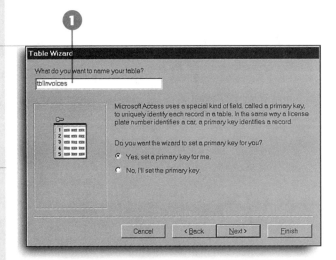

7. The Table Wizard asks whether you want to set your own primary key or whether you want Access to set a primary key for you. If one of the fields that you added should be a primary key, you set the primary key yourself; otherwise, let Access create a primary key for the table. Choose **Next**.

8. If you decide to set the primary key yourself, the dialog box shown in Figure 21.7 appears. In the **What field will hold data that is unique for each record** drop-down list, select the appropriate field. Then specify the type of data the primary key will contain by clicking one of the option buttons.

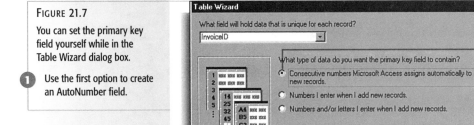

9. Whether or not you let Access choose your primary key or you set one in step 8 after you choose **Next**, Access asks you whether your table is related to other tables (if you have other tables in the database). Access lists relationships found between the new table and existing tables (see Figure 21.8). Choose the **Relationships** button 🔲 to define the additional relationship. When done with the relationship dialog box, choose **OK** and then **Next**.

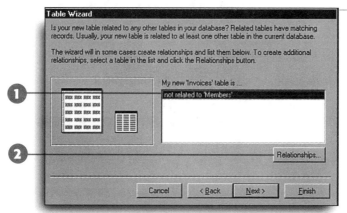

FIGURE 21.8

The Table Wizard searches for and creates relationships between the new table and existing tables.

❶ Choose the table to relate to.

❷ Then click the Relationships button.

10. The last step of the Table Wizard dialog box (see Figure 21.9) asks you whether you want to **Modify the table design**, **Enter data directly in the table**, or **Enter data in the table using a form**. (Because you haven't created a form yet, go ahead and choose this third option.) Choose an option and click **Finish**.

Further customize a table

Use Table Design view to further customize a table that you created with the Table Wizard.

SEE ALSO

➤ *For a background discussion on primary keys, see page 447*

➤ *For more information about primary keys, see page 483*

➤ *To set your own relationship manually (without the wizard), see page 493*

If you chose either of the first two options in the last step of the Table Wizard, you view the table either in Datasheet or Design view. Datasheet view displays the data in spreadsheet format, ready for data entry and editing. Design view enables you to change the structure or appearance of your table. You cannot enter data in Design view. To switch from one view to another, click the View button 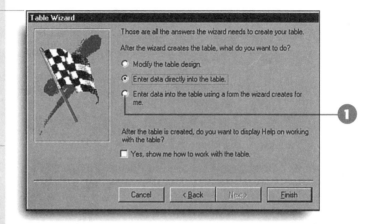, which is the first button on the Table Datasheet toolbar.

FIGURE 21.9

After the Table Wizard creates your table, you can enter data, edit the design, or view table Help.

❶ The wizard can even create a form for you in which to enter data.

Creating a New Table by Importing

In cases where the data resides in another application format and you need to maintain that data in Access from this point forward, you might prefer using the **Import Table** option. Access supports the following file types for importing:

- Access (MDB)
- Text (TXT, CSV, TAB, ASC)
- Excel (XLS)
- Lotus 123 (WK*)
- Paradox (DB)
- dBASE III, IV, 5 (DBF)
- FoxPro (DBF)
- FoxPro 3 (DBC)
- ODBC Databases

One of the time-consuming parts of my consulting business has been importing data from other sources. Although the steps mentioned next take very little time, often the data is not very clean. For example, customer IDs that are supposed to be unique may not be, or customer names that are supposed to be the same

Access doesn't support the file format you need?

Try exporting from the original application to a supported file format.

You may need to install file types

Depending on your installation of Access, you may or may not have the displayed list of file types available for import, export, or linking. You may need to go through the Access or Office setup if your file type isn't available. In setup, select **Microsoft Access**, choose **Change Option**, and then see the options under **Data Access**.

are not. You may see the same company listed many ways as in ABC Inc, A.B.C., ABC Incorporated, and so forth. When you make reports or summary queries of these companies, the data does not summarize properly into one group. Be sure, therefore, to plan a substantial amount of time into cleaning up data that you import.

Don't forget to use the action queries (such as an Update query) mentioned in Chapter 24 to help you. You may also need to use the **Find Duplicates Query Wizard** or **Find Unmatched Query Wizard** if you have multiple tables and need to build relationships. These two wizards appear when you choose the **New** button on the **Query** tab. If you need these wizards, follow the steps on the wizards to complete the tasks.

SEE ALSO

➤ *To understand what results when you use action queries, see page 578*

Create a new table using Import Table

1. Open the Database window, select the **Tables** tab, and select the **New** button.

2. Double-click **Import Table**. The Import dialog box appears (see Figure 21.10).

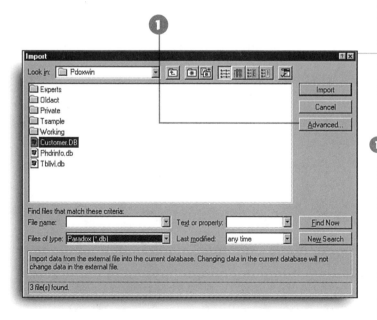

FIGURE 21.10

When you create a table by importing, edits in Access only affect the new Access table, not the original data file.

1 Click Advanced to search for a file if you don't know where it is.

3. In the **Files of type** drop-down list, specify the file format from which you are importing.

4. Specify the location of the file in the **Look in** drop-down list.

5. Select the **File name**.

6. Choose **Import**. A few possible results are as follows:

- If the import is successful, the table appears in the **Table** tab of the Database window. Click the **Tables** tab to see the icon representing the new table.

- If Access encounters any problems, an error dialog box appears to explain the problem. For example, both dBASE and FoxPro have .dbf file extensions. If you import the wrong file type, you may get an error message about the external file format. If you get an error, check the file format (and version) and the names of fields in your source file. For FoxPro, dBASE, and Paradox files, if there are linked index or memo files, you have to import them with the file. When you import a spreadsheet or text file, Access may not be able to determine the correct data type (the file's field starts with numbers but occasionally has a text value). You may need to edit the file before you can import it into Access. If you have an OLE field in Paradox, you cannot import or link the table in Access (delete the field in Paradox).

- If you need to define any import options such as spreadsheet range, or data width, Access prompts you with additional Wizard dialog boxes.

SEE ALSO
➤ *To learn naming rules for fields (and other Access objects), see page 457*

Creating a New Table by Linking

When your data resides in another application format and you need to edit and view that data from Access while others edit and view the data in the other application, you might prefer to use the Link Table option to create a new table. Access supports the following file types for linking:

- Access (MDB)
- Text (TXT, CSV, TAB, ASC)
- Excel (XLS)
- Paradox (DB)
- dBASE III, IV, 5 (DBF)
- FoxPro (DBF)
- ODBC Databases

Create a new table using the Link Table Wizard

1. Open the Database window, select the **Table** tab, and select the **New** button.
2. Double-click **Link Table**. The Link dialog box appears (see Figure 21.11).

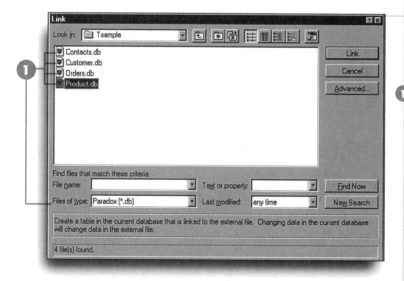

If link doesn't work, try import

You cannot link FoxPro 3 (DBC) and Lotus 123 (WK*) files to an Access table. You can, however, import them.

FIGURE 21.11

When you create a table by linking, edits made in Access affect the original data file.

1 Displayed list depends on **Files of type** selected.

3. Specify the file format from which you are linking in the **Files of type** drop-down list.
4. Specify the location of the file.
5. Select the **File name**.
6. Choose Link. A few results that can occur:

- If the link is successful, the table appears in the **Table** tab of the Database window (see Figure 21.12).

- If Access encounters any problems, an error dialog box appears to explain the problem. (See the earlier section "Creating a New Table by Importing" for some of the errors.)

- If you need to define any link options such as spreadsheet range, or data width, Access prompts you with additional Wizard dialog boxes.

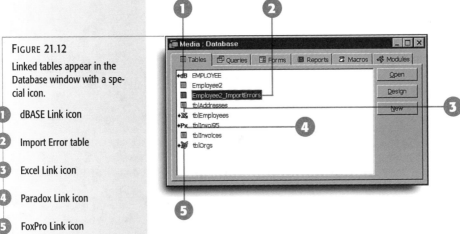

FIGURE 21.12

Linked tables appear in the Database window with a special icon.

1. dBASE Link icon

2. Import Error table

3. Excel Link icon

4. Paradox Link icon

5. FoxPro Link icon

Creating a Blank Table

Create a blank table

1. Display the Database window (press F11).

2. Select the **Table** tab.

3. Choose the **New** button to open the New Table dialog box.

4. Double-click **Design View**. Access displays a blank table in Design view (see Figure 21.13).

5. In the top of the Table window, specify the **Field Name** and **Data Type**, and if desired, provide a **Description** to appear in the status bar. You use the bottom of the Table window to set field properties, such as format, field size, default value, and validation rules. (The following section, "Modifying

Table Design" explains how to design and modify the design of a table.)

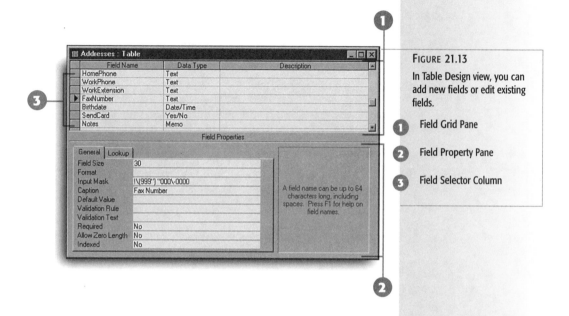

FIGURE 21.13

In Table Design view, you can add new fields or edit existing fields.

1 Field Grid Pane

2 Field Property Pane

3 Field Selector Column

6. When finished, click the Save button 🔲 and give the table a name.

Modifying Table Design

You can view a table in Datasheet view or Design view 📝 ▾. In Datasheet view, you enter and modify data in your table; in Design view, you add or modify fields.

Enter Design View

1. Go to the Database window (press F11).

2. In the Database window, click the **Tables** tab and select the desired table.

3. Choose the **Design** button.

Alternatively, if you are currently viewing the table in Datasheet view, choose the Design View button 📝 ▾ on the toolbar.

Design view contains the following components:

- *Table Design toolbar*. Contains various tools that help you design and work with your table.
- *Field Grid pane*. Contains columns that enable you to define field names, data types, and descriptions.
- *Field Properties pane*. Enables you to set various properties for each field.

The next sections explain how to work with these components.

Working with the Table Design Toolbar

In the Table Design window, the toolbar contains the active buttons listed in Table 21.1.

TABLE 21.1   The Table Design toolbar

Button	Button Name	Description
	Datasheet View	Displays the table in Datasheet view
	Save	Saves the table design
	Cut	Removes the selected text or object from the Design window to the Clipboard
	Copy	Copies the selected text or object from the Design window to the Clipboard
	Paste	Places a copy of the Clipboard contents in the current selection
	Primary Key	Enables users to select a column or columns as the primary key; toggles primary key on/off
	Indexes	Displays the index sheet for the currently selected object
	Insert Row	Inserts a row above the current row
	Delete Row	Deletes the selected row(s)

Button	Button Name	Description
	Properties	Opens or closes the property sheet for the currently selected object
	Build	Helps create an item or property such as a field or input mask property

Working in the Field Grid Pane

The field grid pane enables you to define field names, data types, and descriptions. The grid consists of the field row selector column, the **Field Name** column, **Data Type** column, and the **Description** column (refer to Figure 21.13).

As is true of most objects in an Access database, field names can contain up to 64 characters (letters, numbers, and spaces). Field names must be unique within the table.

SEE ALSO

➤ For a description of naming rules, see page 457

Determining the Data Type

A data type specifies the kind of information that you can store in a field. If you define a field as a Date field, for example, Access does not permit you to enter text in that field. Based on the data type, Access also determines the types of calculations or other operations available for that field.

Access provides the following basic data types:

- **Text**. Alphanumeric characters, up to 255 bytes.

  For numbers containing punctuation (such as hyphens in a Social Security or phone number), you can use the Text data type or change formatting or the input mask, because no punctuation is allowed in a Number data type.

SEE ALSO

➤ For a description of input masks, see page 483

- **Memo**. Alphanumeric characters, up to 64,000 characters. This data type is great for notes.

- **Number**. Any numeric type for storage sizes and range of values permitted (see Table 21.2 following this list).

- **Date/Time**. Dates and times.

- **Currency**. Rounded numbers that are accurate to 15 digits to the left of the decimal point and to four decimal places.

  Be careful when choosing between the Number and the Currency data type. Entries in fields formatted as Currency are rounded, whereas Number fields use floating-point calculation (the decimal point floats as needed). Currency data type uses a faster method of fixed-point calculation (predetermined number of decimal places) that prevents rounding errors.

- **AutoNumber**. Unique sequential (incrementing by one) or random numbering, automatically entered by Access for each record you add. AutoNumber is often the choice for primary key fields.

- **Yes/No**. Logical values (Yes/No, True/False, or On/Off).

- **OLE Object**. OLE objects, graphics, or other binary data. The OLE Object data type is the key to including other Office documents (Word, Excel, PowerPoint) in your Access database. For example, you may need to have an employee database with résumés from each employee or keep track of different budgets from Excel. In Datasheet view or on a form in an OLE field, choose **Insert**, select **Object**, and select an existing document through the **Create from File** choice. Warning: Your database grows very large if you don't choose to **Link** the file.

- **Lookup Wizard**. Walks you through the process to create a field that displays a drop-down list of acceptable values from another table. The Lookup Wizard creates Number or Text data type, depending on the key from the lookup table. (To use the wizard see "Creating a Lookup Field" later in this chapter.)

Access allows the range of values shown in Table 21.2 for numerical data (identified in the Field Size property). Good database design requires that you use the smallest storage size possible to display any potential value in the field.

Example data types

For a Client Number field, use **AutoNumber** so that Access automatically enters consecutive numbers for you. For the Client Name field, use **Text**. For the Phone field, you could use **Number**, but **Text** is easier if you want the phone number field to contain punctuation, such as dashes. For the Invoice Total field, use **Currency** to get the proper dollars-and-cents format, calculations, and for a Notes field. Use **Memo** to get more information into the field than a text field allows.

TABLE 21.2 **Numeric values permitted for the number data type**

Field Size	Storage Size	Range
Byte	1 byte	0 to 255; no fractions.
Integer	2 bytes	–32,768 to 32,767; no fractions.
Long Integer	4 bytes	–2,147,483,648 to 2,147,483,647; no fractions.
Single	4 bytes	Numbers with seven digits of precision. –3.402823E38 to 3.402823E38.
Double	8 bytes	Numbers with 15 digits of precision. –1.79769313486231E308 to 1.79769313486231E308
Replication ID	16 bytes	Globally unique identifier (GUID) used for database replication.

By default, Access assigns the data type Text to a new field. To assign a different data type, click the field's **Data Type** column, click the down-arrow button, and select one from the **Data Type** drop-down list (see Figure 21.14).

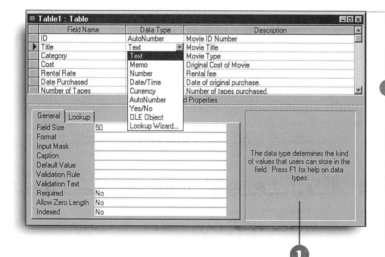

Tip for selecting drop-down options

To speed selection of data types, type the first letter of the data type and press Tab. Access fills in the rest.

FIGURE 21.14

Type the first letter of the data type or select it from the drop-down list.

① The help box gives short help and directs you to F1 for more help.

I recommend that you use the **Description** column to provide further information about a field. The description is optional, but it does appear in the status bar when the insertion point is

in that field in datasheet or form view. The description is also
helpful if you need to go back later and remember what the
fields mean.

Creating a Lookup Field

If you want to create a lookup field (combo box) in Access 2.0,
you can only do that on a form. In Access 95 you can create
lookup fields directly in a table. When you enter data, you can
then click the down arrow or begin typing to choose the value
from the lookup list. When you create a form based on this
table, Access automatically turns this field into a combo box.
Before you begin this procedure, create a table that contains at
least a primary key field and a description.

Create Lookup Field

1. In Table Design view, type the name of the field in the Field
   Name column and press **Tab**.

2. Choose **Lookup Wizard** in the **Data Type** column and
   press **Tab**. The first step of the wizard displays.

3. You have a choice of looking up the values from an existing
   table or query or typing in the values that you want. I recommend that you use an existing table (so you can easily add
   items). Choose that option and the **Next** button.

4. Double-click the table (or query).

5. The next step of the wizard shows you a list of fields in the
   table or query. First double-click the primary key field and
   then pick one or more other fields that help you define your
   record (these are usually description or name fields). Choose
   Next.

6. The wizard then shows your column(s) with data. Usually,
   you do not need to see the primary key, so keep the **Hide
   key column** option checked. If you want to increase the
   width of columns, point to the right edge of the column
   name box (your mouse pointer is a double-headed arrow)
   and drag. When finished, choose **Next**.

7. Type a label for your lookup column and choose **Finish**.
   The label appears in the Caption property for this field.

8. You see a dialog box indicating that you must save the table before relationships can be created. Choose **Y**es.

Setting the Primary Key

Although it is not required, every table should have a primary key so that it works efficiently in Access. The primary key identifies a record as unique. In an Employee database, for example, each employee has a unique Employee number. The Employee number field would be the primary key. You can create a primary key using this procedure if you create a table through Datasheet view or manually through Design view. If you create a table by using the Table Wizard, Access can create one for you.

SEE ALSO

➤ *For a description of primary keys, see page 447*

➤ *To see how to create a table with the Table Wizard, see page 468*

Set a primary key

1. Click the field selector (first column) to select the field that you want to use as the primary key. For a multi-field primary key, hold down the Ctrl key and click the field selector for the remaining field(s).

2. Choose the primary key icon 🔑 . A key icon appears in the field selector column of each primary-key field (see Figure 21.15).

Setting Field Properties

Fields have *properties* that define the way data is stored and displayed. The first field property with which you dealt was field name, followed by data type, and field description; however, you can set many additional properties. By setting field properties, you can provide the following:

- A default caption
- A default value
- A format (display layout) for data entry
- Data-entry validation (rules for entry)

- An index (for fields that can be indexed)
- Various display qualities, such as field size and formats

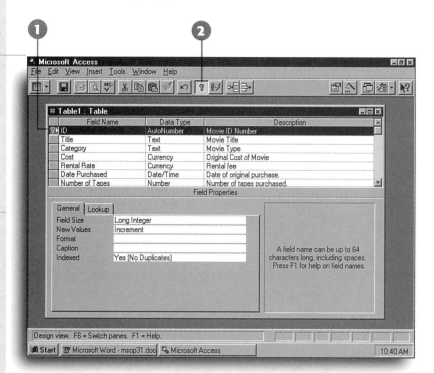

FIGURE 21.15

Access displays a key icon in
the field selector column to
indicate the field(s) that define
the primary key.

❶ Click the field selector to
select the field row(s).

❷ Click to set primary key.

The field properties set at the table level are applied automatically to other database objects that use this table, such as forms, reports, and queries. In Table Design view, field properties are organized on two tabs, General and Lookup (see Figure 21.16).

SEE ALSO

➤ *To see how to set the field name, data type, and description, see page 479*

The following is an overview of the General field properties:

- **Field Size**. Limits Text fields to a specific number of characters such as 2 for two characters in a State field; and limits Number fields to a range of values (refer to Table 21.2).

- **New Values**. Specifies how new values for AutoNumber fields should be generated—incremental or random.

- **Format**. Specifies a specific display format for dates and numbers, such as 2/21/99, Sunday, February 21, 1999, 1234.5, or $1,234.50. The format options are different depending on the data type that you use for the field.

- **Decimal Places**. Sets the number of decimal places displayed in Number and Currency fields, such as 2.99.

- **Input Mask** (Text and Date data only). Specifies formatting characters, such as dashes in a phone number field, to be filled in automatically during data entry.

- **Caption**. Supplies a label to be used in forms and reports and as the header of the datasheet column instead of the field name, such as Movie Tag instead of MovieID.

- **Default Value**. Specifies a default value to be entered automatically in new records, such as the city and state in which a video-rental store is located.

- **Validation Rule**. Restricts data entry to values that meet specific criteria, such as the return date being greater than today's date.

- **Validation Text**. Specifies the error message that appears when data entry violates a validation rule.

- **Required**. Specifies that data be entered in the field, such as the member's ID number.

- **Allow Zero Length**. Permits Text and Memo fields to contain *zero-length strings* (""). By default, Access does not store string values that contain no characters or spaces.

- **Indexed**. Sets up an additional index based on this field. (For more information, see "Setting Index Properties" later in this chapter.)

On the **Lookup** tab, the properties change depending on what data type you choose and what the value is for the first Lookup field property, **Display Control**.

- **Display Control**. Specifies the type of control to use to display the field on a form (only for Text, Number, and Yes/No fields). The types of controls include Text Box (the default), List Box (shows more than one value at a time with scroll bars), and Combo Box (creates a drop-down list of choices

For help on any property

Click the property box and press F1. The help screen displays the property name, a long description, and sometimes includes examples.

with the result appearing in a text box with a drop-down arrow).

- **Row Source Type**. Specifies whether the values in the List Box or Combo Box come from a table or query, a list that you type (Value List), or a list of fields from a table or query.

- **Row Source**. Name of a table, query, or SQL statement used for the List Box or Combo Box.

- **Bound Column**. The column number shown in the Row Source whose value is stored in the current table.

- **Column Count**. Number of columns used for the Combo or List Box.

- **Column Heads**. Displays the name of the fields from the Row Source.

- **Column Widths**. Width in inches of the drop-down or list box columns separated by semicolons. If you do not want a column displayed, type ø for the column width. An example of the Column Widths is 0;1;1.5 where the first column (this could be the Bound Column such as an ID number) does not display.

SEE ALSO

➤ *The items on the Lookup tab are automatically set when you use the Lookup Wizard. For more information, see page 482*

Set field properties

1. Select the field for which you want to set properties. The bottom part of the window displays the General properties for that field (see Figure 21.16).

2. Click the specific General property that you want to set, or press F6 to move to the **Field Properties** pane and Tab to the desired property.

3. Enter the property value, or select it from a drop-down list of values (if available).

4. Continue setting other properties for the field.

5. Select the **Lookup** tab and set properties as needed.

6. Repeat steps 1 through 5 to set properties for other fields as needed.

7. When you finish setting properties, save your table.

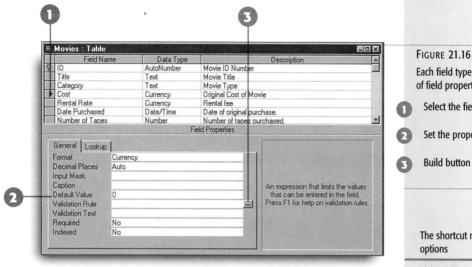

FIGURE 21.16

Each field type has its own list of field properties.

1 Select the field

2 Set the property

3 Build button

The shortcut menu offers useful options

Right-clicking a field property displays a pop-up shortcut menu containing the **Build**, **Zoom**, **Cut**, **Copy**, **Paste**, and **Table Properties** commands. (Some commands are disabled and don't show depending on the property or data type.)

If the property box is too small for the value that you need to enter, press Shift+F2 or click the right mouse button and choose **Zoom** from the shortcut menu to display the Zoom dialog box (see Figure 21.17). The Zoom dialog box is available throughout most of Access.

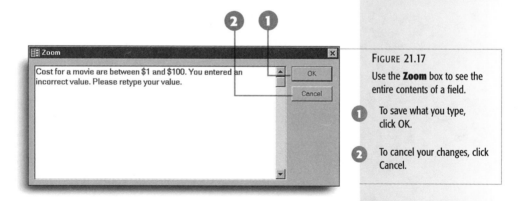

FIGURE 21.17

Use the **Zoom** box to see the entire contents of a field.

1 To save what you type, click OK.

2 To cancel your changes, click Cancel.

The Expression Builder is available for some properties. This feature is also available when you are creating a query. (You can use the Builder in both the Field row and Criteria row of a query.) The Builder is also available when you create formulas in reports. Some of the properties on forms also use the Expression

Builder. You need to click in the Control Source property (located on the Data tab in the Properties dialog box) and click the Build button.

The Build button ▨ on the Table Design toolbar, or to the right of the property in the Field Properties grid, enables you to see available functions or examples. Figure 21.18 shows the Expression Builder dialog box for the **Validation Rule** property. (The same dialog box would be available for the **Default Value** property.)

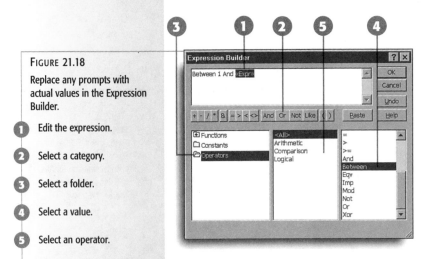

FIGURE 21.18

Replace any prompts with actual values in the Expression Builder.

❶ Edit the expression.

❷ Select a category.

❸ Select a folder.

❹ Select a value.

❺ Select an operator.

The Builder may also give examples from which to choose. If your cursor is in a field name in Design view, the Build button opens a Field Builder dialog box (see Figure 21.19) in which you can select sample field names from different sample tables. This is the same as one of the steps of the Table Wizard. When you choose Build for the Input Mask property, Access gives you a choice of examples that includes phone numbers, social security numbers, passwords, and dates.

SEE ALSO

➤ *In Excel, the feature equivalent to the Expression Builder is the Function Wizard, which is easier to use. See page 260*

➤ *For a more in-depth description of how to use the Expression Builder, see page 595*

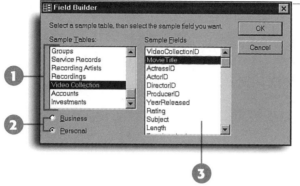

FIGURE 21.19

Choose Business or Personal,
the Sample Table, and the
Sample Field you want.

❶ Table samples for the selected table type

❷ Type of table

❸ Fields in the selected sample
table

Setting Index Properties

Indexes help Access find values. Access automatically creates and
maintains an index for the primary-key fields. You can create
additional indexes by setting the field index property.

If you frequently search or sort certain fields (included in queries
and reports), you can increase processing speed by creating an
index for those fields. You can set up indexes for all field types
except OLE, Hyperlink, Memo, and Yes/No. You can set the
following index properties:

- **Yes (Duplicates OK)**. Creates an index that includes duplicate field values.

- **Yes (No Duplicates)**. Creates an index based on unique
  field values.

- **No**. Has no index.

Set index properties

1. In the **Field Grid** pane, select the field to be indexed.

2. In the **Field Properties** pane, select the **Indexed** property.

3. Select a type of index from the **Indexed** drop-down list of
   index property values (see Figure 21.20).

SEE ALSO

➤ *For more description on input masks and other field properties, see page 483*

➤ *Primary keys are automatically indexed. To see how to create a primary key, see page 483*

**Although indexes speed searches
and sorts, they might slow data
processing**

Each time a record is added,
deleted, or changed, the indexes must be updated. You generally won't notice if you are
adding one record at a time. If
you are doing mass updates,
however, then you see a significant time difference if you have
many records.

FIGURE 21.20

By setting the index property to **Yes**, you speed up your search.

1 Note that you have two choices for Yes.

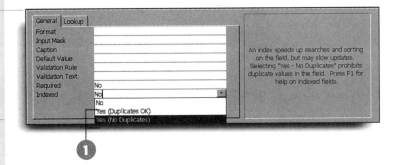

To speed up data entry

Set field properties for default values, and use default patterns (input masks) to format data automatically as it is entered.

Setting Table Properties

Like fields, tables have properties. Table properties apply to the entire table and to all the records that the table contains. You can set the following properties for a table:

- **Description**. Enter a description of the table and its purpose (for more room, use the **Zoom** box by pressing Shift+F2). For example, the Movies table could be described as the inventory of movies purchased. If you click the Details button on the Database toolbar, the description as well as the date and time appear for the table.

- **Validation Rule**. Restricts data entry to values that meet specific criteria for each record in the table—for example, requiring that the ShipDate be after the EntryDate. You use this property when you want to base one field on the value in another field. In the example in Figure 21.22, notice that the field names are in square brackets.

- **Validation Text**. Displays a message when the record-validation rule is violated—for example, describing why the ship date is supposed to be after the entry date.

- **Filter**. Specifies the filter to be loaded with the table—for example, showing only the movies that are currently in stock.

- **Order By**. Specifies the order to be loaded with the table—for example, showing movies in descending order of when purchased.

Set Table Properties

1. In Table Design view, choose the Properties button 🔝. The **Table Properties** window appears (see Figure 21.21).

2. Click any property and type text or expression. This list below provides guidance for the different table properties that you can change:

- For example, type text in the Description property.
- For Validation Rule, type the name of a field in square brackets, an operator (<, =, >), and the name of another field in square brackets.
- For Validation Text, type the text that you want to appear when the user breaks the validation rule.
- For Filter, type the name of a field in square brackets, an operator (<, =, >), and a value. If the value is text, enclose the value in quotes. If the value is a date, enclose the value in pound signs. For example, [Hire Date] < #2/1/99#.
- For Order By, type the name of a field in square brackets. If you want the field sorted in descending order, type DESC after the field name.

3. When finished, click the Close button (x) to close the **Table Properties** window.

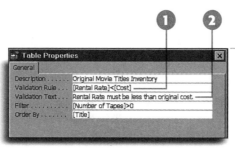

Table Properties
General
Description . . . . . . Original Movie Titles Inventory
Validation Rule . . . [Rental Rate]<[Cost]
Validation Text . . . Rental Rate must be less than original cost.
Filter . . . . [Number of Tapes]>0
Order By . . . . [Title]

FIGURE 21.21

To apply a validation rule to all records in a table, set the table's Validation Rule property.

1 Validation rule when comparing two fields

2 Validation rule when one field is compared with a value

Modifying a Table

Access makes it easy for you to modify your table to meet changing needs. You can add, rename, delete, and move fields. Remember, you should always back up your data before modifying the structure of your table. You should also consider the effects of the following actions on dependent database objects, such as forms, queries, and reports:

- *Deleting a field*. Fields deleted from tables also must be deleted from forms, queries, and reports.

- *Renaming a field*. Renamed fields must be renamed in forms, queries, and reports. In addition, you must rename any references to the field in calculations, expressions, macros, and modules.

- *Changing a data type*. Certain data-type conversions are not allowed, such as converting from any data type to the AutoNumber data type. In other cases, if you convert from a larger data type to a smaller data type, data is truncated (cut off or lost). For example, changing from a Number data type to a Yes/No data type changes all values to Yes or No, and data will be lost. (For more information, refer to "Determining the Data Type" earlier in this chapter.)

- *Changing the field size*. Changes that truncate numbers with decimals are rounded. If a change makes the value too large for the new field, the data is lost (an error message appears before the data is lost).

Modifying Table Elements

1. In Table Design view, position the insertion point in the row for the field.

2. Modify any one of the following table elements:

   - To insert a row above the insertion point, choose the Insert Row button ⊰⋲.

   - To rename a field, select the field name cell and type a new name.

   - To delete a field, choose the Delete Row toolbar button ⊟⋅.

   - To move a field, with the black right-arrow mouse pointer, click the field selector (first column) to select the field row that you want to move. With the white arrow mouse pointer, drag the field row to the new position.

3. Click the Save button 🖫 to save the design changes.

4. Click the Datasheet View button 🖩▾ to see your data in rows and columns.

You cannot make the changes in table design and check Datasheet view before you save the design changes (in case you want to disregard the changes). If you attempt to go to Datasheet view after you make the design changes, Access prompts you to save your changes anyway.

Setting Relationships

A relationship enables you to relate one table to another table. For instance, consider a school database with tables for students and assignments. Each student is listed in the student table only once and has a primary key student ID. In the assignment database, a student can have many assignments. The only necessary information about the student is the student ID, which is listed multiple times for each assignment that the student had. The student ID in the assignment table is a foreign key. By creating a relationship between students and assignments using the common student ID field, you create queries that pull information from both tables (seeing the student's first and last name from the student table and the assignment grade in the assignment table, for example). You can also create a form that shows student information and enables you to have a subform to input each assignment.

When planning a table, I recommend that you use the same field names in all related tables (student ID in both student and assignment tables in the preceding example). Although you can physically create relationships between fields that do not have the same information (connect the student ID with the parent ID for example), this creates incorrect results.

If you create tables with the Table Wizard, Access indicates how your table relates to any other tables in the database. Also, if you use the Lookup Wizard as a data type in table design, Access may create a relationship for you. If you want to view or edit these relationships or create new ones, click the Relationships button 🖼 on the Database toolbar. If no relationships have been set, you enter the Show Table dialog box. Add any tables that you want to the relationship window.

You need to create *relationships* between tables when you have forms and subforms and reports and subreports or when you are using combo or list-boxes to lookup values in another table. When you create relationships in advance, your multiple table queries also know how tables are related.

Most relationships are a one-to-many type where one record (such as a customer record) is related to many records (such as invoices). The primary key on the one side of the relationship is related to a field (that has information in common) in the related table. This field in the related table is called a foreign key and may or may not be a primary key itself. In the example in Figure 21.22, one movie title can have multiple actors, so the MovieID in the tblMovieTitles is the primary key and related to the foreign key MovieID field in the tblMovieActors.

SEE ALSO

➤ *Relationships are what set a relational database apart from a flat file database. For an explanation, see page 446*

➤ *Primary keys and foreign keys are two of the main building blocks of relationships. For an explanation, see page 447*

➤ *To see how to create primary keys, see page 483*

Create a Relationship

1. Choose **T**ools and select **Relationships** ⊞.

2. If necessary, click the Show Table icon ⊞ and choose a table.

3. From the **Relationship** window, drag the primary key field name from one field list (the one side of a relationship) to the related field name in another field list (generally, the many side of a relationship). The Relationships dialog box appears (shown in Figure 21.22.)

4. Choose the options in the Relationships window and choose the **C**reate button when finished. The relationship shows a line between the two tables connecting the common field.

The following are the options in the Relationship dialog box:

- **E**nforce Referential Integrity. If this option is checked, and you change or delete the primary key, you are prompted

either that the change is not possible or that data in the
related table will change.

- **Cascade Update Related Fields.** If this is checked when
  you change the primary key, the related foreign key field
  automatically changes. If not checked, you are warned that
  you cannot make a change when you try to edit the primary
  key.

- **Cascade Delete Related Fields.** If checked when you
  delete the record, any related records that match the primary key are deleted. If not checked, you are warned that you
  cannot delete the record if there are related records.

- **Join Type.** This is the default join for queries, including
  whether you only want to see records that have a common
  key in both tables or want to see all of one table and any
  matching records in the other table.

To delete a relationship, click the relationship line and press
Delete.

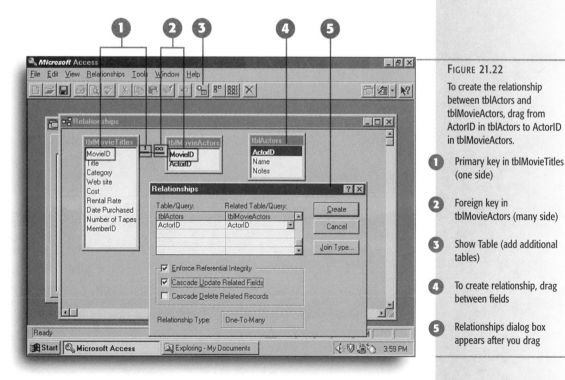

FIGURE 21.22

To create the relationship
between tblActors and
tblMovieActors, drag from
ActorID in tblActors to ActorID
in tblMovieActors.

1. Primary key in tblMovieTitles
   (one side)

2. Foreign key in
   tblMovieActors (many side)

3. Show Table (add additional
   tables)

4. To create relationship, drag
   between fields

5. Relationships dialog box
   appears after you drag

Viewing and Editing Data

Move around a table and query in Datasheet view

Add, edit, and delete data

Locate, sort, and filter data

Import and export data from and to other applications

Change the way your datasheet looks

Navigating in Datasheet View

After you create your table, you are ready to start entering data. Datasheet view enables you to work in a familiar row-and-column format (spreadsheet) in which you can see many records at the same time. To switch from Design to Datasheet view, choose **View** and select **Datasheet**, or choose the Open command button ▦▾ on the database window. Figure 22.1 shows what a new (empty) table looks like. Table 22.1 describes the Active Datasheet toolbar buttons.

FIGURE 22.1

A new table displayed in Datasheet view contains only a blank record with the insertion point in the first field, ready for input.

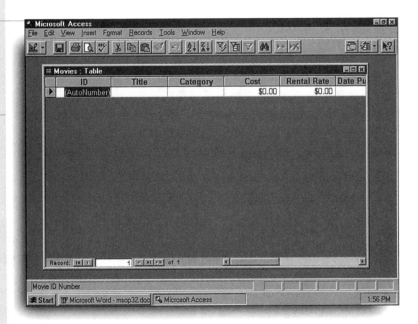

TABLE 22.1   Datasheet toolbar buttons

Button	Button Name	Shortcut	Description
![View]	View		Drop-down list of table views: While In Design shows Datasheet view button and While In Datasheet shows Design View button
![Save]	Save	Ctrl+S	Saves the layout of the current table (in Design view, saves the design of the table)

Button	Button Name	Shortcut	Description
	Print	Ctrl+P	Prints the current table in datasheet format
	Print Preview		Displays the current table in page layout format and enables you to set up the printer and print the current table in datasheet format
	Spelling	F7	Spell-checks the current table
	Cut	Ctrl+X	Deletes selected data and copies it to the Clipboard
	Copy	Ctrl+C	Copies selected data to the Clipboard
	Paste	Ctrl+V	Inserts Clipboard contents
	Undo Current	Ctrl+Z	Reverses the last change to the current field or record
	Sort Ascending		Sorts data in ascending order
	Sort Descending		Sorts data in descending order
	Filter By Selection		Filters data based on selected data
	Filter By Form		Displays the Filter By Form window (a blank version of the active form or datasheet), so that you can enter filter data criteria
	Apply Filter		Turns filter on/off
	Find	Ctrl+F	Searches the current field for user-specified data
	New Record	Ctrl++	Moves to a new record at the end of a datasheet
	Delete Record	Ctrl+-	Deletes the selected record
	Database Window	F11	Displays the database window
	New Object		Displays drop-down list that enables creation of database objects such as forms, queries, and reports
	Help	F1	Displays context-sensitive help

Print or preview the datasheet

Click the Print button 🖨 in the toolbar or choose **File** and select **Print**. To preview the printout onscreen, click the Print Preview 🔍 button or choose **File** and select **Print Preview**.

Entering and Editing Data

Basic data-entry skills include adding, deleting, and editing table records; copying and moving data; and undoing unwanted data changes.

Entering data in Access is similar to entering data in Excel or a Word table. You type your entry in one cell and press Tab or Enter to go to the next field. When you are in the last field, Tab or Enter automatically takes you to the next record.

Access has two modes: Edit mode for editing a field in a record and Navigation mode for moving between records. Some keys act differently in the different modes. For example, in Edit mode, Home takes you to the beginning of a field. In Navigation mode, Home takes you to the beginning of the record. To toggle back and forth between the two modes, press F2.

Access provides many keyboard shortcuts to speed up data entry and table navigation. Table 22.2 lists the shortcut keys for data entry, and Table 22.3 lists the navigation-shortcut keys.

SEE ALSO

➤ *Many of the techniques for entering text apply to all Office products; see page 54*

➤ *A Word table is similar to an Access table in some ways; see page 174*

➤ *An Excel worksheet is similar to an Access table, especially in entering data; see page 210*

TABLE 22.2   **Data-entry shortcut keys**

Shortcut Key	Description
Ctrl+;	Inserts the current date
Ctrl+:	Inserts the current time
Ctrl+Alt+spacebar	Enters the default field value
Ctrl+' or Ctrl+"	Enters the value from the same field in the preceding record
Ctrl+Enter	Inserts a new line in a field, a label, or the zoom box
Ctrl++	Inserts a new blank record
Ctrl+-	Deletes the current record

Shortcut Key	Description
F2	Toggles between edit and navigation mode
Shift+F2	Displays the zoom box
Shift+Enter	Saves changes in the current record
F7	Checks spelling
Esc	Undoes the last change to the current record or field

TABLE 22.3   Datasheet-navigation shortcut keys

Shortcut Key	Description
F5	Moves insertion point to Specific Record box above the status bar. Type the number of the record to which you want to go, and then press Enter.
Enter or Tab	Moves to the following field.
→	Moves to next field when in navigation mode or moves the insertion point to right within field when in Edit mode.
Shift+Tab	Moves to the preceding field.
←	Moves to previous field when in Navigation mode or moves the insertion point to left within field when in Edit mode.
End	Moves to the last field in the current record when in navigation mode or moves to the end of line in field when in Edit mode.
Home	Moves to the first field in the current record when in Navigation mode or beginning of line in field when in Edit mode.
Ctrl+End	Moves to the last record's last field when in navigation mode or end of the last line in a field when in Edit mode.
Ctrl+Home	Moves to the first field in the first record when in Navigation mode or beginning of field when in Edit mode.
↑	Moves up one record in the same field.
↓	Moves down one record in the same field.
Ctrl+↑	Moves to the current field in the first record.
Ctrl+↓	Moves to the current field in the last record.
Page Up	Moves up one screen.
Page Down	Moves down one screen.
Ctrl+Page Up	Moves left one screen.
Ctrl+Page Down	Moves right one screen.

Saving records in Access

As soon as you move from the current edited record to another record, the data is saved. Because changes are saved automatically, if you want to do some testing, you should first make a copy of the database.

You also can use the mouse to select fields, edit fields, and move around the table. Click the navigation buttons to move to the first, preceding, following, or last record (see Figure 22.2). The Record Number box above the status bar displays the current record number You also can use this box to go to a specific record. (Click the Specific Record box, enter the number of the record to which you want to go, and press Enter.) You can use the scrollbars to scroll across columns or rows that do not appear in the current window.

Too many columns to display all at once?

If you have many fields, you can keep column(s) on the left visible. Click the column (or choose multiple columns), choose **Format,** and select **Freeze Columns**.

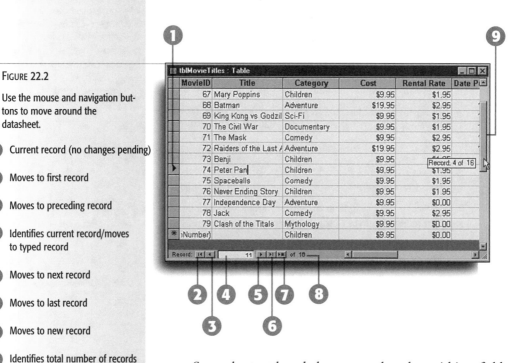

FIGURE 22.2

Use the mouse and navigation buttons to move around the datasheet.

1. Current record (no changes pending)

2. Moves to first record

3. Moves to preceding record

4. Identifies current record/moves to typed record

5. Moves to next record

6. Moves to last record

7. Moves to new record

8. Identifies total number of records

9. Scroll box with tip moves to record

Some shortcut keys help you to select data within a field, a series of fields, or a series of records. (Table 22.4 lists the shortcut keys for selecting data.)

TABLE 22.4 **Selection shortcut keys**	
Shortcut Key	**Description**
Shift	Creates a selection starting from the current point. Use movement keys mentioned in Table 22.2 to expand selection.
Shift+Spacebar	Toggle between selecting field and selecting record when in Navigation mode.
Ctrl+Spacebar	Toggle between selecting field and selecting column when in Navigation mode.
Ctrl+A	Select all records.
F8	Extend mode. Press F8 continuously to select word, field, record, or all records. After F8 is pressed, using any movement keys extends the highlighted selection (without Shift). Press Esc to turn it off.

After you have records selected, you can delete them (Delete), copy or cut them to the Clipboard (Ctrl+X or Ctrl+C), or replace selected records with records from the Clipboard (Ctrl+V). You can use the mouse to select one or more records by clicking or dragging the record selectors. To select one or more columns, click or drag the column selectors.

Adding New Records

Access provides two options for adding records:

- *Edit mode*. Edit mode enables you to add new records at the end of a table or change existing records anywhere in the table. Whenever you change data or enter new records, Access automatically places you in Edit mode.

- *Data Entry mode*. Data Entry mode hides all existing records in the table and displays a blank table, ready for new records.

Add a new record

1. Choose one of the following two options:
    - ▶ Press Ctrl++. This moves you to the bottom of the datasheet and into a new record.

Scrollbar tips

Click the scrollbar once to scroll one screen at a time. When scrolling through a table, scroll tips indicate which record you're on.

- To activate data entry mode, choose the **Records** menu and select **Data Entry**. The Data Entry mode is actually a filter that selects all records with no data (and this shows only the new blank record).

2. Click a field and enter the value that you want. The record indicator changes to a pencil, and Access appends a blank record. If default data already exists in the field, it is replaced by the values that you type. Press Enter or Tab to move to the next field.

3. Continue entering the remaining field data for that record. Access saves each record as you move to a new record; however, you can save the record any time by choosing the **Records** menu and selecting **Save Record** or pressing Shift+Enter.

4. If you chose Data Entry mode, to deactivate Data Entry mode and return to Edit mode (see whole table), choose the **Records** menu and select **Remove Filter/Sort**.

Before you start typing in the new record, any default values show in the record. When you begin to enter data in this row, Access moves the blank record down. If you have an AutoNumber field when you start typing, the number is automatically entered.

The first column on the left of the datasheet is called the record selector column (see Figure 22.3). By clicking this column, you can select the entire row (record).

Access uses the record selector column to display the following record selector symbols:

- The arrowhead ▶ indicates the current record (no new data entry or edits pending).

- The asterisk ✳ marks the blank record that Access keeps at the bottom of the table. When you move to this record, the asterisk changes to an arrowhead, which is the current-record indicator.

- The pencil ✏ indicates that the current record contains data entries or edits you have not yet saved.

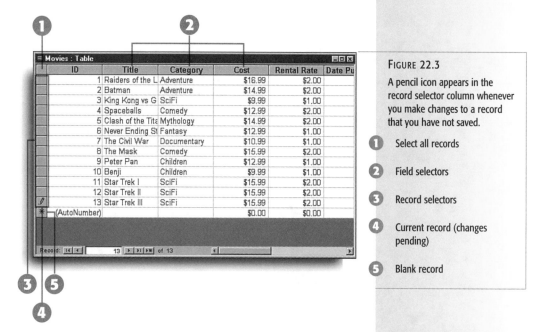

FIGURE 22.3

A pencil icon appears in the record selector column whenever you make changes to a record that you have not saved.

1 Select all records

2 Field selectors

3 Record selectors

4 Current record (changes pending)

5 Blank record

- The record-locked symbol ⊘ indicates that the record is currently being edited by you (on a form or query) or another user in a multiuser environment. This record is read-only to all users except the one who is currently entering data into it.

As you enter data and move from field to field, Access checks data entry for the proper data type and any special properties that you set (such as validation). Access notifies you of any invalid entry when you attempt to move to the next field or record.

Notes for AutoNumber Fields

While you enter information in your table, you may come across AutoNumber fields. The following are some notes to keep in mind when you see these fields:

- You cannot edit data in AutoNumber fields. Access automatically enters a sequential number in AutoNumber fields.

Change the behavior of record locking

Choose **Tools**, and select **Options**. Click the **Advanced** tab, and view the **Default Record Locking** section.

No Locks allows anybody to make changes to any record. If there is a conflict, the user is prompted as to which change takes preference or whether to save the changes to the Clipboard.

Use **All Records** to indicate that all records in the table are locked when one user is editing them.

Use **Edited Record** to lock the current record (and get the record-locked symbol) for the current record (and depending on record size, surrounding records).

Press Tab, Enter, or an arrow key to move past these fields. Access enters the proper value automatically.

- AutoNumber fields may skip numbers. If you start filling in a record and then delete the row, Access skips the AutoNumber field for the next new record. If you delete records, Access also skips AutoNumbers. To reset the AutoNumber field so that no numbers are skipped at the end of a table, compact the database. With no database open, choose the **T**ools menu, select **Database** **U**tilities, and choose **C**ompact Database.

SEE ALSO

➤ *To create fields with AutoNumber and other data types, see page 479*

➤ *AutoNumber fields are usually used as a primary key. See page 447*

Editing Data

Edit existing table data

1. If no data exists in a selected cell, simply start typing.

2. To change existing data, select the field in the record that you need to edit. You can select the field by positioning the mouse pointer on the left edge of the cell until the mouse pointer turns to a white plus, and then clicking. Or, click the I-beam mouse pointer in the cell and press F2. To replace the cell contents with new data, start typing.

3. To navigate in the cell, press F2 again and the cursor changes to an insertion point enabling you to edit as you would in Word.

4. If the data exceeds the width of the cell and you want to see more, use the zoom box (Shift+F2).

5. If you make a mistake while editing and want to start over, press Esc once to delete the changes in the current field. Press Esc again to delete the rest of the changes in the current record.

To check the spelling of your table or data in a form, press F7
![spell check icon]. The spell checker opens and is basically the same as the

---

You do not need to insert records in a particular place in a table

Access automatically inserts new records where they belong in the table, based on the primary key field.

Quickly enter dates

Entering and displaying dates deserve special mention. You can type 5/5 or 5 Spacebar 5 and Access automatically enters the current year and displays the date in whatever format is defined in the Format field property.

Warning: You don't have much time to undo errors

As soon as you begin editing another record, apply or remove a filter, or switch to another window, you cannot use the Undo methods to reverse a change in the last record.

spell checker for other programs. (For more detailed instructions, see the references below.) After you press F7, choose whether you want to **Ignore** the word, **Add** it to the dictionary, or **Change** the word to one that is in the dictionary.

SEE ALSO

➤ *The Access spell checker is almost identical to Word's; see page 100*

➤ *To see how you spell check in Excel, see page 224*

➤ *To see how you spell check in PowerPoint, see page 387*

Replacing Data

Just as in Word, Excel, and PowerPoint, Access has a find and replace feature to edit records.

Replace text

1. Click the insertion point in the field for which you want to replace data. Press Ctrl+H. The Replace in field dialog box appears.

2. In the **Fi_nd** **What** text box, type the text to be replaced. In the **Replace With** text box, type the replacement.

3. Use the **Fi_nd** **Next** button to find and skip entries. Use **Replace** to replace the currently highlighted field. Use **Replace All** to replace all occurrences of the Find What text.

4. When finished, choose **Close**.

Deleting Records

If you need to delete an entire record, click the record selector or use the navigation keys to move to that record, and then choose **Edit** and select **Delete Record** or press Ctrl+-. Access deletes the current record and a dialog box asks you to confirm or cancel the deletion.

To quickly edit existing data in a field, use your mouse

With one click in the middle of text in a cell, you can select the record, select the field, and position the insertion point in the cell.

If you can't add new records, you might not have user rights to insert data

Check to see what rights you have by choosing **Tools**, selecting **Security**, and choosing **User and Group Permissions**. On the **Permissions** tab for the table, make sure that the **Update Data**, **Insert Data**, and **Delete Data** check boxes are selected. If not, you might not have access rights to the table. If that is the case, ask the database manager to grant you editing rights to the table.

You can delete more than one row at a time

To select more than one contiguous record, click the first record selector and then drag to extend the selection. Then press Delete to delete all the selected records.

Manipulating Data

Moving, copying, locating, and sorting data can be overwhelming tasks, unless you are using Access. Data manipulation is one of the database automation operations at which Access excels.

You can find most of the program's data manipulation features in the Table Datasheet toolbar, which is active when you are in datasheet view (refer to Table 22.1).

Cutting, Copying, and Pasting Data

The standard Windows cut, copy, and paste operations work the same way in Access. You can cut, copy, and paste data from one cell to another or from one table to another.

SEE ALSO
➤ *For an introduction to copying, see page 62*
➤ *To see how to move data in Excel, see page 217*

Cut or copy an entire record

1. Click the Record Selector (the gray box on the left of the record) to select the entire record.
2. Choose the Cut ✂ or Copy 📋 button on the toolbar to place the record on the Clipboard.
3. Move to the target table.
4. Do one of the following:
   - Select records to be replaced, choose the **Edit** menu, and select **Paste.**
   - To add the records to the target table, choose the **Edit** menu, and select **Paste Append.**

Be careful when copying records between tables. To move or copy an entire record to another table, the fields must be the same data types, in the same order in the datasheet, and target datasheet fields must be long enough to receive the data; however, the field names might be different. You cannot paste data into hidden fields.

If your Paste Operation fails, you get an error message saying that the records are put in a table called Paste Errors. A paste operation fails if the data violates a validation property or creates a duplicate primary key (or a duplicate index value for which no duplicates are allowed).

SEE ALSO

➤ *If your fields in the two tables are different, use an Append Query instead of using paste. See page 578*

Dragging and Dropping Tables

Access presents users with a handy drag-and-drop feature that's sure to save you time.

Drag and drop to Word or Excel

1. Open the desired Word or Excel document.

2. Tile or arrange windows as needed so that you can see both applications onscreen.

3. Do one of the following:

- Switch to the Access Database window and drag the table or query icon to the Word or Excel document window.

- To drag and drop a range of cells in a Datasheet window, use the white arrow mouse pointer (point to the left edge of the range) to drag the selected data and drop it in the Word or Excel document (see Figure 22.4).

You can also drag and drop an Access object onto the desktop as a shortcut icon. When you double-click the desktop shortcut, Windows opens Access, the database associated with the object and the object. For example, if you commonly work with a certain table, you could drag and drop it on the desktop. Double-click the table icon and you're ready to start working on the table right away!

SEE ALSO

➤ *For an introduction to drag and drop in Word, see page 64*

➤ *To see how to use the drag and drop feature in Excel, see page 212*

Paste ignores AutoNumber fields

When you paste a record into a table with an AutoNumber field, Access ignores the field in the Clipboard and enters the next number in the AutoNumber sequence.

Having problems selecting a range?

To select a range of records and fields in Access, click the first cell, hold down Shift, and click the last cell.

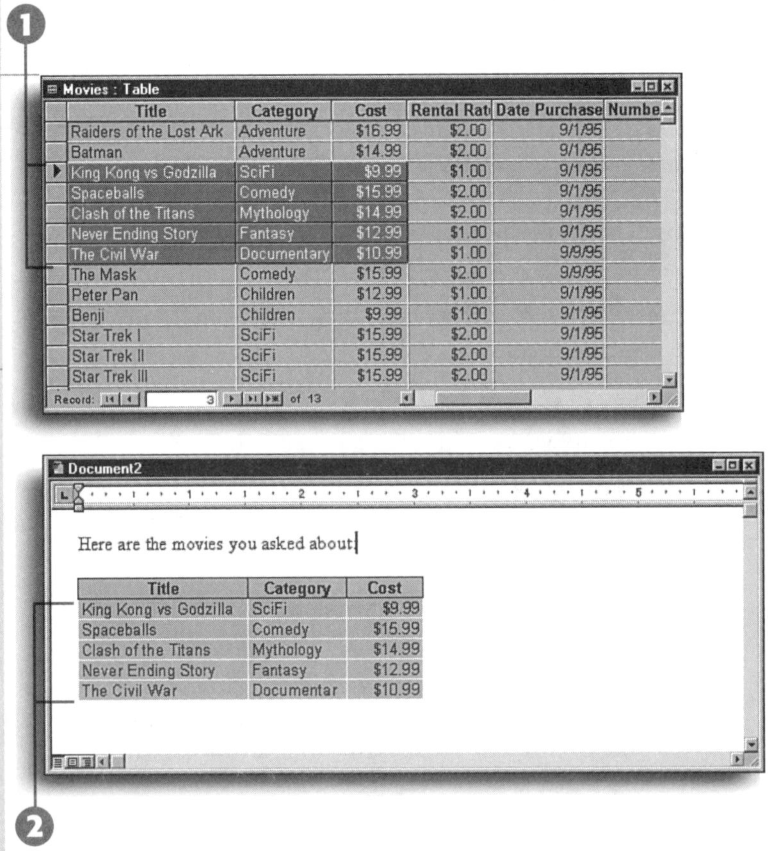

FIGURE 22.4

When you drag and drop selected cells into Word, the formatting is preserved.

1 First, select cells in Access

2 Then, drag and drop to Word or Excel

Locating Data

A common database task is finding a record based on a field value. Suppose a customer calls and asks whether you have a certain movie in stock. Using the Find feature of Access, you can locate the movie based on the movie title.

SEE ALSO

➤ *To see how to use the Find and Replace feature in Word, see page 107*

➤ *To see how to use the Find and Replace feature in Excel, see page 222*

Find a record

　1. Click the Find button 🔍 or press Ctrl+F. The Find in Field dialog box appears (see Figure 22.5).

FIGURE 22.5

The Find feature can help you locate data matching the exact case, if necessary.

2. Enter a string to search for in the **Find What** box.

3. Specify the **Search** direction (**All**, **Up**, or **Down**).

4. Select the **Match** criteria (**Whole Field**, **Any Part Of Field**, or **Start Of Field**).

5. If desired, select **Match Case** to duplicate your capitalization in the **Find What** text box.

6. If desired, select **Search Fields As Formatted** (use if you want dates exactly as you type them, versus a match independent of format—for example, 2/21/59 compared to February 21, 1959).

7. If you want to search only the current field, check the **Search Only Current Field** check box.

8. Choose **Find First** to start the search. Access displays the first record that matches your search criteria.

9. Choose **Find Next** to continue the search and display the next match.

10. To end the search, choose **Close**.

Sorting and Filtering Data Overview

Access enables you to sort and *filter* data in Datasheet view. These features can be handy for generating a list of records based on some filtering or sorting *criteria*. When you filter records, only those records that meet your criteria show; therefore, your table looks smaller. Whereas the Find feature operates on only one criterion, the filter features enable you to specify criteria in multiple fields.

Access provides the following filtering and sorting features in Datasheet view:

Don't know how to spell the word?

You can enter an asterisk in the **Find What** text box as a wild card for any number of characters. For example, **Sm*th*** shows Smith, Smythe, and Smoothers.

When speed is important and your database is large

If the field is indexed, Access finds the value quicker if you select **Whole Field**.

Again, if speed is important…

Selecting the **Search Only Current Field** box speeds up your searches significantly.

- *Sort Ascending* ![icon]. Sorts records in ascending order based on the field(s) selected. When the table is saved, Access saves the sort order. For example, sorting on Movie ID number places the records in the order 1, 2, 3, and so on. If the data is a text field, numbers appear first and then letters; however, anything that starts with 1 is grouped together, (1, 10, 100, 11, 110) then 2's are grouped, and so forth.

- *Sort Descending* ![icon]. Sorts records in descending order based on the field(s) selected. When the table is saved, Access saves the sort order. For example, sorting on Movie ID number places the records in the order 9, 8, 7, and so on.

- *Filter By Selection* ![icon]. Searches for records that meet one criterion. You can perform multiple criteria AND searches (not OR) by specifying the criteria one at a time. You cannot enter expressions as criteria.

- *Filter By Form* ![icon]. Searches for records that meet several criteria. The criteria can be AND searches as well as OR searches. You can also enter expressions as criteria.

- *Advanced Filter/Sort*. Combines the power of the sort and filter features into one search engine. You can specify multiple criteria, perform AND as well as OR searches, enter expressions as criteria, and sort records. The advanced sort feature enables you to sort records in ascending or descending order, or some fields in descending order and others in ascending order.

SEE ALSO

➤ *To learn another saved filter option, a query, see page 562*

Sort in Datasheet View

While in Datasheet view, you can sort records in ascending order or descending order. (Figure 22.6 shows how the list of movies has been sorted by Category.) At any time while in Datasheet view, you can change the sort order or the field on which to sort. Access saves the sort order when you save the datasheet.

Filters do not change the table structure

The subset of data created by a filter is a temporary view of your table data. This view does not change the underlying table structure. You can, however, edit, delete, and add records in this view.

Sort records in Datasheet view

1. Select the field or contiguous fields that you want to sort.

2. To sort in ascending order, click the Sort Ascending toolbar button (shown in Figure 22.6).

FIGURE 22.6

Use the Sort Ascending and Sort Descending toolbar buttons to quickly re-sort data as needed.

❶ Select field(s)

❷ Then, click Sort Ascending

3. To sort in descending order, click the Sort Descending toolbar button .

4. To remove the sort, click the Remove Filter button .

SEE ALSO
➤ *For information on working with forms, see page 531*
➤ *For more information on sorting, see page 531*

Filter by Selection

The Filter by Selection feature enables you to select the data you are looking for and view a list of records matching that data

The sort toolbar buttons enable you to sort on more than one field

In Datasheet view, you can select two or more adjacent fields (columns) at the same time and then sort them in ascending or descending order. Access sorts records starting with the leftmost selected column. In Form view, however, you can sort on only one field at a time.

Fields not in the right order for a multiple field sort?

Use the white arrow mouse pointer in the column header to drag and drop nonadjacent columns together in the desired sort order. Then highlight the multiple columns to sort multiple fields in ascending or descending order.

value. For example, if you can see a list of all children's movies, you can just select the word "children" and filter as shown in the following steps.

Filter by what's in the field

1. Move to the field that you want to use as a filter, or select partial text in a field.

2. Click the Filter by Selection button ▓ (see Figure 22.7).

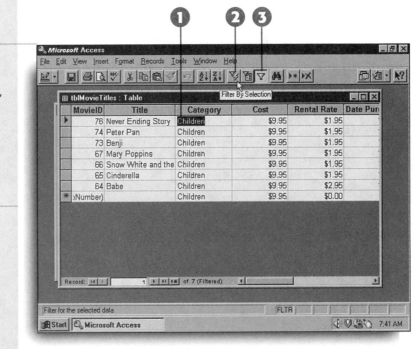

FIGURE 22.7

The Filter by Selection feature shows you a subset of your table, based on the data you selected.

1 Select data to filter on

2 Then click Filter By Selection

3 Apply/Remove Filter toggle

Tip for quickly removing records

Use a filter to show all records that you want to delete or copy, and then select all the records that show when the filter is applied.

3. Repeat step two as many times as necessary to get the snapshot of the data that you want. When you filter your second choice, both conditions must be true.

4. When you want to return to full Table view (see all records), click the Remove Filter toolbar button ▓ .

5. To return to the filtered data, click the Apply Filter Button.

Filter by Form

The Filter By Form feature gives you more options than Filter by Selection. When you have many fields that you are using to filter, this feature is quicker than using successive Filter by Selection. When you use Filter by Selection successively or Filter by Form all on one tab, this is an AND filter, in which all conditions have to be true.

Filter by Form also has another tab called **Or** in which any of the conditions can be true. When you fill in the **Look For** tab, Access searches for a match that includes every criterion on the tab. Use the **Or** tab to specify alternative record values that you want included in the filtered list. Access provides multiple Or tabs for multiple OR criteria. When you use the **Or** tab(s), the filter lists the records that have any of the values in the **Look For** tab or that match the values in the first **Or** tab, the second **Or** tab, and so on.

Filter by form

1. Open the table in Datasheet view, as shown in Figure 22.8.
2. Choose the Filter By Form button 🖼 . The Filter By Form window appears.
3. On the **Look For** tab, click the desired field.
4. Type the criteria value or select the value from the drop-down list.

SEE ALSO

➤ *Filters work very similarly to queries; see page 562*
➤ *Filter criteria work in the same way as query criteria; see page 575*
➤ *To see how to use the expression builder to create criteria, see page 595*

5. Continue specifying as needed the filter criteria in other fields on the **Look For** tab (see Figure 22.9).
6. If you need to specify alternative criteria values, click the **Or** tab and fill in any other values to be included in the filtered list. Additional **Or** tabs appear as needed.

Northwind is a great sample file

The Northwind database comes with Access and is a great sample file to play with. The file is installed in the same folder as Access but in a subfolder called Samples.

FIGURE 22.8

The Northwind Orders table before any filter is applied.

❶ Filter by Form button

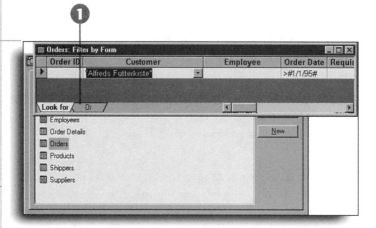

FIGURE 22.9

This Filter by Form finds all the records that have Alfred Futterkiste as the Customer whose orders were purchased after 1/1/95.

❶ Click the Or tab if you want to see a different set of records

7. To save the filter, click the Save button . This saves the filter as a query that you can view from the queries tab of the database window.

8. Click the Apply Filter button ▽ to view the filter results (see Figure 22.10).

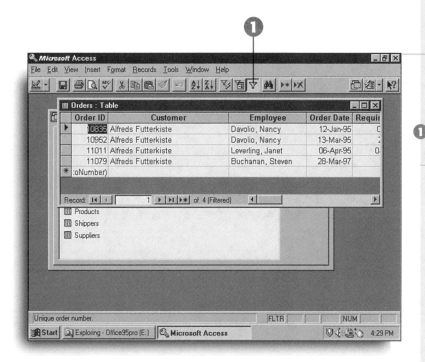

FIGURE 22.10

This table shows the Orders table filtered by the criteria from Figure 22.9.

1 Click the Remove Filter button to display all records

9. To show all records, click the Remove Filter button ⧩.

Performing Advanced Filters and Sorts

The Advanced Filter/Sorts feature provides you with all the power of the filter and sort features through one window. The toolbar and menu options are the same as those in the Filter By Form window.

Filter records using the Advanced Filter/Sort:

1. Choose **Records**, select **Filter**, and choose **Advanced Filter/Sort**. The Filter window appears (see Figure 22.11).

2. In the table's list of fields, double-click each field name that you want to add to the filter.

3. To specify a sort order, click the **Sort** cell for a field, and select a sort order from the drop-down list (**Ascending**, **Descending**, or **Not Sorted**).

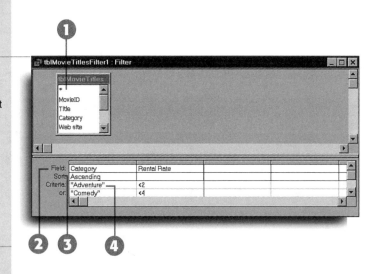

FIGURE 22.11

By specifying sort order and criteria in your queries, you can extract specific data in a special order.

1. Field list box

2. Field(s) to search

3. Sort Order

4. Criteria

4. To specify filter criteria, click a **Criteria** cell for a field and enter the value or expression.

5. To save the filter, click the Save button.

6. Click the Apply Filter button to view the filter results.

7. To show all records click the Remove Filter button 🔽 .

If your filter doesn't list any data

Return to the filter window. Make sure that you listed the proper fields and criteria. Check the criteria against the table data to see whether at least one record meets your search criteria.

SEE ALSO

➤ *To see how the query window is almost identical to the advanced filter window, see page 568*

Importing and Exporting Data

You can transfer data in and out of Access. This capability enables you to use data from another computer system or application, such as from a mainframe computer or a spreadsheet application. Likewise, you can transfer data you store in Access to other computer systems or applications. The Import and Export features enable you to copy data from and to text files, spreadsheets, Access databases, and other database files. The Link Table feature creates a link to a table in another database application so that you can work with the data directly (which we discussed in Chapter 21). This section discusses importing data to existing tables and exporting data from Access.

Table 22.5 lists the application versions and file formats that Access 95 supports for importing, exporting, and linking. Depending on your installation of Access, you may need to rerun Access or Office setup to import, export, or link one of the following file formats.

TABLE 22.5   Import/export/link formats supported

Application	Version
Access	1.x, 2.x, 95
FoxPro	2.0, 2.5, 2.6, 3.0 (import/export only)
dBASE	III, III+, IV, 5
Paradox	3.x, 4.x, 5
Btrieve	5.1x, 6.0 (requires FILE.DDF, FIELD.DDF, and WBTRCALL.DLL files present)
Excel	3.0, 4.0, 5.0, 95
Lotus 123	WKS, WK1, and WK3
Delimited text files	MS-DOS or Windows ANSI text format
Fixed-Width text files	MS-DOS or Windows ANSI text format
Open Database Connectivity	ODBC formats (ODBC) applications (such as SQL Server, Sybase, Oracle)

SEE ALSO

➤ *For more information on creating a new table by linking, see page 474*
➤ *For more information on creating a new table by importing, see page 472*

Importing Data to Existing Tables

Sometimes you have an existing table you need only update with information from another application. The process of adding data to a table is called *appending* data. Unfortunately, Access enables you to append data to existing tables only when importing a spreadsheet or text file. To append data from other sources to an existing table, you must first import the data into a new table and then create an *append query* to add the records from the new Access table to your existing Access table.

If you are importing to an existing table, the data validation and required properties of the table may cause errors if the imported data doesn't follow the rules. Make sure that you back up your database or table before you attempt to import for the first time on this table.

SEE ALSO

➤ *Append queries are a subset of Action queries, see page 578*

Import spreadsheet or text data into an existing Access table

1. Open or switch to the Database window.

2. Choose the **File** menu, select **Get External Data**, and choose **Import**.

3. Specify the file format from which you are importing in the **Files of type** drop-down list.

4. Specify the location of the file.

5. Select the file name.

6. Choose the **Import** button.

7. Follow the directions in the Import Wizard dialog boxes. When the wizard asks where you would like to store your data, choose **In an Existing Table** and select the name of the table (see Figure 22.12).

FIGURE 22.12

Rather than retype data from a spreadsheet, import the information into your database.

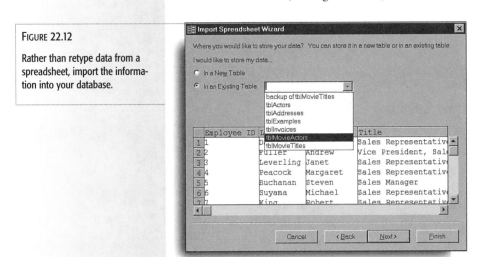

Exporting Data

Often others in your organization will need to use in another application data you store in Access tables. The Export feature enables you to provide them with the Access table data in a variety of file formats.

If you export to an application with different field-naming rules, Access automatically adjusts the names. For example, when exporting to a dBASE table, field names longer than 10 characters are truncated. Field names that have spaces are converted into underscores in some cases.

You also have to be careful that you don't override a file that you intend to keep. Exporting to an existing filename replaces (deletes) the existing file with the new data being exported.

Export data from Access

1. Open or switch to the Database window.

2. Select the table that you want to export.

3. Choose the **File** menu and select **Save As/Export**. The Save As dialog box appears.

4. Choose the option button **To an external File Or Database**.

5. Click **OK**. The Save Table In dialog box appears (see Figure 22.13).

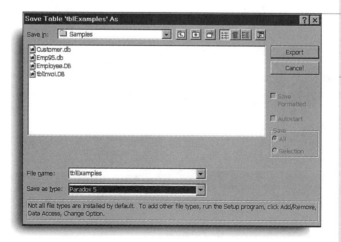

FIGURE 22.13

Select the export file format in the Save As Type text box.

6. In the **Save as type** drop-down list, select a file format to export to.

7. Specify the drive, folder, and filename in which to save the exported data.

8. Choose the **Export** command button.

9. If an Export Wizard dialog box appears, follow the directions.

Changing the Datasheet Layout

By modifying the datasheet formatting, you can customize the layout of your table's Datasheet view. Changing the view of the datasheet does not affect the underlying table data. For example, decreasing the width of a column in Datasheet view does not truncate data in the table or change the field width of data.

Change datasheet layout

1. If you want to change the font type, style, size, color, or underline, select the **Format** menu and choose **Font**.

SEE ALSO

➤ *The format dialog box works similarly to the one in Word, except that you have to change the format for the entire datasheet. See page 78*

2. If you want to change cell appearance, such as gridlines, color, and special effects, from the **Format** menu, select **Cells**. The Cells Effects dialog box appears (shown in Figure 22.14).

If you export the same file continually, save the specifications

While you are exporting, click the Save As button and save the specification. The next time you need to export the table, launch the Export Text Wizard and click **Advanced**, click **Specs**, and select the desired specification file.

FIGURE 22.14

Choose **Format**, **Cells** to work in the Cell Effects dialog box. Access shows you the cell appearance in the **Sample** pane.

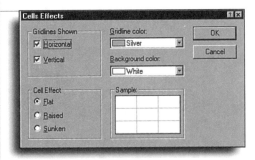

3. To change the row height of all rows, move the mouse pointer between two rows and drag. (You cannot change the row height of just one row.)

4. To change a column's width, move the mouse pointer between two columns and drag. You can double-click to automatically make the column width fit the widest entry (see Figure 22.15).

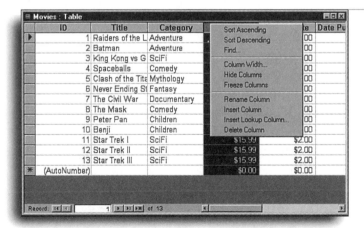

FIGURE 22.15

You can also double-click the double-headed black arrow to automatically adjust the column to the widest entry.

①   Column resize arrow

5. To hide a column, right-click the column header and choose Hide Columns (see Figure 22.16).

FIGURE 22.16

The shortcut menu for a selected column enables you to sort data, find data, and manipulate the column.

6. To display hidden columns, choose the **Format** menu and select **Unhide** Columns. In the Unhide Columns dialog box, check the columns that you want to redisplay (hidden columns have blank check boxes, displayed columns have check marks).

7. To freeze columns so that columns to the left stay onscreen while you scroll to the right, click the column that you want to stay on the left, choose the **Format** menu, and select **Freeze Columns**.

8. To unfreeze columns, choose the **Format** menu, and select **Unfreeze Columns**.

9. To change the order of columns, select the column and drag it to the new location (see Figure 22.17).

FIGURE 22.17

Drag one or more columns to move them in Datasheet view.

1 White arrow mouse pointer

2 Thin vertical line indicates where column will move

MovieID	Title	Category	Rental Rate	Cost	Date Purcha
55	Raiders of the Last A	Adventure	$2.95	$19.95	11/15
80	Independence Day	Adventure	$0.00	$9.95	5/2
51	Batman	Adventure	$2.95	$19.95	11/25
48	Cinderella	Children	$1.95	$9.95	1/6
59	Never Ending Story	Children	$1.95	$9.95	1/6
49	Snow White and the	Children	$1.95	$9.95	1/6
57	Peter Pan	Children	$1.95	$9.95	1/6
56	Benji	Children	$1.95	$9.95	1/6
50	Mary Poppins	Children	$1.95	$9.95	1/6
46	Babe (Movie)	Children	$2.95	$9.95	1/5
54	The Mask	Comedy	$2.95	$9.95	11/15
58	Spaceballs	Comedy	$1.95	$9.95	1/6
61	Jack	Comedy	$2.95	$9.95	5/2
53	The Civil War	Documentary	$1.95	$9.95	11/15
62	Clash of the Titals	Mythology	$0.00	$9.95	1/6
52	King Kong vs Godzil	Sci-Fi	$1.95	$9.95	11/10

Record: |◄ ◄| 1 |► ►| |►* of 16

10. To save datasheet layout changes while you work, choose the Save button 🖫 to save the layout changes.

11. If you make any changes that have not been saved when you close the table, Access asks whether you want to save the datasheet layout changes. Choose **Yes** to save the changes, **No** to discard the changes, or **Cancel** to return to the datasheet.

Change layout for all datasheets

1. From the **Tools** menu select **Options**.

2. Select the **Datasheet** tab (see Figure 22.18).

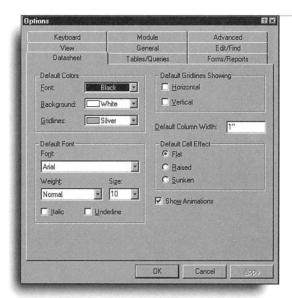

FIGURE 22.18

Use the Datasheet tab of the Options dialog box to customize all newly created datasheets.

3. In the **Default Colors** section, choose the colors that you want for the **Font**, cell **Background** color, or **Gridlines**.

4. Change the **Font** style, **Weight** (boldness), **Size**, and **Italic** or **Underline**.

5. You can also choose whether you want to see gridlines, the default column width, and cell effects (flat, raised, or sunken).

6. When finished with the dialog box, choose **OK**.

Creating Forms and Report Basics

Plan forms for efficient viewing, adding, and editing data

Use Form Wizards for the quickest way to get started

Create a blank form for more design flexibility

Modify a form or report design

Set form and report control properties for easier use

Create drop-down lists, list boxes, and command buttons

Planning Form Design

The key to many information systems (manual and computerized) is the *form* used to gather and maintain data. Forms seem to be everywhere we go. Some forms, such as employment applications, simply gather information; others, such as computerized tax forms, also perform calculations. And some forms function as reports (invoices or customer receipts, for example).

Because Access uses the same toolbar buttons and many of the procedures for forms apply to reports as well, some report basics are covered in this chapter.

Forms are just another way to view table data, so the first step in designing a form is to create the table(s) or review the design of the table(s). Form problems often can be attributed to an improperly designed table. Remember that table properties and field properties, such as *data validation* and *field type*, help you improve the quality of your data (they are your first line of defense against GIGO—garbage in, garbage out).

SEE ALSO

➤ *For more information on using Access to create reports, see page 581*

➤ *You have to have a table before you create most forms. See page 464*

➤ *To set validation rules and other field properties in a table (that will carry over to a form), see page 483*

➤ *Validation rules for a whole record will also carry over to the form. See page 490*

➤ *Before you create a form, you should be mostly done with your table design. See page 491*

After you complete the table designs (and you have tested them on end users and data), you are ready to start designing forms. Forms offer several advantages compared with the Datasheet view of your table data:

- Forms can display one complete record at a time, usually in a vertical format.

- Forms allow you to customize the appearance in much more detail than a table with fonts, colors, and graphics.

- Forms can display fields that the user cannot edit, as well as fields that the user can edit.

- Forms can be designed to resemble paper forms you currently use.

- Forms enable you to rearrange fields (to make data entry easier and more accurate).

- Forms can contain fields from more than one table. (A table datasheet shows the data for only one table.)

- Forms provide special field display functions, such as drop-down lists, word wrapping in fields, and calculated fields.

- Forms can contain graphs.

- Forms enable you to automate tasks and display custom menus.

A well-designed form is easy to use. You should design forms in ways that facilitate data entry. For example, "busy" forms that contain too many fields crammed into a small screen tend to irritate users and lead to data-entry errors. To prevent these problems, consider using several different forms or spreading data entry over several pages of a single form.

Following are some general guidelines for designing forms:

- Keep the form simple. Use easy-to-read fonts and colors. Use graphics and other objects to enhance the form, but don't clutter the form with too many objects.

- If your form will be printed on a black-and-white printer, adjust the colors and layout as needed to present a clear printout. Although forms can be printed, it is better to use reports because reports are designed for printing and do a better job.

- Be consistent across forms. For example, use the same design for the customer data-entry form and the customer order form.

- Clearly show where data is to be entered and what data should be entered.

Use Watermarks

Access allows you to place a graphic (called a *watermark*) in the background of a form. If you have an existing paper form you want to continue using, you can scan the form to convert it to a graphic file. Then, bring the graphic into the background of a new form and drop field controls down where needed on the graphic. For more information, see the "Modifying Form and Report Design" section later in this chapter.

Using the Northwind Forms as a Learning Tool

One of the most helpful ways of learning Access is to use the Northwind database for examples. This file is located in the folder where Microsoft Office is installed under the Access\ Samples\ subfolders. If you don't know where the file is, you can use Windows' Find feature to locate the file.

Find Northwind sample file

1. Click on the Windows **Start** button, choose **Find**, and select **Files or Folders**. The Find: All Files dialog box is displayed.

2. In the **Named** text box, type Northwind and press Enter. After the program searches, Northwind should display in the bottom half of the Find: Files Named Northwind dialog box (if not, you might need to change the drive in the **Look in** drop-down list).

3. Double-click on the Northwind file.

To edit any form, you need to go to Design view.

Edit a Northwind form

1. Click on the Forms tab in the Database Window.

2. Choose the form name and click the **Design** button.

The following list describes some of the Northwind forms and suggests which ones to use for the discussions in this chapter:

- *Customers*. This is a standard vertical form with one combo box field. Use this form for most of the discussions in the chapter, including how to move, delete, and add controls.

- *Employees*. This form shows a picture bound to field in a record. A command button navigates to a different part of the form.

- *Main Switchboard*. This is a startup form. There are command buttons to open other forms, print reports, and exit Access. This is a good example to use with the "Using the Form Design Toolbox" section in regard to command buttons.

- *Orders*. This shows a main form with a subform (Orders Subform). There are combo boxes, check boxes, group boxes, and a button to print the form. There are also calculated text boxes. Look at this form when working with many of the controls mentioned in the section "Using the Form Design Toolbox."

Creating New Forms

You can create new forms using the toolbar 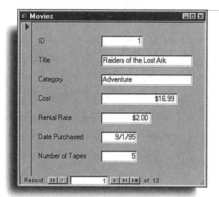 or the **New Form** dialog box. The AutoForm button on the New Object drop-down button creates a simple columnar form based on the current table or query and displays the completed form with data in Form view (see Figure 23.1).

New Object button changes

By default, the New Object button shows the AutoForm button. However, if you choose a different button, that button remains the default choice until you use a different option on the New Object button or exit and return to Access.

Quick Forms

The easiest way to create a form is to use AutoForm and then customize the result by deleting and moving fields and labels.

FIGURE 23.1

Columnar forms let you focus on one record at a time.

You create all other new forms in the **New Form** dialog box. To display the **New Form** dialog box, select the New Form button from the drop-down New Object button on the toolbar. Or, switch to the Database window, select the **Forms** tab, and click the **New** button. Either way, the **New Form** dialog box appears (see Figure 23.2).

Reviewing the New Form Dialog Box

The New Form dialog box allows you to select the table or query on which you want to base the form and provides the following new form options:

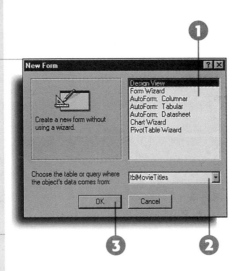

- **Design View**. Allows you to create a custom form design from scratch.

- **Form Wizard**. Assists you in creating a form by asking you questions and using predesigned form templates. (See the section "Creating a New Form with Form Wizard" later in this chapter).

- **AutoForm: Columnar**. Displays one record at a time in a vertical format (each field label and value on a separate line, in a single column). The resulting forms are the same as those generated by the AutoForm button on the toolbar.

- **AutoForm: Tabular**. Displays multiple records in a row-and-column format (see Figure 23.3).

- **AutoForm: Datasheet**. Displays records and fields in the familiar row and column layout of the Datasheet view (see Figure 23.4). This type of form is often used as a subform within another form.

- **Chart Wizard**. Displays a form with a graph or chart of the data.

- **PivotTable Wizard**. Creates a form based on an Excel Pivot Table.

SEE ALSO

➤ *To see how to create a chart with a wizard, see page 320*

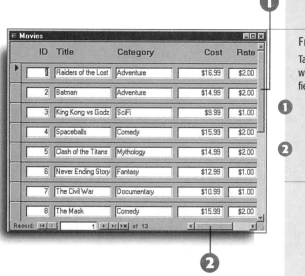

FIGURE 23.3

Tabular forms allow you to work with multiple records and multiple fields at once.

1 To see more records, use the vertical scrollbar

2 To see more fields, use the horizontal scrollbar

FIGURE 23.4

You can even create a Datasheet layout form.

1 Don't type in AutoNumber field. It will automatically display 14 in this example when you type the title.

Creating a New Form with Form Wizard

The Form Wizard generates a form design for you, based on your specifications. The Form Wizard asks you a series of questions to determine what table(s) you want to use and what type of form you want to create.

Use the Form Wizard

1. In the toolbar, click the New Object drop-down button 🔲▾ and select the New Form button 🔲. The New Form dialog box appears (refer to Figure 23.2).

2. Type or select the name of a table or query in the drop-down list box (Figure 23.2 shows tblMovieTitles).

3. Double-click **Form Wizard**. The **Form Wizard** appears (see Figure 23.5).

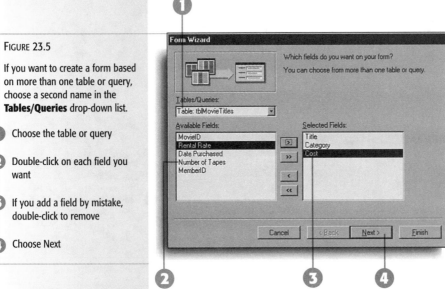

FIGURE 23.5

If you want to create a form based on more than one table or query, choose a second name in the **Tables/Queries** drop-down list.

1 Choose the table or query

2 Double-click on each field you want

3 If you add a field by mistake, double-click to remove

4 Choose Next

4. In the **Tables/Queries** drop-down list, select the table or query you want to include on the form.

5. In the **Available Fields** list, select the fields to be included in the form. Select individual fields (>) or all fields (>>). As you select the fields from the **Available Fields** list, they appear in the **Selected Fields** list. To remove fields from the **Selected Fields** list, use the < arrow key to remove one field or the << arrow button to remove all fields. Choose **Next** to continue.

6. In the next **Form Wizard** dialog box, select a layout
(**C**olumnar, **T**abular, or **D**atasheet) and choose **N**ext
(see Figure 23.6).

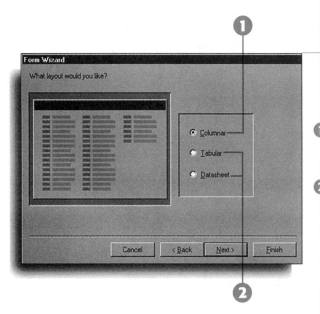

FIGURE 23.6

You can use the **Form Wizard** to create columnar, tabular, or datasheet forms.

❶ Columnar is generally to view one record at a time (you see more fields onscreen)

❷ Tabular and Datasheet view many records at a time (and you see fewer fields)

7. In the next **Form Wizard** dialog box, select a style for the
form and choose **N**ext (see Figure 23.7).

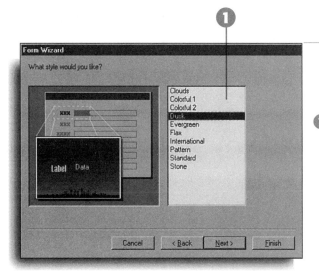

FIGURE 23.7

Each form style has a different background and control appearance.

❶ Clouds, Dusk, and International include graphics, which make the form take longer to load

It might be tempting to choose graphical forms

However, if your computer does not have a lot of memory or is slow, you might want to choose the Standard style, which is the simplest design and loads the fastest. If you want to change the style after you create the form, from Design view choose **Format** and then **AutoFormat** and select the style.

8. In the next Form Wizard dialog box, enter a title for the form in the **Form** text box and select the **Open the form to view or enter information** option or the **Modify the form's design** option.

9. If you want to display Help on working with the form, select that check box.

10. Choose **Finish**. Figure 23.8 shows the completed form.

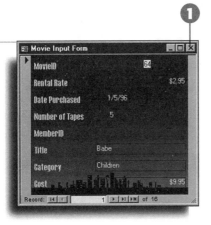

FIGURE 23.8

The **Form Wizard** creates a more stylish, polished form than the AutoForm feature.

1 Click the X to close the form when finished (if prompted, choose Yes to save the design).

SEE ALSO
➤ *To see how to relate tables, see page 493*

If the Form Wizard won't allow you to create a form based on two tables

On the first step of the Form Wizard, you can choose fields from more than one table, but they have to be related. If they are related, the wizard will lead you through different steps. If you get a message that says you are not allowed to use more than one table, try the following. First, check the tables to make sure they have a relationship (a key field in common). Then launch the Form Wizard. Select the first table and desired fields from that table to be included on the form. Select the second table and the desired fields from the second table to be included in the form. The Form Wizard will automatically search for the common key fields and establish the relationship for you.

Creating a New Form with Design View

You can use a Design view to create a new custom form that displays data in specific locations; this cannot be achieved by using generic templates in Form Wizard. For example, you might need to create a form that matches a required government form, such as a W-4 form. Or, you might need to create a form that includes pictures in the employee application form. You might also want to create a form that just has labels and command buttons to create a switchboard menu for other forms and reports.

For an example of a switchboard, go to the Northwind example database and open the Main Switchboard form. This form has a series of command buttons that open other forms. These include

forms for data entry and other forms that act as dialog boxes
(click on **Print Sales <u>R</u>eports**, for example).

Create a new form using Design view

1. In the toolbar, click the New Object drop-down button
   and select the New Form button. The **New Form**
   dialog box is displayed.

2. In the drop-down list box, select the table or query for
   which you want to create a form.

3. Double-click **Design View**. Access displays a blank form in
   Form Design view (see Figure 23.9).

Continue on with the next sections to make design changes to
the form.

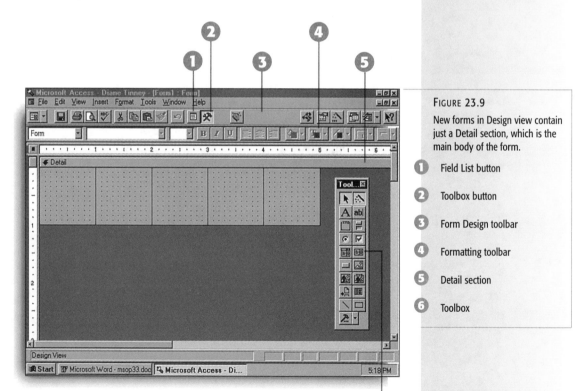

FIGURE 23.9
New forms in Design view contain
just a Detail section, which is the
main body of the form.

❶ Field List button

❷ Toolbox button

❸ Form Design toolbar

❹ Formatting toolbar

❺ Detail section

❻ Toolbox

SEE ALSO
➤ *For a general description on how to add command buttons to a form, see page 541*

Modifying Form and Report Design

The Design view of Reports and Forms is similar. Both objects have a Design toolbar, Formatting toolbar, a Toolbox, detail sections, page header/footer, and report/form header and footer sections. Because of the similarities, this section discusses both form and report design. More details specific to reports are mentioned in Chapter 25.

SEE ALSO
➤ *For a summary of how to change a report's design, see page 590*

Working with Form and Report Sections

Form and Report Design view is where you can create and modify forms and reports. Although new forms in Design view contain only a detail section, you can add other sections to your form design (see Figure 23.10).

Add a form or report header/footer section

1. Choose **View** and select **Form Header/Footer**. (For a report, select **Report Header/Footer**.) A check mark appears next to the item on the **View** menu. You get two additional bands that display across your form or report. Figure 23.10 shows a form header with labels and a form footer with nothing added.

2. To remove form or report headers and footers, repeat step 1.

New reports in Design view automatically contain a Page Header and Footer section. Forms do not. A page header and footer display on top and bottom of each printed page for the form or report. In Form view, you do not see a page header or footer.

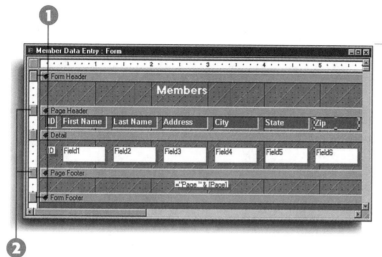

FIGURE 23.10

Knowing the sections of a form or report helps you navigate in Form Design view.

1 Choose **View**, **Form Header/ Footer** to add both form header and footer

2 Choose **View**, **Page Header/ Footer** to add both page header and footer

Add a Page Header/Footer section

1. Choose **View** and select **Page Header/Footer.** A check mark appears next to the item on the **View** menu. You get two additional bands that display across your form or report. Figure 23.10 shows a page header with nothing and a control for the page number.

2. To remove page headers and footers, repeat step 1.

Following is an overview of each section that can appear in a form or report:

- *Form or Report Header.* Appears at the top of the screen. Prints at the top of the first page.

- *Page Header.* Appears only when printed. Prints at the top of each page.

- *Detail Section.* Displays data.

- *Page Footer.* Appears only when printed. Prints at the bottom of each page.

- *Form or Report Footer.* Appears at the bottom of the screen. Prints at the bottom of the last page.

- *Report grouping headers and footers.* Appear only on reports and organize report into categories.

Although you have to choose to have both a header and footer from the **View** menu, you can choose not to display the area for the header or footer.

Hide header or footer

1. Click on each control in the section and press Delete.

2. Move to the bottom of the section until the mouse pointer changes to a double-headed arrow and drag the section so it has no height.

   Sometimes after deleting items on a form or report, you end up with a section width or height that is too large. If you have a large gap on the screen or on the printed page, blank printed pages, or a scrollbar that leads to an area with no items, you will want to change your section size.

Change section height or width

1. Move to the far right or bottom of a section until your mouse pointer changes to a double-headed arrow.

2. Drag the mouse pointer to the left or up to reduce the section's size.

SEE ALSO

➤ *Reports also have the possibility of additional group sections. See page 591*

The Design View Toolbar

Many of the buttons on the Design toolbar are also on the Table Design and Table Datasheet toolbars. The Form and Report Design toolbars provide additional buttons to speed up your form design work. Table 23.1 briefly describes these buttons.

TABLE 23.1   **Design toolbar buttons**

Button	Button Name	Description
	View	Drop-down list of views: Form view, Design view, or Datasheet view for Forms; Design view, Print Preview, and Layout Preview for Reports.
	Format Painter	Picks up format from the selected object and applies format to next objects selected.

Button	Button Name	Description
🔲	Field List	Displays a list of the fields linked to the form or report. Drag a field name from the list to place in the form or report.
🔨	Toolbox	Displays or hides the Toolbox, which contains design objects.
📝	AutoFormat	Applies predesigned styles.
🔧	Code	Displays the Module window (programming statements) for the form or report.
📋	Properties	Displays the Properties window, where you can set characteristics of controls.
🔨	Build	Invokes a Wizard or Builder.

SEE ALSO

➤ *For a description of additional buttons in Design view, see page 478*

➤ *For a description of additional buttons in Form view, see page 498*

Working with Controls

Changing an existing form or report design, whether it was created with wizards or is a blank form or report, is a relatively easy task. In most cases, you just need to click and drag, improve appearance with color, or set some properties.

Objects you place in a form or a report are called *controls*. You move, delete, or change the characteristics of these controls to modify your form or report's design. Controls include text boxes, lines, option buttons, and even page breaks. A description of the specific types of controls is in the section "Using the Toolbox" later in this chapter.

Figure 23.11 shows a columnar form created with AutoForm (in Form view). Although adequate, you can improve the form's appearance. For example, the awkward, extraneous text describing the fields could be modified (or deleted, in some cases). The fields also could be rearranged to fit more on the screen (notice the scrollbar indicating more fields). You can use the formatting toolbar buttons to enhance the appearance of the controls.

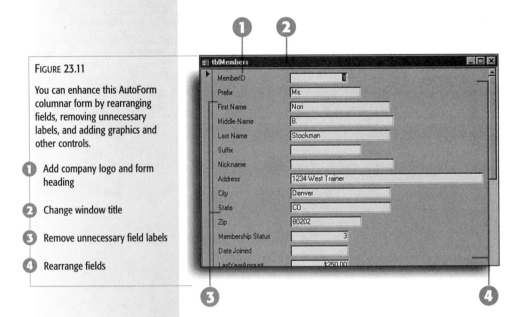

FIGURE 23.11

You can enhance this AutoForm columnar form by rearranging fields, removing unnecessary labels, and adding graphics and other controls.

1 Add company logo and form heading

2 Change window title

3 Remove unnecessary field labels

4 Rearrange fields

In the next few sections, you learn how to enhance the appearance of this columnar form to produce the enhanced member form shown in Figure 23.12.

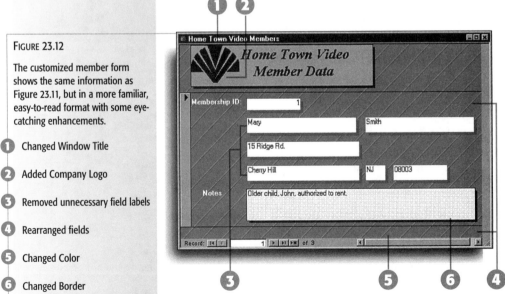

FIGURE 23.12

The customized member form shows the same information as Figure 23.11, but in a more familiar, easy-to-read format with some eye-catching enhancements.

1 Changed Window Title

2 Added Company Logo

3 Removed unnecessary field labels

4 Rearranged fields

5 Changed Color

6 Changed Border

Editing a Control

When you click on a text control once in Design view, you select it. When a control is selected, you can move, size, and change the appearance. For examples in this section, open the Customers Form in Design view.

Selecting and Adjusting Controls

Before you start modifying controls in your form and setting form properties, you need to know how to select a control and how to select the form. Figure 28.11 shows the member form, a single-column form created by Form Wizards, in Form view. As you can see, Form Wizards creates a label box and a text box for each field. You can select the text-box control (where data is entered and displayed) or the attached label box.

Select a Control

1. Click on the control. If the control is difficult to get to, select the control name from the Select Object toolbar button `[App ▼]`. Access displays handles around the control to indicate that it is selected (see Figure 23.13).

> **FIGURE 23.13**
>
> When you select a field object, both the attached label and the text box are selected.
>
> **1** Sizing handle
>
> **2** Control border
>
> **3** Move handle

2. If you want to select more than one control, hold down the Shift key and click on another control.

3. To deselect control(s), click the background of the form or report.

The smaller black handles are the resizing handles.

Resize a Control

1. After a control is selected, move the mouse pointer to one of the small black handles (sizing handles in Figure 23.13) surrounding the control until the mouse pointer is a double-headed black arrow.

2. Drag the mouse to increase or decrease the size of the control. If you have more than one control selected, they all change in size.

The larger boxes around a selected control are move handles. When you click on one control, the move handle of the associated label or control also displays (with no other handles).

Change Text in a Label

1. Click on a label control in Design view (such as the Customers label in the Form Header of the Customers Form). You get handles showing you the control is selected.

2. Click inside a control a second time. You are in Edit mode. You can use Backspace and Delete to delete characters and type new characters.

3. You can also use navigation keys to move around the label. For example, press Home and type to insert new text (such as Northwind). The example would say Northwind Customers.

4. Click outside the label to deselect it.

You will often edit label controls and rarely edit text boxes unless you are creating calculated expressions.

Move a Control

1. To move the control and the associated label, move your mouse pointer to the edge of a control (control border in Figure 23.13) until a hand displays, and drag.

2. To move only the control or the associated label, move your mouse pointer to the upper-left handle at the edge of the control (move handle in Figure 23.13) until the mouse pointer becomes a finger, and drag.

Warning: Don't edit the name of a field inside a text box (unless you are creating a calculated expression)

If you do edit the name, the text box will no longer know which field to use in the underlying table or query.

Labels help input

Your labels on the form should help whoever is adding data. When you originally create the form, the labels will be the names of the fields (or captions). Some of this text might not be descriptive enough to explain what data should go in the fields. When you edit the label on the form, it does not affect the data in the table.

Delete a control

1. Click on the control to select it.

2. Press Delete. If the control selected is a label, it deletes the label only. If it is another control with an attached label (for example, the ContractName text box on the Customers form), both the control and its attached label are deleted.

3. To undelete, click the Undo button 🔙 immediately.

To select more than one control, hold the Shift key down while you click each control. After you select all the controls you want to change, you can drag them to a new location, resize, or delete them as necessary.

Select the entire form or report

1. Click the upper-left corner (see the Form Selector later in Figure 23.14) of the form or report.

2. Change any properties you want (see "Setting Control and Form Properties" later in this chapter).

3. Drag (when the mouse pointer is a hand) to move all the selected controls at once.

Copy the formatting of a control to other controls

1. Select the control whose format you want to copy.

2. Click the Format Painter button 🖌️ . To apply to multiple controls, select the control with formatting to copy, and double-click the Format Painter.

3. Click on the next control to which to apply the format.

4. If you double-clicked on the Format Painter button in step 2, continue clicking on other controls and click on the Format Painter button again to turn it off.

Line up multiple controls

1. Select more than one control.

2. Choose the **Fo**rmat menu and then select **Al**ign.

3. Choose **L**eft, **R**ight, **T**op, or **B**ottom to line up the controls with one another.

Can't drag a control where you want it?

In some cases, you can drag the controls to a different section (from page header to form header, for example). In other cases, you need to choose **Edit** and select **Cut** ✂️ and **Paste** 📋 to move the selected controls.

Yeehaw! You can also lasso controls to select more than one

You can also use the mouse to draw a box around multiple controls (start outside a control) to select the controls. In addition, you can click or drag in the horizontal or vertical ruler to select multiple controls.

Size controls

1. Select more than one control.

2. Choose the **F**o**rmat** menu and then select **S**ize.

3. Choose **to** **T**allest, **to** **S**hortest, **to** **W**idest, or **to** **N**arrowest to make the size uniform.

Equalize space between controls

1. Select more than one control.

2. Choose the **F**o**rmat** menu and then select **Make** **E**qual to equalize the space between controls.

3. When the spaces are equalized, you can choose **F**o**rmat,** select either **Hori**z**ontal Spacing** or **V**ertical Spacing, and then choose **I**ncrease or **D**ecrease to change the spacing between the controls.

You can use the features on the Formatting toolbar to change the appearance of the selected control or controls. The features of the Formatting toolbar are described in Table 23.2.

You can change the properties of multiple controls selected at one time. For more information on properties, see the later section "Setting Control and Form Properties."

Using the Formatting Toolbar

Use the Formatting toolbar to enhance the appearance of the form and its contents. You can customize the color of text, background, and border for each control you place in a form. Table 23.2 defines all the tools available on the Formatting toolbar.

Use the Formatting toolbar

1. Select an object in the form with one of the following methods:

   - Click on a control. Hold down Shift and click on additional controls.

   - Click in one of the rulers to select controls directly below or to the right of the ruler (or drag in the ruler to select more controls).

   - Click on a section bar (Details, Header or Footer).

Don't waste too much time trying to move and size a bunch of controls by hand

Use the menus instead. To make selected controls uniform, choose **Format** and then one or more of the following menu items: **Align**, **Size**, **Horizontal Spacing**, or **Vertical Spacing**.

- Click on the Form selector button in the upper-left corner of the form to select the form itself.

2. You then can change the color of the foreground, background, or border by clicking on the buttons described in Table 23.2. As you click the various formatting buttons, the appearance of the selected object instantly changes to reflect your selections. This way, you can see the effect and decide what appearance you want to give the object.

TABLE 23.2 Formatting toolbar

Button	Button Name	Description
App ▾	Select Object	Drop-down list of all objects on the form or report. Used to select specific objects. (You can also select objects with mouse.)
Arial	Font Name	Changes font of selection with drop-down list of available fonts.
8 ▾	Font Size	Changes font size with drop-down list of font sizes.
B	Bold	Boldfaces selection.
I	Italic	Italicizes selection.
U	Underline	Underlines selection.
▤	Align Left	Aligns selection to the left within control.
▦	Center	Centers selection within control.
▤	Align Right	Aligns selection to the right within control.
🖻 ▾	Fill/Back Color	Displays palette of colors from which you can select and apply to the background of the selected control(s).
🅰 ▾	Font/Fore Color	Displays a palette of colors from which you can select and apply to the text of the selected control(s).
◩ ▾	Line/Border Color	Displays a palette of colors from which you can select and apply to the border of the selected control(s).

continues...

TABLE 23.2 Continued

Button	Button Name	Description
	Line/Border Width	Displays a variety of line widths from which you can select and apply to the selected control(s).
	Special Effect	Displays a variety of special effects from which you can select and apply to the selected control(s) such as Raised, Etched, Chiseled, Flat, Sunken, and Shadowed.

Setting Control and Form Properties

Every object in Access has properties. *Properties* determine the appearance and behavior of an object. In Form and Report Design view, you can view and change the properties of controls, sections, and of the form or report itself.

To display the properties of a control, double-click the control, or select a control and then click the Properties button on the Database toolbar. To view the Form's or Properties Sheet window, double-click the upper-left corner (Form/Report Selector).

After the Properties window opens, each time you select a different object, the contents of the window changes.

The Properties window has five tabs:

- **Format**. To change formatting and layout properties, choose options on the Format tab.
- **Data**. To change the source of data, how the data is organized, or rules for data entry, choose the Data tab.
- **Event**. To program what happens when an event happens (a click or change in data, for example) to an object, choose the Event tab.
- **Other**. For user help and other properties, choose the Other tab.
- **All**. If you don't know where a property is and want to see all properties for the selected object, choose the All tab.

To select the form or report and display the form's or report's properties, double-click the Form/Report Selector (immediately

Don't forget the shortcut menu

Right-click a control for quick access to features such as the Properties sheet.

You can copy a form or report that uses a different table or query

In the database window, press Ctrl+C and then Ctrl+V, and type the new name. Go to the new Form or Report's Record Source property and choose an existing table or query from the drop-down list or create a new query with the Build button. For each field with a different name, go to the Control Source property and choose the field name from the drop-down list.

to the left of the horizontal ruler). The Form or Report Properties window is displayed (see Figure 23.14). You use this window to change the caption at the top of your form or report window (the caption property). For example, the Customers form has Customers as the caption. You could type in Customer Information as an alternative for the title bar in Form view.

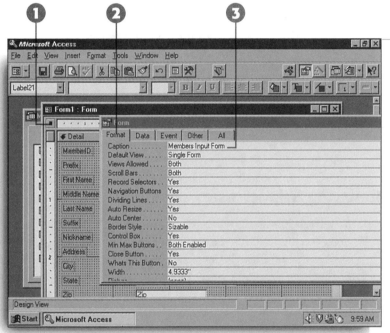

FIGURE 23.14

By setting form properties, you can customize the appearance and behavior of each form.

1. Form Selector

2. Choose tab for the type of property

3. Title bar caption changed

Many property settings are "inherited" from the associated table or query. Some properties are set through the Toolbox and Formatting toolbar, and some properties have no settings.

For more information on a specific property, place the insertion point in that property's field and press F1.

Change a property

1. Right-click the object (control, section, form/report) and choose **Properties** 📇 .

2. Click in the cell of the property you want to change.

3. Do one of the following:

- Type the new property.
- Choose from the drop-down list of options.
- Double-click to cycle through the list of options.
- Click the Build button ![Build button icon] to the right of the property or on the Design toolbar.
- Paste a result from a previously copied property.

4. To change properties for another control or section, click on the item. The title bar of the property sheet changes to reflect the new item. Repeat steps 2 and 3.

5. When finished with the properties, click the close button (x) to close the property sheet.

The following sections describe some of the most used properties. You change any of the properties by the methods in the steps mentioned previously.

Mouse tip for choosing properties

Double-click Yes/No (or other) properties to alternate between the possible values.

Displaying Help for Users

By default, the status bar in Form view displays the field descriptions you entered in the associated table. You might find, however, that the field name is not enough to direct data entry. Instead of changing the field name, you can override this description and enter new text in the Status Bar Text property for that control (on the Other tab).

Use the ControlTip Text property to display a pop-up message when the user moves the mouse pointer over a control.

Limiting User Input

In addition to security options, you can limit user input through form and control properties. On the form, you can change **Allow Edits**, **Allow Deletions**, or **Allow Additions** to **No**. Using the Data Entry property is the same as choosing **Records** and then selecting **Data Entry** in Form and Table Datasheet view. If you want users to be able to only add records rather than edit them, change the **Data Entry** property to **Yes**. For an individual control, you can change the **Visible** property to **No** (if you are using the control in a calculation), change the **Display When** property to only show for printing or for the screen, change the **Enabled** property to **No** (unable to get into field), or change **Locked** property to **No** (unable to change field).

Setting Default Values and Validation Rules

Access enables you to set default field values and validation rules, in both tables and their associated forms. Generally, you should place such data properties at the table level, but in some cases, the default value or validation rule might apply only to a particular data-entry form. In these cases, you can set default values and validation rules in the property sheet of a control.

For assistance in writing expressions, click the Expression Builder button ![icon] next to the property. The Expression Builder helps you write expressions and offers common validation expressions you can use.

SEE ALSO

➤ *To see how to set validation rules in a table, see page 483*

➤ *To see how to use the Expression Builder, see page 595*

Changing Tab Order

Tab order refers to the order in which you move from control to control when you press the Tab key. The default tab order of Access forms starts at the upper-left object and moves from left to right and then from top to bottom. At times, the default tab order might not meet your needs or is changed when you move or add fields. For example, you might be entering data from a source that displays the information in a different order. Rather than rearrange the field controls in your form, you could rearrange the tab order. You also might want to change tab-order properties when your data-entry task starts in the middle of a form. Rather than tab several times to the desired field, you could assign that field a tab-order index of 1.

To change the default tab order in a form, set the **Tab Stop** and/or **Tab Index** property of a control. A **Tab Stop** value of **Yes** enables users to tab to the control; **No** causes the tab to skip the control. The **Tab Index** value stipulates the exact numerical tab order (see Figure 23.15).

You also can set the **Auto Tab** property. The **Auto Tab** property controls whether the field automatically tabs to the next field when you type the last allowable character. For example, if a Social Security number field can contain only 11 characters and the **Auto Tab** property is set to **Yes**, Access automatically tabs to the next field when the user types the 11th character.

You can set the tab order for your entire form

After you make changes on a form, your tab order might be incorrect. Choose **View** and select **Tab Order**. In the Custom Order list, you can drag fields to the desired order. Alternatively, to reset the order to left to right and top to bottom, choose the **Auto Order** button.

FIGURE 23.15

Use the Tab Index property of a control or choose **View** and then select **Tab Order** to change the tab order of your form.

❶ Drag field selector to change order of tab

❷ Change **Tab Index** property on Other tab

❸ Choose **Auto Order** to reset tab stops to default order

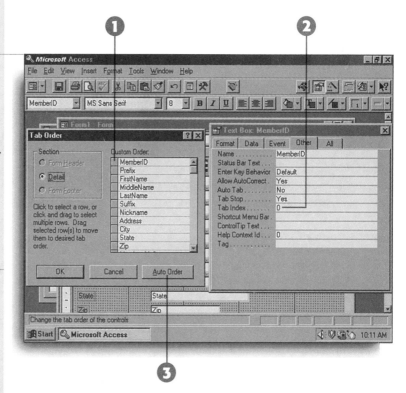

Creating New Controls

If you accidentally deleted a control or you are creating or modifying a form or report, you need to add new controls.

Add a control to a form or report from the Field List

1. If the Field List does not display, click the Field List button 🔲 on the Form Design toolbar.

2. Drag a field name from the Field List on to the form or report.

When you drag a field from the Field list (see Figure 23.16), Access creates a default type of control (check box for yes/no data types, Bound Object Frame for OLE data types, combo boxes for fields with Lookup properties set, and text box for all other data types). There are three categories of controls:

- *Bound controls*, which are linked to a field in a table or query.
- *Unbound controls*, which are not linked to any field in a table or query.
- *Calculated controls*, which are unbound controls that use field data or functions to perform calculations onscreen. The result of the calculation is not stored in any table or query.

If you want a different kind of control after you placed the control on the form, choose **F͟ormat** and select **Change T͟o**. To turn off or on the Field List, click the Display/Hide Field List button.

If you want to add a control other than the default control for a field, you need to use the toolbox.

Create a calculated control

1. Create the unbound Text Box control (one not linked to a field in the table) for the calculated field.

2. Type the expression in the control, or set the control's Control Source property to the expression, as explained in the next section. An example of an expression is `=[Price]*[Quantity]`, where Price and Quantity are fields in the underlying table (or names of controls) and are multiplied to come up with an extended price. Notice that field names are enclosed in square brackets.

> **You cannot edit data in calculated fields in Form view**
>
> A calculated field is a control in a form or report that displays the result of an expression, rather than stored data. This is because Access enters the appropriate value automatically. Press Tab, Enter, or an arrow key to move past these fields or change their **Enabled** property or **Tab Stop** property to **No**.

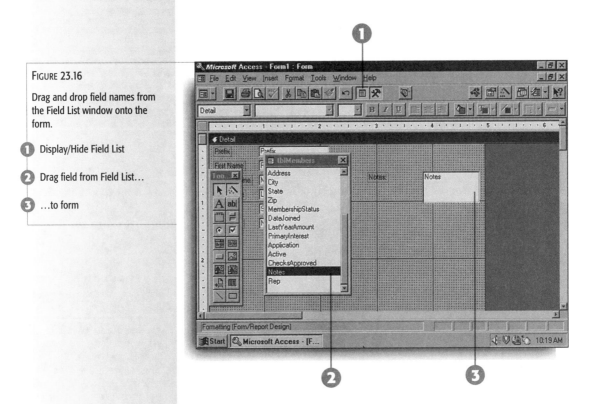

FIGURE 23.16

Drag and drop field names from the Field List window onto the form.

1 Display/Hide Field List

2 Drag field from Field List...

3 ...to form

Using the Toolbox

The toolbox contains design objects (such as fields, text, and boxes) that you can place in a form or report. This section briefly describes each item in the toolbox. Most of the toolbox buttons are used in forms, but not all are used in reports. The buttons displaying fields as alternatives to text boxes (option group, combo box, list box) would not be likely for reports. Figure 23.17 shows a form in Design view that requires many of the tools on the toolbox to be used. The Form view is shown later in Figure 23.18, which is included in the "Navigating Form View" section of this chapter.

The toolbox is a toolbar you can move around and resize just like any other toolbar. To display the toolbox, click the Toolbox button on the Form Design toolbar. By default, the Select Objects tool is selected. Use this tool to select the object in your form or report with which you want to work. Access displays handles around the selected object.

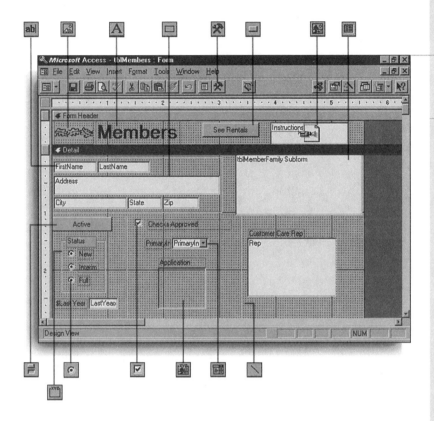

FIGURE 23.17
Each tool used to create the form is shown.

To place a new control in the form or report, select the appropriate tool in the toolbox. The mouse pointer changes to a crosshair and displays the tool's icon. If desired, choose a field name from the field list, move the crosshair to the desired location, and then click and drag the control to the desired size.

The following paragraphs briefly describe each tool in the toolbox:

Select Objects. Selects objects.

Control Wizards. Turns Control Wizards (help for other tools) on and off. It's usually best to keep the Control Wizard on to help you through the difficult process of creating option groups, combo and list boxes, and subforms or subreports.

Label. Creates a text control. Use the Label tool to type text in your form or report (such as a title). After you click the form or report and start typing, the label expands to fill the text. Click

Don't worry about sizing something manually

After you change the font of a label, you might need to resize it. Instead of using the resizing handles, choose **Format**, select **Size, and choose to Fit** or double-click one of the sizing handles.

Toolbox buttons have properties just like controls

For example, the Default Text box has an **Auto Label** property that automatically adds a label when you create a text box. There are also a **Label X**, **Label Y**, and **Label Align** properties, which identify the location and justification of the attached label. To show and edit the default properties for each of the Toolbox controls, turn on properties by clicking the Form Design toolbar and then click the [icon] tool in the toolbox.

Stick to Windows conventions to help users understand your form

Although you can put check boxes within an option group and have option buttons represent yes/no responses for multiple questions, it is better to stick to the standard Windows interface design, in which option buttons represent one of many choices and check boxes represent yes/no answers.

outside the label and back on the label again to format it. You might need to reformat the label with the Font, Bold, and Font Size text boxes.

[icon] *Text Box.* Displays field data (label and text box). Because you can just drag a field from the field list, you won't have to use this option much except for calculated controls. To create an expression, type = and the expression. Alternatively, go to the **Control Source** property and use the Build button [icon].

[icon] *Option Group.* Use the Option Group control when you want to place option buttons or toggle buttons in a group where only one choice is possible within the group. Placing an option group in the form displays the Option Group Wizard, which helps you define the option group and set the desired properties.

[icon] *Toggle Button.* Creates an on/off button, which appears depressed when in the on position. A toggle button can be part of an option group or by itself if the answer is yes or no. If you use toggle buttons, make sure you set the **Caption** property so you can tell what the button indicates.

[icon] *Option Button.* Usually used as an option within a group. If you use the Option Group tool, option buttons are created for you. If you want to add an option button manually to a group, first create the option group. Then choose the Option Button tool and click inside the option group (the option group becomes highlighted).

[icon] *Check Box.* Creates a check box and a true/false control. You can drag a yes/no field from the field list to create a check box. A check mark indicates yes and a blank indicates no. If you want new records to automatically display yes or no, type Yes or No in the **Default Value** property.

[icon] *Combo Box.* Creates a drop-down list of predefined choices but also enables the user to type values. The combo box and list box are often used when you want to look up values from another table or query. For example, on an orders table you might want to identify an employee. Instead of typing the whole employee's name in, create a combo box based on the employee's ID.

When you choose the Combo Box tool, a wizard asks you for the table to use to display the choices and the fields you want to

see. The first field you choose should be the one you want to
see after the combo box is closed. You can use any other fields
to help identify the employee. For example, you could use
Employee Last Name, First Name, Extension, and ID fields for
the combo box.

The following properties are important to review if the combo
or list box doesn't work:

- *Control Source.* Field in your table where you're storing the
  answer.

- *Row Source.* Name of table or query used to lookup values.
  You can click the build button to access the query builder,
  choose the fields, and sort order of the items that are in the
  drop-down list.

- *Column Count.* Number of columns from the row source
  used for the list.

- *Column Widths.* Display width for each column in the list; 0
  will not display column.

- *Bound Column.* Which column from the row source that will
  be placed in the field on the form.

- *List Width.* Width of the entire drop-down list.

- *Limit to List.* Determines whether you want to limit values to
  the table/query/list for your combo box or allow the user to
  type other values as well.

List Box. Creates a drop-down list of predefined choices but,
unlike combo box, does not enable the user to type new values.
The list box also is different because you see multiple rows and
columns even when the control does not have the focus. Because
the list box takes up so much room on a form, I don't use it very
much.

Command Button. Creates a button that runs a macro or calls
an Access procedure when clicked. When you place this tool on
a form, the Command Button Wizard steps you through the
most used options such as moving to another record, adding and
deleting the record, opening a form, and running a report.
Access automatically creates a Visual Basic procedure that goes
with the button. You could edit the procedure or create a macro
to attach to the **On Click** property of the button.

Image. Creates a frame to display a static image. When you choose this tool, Access takes you into the Insert Picture dialog box to find the picture file. You might have to change the **Size Mode** property to display the picture properly.

Unbound Object Frame. Creates a frame to display pictures, graphs, and OLE objects that are not from the database. Access takes you into the Insert Object dialog box, where you can create a new object using one of the registered programs or find the file that contains the object.

Bound Object. Creates a frame to display an OLE object from the database (changes with each record). The Bound Object Frame tool displays pictures, graphs, or other OLE objects stored in an Access database. This type of control is automatically created when you drag an OLE object from the field list. To add a new OLE object into the field for a record, you need to be in the Field in Form view and paste the object from the Clipboard or choose the **Insert** menu and select **O**bject.

Page Break. Creates a page break in the form or report. Anything below the control prints on the next page.

Subform/Subreport. Creates a frame to display an embedded form or report. A common use of the Subform/Subreport tool is to show a one-record-to-many-records relationship between related tables—for example, to show the movie rentals for each customer. When you want to embed a form in another form, use the Subform/Subreport tool in the main form. You can save time by using Form Wizards to create both the embedded form and the main form.

Line. Draws a line. To draw a straight line, hold Shift down as you drag the mouse. Use the Line/Border Width button to change the thickness of the line.

Rectangle. Draws a rectangle. If you want options within a box, use the Option Group tool instead. Use the Line tool to draw lines and the Rectangle tool to draw boxes that visually group items or draw attention to an item.

Which control properties are important?

The important control properties for the Subform/Subreport control are the Source Object (name of subform or subreport) and the Link Child Fields (name of field on subform/subreport), whose value matches the main form's primary field identified by the Link Master Fields property. In some cases, there is no link. For example, you might want two unrelated summary reports to appear on one page. You can also create subforms or subreports by dragging a form or report from the Database window to the form or report you are building.

Adding Controls through the Toolbox

To add one of the controls mentioned in the previous section, you use the Field List in conjunction with one of the buttons from the Toolbox.

Add a control to a form or report

1. Click the Toolbox button 🛠 to display the toolbox.

2. Click the desired control tool in the Form Design toolbox.

3. For unbound or calculated controls, position the mouse pointer in the form where you want to add the control. Click to create a default-size control; click and drag to create a custom-size control.

4. For bound controls, display the field list by clicking the Field List button 🔲. Click and drag the desired field name to the appropriate position in the form.

5. If a wizard is displayed, answer the steps in the wizard (described with the specific control) to create properties for the control.

Navigating Form View

Entering and editing data in Form view is the same as in Datasheet view. All the data-entry shortcuts and tools, such as Find and Filter By Form, are available in Form view. By using the View drop-down toolbar button, you can easily move between Datasheet, Form, and Design view.

Figure 23.18 reviews some of the record navigation features.

SEE ALSO

➤ *For a description on how to enter data into a table (and a form), see page 500*

➤ *For notes on adding a record to a table (which also applies to a form), see page 503*

➤ *To display records in your table (or form) in order or selected records, see page 508*

FIGURE 23.18

Navigating on a form is very
similar to navigating in
Datasheet view.

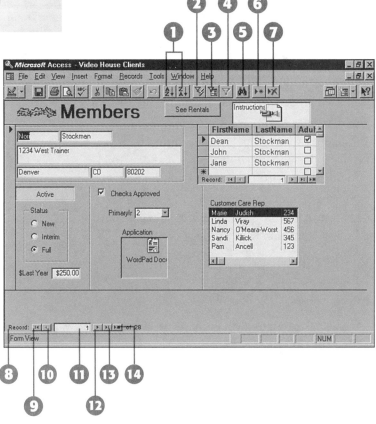

1	Sort current field	**8**	Record Navigator (in order of buttons):
2	Filter by current field	**9**	First record
3	Choose filter criteria	**10**	Previous record
4	Apply/Remove filter	**11**	Choose record
5	Find record	**12**	Next record
6	New record	**13**	Last record
7	Delete record	**14**	New record

Querying Databases

Create and save a query to display a subset of your table

Perform calculations to add, multiply, and sum your data

Specify query criteria to limit which records you see

Update, delete, or add records with action queries

Exploring Queries

So far, this section of the book has focused on the ways in which you can enter data into your database. Now it's time to explore ways of getting information out of your database.

One of the most useful features of modern database applications is the *query*, which provides you a way to question your database. The result of a query (the answer) then can be printed or viewed onscreen. A query is a statement that indicates for Access the kind of information that you need to extract from one or more tables. A query also can perform an action on the data in the table(s) and summarize data in spreadsheet format.

You can use queries, for example, to accomplish the following tasks:

- Compile a list of employees who live in a certain state.
- Show customer names, demographics, and purchasing information in one report.
- Determine the frequency of movie rentals.
- Calculate the total cost of movies by category.
- Purge the database of customers who have not rented in the past year.
- Add old customer records to a history database.

Queries can be used as a source of information for forms and reports. In such a case, the query enables you to include specific data from more than one table. Access executes the query each time you open the form or report, so you can be sure that the information you see is up-to-date.

Access enables you to create the following types of queries:

- *Select queries*. Used to extract data from tables based on criteria specified in the query object. This type of query is the most common. A select query could be used to list all customers in New York, for example. You can use select queries to display fields from more than one related table. (For an example of a select query, see Current Product List in the Northwind database.)

- *Action queries.* Used to perform an action on records that meet criteria specified in the query object. This type of query enables you to change or move data, create new tables, or purge records from a table. You could use an action query to purge inactive customer records.

- *Totals queries.* Used to group data with sums, averages, or other summary calculations. (For an example of a total query, see Category Sales for 1994 in the Northwind database.)

- *Crosstab queries.* Used to summarize data in a spreadsheet format based on criteria specified in the query object. Crosstab queries are often used to calculate data for a graph. (For an example of a crosstab query, see Quarterly Orders by Product in the Northwind database.)

- *Union queries.* Used to combine sets of records from different tables with common fields. For example, you can create a query that combines present and past invoice data. (For an example of a union query, see Customers and Suppliers by City in the Northwind database.)

- *Pass-through queries.* Used to send commands to a Standard Query Language (SQL) database.

- *Data-definition queries.* Used to perform actions on Access databases with SQL statements.

For each query type, you can specify query parameters that prompt the user to specify criteria before the query executes. In the video-store application introduced in Chapter 20, for example, you could create a query that lists movies based on each customer's preferences.

Access places the results of some query or filter operations in a dynaset. A *dynaset* looks and behaves like a table, but it actually provides a dynamic view of the data in one or more tables. You can enter and update data in a dynaset. After you do so, Access automatically updates the data in the associated table or tables. A dynaset is similar to a snapshot, which also looks like a table but is not updatable. Crosstab and total queries are examples of snapshots.

Beyond the scope of this book

Crosstab, Union, Pass-through, and Data-definition queries are beyond the scope of this book. For more information on these types of queries, see Que's *Special Edition, Using Access 95*. This chapter just discusses the basics of queries and talks about select, total, and action queries.

You see the changes other users make, too

In a multiuser environment, changes made by other users are reflected in the dynaset and its associated tables.

SEE ALSO

➤ *To learn more about the basics of creating your own database, see page 446*

➤ *For more information on the Northwind sample database provided with Microsoft Access, see page 530*

Things to Consider When Creating a Query

It helps to spend some time designing the query before you actually create one. Think about some of the following factors before getting started:

- Which table(s) contain the information you need
- Table relationships (are the tables properly keyed?)
- The type of query you want to perform
- The field conditions and criteria that the records must meet
- Calculations, if desired
- Sort order
- The name under which you want to save the query

Create New Query

To create a new query, click the New Object, New Query button 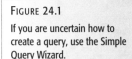 on the toolbar, or switch to the Database window, select the **Query** tab, and then click the **New** button. The New Query dialog box appears (see Figure 24.1). As with tables and forms, Access provides several methods for creating queries.

FIGURE 24.1

If you are uncertain how to create a query, use the Simple Query Wizard.

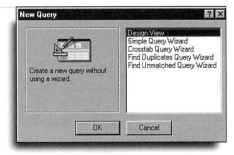

The New Query dialog box provides five basic types of generic queries (refer to Figure 24.1):

- **Design View**. Enters Query Design by displaying a blank query form for the table(s) that you select.

- **Simple Query Wizard**. Creates a select query from fields that you pick.

- **Crosstab Query Wizard**. Summarizes query data in a spreadsheet format.

- **Find Duplicates Query Wizard**. Locates duplicate records in a table.

- **Find Unmatched Query Wizard**. Locates records in one table that do not have matching records in a related table.

Each wizard prompts you for specific information needed to create its particular type of query. In each case, you must identify the table(s) or queries on which the new query will be based.

Creating a Query with the Query Wizard

The easiest way to create a query is to use the Simple Query Wizard. This walks you through the process step-by-step.

Create a query with the Simple Query Wizard

1. On the Queries tab in the Database Window, click the **New** button. The New Query dialog box opens.

2. Double-click **Simple Query Wizard**.

3. In the first screen of the dialog box, choose the underlying table (or query) for your new query from the **Tables/ Queries** drop-down list. For example, if you are using the sample Northwind database, choose the Categories table (shown in Figure 24.2).

4. Double-click each field that you want in the new query. The field moves from the **Available Fields** list to the **Selected Fields** list. If you accidentally add too many fields, double-click the field in the **Selected Fields** list to remove it. When you've finished choosing fields, click the **Next** button.

5. Type a name for the query in the last step of the wizard and choose **Finish** to open the query and see the results.

Alternatively, you can change the option to Modify the query design, go to Design view, and change the query according to the instructions in the following section, "Using Design View."

FIGURE 24.2

Choose the table and fields that you want for your query.

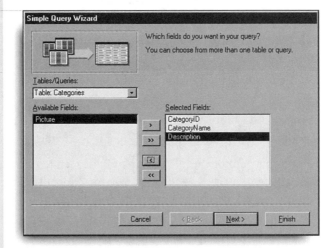

Using Design View

A new query can be started different ways using Design view. Generally, all queries start as a select query and to start, the steps are the same. Because I usually don't remember, however, which table I should use, I use the following method.

Create a select query with Design View

1. In the Database window, double-click the table or query on which you want to base the new query. If you're using the Northwind database, start with the Customers table.

2. From the New Object drop-down button 🔲▾, choose New Query 🔲. The New Query dialog box opens.

3. Double-click **Design View**. Access displays the select query: Query1 window. The name of the original table or query displays on a title bar of a list of fields.

4. If you want to add another table to the query, click the Show Table button 🔲. The Show Table dialog box appears (see Figure 24.3). Double-click each table that you want to

add. As you select tables, Access places a field list for the
table at the top of the Select Query window. Click **Close**
when you're finished adding tables. If you're using the
Northwind database, try adding the Orders table. If you add
more tables and the tables are related, you see lines joining
tables (see Figure 24.4).

FIGURE 24.3

The Show Table dialog box
enables you to add tables and
other queries to your new
query design.

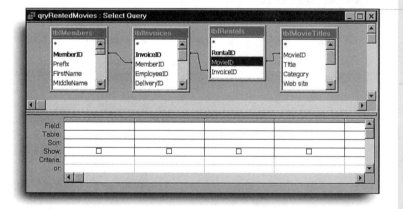

FIGURE 24.4

The added tables appear in the
top portion of the Query
Design view.

5. Access automatically finds table relationships and draws a
line between the matching key fields (same field name and
field type). These lines are called join lines. *Join* lines apply
only to multitable queries. You can create join lines yourself
by dragging and dropping a key field from one table to
another.

6. Double-click each field that you want in the field list(s) to
add the fields to the lower half of the Query Design window.

7. If you want to sort the query, change the Sort row of any fields to Ascending or Descending.

8. Add any criteria or calculations you want.

9. Click the Save button 🔲 and type a name for the query.

The bottom half of the window contains the Query-by-Example grid, in which you define the criteria of the query. Query-by-Example (QBE) enables you to define query criteria by providing practical examples of the type of data that you need. To find all employees in the state of New Jersey, for example, you would type the example element NJ. (For a more thorough discussion of the QBE grid, see "Specifying Query Criteria" later in this chapter.)

SEE ALSO

➤ *Your tables should already have relationships established before creating queries, see page 493*

Exploring the Query Design Window

While you are creating a query, you are in the Query Design window (which is also called the Query-By-Example grid). If you just completed the task in the preceding section, you are in the Query Design window. Otherwise, follow the steps to edit an existing query.

Bring a query into Query Design mode

1. From the Database window, click the Queries tab.

2. Select a query.

3. Click the Design button. You enter Query Design mode.

The Query window enables you to see queries in several views (available via the View menu or toolbar):

- *Design view.* 📝▾ Used to define the query

- *SQL view.* **SQL** Used to view or modify the SQL query-language definition of your query

- *Datasheet view.* 🞖▾ Used to display the results of your query

The Query Design window toolbar provides many buttons that speed your query work. Table 24.1 describes these buttons.

You can also easily choose other types of queries

By default, Access sets the query type to Select query. You can change the query type by making a different selection from the Query menu or Query Type button 🖽▾ on the toolbar.

Queries are useful for forms and reports

Remember that in addition to Datasheet view, query results can be used as the basis for a form or a report.

You can drag and drop queries into Word and Excel

From the Database window in Access, drag a query icon or selected data in Datasheet view to the Word or Excel document. (The document must be open.)

TABLE 24.1   Query window toolbar buttons

Button	Button Name	Description
	View	Drop-down list of views: Design view, SQL view, or Datasheet view
	Save	Saves the query design
	Print	Prints the query datasheet (in Datasheet view)
	Print Preview	Displays the query as it appears when printed
	Spelling	Spell checks the query in Datasheet view
	Cut	Deletes the selected data or object and copies it to the Clipboard
	Copy	Copies the selected data or object to the Clipboard
	Paste	Inserts the Clipboard contents
	Undo Current	Reverses the last change
	Query Type	Drop-down list of query types: Select, Cross-Tab, Make Table, Update, Append, and Delete
	Run	Executes the query
	Show Table	Displays the Show Table dialog box listing available tables and queries for use in the current query design
	Totals	Displays or hides the totals row in the Query grid pane
	Top Values	Drop-down list of filter values (top 5, 100, 5%, 25%)
	Properties	Displays the Properties window

continues…

TABLE 24.1   Continued

Button	Button Name	Description
	Build	Invokes a wizard or builder
	Database Window	Displays the Database window
	New Object	Drop-down list that enables creation of database objects such as forms, queries, and reports
	Help	Displays context-sensitive help

Editing a Query

After you start a new query or click the Design button in the Database window for an existing query, Access displays the Query window in Design view. Query Design view (see Figure 24.5) is split into two main sections. The top section contains a field list box for each table being used in the query definition; the bottom section contains the QBE grid, where you define your query. Each column of the QBE grid is a field. For each field, you define the query parameters, such as criteria and sorting, in the rows of the QBE grid. Because most queries start as a select query, the following discussion applies to the beginning of all queries.

Selecting Fields

The QBE grid consists of columns and rows. Each column represents one of the fields used in your query. To add a field to the QBE grid, double-click the field in the field list box, or drag the field name to a column. Access fills in the field name and checks the **Show** check box. If you want to use the field in sorting or criteria but not display the field in the dynaset, deselect the **Show** check box.

To start these procedures you need to be in Query Design view. (See the preceding sections, "Using Design View" or "Exploring the Query Design Window.")

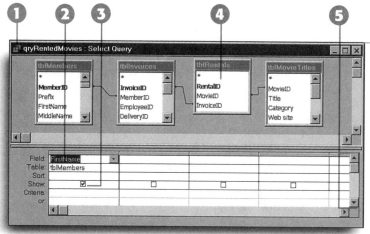

FIGURE 24.5

Define the query in the QBE grid by adding fields and setting query parameters.

❶ Query type and title

❷ Field selector

❸ Check to include field in query results

❹ Tables added

❺ Query-by-Example (QBE) grid

Edit fields in Query Design

1. To select all the fields in a field list box, double-click the Table name and drag the highlighted area to the QBE grid.

2. To add one field, double-click the field in the field list.

3. To remove a field, select the field selector and press Delete.

4. To change the order of the field columns, select a field column by clicking the field selector in the QBE grid and dragging the column to the new location.

5. If you want to start over, choose the **Edit** menu and select **Cle a r Grid**.

The QBE grid contains another row that is hidden by default: Totals. To display this row, choose **View** and select **Totals** Σ . The Totals row appears below the Field row in the QBE grid. (See the later section, "Adding Group Calculations.")

Adding Calculated Fields

You also can add calculated fields to the QBE grid. To start with, you are still working with a select query (but you can use this query later for a totals query). Calculated fields are temporary fields created in the dynaset when a query executes. You can use

Does your table have too much information?

Suppose that you want a list of your friends' names and phone numbers, but not their addresses and birthdays. Even though all that data is stored in your FRIENDS table, you could get a subset of information by creating a query and selecting only the Name and Phone Number fields.

a calculated field, for example, to calculate a markup on products or to concatenate text fields.

Create a new calculated field

1. Select an empty field-name cell in the QBE grid.

2. Type a name for the new field and a colon. Using a new query based on the Order Details table, from the Northwind database; for example, type Extended Price:.

   If you do not type a field name and just skip to step 3, Access creates a default name such as Expr1, which you can later edit.

3. Type the expression (calculation). Field names used in the calculation should appear in brackets ([ ]), and spaces must be in quotes, but numeric and arithmetic operators do not require any special notation. For example, if you were using the Order Details table database, you would type [Quantity]*[UnitPrice].

4. Click outside the Field cell to see whether Access accepts your expression.

5. Continue with additional fields or save 🖫 your query.

For more help on naming fields, search for the help topic **Renaming a Field in a Query**. For assistance on writing expressions for calculated fields in a query, search for the help topic **Calculated Fields, customer calculations in queries**. You also can click the Build button 🔨 on the toolbar to launch the Expression Builder, which can help you create the expression.

The following are some calculation examples:

- Increase price by 5%: [Price]*1.05
- First five characters of zip code: Left([ZipCode],5)
- Name combined: Salesperson: [FirstName] & " " &[LastName]
- Extended price: [Price]*[Quantity]*(1-[Discount])/100)*100
- Year: Format([ShippedDate],"yyyy")
- Month: Format([ShippedDate], "mmm")
- Days between dates: DateDiff("d", [OrderDate], [ShipDate])

The crosstab query summarizes one field by changes in two other fields.

When you click the Crosstab Query Type button 🔲, two new rows appear in the QBE grid: **Total** and **Crosstab**. The Total row has the same values mentioned later for group calculation queries (**Sum**, **Avg**, and so on). Choose this for the value to be summed (usually a numeric data type field) and **Value** in the **Crosstab** row. In the other two fields (usually text data types), choose **Group By** in **Total** row and **Row Heading** and **Column Heading** in the **Crosstab** row. An example could be Employee (Group By, Row Heading) by Country (Group By, Column Heading) summing Amount (Sum, Value).

If your query has way too many records from what you were expecting and it takes an extreme amount of time to run

You probably have not created a join between your tables. Return to Design view and either delete the unnecessary tables or drag a field between tables to create a join.

Can't read a calculation formula?

To change the width of a column, position the mouse pointer above the Field row, on the vertical grid line. The pointer changes to a set of opposing arrows. Drag the grid line to the desired width. You can also press F2 to enter the Zoom window.

Sometimes you need to add two text fields together (you don't want to see two separate columns for a name, for example). This is called *concatenation*. In an empty field cell, type the new field name, followed by a colon. After the colon, type the field names, enclosed in brackets if necessary. Between the field names, type an ampersand (&). If you want to insert a space or text between the fields, use two quotes and another ampersand: [field1] & " " & [field2]. Figure 24.6 shows a string concatenation of a member's first and last name and a calculation that computes projected sales based on a price increase of 10 percent.

Access is helpful when creating some calculations

When you create calculations or expressions using field names, Access automatically adds square brackets to identify a field when the field is one word. For this reason, it is a good idea to keep your field names to one word (FirstName, for example). You can, however, always enclose field names in brackets to ensure that Access correctly includes field names in calculations.

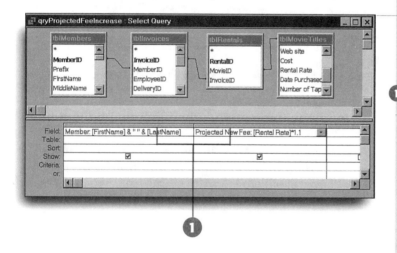

FIGURE 24.6

Calculated fields enable you to perform calculations in queries and concatenate text fields.

❶ Calculated fields

SEE ALSO

➤ *For more detail on naming rules, see page 457*

Adding Group Calculations

Query results sometimes need calculations included for groups of records rather than for each record (see Figure 24.7). You might want to see total sales by state, for example, or advertising cost by product. Access enables you to perform sophisticated calculations on groups of records. For example, you could determine the average salary by department or the maximum hours by job order. During the process of creating group calculations, you change a Select query into a totals query. For an example of a totals query, see the Category Sales for 1994 query in the Northwind database.

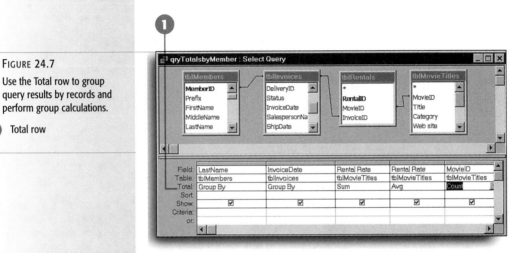

FIGURE 24.7

Use the Total row to group query results by records and perform group calculations.

① Total row

To calculate totals for several groups

Use multiple **Group By** total types.

You define groups in the **Total** row. To display the **Total** row, click the Totals button ∑. After you add the **Total** row to your QBE grid, Access automatically adds the words **Group By** in each field. Use **Group By** to identify the fields (groups) by which you want to perform the calculation. You can change this selection to any of the following types of calculations:

- **Sum**. Totals the field values.

- **Avg**. Computes an average field value.

- **Min**. Finds the minimum field value.

- **Max**. Finds the maximum field value.

- **Count**. Returns the number of values in a field, disregarding null values.

- **StDev**. Computes the standard deviation (square root of the variance) of the field values.

- **Var**. Computes the variance of the field values.

- **First**. Returns the first value in a field.

- **Last**. Returns the last value in a field.

- **Expression**. Enables you to create a calculated field for a group.

- **Where**. Enables you to specify criteria for a field you are not using to define groupings. (See the following section, "Specifying Query Criteria.")

Perform group calculations

1. Create a select query (see the preceding sections, "Creating a Query with the Query Wizard" or "Using Design View").

2. In Design view, display the **Total** row by clicking the Totals button ▣.

3. In the **Total** cell, select **Group By** for each category that you want to combine (this is usually a text field).

   If the totals are for all records, no total cells should be of the type **Group By**.

4. In the Total cell, select fields that you want to add, count, or do other math functions, such as **Sum** (usually number fields) or **Count** (can be either numeric or text fields).

5. Click the Save button ▣ to save the query.

6. Click the Datasheet View button ▣▾ to see the results of the query.

With what fields do the calculation types work?

Calculation types—such as Sum, Avg, and Var—that calculate totals can be used only for fields of the following data types: Number, Date/Time, Currency, Counter, and Yes/No. The data type Text also is valid for Count, First, and Last.

Specifying Query Criteria

The Criteria row (see Figure 24.8) of the QBE enables you to include, in your query results, only records that meet specific conditions. Criteria are conditions used to select records but can be used with any type of query. This query feature is probably used more often than any other.

You can select records by entering any of the following conditions:

- *Exact Match*. Use a literal value, such as the text string **NJ** or the currency amount **1000**, which the field value (not case-sensitive) must match.

- *Wildcard Pattern Match*. Use a combination of literal characters and wildcard characters (see Table 24.2, which follows this list), such as **N*** or **Like "1###"**, which the field value must match.

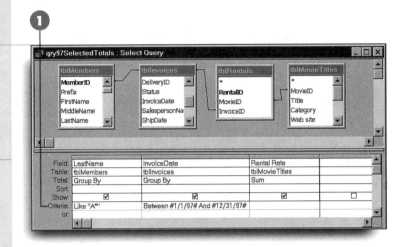

1

FIGURE 24.8

Limit the records included in your query results by specifying criteria in the **Criteria** row.

1   Criteria row

Need a criteria example?

To find all rentals in 1997, you could enter the criteria * / * / 97 or Between 1/1/97 and 12/31/97.

- *Elimination Match*. Use the NOT operator to eliminate records that meet the criteria (for example, not NJ).
- *Date Match*. Use an exact date or the Date( ) operator, which represents today's date (according to your computer's clock). For example, you could use the criteria 12/1/99 or Date( ).
- *Blank Values*. Use the NULL operator to specify that you want to see only blank values. Conversely, use NOT NULL to specify that you do not want blank values in your query results.
- *Comparison Operators*. Use any of the comparison operators (see Table 24.3, which follows this list) to compare record data with a specific condition. For example, you could enter <DATE( ) to see only records with dates before today's date.
- *Yes/No Values*. Use Yes, True, On, or -1 to specify Yes values. Use No, False, Off, or 0 to specify No values.
- *Multiple Criteria*. Use the logic operators (see Table 24.4) to establish multiple criteria within the same field. Use the same criteria row to establish multiple criteria based on multiple fields (where all fields must match). Use different criteria rows (or) where any of the values match.

TABLE 24.2 Wildcard operators

Operator	Description
*	Use in place of any number of characters.
?	Use in place of any single character.
#	Use in place of any single digit (for example, Like "1###").
[ ]	Use to specify characters within the brackets (for example, N[JY]).
!	Use to match any character not in the list (for example, N[!JY]).
-	Use to match one character in a range of characters (for example, N[J-Y]).
LIKE	Use to match any characters (for example, use LIKE "[A-D]*" to see a list of members whose names begin with A, B, C, or D). Often, Access automatically adds the word Like in the grid.

Need help with operators?

For more information on operators, refer to online Help (press **Shift+F1** and click the criteria row).

TABLE 24.3 Comparison operators

Operator	Description
>	Greater than
<	Less than
<=	Less than or equal to
=>	Greater than or equal to
< >	Not equal to
=	Equal to

TABLE 24.4 Logic operators

Operator	Description
AND	Requires that all criteria be met.
OR	Requires that either criterion be met (either/or).
NOT	Requires that criteria not be met.
BETWEEN X and Y	Requires that values be within a specified range. Note that both x and y are included.
IN	Requires that value be within the same field. An example would be In("TX","OR","CO").

You can specify multiple rows of criteria for each field

Multiple rows of criteria create an OR condition. Multiple criteria in the same row create an AND condition unless the keyword OR is specified.

Specifying Query Properties

You can view and modify the properties of a query, of the table field lists that a query uses, or of individual fields. To view and modify the properties of any of these objects, choose **View** and select **Properties** to open the Properties window 📷. Then click the object for which you want to set properties. The contents of the Properties window change to reflect that object's properties.

(You might want to specify the format of a calculated field—for example, to specify the number of decimal places to be displayed.)

An important query property is the **Unique Values** property (see Figure 24.9). By default, this property is set to **No**, indicating that duplicate records, if they exist and meet your criteria, are listed in the dynaset. To exclude duplicate values, set the **Unique Values** property to **Yes**.

FIGURE 24.9

Set the query property **Unique Values** to **Yes** to exclude duplicate values from the dynaset.

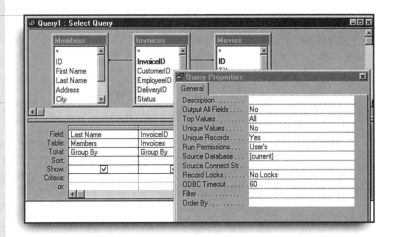

If your query takes too long to run

Within Access, you can improve the efficiency of queries by using Rushmore Technology. Basically, this technology has you create an index for the fields used in your query. For more information on Rushmore Technology, search for the help topic "Optimize Query Performance."

Using Action Queries

If you want to update a number of records at one time, Access provides action queries. To create an action query, first create a select query and then modify the query to an action query. Table 24.5 shows the different kinds of action queries available.

TABLE 24.5 **Query types**

Icon	Query Name	Description
	Select Query	Use a select query before you create any action queries.
	Make-Table Query	Creates a new table with the fields that you identify in your QBE grid. Type in the table name after you click the Query Type button.
	Update Query	Changes the value for the field(s) that you identify. After you click the Query Type button, a new row, **Update To**, appears in the QBE grid. Type the expression in this row. For example, in the Price field column, you could type [Price]*1.25 to increase the price by 25 percent.
	Append Query	Adds records to the bottom of the table that you identify. After you click the Query Type button, choose the name of an existing table. You see a new row, **Append To**, in the QBE grid. If the field names are different between the two tables, choose the name of the append to field below the name of the current table's field.
	Delete Query	Deletes any records that match your criteria.

Create an action query

1. First, create a select query that lists all the fields and necessary criteria.

2. Display the results of the select query in Datasheet view to make sure you are choosing the correct fields and records.

3. Change the query to an action query by choosing one of items on the **Query** menu or by clicking the Query Type button (see Table 29.5).

4. If prompted for a table name (Make-Table Query or Append Query), type or choose the table in the Table Name drop-down list.

5. Click the Run button .

6. Read any warning messages and reply carefully (see Figure 24.9).

FIGURE 24.10

Notice that the dialog prompt indicates that you cannot undo any of the changes and is checking to make sure that you really want to go ahead.

When working with action queries, be extra careful

After you reply to any warning messages, you are not able to undo your changes and risk deleting or changing the wrong data. Until you are absolutely confident that you won't mess up your data, have a backup copy of the database or a backup copy of any tables affected by the action queries. To make a backup copy of a table, go to the Table tab of the Database window, choose the table, and press Ctrl+C. Press Ctrl+V to paste the new table and give it a name, such as Backup of Members.

Table 24.5 shows the different kinds of action queries available. Click the Query Type button and choose the icon shown in the first column. If you save these queries, the query name in the Database window is preceded by the same icon in the first column, with the exclamation point warning you that Access makes major changes to your data if you run the query. Be careful; you run the query again just by opening it from the database window (choosing **Open** or double-clicking the query name).

Creating Reports

Creating a New Report

Whereas forms are primarily for input, reports are only for output. Reports present data in print better than forms or datasheets do. You have more control of the design layout and print output. For example, you can design a report that prints in landscape orientation on legal paper and that subtotals by page or by group.

Before creating a new report, take some time to plan its design. Consider the following items:

- Review the tables, forms, and queries currently used in your database.

- Identify the data components of your report.

- Be sure that all necessary data is entered in the appropriate tables.

- Use a form instead of a report if you need to perform any data entry. You cannot enter or modify data in a report.

- Consider creating a query as a preliminary step if your report contains fields from more than one table or if there are derived fields.

- Review existing printed reports, and get feedback from the people who use the reports on outstanding issues or areas that need improvement.

Report creation is very similar to form creation. To create a new report, display the Database window, select the **Report** tab, and click the **New** button. The New Report dialog box appears (see Figure 25.1).

The following New Report options are listed:

- **Design View**. Enables you to create a custom report from scratch

- **Report Wizard**. Assists you in creating a form by asking you questions and using predesigned report templates (see the next section, "Creating a New Report with Report Wizard")

- **AutoReport: Columnar**. Displays one record at a time in a vertical format (same layout as AutoForm: Columnar)

Hidden feature: You can save a form as a report

This feature is available as a custom toolbar. First, open the form in Design view, choose **View**, and select **Toolbars**. Click **Customize** and select the **Form & Report Design** category on the **Commands** tab. Drag the Save As Report button to the Form Design toolbar and click **Close**.

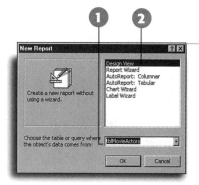

FIGURE 25.1
The New Report dialog box enables you to choose a Table or Query for your report, and the next step provides related tables and queries if you select Report Wizard.

1 Choose the table

2 Double-click the report type

- **AutoReport: Tabular**. Displays multiple records in a row and column format (same layout as AutoForm: Tabular)

- **Chart Wizard**. Displays a report with a graph or chart of the data

- **Label Wizard**. Creates label reports in a variety of formats

SEE ALSO

➤ *To create a form, see page 531*

➤ *To see the steps of the chart wizard, see page 320*

Creating a New Report with Report Wizard

When you select a Report Wizard, Access presents a series of dialog boxes that ask you for the report specifications. The Report Wizard functions much the same as the Form Wizard, so many of the dialog boxes are familiar.

Create a new report using the Report Wizard

1. Click the New Object Report button ▣ in the toolbar and select **New Report**.

2. Type or select the name of the table or query on which to base the report.

3. Double-click **Report Wizard**.

4. Select the fields to be included in the report from the **Available Fields** pane (they appear in the **Selected Fields** pane). Select **Next**.

5. Specify any desired grouping levels (see Figure 25.2) and select **Next** (see "Choosing Report Wizard Grouping Options" later in this chapter).

FIGURE 25.2

If you choose grouping levels, the Grouping Options button enables you to change intervals for grouping.

1 Double-click a field in the list

2 Grouping Options button displays box in Figure 25.4

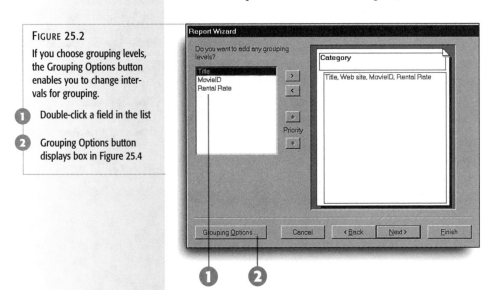

6. Specify any fields on which you want to sort within the groupings. Click the AZ button next to the field name if you want to change the sort from ascending to descending. Choose **Next**.

7. Select the desired layout (**Vertical**, **Tabular**, or for grouped reports, various step, block, and outline layouts are available) and decide whether you want **Portrait** or **Landscape** orientation.

8. If desired, select **Adjust the field width so all fields fit on a page** and choose **Next**.

9. Select a style (**Bold**, **Casual**, **Compact**, **Corporate**, **Formal**, or **Soft Gray**) and choose **Next**.

10. Type the report title and choose **Preview the report** or **Modify the report's design**.

11. Select report Help if desired.

12. Choose **Finish**. (Figure 25.3 shows a finished single-table report.)

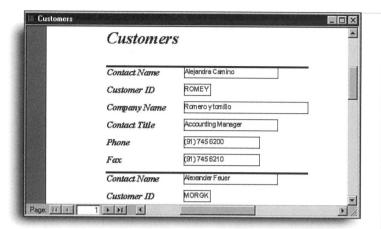

FIGURE 25.3

The Report Wizard created this customer contact report in just a few minutes.

SEE ALSO

➤ *For similarities to forms, see page 533*

Choosing Report Wizard Grouping Options

If you chose grouping levels in step 5 of the preceding procedure on the Report Wizard, the report breaks into different sections. Each change in the grouping value produces a group header (usually a title) and a group footer (usually subtotals).

The **Grouping Options** button opens the Grouping Intervals dialog box (see Figure 25.4). For each text grouping field, you can choose to group on the entire value or the first few characters. For example, if you choose 1st Letter, all the As are grouped, followed by the Bs, instead of a break on every last name. If the grouping field is numeric, the grouping intervals enable you to group by 10s, 50s, 100s (1–10 can be grouped together, 11–20, and so on). If the grouping field is date, you can group by Year, Quarter, Month, and other time periods.

On the next step of the Report Wizard (step 6 in the preceding procedure), the **Summary Options** button is available if you choose grouping (see Figure 25.5). For each numeric field, you can choose to have subtotals and other subcalculations for each break in the group, and you can create **Sum**, **Avg**, **Min**, and **Max** calculations. In addition, you can choose between seeing the calculations only (**Summary Only**) or seeing the records as well as the calculations (**Detail and Summary**). You can also obtain percentages by selecting **Calculate percent of total for sums**. (To modify the groups on your report, see the following section, "Sorting and Grouping in Reports.")

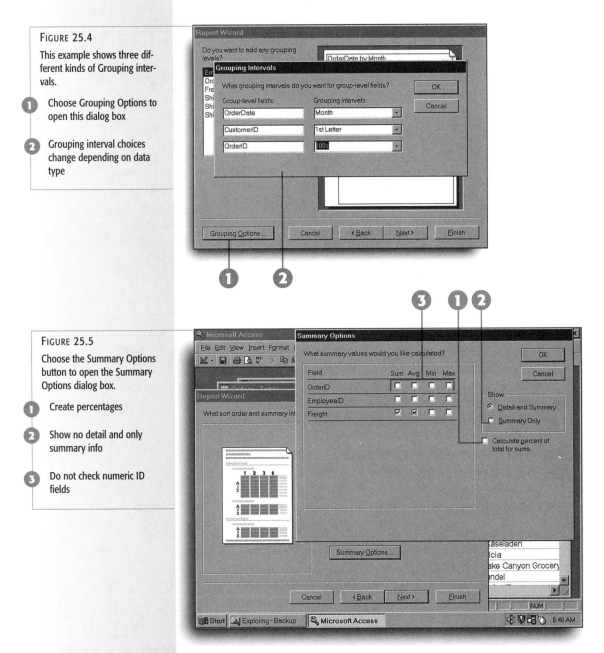

FIGURE 25.4

This example shows three different kinds of Grouping intervals.

1 Choose Grouping Options to open this dialog box

2 Grouping interval choices change depending on data type

FIGURE 25.5

Choose the Summary Options button to open the Summary Options dialog box.

1 Create percentages

2 Show no detail and only summary info

3 Do not check numeric ID fields

Creating Mailing Labels

Figure 25.1 showed a Label Wizard as one of the options on the New Report dialog box. Because much of your data potentially has names and addresses, this wizard helps you create mailing labels for your clients, associates, suppliers, or anyone to whom you need to send letters.

Create Mailing Labels

1. Click the New Object button ![] and choose **New Report**.
2. On the New Report dialog box, choose the name of the table or query containing the addresses (or other fields) that you want to use. If you are using the Northwind database, try the Customers table.
3. Double-click **Label Wizard**.
4. Choose the label size (look on the box your labels come in) and choose **Next**.
5. If desired, change the text appearance and choose **Next**.
6. Choose the fields and type text (as shown in Figure 25.6) to create your Prototype label. Make sure that you type a space and other punctuation between field names. When finished, choose **Next**.

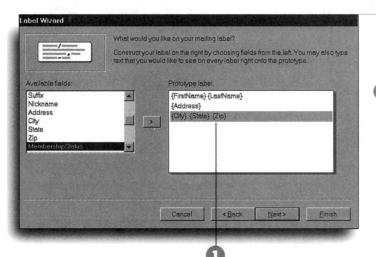

FIGURE 25.6

Double-click the fields in the Available Fields list to add them to the prototype label.

1 Note a comma and space between city and state and space between state and zip code

7. Choose the fields by which you want to sort the list (for example, zip code) and choose **Next**.

8. Give your report a name and choose **Finish**.

SEE ALSO

➤ *You can also create mailing labels (and letters and envelopes) through Microsoft Word; see page 135*

Print Preview

You can access Print Preview by clicking the Print Preview button 🔍 on the toolbar in the Database window when in Report Design view or Report Wizards. Alternatively, if you selected to preview the report in the last Report Wizard dialog box, Access displays the print preview of the report (see Figure 25.7). Print preview shows onscreen how the report will look when printed. The mouse pointer resembles a magnifying glass. Click the report to zoom the view in at the location of the mouse magnifying glass. Click again to zoom out.

The navigation buttons on the bottom of the screen are similar to those for reports and forms, except that now they are used for pages. Choose them to go to the first page, previous page, specific page, next page, or last page.

Don't forget commas, spaces, and other punctuation when you create a label

Type these directly in the **Prototype label** box (as opposed to clicking the space and comma buttons in version 2 and earlier).

FIGURE 25.7

Click the magnifying glass in the report to zoom in or out.

1 Click for next page

2 Click for last page

3 Type a page number and press Enter

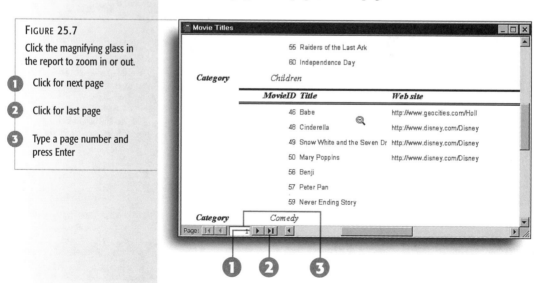

The Print Preview toolbar contains the buttons shown in Table 25.1.

TABLE 25.1   Buttons in the Print Preview toolbar

Button	Button Name	Description
	Print	Prints the report
	Zoom	Toggles zoom in and out
	One Page	Shows one page at a time
	Two Pages	Shows two pages at a time
100%	Zoom	Sets the reduction/enlargement percentage for zoom
Close	Close Window	Closes the Print Preview window
	Office Links	Displays a drop-down button list of available Office Links: Publish It with MS Word, Analyze It with MS Excel
	Database Window	Switches to the Database window
	New Object	Displays a drop-down button list that enables you to create various objects such as tables, forms, and reports
	Help	Displays context-sensitive help

SEE ALSO

➤ *To compare how to preview a Word document, see page 109*

Seeing an Example Layout with Layout Preview

In addition to Print Preview, there is Layout Preview. If you have a lot of data and Access takes a significant amount of time to run Print Preview, choose **View** and select **Layout Preview** to get an idea of what your report will look like. Click the Last Page navigation button at the bottom of the screen to see

Outputting your report

You can print your report like you do any other office documents by clicking the Print button on the toolbar or pressing Ctrl+P and choosing the **OK** button. If you have email installed, you can also send your report to an email recipient by choosing the **File** menu, selecting **Send**, and filling in the format and mail dialog boxes. You can also convert your report to a Word or Excel document by clicking one of the choices on the Office Links button.

how the totals appear in the Report Footer. You see all sections and sorts, but only for a sample set of data. Make sure that you do not print this view because the totals will be incorrect.

Modifying a Report

If you have not read Chapter 23, "Creating Forms and Report Basics," you may want to now. Working on forms and reports in Design view is almost identical. Chapter 23 shows you how to work in sections; how to move, align, and set properties for controls using the Design and Formatting toolbars and the Toolbox; and how to work with expressions. The following is a quick summary of what you need to know for reports:

- If necessary, click the Field List button ▦ to display the Field List and then add fields by dragging them on to the report.

- Select multiple controls with Shift, by dragging the mouse, or by dragging the mouse in the rulers.

- Delete controls by selecting them and pressing Delete.

- Move controls by dragging them with the hand mouse pointer (both field and label) or the finger mouse pointer.

- Align and size controls with **Fo̲rmat** menu items.

- If you want additional lines that the Report Wizard did not draw for you, use the Line tool ＼ (hold Shift for straight lines).

- Access the properties window by right-clicking the object and choosing **Properties** ▣.

- Create a calculated new field with the Text Box tool ⓐⓑ and type = and the formula directly in the Text Box or its **Control Source** property.

- Change the appearance of a control with the Formatting toolbar, and change the format of a number with the **Format** and **Decimal Places** properties.

- To hide a section of a report (to turn a detail report into a summary report, for example), change the Visible property to **No**.

- To set page breaks, use the Page Break tool or change either the **Force New Page** or **Keep Together** properties.

- If the text for a field is not large enough to display, change the **Can Grow** property to **Yes** so that the text wraps on more than one line.

Sorting and Grouping in Reports

Access enables you to organize report records in a particular sort order or in specified groups. For a mailing-list report, for example, you can print the labels by zip code. For a marketing report, you can group customers by state or region.

The grouping feature is available only when you are designing reports (not forms). Grouping divides data into separate groups and sorts records within the groups based on your specifications. In a company phone-list report, for example, you can use the grouping feature to list employees by department. You also can alphabetize the list by department, and alphabetize the names of employees within each department. You can group on multiple fields. For example, you can use the grouping feature to create a report that lists all employees' names and phone numbers by division, by department within the division, and by position within the department. You can add grouping to your report through the Report Wizard (see the preceding section, "Choosing Report Wizard Grouping Options") or manually through the Sorting and Grouping window.

Manually add Grouping to a Report or Edit Existing Options

1. Click the Sorting and Grouping button 📧 to display the Grouping dialog box (see Figure 25.8).

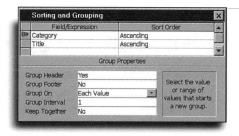

FIGURE 25.8

Use the Sorting and Grouping feature to divide and sort records in your report into meaningful sections.

2. In the top section, select the field on which you want to group, and select either ascending or descending sort order.

3. In the bottom section, set the Group Properties for the grouping as follows:

    - Choose **Yes** or **No** in **Group Header** and **Group Footer** to display or not display a header or footer for that group.

    - Choose the **Group On** choices depending on the data type (Prefix characters for text, Interval for numbers, and Time intervals for date). Looking at the Summary of Sales by Year report in the Northwind Database, you notice two Group Ons for the same field ShippedDate—one by Year and one by Qtr.

    - The **Group Interval** property enables you to choose how many prefix characters or how many of the intervals you want to keep together. If you select **Group On** Year and **Group Interval** of 5, then your report has a new group header and footer at every five years.

    - The **Keep Together** property enables you to try to fit an entire group on one page (**Whole Group**) or at least make sure the first line of the detail section prints with the group header (**With First Detail**).

4. When finished with grouping properties, you can close the Sorting and Grouping box (you don't have to) and preview ⬚ or print ⬚ the report.

When you use the Report Wizard to create groups, Access automatically adds a group header and footer. You can activate or deactivate one or both of these sections in the Sorting and Grouping window. If you chose the Group Options command button during the Report Wizard, Access also automatically adds the Group On and Group Interval Group Properties.

When you want to exclude the detail section and show only the group headers and footers

Change the **Visible** property of the Detail section to **No**.

Working with Expressions

Calculated field expressions generally are more common in reports than in forms because forms are used for data entry but reports are used to see the results (and summary) of data.

AutoReport or the Report Wizard often creates subtotals and totals for you. This may even include fields that should not have calculations such as numeric ID fields. To delete unwanted calculations, click the control in the group or report footer section and press Delete.

Create a Calculation

1. In Report Design view, choose the Text Box tool [abl] and click where you want the calculation to go in the report.

2. Type the expression or use the Build button in the Control Source property. A simple example is =Sum([Subtotal]) on the Summary of Sales by Year report in the Northwind database.

The placement of the calculation in a section is critical (see Figure 25.9). The following are guidelines for placing calculation controls:

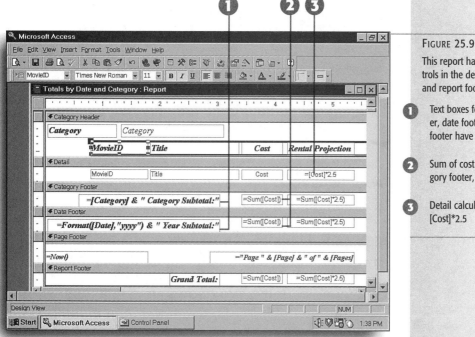

FIGURE 25.9

This report has calculated controls in the detail, grouping, and report footer sections.

1 Text boxes for category footer, date footer, and page footer have text calculations

2 Sum of cost in detail, category footer, date footer

3 Detail calculation shows [Cost]*2.5

- To change the value of a field for every record or create a new calculated field for every record, place the text box in the **Detail** section. Common examples include =[FirstName] & " " & [LastName] (name in one field) and =[Quantity]*[Price] (amount). Use the ampersand (&) to combine text data types and the arithmetic operators (+, -, *, and /) for numeric types. The example in Figure 25.9 is =[Cost]*2.5.

- To have subtotals for a grouping, include the text box in the Group Header or Group Footer section. Common examples include =Sum([Quantity]) and =Avg([Quantity]). The example in Figure 25.9 is =Sum([Cost]). Note that the functions include both parentheses and brackets. If you want to subtotal a calculated field, use the sum function with the calculation: =Sum([Quantity]*[Price]).

- You can use identical expressions in the different group footers to create subtotals for each grouping and to create grand totals in the report footer section.

- If you are grouping on intervals, the group header usually has an expression showing the interval. Examples include =Format$([Date],"yyyy") and =Left$([Name],1). The Format$ expression shows the year (mmm is the three-letter month, mmmm is the full month name, q is the quarter number). The Left$ expression displays the first character from the Name field.

- Page headers or footers usually have some sort of date reference. For today's date, type =Now() in the text box (or **Control Source** property) and change the Format property to the desired format—Long Date is the default when created with a Report Wizard.

- Page headers or footers also usually have page number reference. Use [Page] for the page number and [Pages] for total number of pages. An example is ="Page " & [Page] & " of " & [Pages]. The first page would show Page 1 of 20 in a 20-page report.

- Do not put summary calculations in page footers; a simple =Sum([Quantity]) formula does not work. Advanced users create a Visual Basic procedure to accomplish the task.

Building Expressions with the Expression Builder

Instead of typing in an expression, you can use the Expression Builder to help you remember functions, common expressions, and field names. You can also use the Expression Builder in table properties, queries, and forms.

Use the Expression Builder

(Note: If you want to create an example with these steps, use the Northwind database. Use the New Report dialog box and choose **AutoReport: Tabular** with the **Order Details** table.)

1. Save the report before you start the Expression Builder.
2. Create a text box, using the Text Box 🔘 button.
3. Click the Properties button 🔘.
4. Move to the **Control Source** property for the text box.
5. Click the Build button to the right of the **Control Source** box or on the toolbar 🔘.
6. Choose items from the yellow file folders, the operation buttons (+, - , and so on), or type text in the upper part of the Expression Builder (see Table 25.2).
   - For the Northwind example, double-click the Functions folder and click the Built-In Functions subfolder.
   - In the second column choose **Conversion**.
   - In the third column, choose **Ccur (convert to currency)** and click the **Paste** button. Ccur(<<expr>>) appears in the top half of the Expression Builder.
   - Click the middle of **<<expr>>** to select the text and brackets and press **Delete**.
   - In the first column, choose the top folder (it gives the name of the report).
   - In the second column, choose **<Field List>** to show a list of fields from the underlying record source.
   - In the third column, double-click **Quantity**, click the * button (multiply), and then double-click **UnitPrice** in the third column.
7. When finished building the expression, click the **OK** button.

TABLE 25.2   **Items in the Expression Builder**

Section	Description
Report Name	The first yellow file folder includes the name of the current report. Any subreports are listed as an indented level under the report name. In the second column, you can choose a name of a control or **<Field List>**, and the names of the fields in the report are listed in the third column (see Figure 25.10).
Tables, Queries	Shows a list of tables and queries in the database. To refer to a field in a table or query, choose an item in the second column.
Forms, Reports	Shows a list of forms and reports in the database. Choose a control from the second column or **<Field List>**, and a name of a field from the third column.
Functions	Choose a category in the second column (or keep <All> highlighted and then choose a function in the third column). Any prompts you need to fill are indicated by <<>>.
Constants	Choose a value such as True or False.
Operators	The third column includes the same operators that appear as buttons in the middle of the Expression Builder. Some additional operators, such as Between and >=, are included.
Common Expressions	These expressions generally include items that appear in the report or page header or footer. Choose a page number, date, or user item in the second column, and the third column shows the syntax.

FIGURE 25.10

The Trim function removes any extra spaces before or after the expression in the parentheses.

1 Choose Labels tblMembers or the current report name to see items on the report in the second column

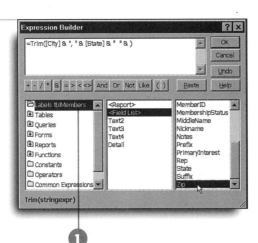

Using Subreports

A report within another report is called a *subreport*. You can use subreports to create a multitable report in which detailed subreports display records related to the main report's current record. You also can use subreports to combine two or more unrelated reports in an unbound main report.

Create a subreport

1. Create the detailed report you want to use as the subreport.

2. Display the main report in Report Design view. For practice, open Northwind's Sales by Year report in Design view and delete the subreport in the ShippedDate Header.

3. Display the Database window.

4. Drag the detailed report object icon to the desired section in the main report (see Figure 25.11). In this example, drag **Sales by Year Subreport** to the **ShippedDate Header** section. Delete the label.

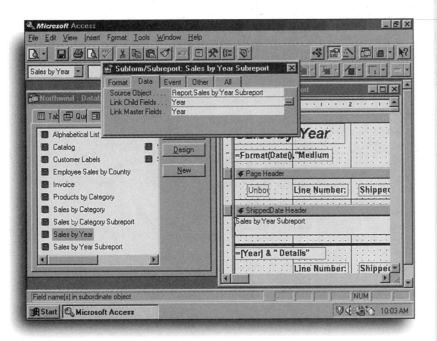

FIGURE 25.11
Drag the subreport to the report.

5. If the subreport records are related to the main report, link them by setting the **Link Child Fields** and **Link Master Fields** properties in the subreport's property sheet. The child field is a field on the subreport and the master field is the related field on the main report. In the Northwind example, type Year in both properties.

6. Resize the subreport and edit or delete the label attached to the subreport control if necessary.

7. Print 🖨 or preview 🔍 the report. (Figure 25.12 shows the report and subreport.)

FIGURE 25.12

The Sales by Year report shows the summary for 1994, which is a subreport.

1 Subreport

2 Inside of main report

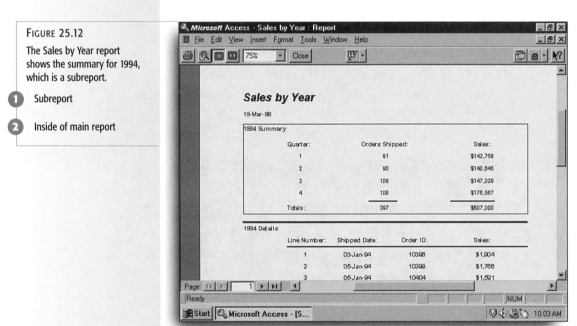

8. Save 💾 the report design.

Glossary

absolute references A reference in a formula used to refer to data in a specific cell, rather than allowing the reference to change based on the column or row (relative reference).

action query An Access query that updates a table (such as deleting records, updating records, creating a new table, or appending records to an existing table).

activation An OLE term meaning to run an object. You usually activate an OLE object by double-clicking it.

active cell In Excel, the selected cell to receive the data or formula.

add-in A wizard (such as the Report Wizard) or a builder (such as the Expression Builder) that helps users perform a potentially complex operation.

aggregate functions Functions you use to summarize data on a query, report, or form. These include Sum(), Avg(), Min(), Max(), and Count().

alias When you use a *self-join*, a temporary name assigned to an Access table to help differentiate one table joined to itself.

alignment How an entry is positioned on a line, in a text box, or label horizontally (or vertically) on a document.

animation A text effect that makes the text move or flash and is useful for onscreen presentations.

append To place data at the bottom of a file or table.

append query an Access *action query* that copies records from one table and places them on the bottom of another table.

arguments Inputs used to calculate functions and procedures. Arguments are enclosed in parentheses. Arguments passed to procedures are also called *parameters*.

arrays Rectangular ranges of formulas or values that Excel treats as a single group.

attribute   Any characteristic that is applied to an object, such as color, border, fill, and shadow.

AutoCaption   A feature that automatically adds a caption with a sequential number to items of a particular type as you insert them in a document.

AutoCorrect   A Microsoft Office feature that automatically corrects common typographical or spelling errors as you type them.

AutoFormat   A feature that applies a set of predefined formatting choices to documents.

AutoNumber   An Access data type that automatically increments by one for every new record. This data type replaced Counter in Access 1.x and 2.0. AutoNumber fields are usually primarily for *primary keys*.

AutoText   This feature enables you to store frequently used text or graphics so that they can be quickly inserted in a document as needed.

axis   The horizontal or vertical line containing category or value labels on a chart. The x-axis is usually the horizontal, category axis; the y-axis is usually the vertical, value axis.

bookmark   A named marker for a block of text, table, graphic, or a position in a document that helps you move to the location quickly.

bound   On an Access form or report, data is bound to a *control* when the data is linked to an underlying query or table.

Thus, for every record, the value in the control changes.

Briefcase replication   A Windows 95 and NT 4 feature that creates more than one copy of a document (on a network and laptop for example) where changes in any copy can be updated to other copies. In Access, data merge to get the latest data from both databases. In other Office products, the user can choose which (entire) file she wants to keep.

builder   An Access help feature that provides assistance in creating expressions for formulas and properties. The Expression Builder is an example.

caption   The text that appears in the title bar of an Access window. The caption property of a field in Access table design becomes the label associated with a text box or other control. The label itself has a caption property that is the text that appears on the form. In Word, the caption is the text that goes at the bottom of a figure.

cascade delete   When *referential integrity* is set in an Access table relationship, the property that causes records on the many side of a relationship to delete when the related record is deleted.

cascade update   When *referential integrity* is set in a Access table relationship, the property that causes the related key on the many side of a relationship to change to the new value on the related record.

cell(s)   The intersection of a row and column.

cell reference   The alphanumeric name of the cell.

character styles   A collection of character formats identified by a single name.

Chart Wizard   An Excel and Access feature that automates the creation of a chart.

check box   On a form or dialog box, a small square that the user can click to turn on or off. A check box is usually associated with a Yes/No field.

child   Data or an element related to another object but lower in hierarchical level than the related (parent) object. An Access subform is related to an Access form. The Link Child Fields property indicates the field that links the Child to the master (Parent) form (which is related to the Link Master Fields property field).

client   An application in which you can create a linked object or embed an object through *object linking and embedding (OLE)*.

client/server   A type of network where servers store files and allocate resources. Servers typically control who can access the information and use the resources. Servers can refuse to let computers or users into the system. Clients connect to the servers and request information or resources.

clip art   A collection of graphics and pictures available for use in Office applications.

Clipboard   A temporary storage area for cut or copied items in Windows applications.

code   The text you enter in a program to create your application. In Access, you enter code in modules. In Excel, you enter code on module sheets. In Word, you enter code on a template.

color scheme   A set of colors that are chosen because they complement one another.

column   A vertical set of text or objects. In an Excel worksheet, a column is a vertical block of cells and columns are labeled with letters (A through IV). In an Access table, a column represents a field.

combo box   On a form or dialog box, a combination of a text box and a list box where the user can type a value or choose one from a list.

command button   On a form or dialog box, a rectangular object a user can click that confirms the choices, cancels the choices, or causes another action. The most common command buttons are OK and Cancel.

comment   A comment added to a document. In Word and Excel, also called Annotation and Notes. A comment mark is inserted in the document and the comment is displayed in the comment pane.

compound document   In *OLE*, a document containing objects from one or more other applications.

concatenation   Combining text, numbers, or dates within a text box. In Access and Excel, you use the ampersand (&) symbol to join the contents of multiple cells.

controls   Data-entry objects commonly used in forms, such as text boxes, combo boxes, and check boxes.

counter   In Access versions 1.x and 2.0, a data type that increments by one for every new record that is now called AutoNumber.

criteria   In a Word mail merge query and an Access query or filter, characters that provide conditions on which data to view.

data form   Used to represent one data record, this form enables you to add, delete, or modify a record in the data source.

data labels   Identifiers that you can attach to data points on a chart.

data series   In an Excel worksheet or chart, a collection of values that pertain to a single subject.

data source (Access)   Where an object gets its information. The data source for an Access form or report is called the record source. The data source for a text box or other control is called the control source.

data source (Word)   This term is used in merging to refer to information that changes in each letter, for example, names and addresses.

data type   A description on an Access field that determines what kind of information you can enter in the field. Field data types include Text, Memo, and Number.

database   A set of related tables, queries, forms, reports, macros, and modules. In Access, the database is a single file indicated by a MDB extension. A database can also be defined more generally in Excel, Word, or Schedule+ as a list of rows and columns where each row is a record and each column a field.

database management system (DBMS) a computer application that helps you store, retrieve, sort, analyze, and print information in a database. It is an application, like Access, that has the menus, toolbars, and other features that help you manage your database.

database window   The primary window visible in Access where you can view or design all objects, such as tables, queries, and other objects. To view the Database window, press F11.

Datasheet view   A row and column view of an Access table, query, or form where you can generally input data.

debug   The process of removing errors in a program.

debug window   A window that enables you to test code statements and expressions as well as check on the values of variables within your procedures.

dependents   Cells that include a formula reference to the current cell.

Design view   The view of an Access table, query, form, and macro objects that enables you to create or change the object.

desktop publishing   A term used to define printed and electronic marketing media such as fliers, brochures, catalogues, business cards, letterhead, mailers, and newsletters.

dialog box   A form within the Windows application or created in Access, Excel, or Word that accepts input from the user. Also called a dialog, this form is usually modal, which means it stays in front of other objects until it is closed.

Document Map   A new way to move quickly through long or online documents.

drag and drop   A method of copying or moving items by selecting and dragging, using the mouse.

drawing object   An object you create by using one of the tools on the Drawing toolbar.

drop cap   A large capital letter in the first word that is set into a paragraph.

dynaset   Short for dynamic set of data. A dynaset is the datasheet (row and column) view of an Access query that you can edit.

embedded object   A document (the source) stored inside another document (the container). For example, a Word document could be stored in an OLE field of the Access database. The

information is actually stored in the container rather than pointing to a *linked* document elsewhere on a disk.

encryption   The process of rendering a file unreadable without the use of a key to decrypt the file.

end-of-cell mark   The point beyond which no text can be entered in the cell of a table.

event   An action taken by a user, such as a mouse click or keystroke, that is recognized by one of Access's event properties such as OnClick or OnDblClick. Events can also be triggered by the program such as when a form opens or the Timer Interval is reached.

expression   A combination of field or variable names and arithmetic or other operators used to perform a calculation, manipulate characters, or test data. For example, =Date() [Price]*[Quantity], and =[FirstName] & " " & [LastName] are expressions. See also *builder*.

external link   A hyperlink that jumps to a Web or FTP site or is located on another computer in a network, an intranet, or Internet site.

field   The information in one column of a list or database. Also, a single item of information in a record.

field code   A code or marker representing a Word field; you can view the codes or view the results of the codes.

field name   The identifier for an Access field.

file management system Sometimes called *flat file database*; stores data in files without indexing, which means that data is processed sequentially. Contrasted with relational database management system.

file sharing Allowing others to have access to your files. This can be accomplished by placing files on a network.

file sharing options Options for assigning passwords to a document or for suggesting that it be opened as a read-only document.

fill color The color inside an object.

filter To show only certain records from an Access table or Excel range. A filter in Access can also include sorting information. An Access filter is not stored in the Database window, while a query is.

flat-file database A nonrelational database. Usually consisting of one large table with values repeated in many places (the same company name, address, phone number could be repeated in many records).

flip Turning an object over, either horizontally or vertically, to create a mirror image of that object.

focus The capability of a control, form, or dialog box to receive keyboard or mouse input. Only one object, such as a text box, can have the focus at a time.

font settings The font, style, size, color, or effect on text characters and slides.

foreign key An Access field (or fields) on the many side of a one-to-many relationship between tables that relates to the primary key of the other table. Foreign keys do not need to be unique within the table.

form An organized and formatted document that facilitates data entry.

Form view The view of an Access form where users can input data. This is opposed to Design view where you can create and modify the form.

Formula Bar The area on the Excel window where cell contents are displayed and can be used for editing.

freeform shape An object that can consist of curved lines, straight lines, or a combination of the two. You might use the Freeform tool to draw a cartoon, create an unusual shape, or write your name.

front-end The visible, user-entry part of an application. Access can act as a front-end with the forms, reports, and queries attached to a back-end database on another system such as SQL Server.

FTP (File Transfer Protocol) A set of rules that governs the transfer of files between computers.

function A predefined formula that performs a specific operation. Sum() is the most used function in both Access and Excel.

GIF (Graphic Interchange Format) A format for compression of graphic images, especially continuous tone and line art images.

grid   In PowerPoint, the invisible series of dots on a slide that helps align objects. On an Access form, a set of nonprinting lines that aids the user in aligning objects such as text boxes and other controls. In Design View, Access shows the grid as a series of dots.

gridlines   On an Excel worksheet, a Word table, or Access datasheet, the lines that indicate the rows and columns. On a chart, the lines that start at and are perpendicular to the category and value axes.

group   In an Access report, one or more records that are combined together and identified with a group header and summarized with a group footer.

guides   Horizontal and Vertical nonprinting lines that help line up objects.

handles   Small square boxes attached to graphic objects, used to re-size, move, and select objects.

horizontal page breaks   In Excel a command to break the page at the current row.

HTML (Hypertext Markup Language)   The underlying code of Web pages.

hyperlink   A graphic or text that connects to another file, a named location in a file, or a Web page.

index   In an Access table, the property that will speed up searches and sorts. One or more fields can be part of an index.

inner join   In an Access query, the link between two related tables, that only returns related fields that are common in both tables.

input mask   An Access input aid that adds characters, such as dashes for social security numbers or parentheses for phone numbers. An input mask can also force the user to input text or numeric characters.

insertion point   A blinking bar that indicates where the next character you type will appear. Sometimes referred to as the cursor.

integer   A number with no decimal places. Access integer data types include integers that can be numbers +/- 32,000 or long integers that can be +/- 2 billion.

internal link   A hyperlink that jumps to a document on the same computer as the page containing the hyperlink, or to a named location with the page.

Internet   A worldwide network of smaller computer networks connected using communication lines to allow transfer of information to and from many resources.

intranet   A communication network within an organization that uses Internet technologies to share information.

ISP (Internet service provider)   Provides access to those things available on the Internet—newsgroups, Web sites, and email.

join   Connects two Access (or another application in Microsoft Query) tables together in a query on a common field. The field is usually a primary key in one table and a foreign key in the second table.

JPG (Joint Photograph Group) A format for compression of graphic images, especially photographic images; this is the native format that Word uses to store images.

key or key field A field that identifies a record. Access tables are indexed and sorted on key fields. Within a sort, the fields that determine sort order.

label Text on a chart. Also, text on a form or report that appears for every record. A label can be a title on the top of the form or attached to a control such as a text box identifying the contents of the control. Last Name: is an example of a label.

landscape orientation Information arranged horizontally on the page.

leader The characters that fill in the space between the end of the text and "leads" up to the left side of the tab position.

legend A chart or map element that explains the markers or symbols used in a chart.

line style Defines the width or style of the object's frame.

linked table Within an Access database, a table whose data originates in another file. The file could be another Access file or a file from a different database application.

list One set of items after another. If the list is structured in a table format with the names of fields at the top and each item in a row, a list in Excel can be converted into a database table.

list box On a form or dialog box, a rectangular area that enables the user to choose one from a choice of many values. When the list of values is larger than the space provided, the application provides a scroll bar to see more of the values.

lookup column A combo box within a field of a table. By choosing Lookup Wizard in the Data Type column in Access Table Design View, you create a lookup column for the field.

macro A stored list of commands automatically executed by an Office application.

mail merge The process of combining a list (usually of addresses) into another document (usually a letter or envelope).

main document The document that contains boilerplate text and graphics and holds field codes for variable information when creating a merge.

master In Access, the main form or report. The subform becomes the child form. In the subform's properties, the Link Master Fields property is a field from the main form that links to the subform's field mentioned in the Link Child Fields property.

master document A document you divide into subdocuments.

masters Masters correspond directly to the slides, speaker's notes, and handout components of a presentation. Masters contain the elements (text or pictures) that you want to appear on every component page.

memo An Access data type that can hold a great deal of text (up to 64,000 characters).

merge field Used to identify which category of data source information will be printed in its location.

modal A form (or dialog box) that keeps the focus until it is closed.

modeless A form (or dialog box) that can be minimized or can lose the focus to another form or dialog box. A pop-up modeless form remains on top of other forms, yet allows you to input in the other forms.

module A collection of stored procedures in Access and Excel. Modules are named on the Modules tab in the Database window. In Excel, module sheets store procedures. However, Access forms and reports also have modules associated with them. Form and report modules are also called class modules.

name box In Excel, the area located at the left end of the formula bar.

null An Access field with no value. This is not the same as a 0 or a zero-length string. Use Is Null in the criteria grid of a query to find fields without an entry.

object On one level in Access, the specific tables, queries, forms, and any other items listed in the Database window. On another level, anything that can be manipulated in Access including controls, procedures, and the database itself. An object in other Office documents also refers to anything on a document, especially a graphic such as a picture, organization chart, or other visual item.

object linking and embedding (OLE) The ability to link or embed contents of one file in another (the data is considered the object). Linking leaves the data in the original location and is accessed when the link is activated, reducing the size of the second file. Embedded data is actually placed in the second file, increasing its size, but not requiring access to the original file.

object placeholders The frame placed on a slide in PowerPoint to designate the location of different objects.

OLE1 An alternative method for linking and embedding objects.

operator A mathematical symbol (such as +) or logical keyword (such as AND) that is a part of an expression.

optimization The process of improving the application's performance.

option button On a form or dialog box, a small circle that the user can click to turn on, usually associated with an option group. Also called a radio button. A check box is usually associated with an option group but can also represent a Yes/No value.

option group On a form or dialog box, a group of controls where only one of them can be selected at once. Usually the controls inside an option group are option buttons but they can also be toggle buttons or check boxes.

order of precedence   The order in which applications perform mathematical operations.

Organizer   A dialog box that enables you to copy, delete, and rename styles, AutoText entries, toolbars, and macros between documents and templates.

orientation   The direction of printing on a page. Landscape orientation prints along the length of the page. Portrait orientation prints along the width of the page.

outer join   In an Access query, the link between two related tables that returns all the records from one table and records from related fields that are common in both tables.

outlining   A feature in Word that makes it easy to organize and manage documents by using different levels.

paragraph styles   A collection of paragraph formats identified by a single name.

parameters   In an Access query, prompts for user input. In a Visual Basic or WordBasic procedure, variables that are supplied to the procedure from outside the procedure.

path   Used to specify the exact location of a file; this might include drive and folder information.

pattern   A design (such as lines, dots, bricks, or checkerboard squares) that contains two colors: a foreground color and a background color.

permissions   In Access security, authority given to perform operations (such as read or modify) on a database object.

pivot table   An Excel feature that enables you to summarize and analyze data in lists and tables. Pivot tables are called that because you can quickly rearrange the position of pivot table fields to give you a different view of the table.

PivotTable Wizard   An Excel and Access feature that automates the creation of a pivot table.

PNG   This format is used by Word to convert raster images.

polygon   A closed shape made up of straight lines.

portrait orientation   Portrait orientation prints along the width of the page.

precedents   In Excel, cells referred to by the formula in the active cell.

presentation template   A saved presentation file that contains predefined slide and title masters, color schemes, and graphic elements.

primary key   The field (or fields) that uniquely identify a record in a table. You cannot have duplicate primary keys within a table.

private   Within Schedule+, the ability to see an item in your schedule, but not allow others to see the item description when they look at your Schedule+ file through the network.

property   An attribute or characteristic of an object. Properties can define the appearance of an object (such as color) or what happens when the user performs an action on the object (such as click).

query In Access, an object that chooses and sorts selected records and fields from another query or table. A query can also modify a table (see *action query*).

range A group of cells that can be acted upon with Excel commands.

record The information in one row of a list or database.

record locking In a multiuser system (such as Access), when one person is modifying a record, you can set the record locking properties to lock other users out of the record or to verify changes made when two users edit the same record at the same time.

reference operators Enables you to refer to several different cells in a single formula.

referential integrity Rules between primary and foreign keys of tables. Referential integrity requires that every foreign key must have a related field in the primary table. Access accomplishes this through *cascade delete* and *cascade update*. If these properties are not set in the relationship window, Access will not allow deletions or updates of primary keys that have related records in a foreign table.

relational database Usually consisting of many tables that have relationships between them. The relationships help avoid duplication and improve data validity.

relational database management system An application, such as Access, that has the capability to create relational databases and the tools to make the application work.

relationship Between two Access tables, the common field (or fields) that identify how they are connected.

relative reference By default, when you copy a formula that contains cell references, the cell references adjust to their new location.

replication The process of copying an Access database in more than one location. After the two (or more) databases are updated, changes can be propagated to both databases.

report An Access object used for printed output that details or summarizes records in a table or query. More generally, any kind of printed output in an Office application.

resize handles Small boxes that appear at the four corners and on each of the four sides of the rectangle around a selected object (such as a picture). When the object is selected, you can move it or change the size or shape by dragging the handles.

revision marks Editing marks in a document entered by protecting or marking a document for revisions, or by choosing Format, AutoFormat.

revisions A means of tracking changes in a document; the document must be protected or marked for revisions.

RGB (Red, Green, Blue)   The color mode used to create custom colors for Web pages. In the HTML, RGB colors are converted to hexadecimal code.

rotating   Turning an object around a 360-degree radius.

row   The horizontal divisions in a Word table, an Excel worksheet, or an Access table.

ruler   Numbered vertical or horizontal guide that indicates your position on the document. Usually, rulers appear at the top and/or left side of the document window if visible.

ScreenTips   The small pop-up labels that appear next to a toolbar button, revision, or comment when you move the mouse pointer onto the button, revision, or comment, and pause.

section break   Contains all formatting, such as margins, line numbers, and page size, for the section immediately preceding it.

sections (Access)   Divisions in an Access form or report that each have their own properties. Sections include the form or report header and footer, page header and footer, details, and in reports group headers and footers.

sections (Word)   Divisions in a document that enable you to change formatting elements only within that portion of the document.

self-join   In an Access query, a table related to itself by two different fields. For example, an employee table can include the ID of a manager who is also in the same table.

server   An application capable of creating objects that can be embedded in or linked to documents created by another application.

servers   Computers on a network that are not used by one individual to do local work but rather are used by multiple users on the network. Servers provide resources, control network access, store network files, and perform network processing.

shaded color   A dark-to-light or light-to-dark variation of an object's color.

shadowing   A means to enhance text or drawn objects.

sheet tabs   The object in Excel used to switch to different worksheets in a workbook.

SQL (Structured Query Language)   Pronounced "sequel." A standard computer language used by many programs, including mainframes and client/server databases. The SQL used in Access and Microsoft Query are subsets of the available language. To see a SQL statement, choose SQL View on the View button while you are in Design View of a query.

status bar   The bottom portion of the application window where application and user messages appear.

style   A collection of formats identified by a single name.

subdocument   A section of a master document.

subform   An Access form that is inside a main form. Usually, the subform displays in Datasheet view and many records can be related to the one in the main form.

subqueries   An Access query that is used within another query. This can be where the second query was created using the first as the data source or where a SQL statement is typed in a criteria cell.

subreport   An Access report that is inside another report.

syntax   The rules for writing functions or programming statements. For example, you need to include parentheses with the Sum function and include a range in Excel or field name in Access in the parentheses. If the field name includes a space, you must surround the field name with brackets.

tab order   The order of the fields on a form accessed when you press Tab or Enter.

table   The primary building block within a database where data is stored. You must have at least one table before you can create a query, form, or report in Access.

Table AutoFormat   A feature that automatically formats and sizes tables.

table of authorities   A list that contains the locations where citations occur in a legal brief generated by Word based on marks inserted in the document with the Insert, Index and Tables, Mark citation command.

table of contents   A list of the contents of a document generated by Word based on built-in heading styles.

table of figures   A list of figures or other items in a document generated by Word based on captions inserted with the Insert, Caption command.

template   A generic document for text, graphics, and formatting used to standardize and avoid repetitive work.

template wizard   The series of dialog boxes that lead you through the steps of creating a document.

tentative   Not definite. In Schedule+, you can create tentative appointments that do not show your time as busy.

text box   A type of drawing object that can contain text or an imported graphic. On a form or dialog box, a rectangular area where the user can type an entry.

toggle button   On a form or dialog box, a rectangular button that appears pressed or unpressed. A toggle button usually is attached to a Yes/No field or is part of an option group.

Toolbox   In Access form and report design, a toolbar that contains buttons for adding controls such as check boxes, combo boxes, and text boxes to the design.

ToolTips   The small pop-up labels that appear next to a toolbar button when you move the mouse pointer onto the button and pause.

unbound   On an Access form or report, data that is not connected to a particular record in a table. The most common unbound control is a label, but you can also have graphics such as a logo on your form or report as well.

UNC (Uniform Naming Convention)   The method of identifying files on computers within a network. Type two backslashes (\\), the name of the shared directory, and then the path to the file.

uniform arc   The shape of the arc you draw (regardless of the size) always is a quarter-circle.

union query   An Access query that combines two tables with multiple common field names. The union query is most often used with a history table and a current table where the field names correspond to each other. The two tables remain in separate locations but the Datasheet view of the union query shows the records from one table below the other.

URL (Uniform Resource Locator)   An address for an Internet site.

validation   A rule for correct data entry within a series or range of acceptable values. If an Access field's Validation Rule is broken, the Validation Text appears in a message box to the user.

variable   The name given to a symbol that represents a value that can be a string, number, or Access object. The value of a variable can change during program execution.

VBA (Visual Basic for Applications)   The programming language provided with Access 95 and Excel 95.

vertical page breaks   In Excel, a way to break the print range at the current column.

view   The different ways to see and edit the document onscreen.

wildcard   A symbol that can represent one or more characters. You use the * wildcard to represent multiple characters in the criteria row of an Access query.

wizards   A series of dialog boxes that lead you through the steps of creating a document or performing a function.

WMF (Windows Metafile)   A format for compression of graphic images that is used by Windows applications.

WordArt   A supplementary application supplied with Office 95 that can be used by Word, Excel, PowerPoint, and Access to create special text effects.

workbook   The main document used in Excel for storing and manipulating data. A workbook consists of individual worksheets, each of which can contain data.

workgroup   In Access, a group of users that are part of the same security file who share database files. The names of the users and their passwords are stored in the workgroup file (the default is SYSTEM.MDW). In Word, a group of users who share common templates.

worksheet Made up of 256 columns and 16,384 rows. The columns are lettered across the top of the document window, beginning with A through Z and continuing with AA through AZ, BA through BZ, and so on, through column IV. The rows are numbered from 1 to 16,384 down the left side of the document window.

World Wide Web (WWW) A vast system of computers throughout the entire world connected electronically by modems that allows information in the form of text, graphics, sound, and animation to be accessed from any other computer that has an Internet connection.

Yes/No field An Access field data type that can accept one of two responses such as Yes/No, True/False, or On/Off.

zero length string Also called empty string, an Access zero length string indicates no data and is entered with two double quotes with no space between them(""). A zero length string generally represents that you know that there is no value for the field. This is contrasted with the *null* value where the value could be unknown.

Index

Symbols

= (absolute references), 264

* (asterisk) symbol, 504

$ code (currency symbol), 234

% code (percent sign), 234

. Code (placeholder for decimal point), 234

\# code (placeholder for digits), 234

0 code (placeholder for digits), 234

1.5 Lines option (Paragraph dialog box), Word, 86

3D charts (Excel), 324, 337-338

35-mm slides, 426

A

A4 Paper option (Slides Sized for drop-down list), 426

abbreviations, Replace text box (Word), 103

ABS() function (Excel), 295

absolute references, creating, 263-264

accepting data entries (worksheet cells), 195

Access. *See also* databases
compared to other Office applications
Excel, 447, 450
Schedule+, 451
Word, 450-451
dialog boxes. *See* dialog boxes, Access

documents. *See* documents, Access
features, 451-452
link formats supported by, 519
queries. *See* queries (Access databases)
Query Design window, 568-570
starting, 452-453, 457
toolbars. *See* toolbars, Access
wizards. *See* wizards, Access

Access Form command (Data menu), Access, 315

Access icon, displaying, 453

Access Report command (Data menu), Access, 315

action queries (Access), 563
creating, 578-580
types of, 579

activating. *See also* starting
cells in worksheets (Excel), 193
toolbars, 18-19

Add button (Word), 57

Add Custom AutoFormat dialog box (Excel), 329

Add Field Name button (Mail Merge), 125

Add New button (Mail Merge), 126

Add option (Spelling dialog box), Excel, 225

Add Report dialog box (Excel), 315

Add to Document option (Envelopes and Labels dialog box), 117

Add to Favorites button, 38

Add View dialog box (Excel), 314

Add Words To option (Spelling dialog box), Excel, 225

add-ins, Excel, 313
installing, 313-314
Report Manager, 313-316
View Manager, 313-314

Add-Ins command (Tools menu), Excel, 313

adding. *See also* inserting
animation to slides (PowerPoint), 439-441
bar numbers to charts (Excel), 339-340
bullets to paragraphs (Word documents), 93-94
comments to slides (PowerPoint), 438-439
controls to forms, 559
current date to main document (Mail Merge), 124
data labels to charts (Excel), 339-340
fields to database tables (Access), 477
footers, 538-539
formats, 161-166
to forms, 538-539
to reports, 538-539
gridlines to charts (Excel), 341

adding

Currency format (Style dialog box), Excel, 232

Currency symbol ($), 234

Current Page option (Print dialog box), Word, 114

custom footers, creating, 308-310

custom formats, creating
dates, 235-236
numbers, 233-234
times, 235-236

custom headers, creating, 308-310

Customers form (Northwind), 530

Customize command (Toolbars menu), Excel, 233

customizing, 247. *See also* formatting
charts (Excel), 328
labels (Excel), 341

Cut button
Datasheet toolbar, Access, 499
Standard toolbar, 21
Table Design toolbar, 478
Word, 63

Cut command (Edit menu), Excel, 217

Cut command (shortcut menu), Word 63

cutting data in databases (Access), 508-509

D

D code (day of month with no leading), 236

data. *See also* numbers; text
alignment (Excel worksheets), 240-245
charts (Excel)
identifying, 330-331
selecting, 320-322
criteria, rule specification in data sources, 137-138

databases. *See also* databases
cleanup for database import, 473
copying, 508-509
cutting, 508-509
editing, 500-502, 506-507
exporting, 521-522
filtering, 511-518
finding in records, 510-511
importing, 518-520
inserting, 500-502
manipulating, 508
normalization, 457
pasting, 508-509
redundancy, 446
replacing, 507
selecting, 503
sorting, 511-513, 517-518
importing, 35
inserting into worksheet
cells, 194-195
dates, 196
numbers, 195
series, 199-204
text, 195
times, 196
labels, charts (Excel), 339-340
sharing across applications, 10
worksheets. *See also* worksheets
attributes, 246-247
copying, 212-216
deleting, 211
formatting characters, 247

Data Entry command (Records menu), Access, 504

Data entry mode (Access), 503

Data Form dialog box (Word), 126

Data Labels command (Insert menu), Excel, 339

Data Map charts (Excel), 341

Data menu commands (Access)
Access Form, 315
Access Report, 315

data sources (Mail Merge), 120, 124
Access data as, 135
adding information to, 125-126
address books as, 136-137
creating, 123-125
editing, 126-127
inserting merge fields, 127-128
merging with main document, 130
to email addresses, 132-133
errors, 130-131
to faxes, 132-133
to new documents, 131-132
to printers, 131-132
worksheets, 133-134
rule specification, 137
data criteria, 137-138
fields, 137
sorting records in, 128-130
viewing, 130

Data tab (Properties window), Access, 548

data types
database fields
changing, 492
defining, 479-482
Lookup, creating, 482-483
setting index properties, 489
setting properties, 483-489
setting table properties, 490-491
types, 479-480
database tables, editing, 466

data-definition queries (Access), 563

database management system. *See* DBMS

Database Utilities command (Tools menu), Access, 506

Database window, 455

Database Window button
Datasheet toolbar, Access, 499
Print Preview toolbar, Access, 589